One of the Family

One of the Family

Metis Culture in Nineteenth-Century Northwestern Saskatchewan

BRENDA MACDOUGALL

UBC Press • Vancouver • Toronto

20 19 18 17 16 15 14 13 12 11 10   5 4 3 2 1

Printed in Canada on FSC-certified ancient-forest-free paper (100% post-consumer recycled) that is processed chlorine- and acid-free.

Library and Archives Canada Cataloguing in Publication

Macdougall, Brenda, 1969-
   One of the family : Metis culture in nineteenth-century northwestern Saskatchewan / Brenda Macdougall.

Includes bibliographical references and index.
ISBN 978-0-7748-1729-5

   1. Métis – Saskatchewan – Île-à-la-Crosse – History – 19th century. 2. Métis – Kinship – Saskatchewan, Northern – History – 19th century. 3. Métis – Saskatchewan – Île-à-la-Crosse – Social life and customs – 19th century. 4. Métis – Saskatchewan, Northern – Social life and customs – 19th century. 5. Métis – Saskatchewan, Northern – Ethnic identity. 6. Fur trade – Saskatchewan, Northern – History – 19th century. 7. Catholic Church – Saskatchewan, Northern – History – 19th century. 8. Île-à-la-Crosse (Sask.) – Genealogy. I. Title.

FC113.M33 2010   971.24′100497   C2009-903399-2

Canada

UBC Press gratefully acknowledges the financial support for our publishing program of the Government of Canada (through the Canada Book Fund), the Canada Council for the Arts, and the British Columbia Arts Council.

This book has been published with the help of a grant from the Canadian Federation for the Humanities and Social Sciences, through the Aid to Scholarly Publications Programme, using funds provided by the Social Sciences and Humanities Research Council of Canada.

UBC Press
The University of British Columbia
2029 West Mall
Vancouver, BC V6T 1Z2
www.ubcpress.ca

To Gael Isobel (Irving) Macdougall and Jeffery Morin

I think you would have liked this

Contents

Illustrations

PHOTOGRAPHS

TABLES

Acknowledgments

At a convocation banquet hosted by the University of Saskatchewan several years ago, a gentleman seated at my table casually asked me about my current research. I gave a rather vague answer about the social and cultural history of the Metis from the northwestern Saskatchewan community of Île à la Crosse and the use of genealogical reconstruction. His interest piqued, my seatmate then asked what my central thesis was regarding those particular Metis and their community. I explained that, historically, the Metis concept of family was not only a means of internal social organization but also a mechanism that permitted them to assert a level of autonomy against the Hudson's Bay Company and Roman Catholic Church. At this point, he looked at me with a somewhat confused but still interested look and asked, "Didn't *anything* good happen in Aboriginal history?" He further elaborated that it was unfortunate Aboriginal history was so negative, and he expressed a wish that people would talk about things that were positive. Now *I* was confused. Certainly greater knowledge and understanding of an Aboriginal construction of family would not only give us greater insight into Aboriginal worldview and epistemology but would also transform our understanding of both fur trade and mission history. Such an approach situates Aboriginal history – in this case Metis history – within a space where people developed institutions and responded to external forces in ways that affirmed their values and sense of distinctiveness.

My intent when I began this research was to contribute in some fashion to the development of methodologies and models by which we could interpret historical documents in a manner that reflected the perspectives, realities, and experiences of Aboriginal communities. After completing a master's degree in colonial American history at the University of North Carolina-Greensboro, I felt that the discipline of Native Studies afforded the best opportunities to pursue that goal. One of the central epistemological purposes of Native Studies as a discipline is to evaluate and challenge colonialism, but I do not place this research exclusively within that theoretical framework. Importantly, Native Studies encourages research located and grounded in Aboriginal knowledge systems and in Aboriginal understandings of how to establish relationships to function in this world. By taking this approach, scholars are placing Aboriginal people at the centre, not the periphery, of discourse or analysis. On the surface, this appears to be a fairly straightforward statement, yet it has taken me many years to come to an understanding of what it means to approach research from an Aboriginal perspective. The most obvious method is to engage in extensive interviewing of traditional knowledge holders, and while this is a valuable approach, it was not one selected here. Another way to generate an Aboriginal perspective is to balance traditional knowledge and values with documentary evidence.

This study uses the lens of Metis family systems, as captured in the Cree term *wahkootowin,* to examine how the Metis of northwestern Saskatchewan understood their relationships with fur companies and Christian churches. As an integral facet of an Aboriginal worldview, wahkootowin is a concept that is invoked in ceremonies, prayer, and daily conversation. However, the term did not appear in any of the historical records used in this study. Rather, I encountered it in spiritual teachings about family first imparted to me by Metis elder Maria Campbell. For this reason, I am first and foremost grateful to Maria Campbell and, subsequently, others who have shared with me the teachings or simply expressed the sentiment of wahkootowin. Once I gained a suitable understanding of wahkootowin, I was able to read and interpret documentary evidence located in fur trade, mission, and government records in a manner faithful to the worldview of this Metis society. Using this lens does not dismiss colonialism, oppression, exploitation, or victimization as outcomes of the Metis relationship with the fur trade and the Church, but it does demonstrate that, most of the time, Aboriginal people lived their own lives and were not always responding and reacting to external (and negative) forces.

This book is an outgrowth of doctoral research conducted with Dr. Frank Tough, formerly a faculty member in Native Studies at the University of Saskatchewan and now with the Faculty of Native Studies at the

University of Alberta. For his guidance, assistance, expertise, and the loan of his databases, I extend a heartfelt thank you. There are several others who contributed to this book by assisting in the development of my interest in academia and this research program, and they must be acknowledged, including the late Drs. F. Laurie Barron, Howard Adams, and Converse D. Clowse. These three scholars served as important mentors during my undergraduate and graduate years. Drs. J.R. Miller, James B. Waldram, and Winona Wheeler all provided firm but supportive encouragement and shared their knowledge of kinship structures, social and cultural systems, and local Aboriginal communities and oral traditions, each of which offered unique insight into the knowledge systems of Metis Cree peoples. Additionally, Drs. Nicole St-Onge of the University of Ottawa, Laurie Meijer Drees of Victoria Island University, Jennifer S.H. Brown at the University of Winnipeg, and Carolyn Podruchny at York University have all provided insightful and invaluable comments, as well as wonderful support, as I worked to revise this study for publication. Furthermore, Darcy Cullen, Ann Macklem, and Audrey McClellan, along with the entire team at UBC Press that has worked with me on this book, have been unfailingly patient and helpful in this process. I must extend a special acknowledgment to my cultural mentor and teacher, Maria Campbell, whose willingness to share her knowledge of wahkootowin, language, and landscape gave me important entry points into ethnohistorical research.

To the families of northwestern Saskatchewan, especially those from Île à la Crosse, Beauval, Pinehouse, and Buffalo Narrows who permitted me into their homes and allowed me access to their knowledge and history, it has been an indescribable honour. Over the last several years, I have been privileged to visit the communities and spend time with many residents of the northwest, including Alan Morin and his family, Jim Favel, Don and Marie Favel, Duane Favel, Philip Durocher, Alan (Spud) Morin, Georgina Morin, Mrs. Bouvier, Alex Maurice, Ray Laliberte, Clem Chartier, Philip Chartier, Rosa Tinker, and Rita Bouvier. I hope that I have in some way reflected the spirit and integrity of your families, communities, and histories. If I have failed in any way, the fault is entirely mine.

Several agencies and individuals provided me with valuable technical support for this work: Gilles Lesage, director, and the staff at the St. Boniface Historical Association provided me access to the Oblate records from The Pas Diocese, which includes northwestern Saskatchewan; the volunteer staff at the Reading Room of the Mormon Temple in Saskatoon, Saskatchewan, dealt with microfilm orders and provided me with the space to copy all the registries for the region; and the staff at the interlibrary loan office at the University of Saskatchewan Main Library efficiently managed all my loans from the Hudson's Bay Company Archives. Andrew Dunlop at the University of Saskatchewan produced the fine maps for this work while Neil Soiseth produced the genealogical charts and tables.

This research could not have been accomplished without financial assistance from Studentships in Northern Studies (2000), the Metis Nation-Saskatchewan (intermittent between 1999 and 2003), and a University of Saskatchewan Graduate Scholarship (1998-2000). I was also generously offered a Social Sciences and Humanities Research Council Graduate Fellowship (1999), a fellowship that I had to turn down after obtaining a faculty position at the University of Saskatchewan. Over the years, the Northwestern Saskatchewan Métis Land Committee, Matri-X, the Metis Nation-Saskatchewan, the Canadian Northern Studies Trust, and the University of Saskatchewan's Department of History's Messer Fund provided assistance so I could travel to the archives in Ottawa as well as to northwestern Saskatchewan. A Hudson's Bay Company visiting scholar position in Metis Studies at Carleton University (2005) took me away from my regular teaching duties and gave me the space to complete the original manuscript. Since 2003, I have benefited from some additional funding provided by Otipimsuak – the Free People: Métis Land and Society in Northwest Saskatchewan, a research project funded by the Community-University Research Alliance program of the Social Science and Humanities Research Council (CURA 833-2003-1034 Tough). More recently, I received financial assistance to complete extensive revisions to this manuscript from Dr. Nicole St-Onge via an Indian and Northern Affairs Canada–University of Ottawa Contribution Agreement, "Post Powley Research Funds on Métis Identity and Métis Territoriality Past and Present."

Thanks must go to my colleagues in the Native Studies Department, including Gail MacKay and Roger Maaka, who unfailingly supported my research. In particular, my heartfelt thanks goes to Ron F. Laliberte, who survived the war with me; we're both the better for it. Special thanks must go to Robert Alexander Innes, one of my first students, who has since obtained a PhD in American Indian Studies and become a colleague in the Department of Native Studies. It has been a pleasure to have you as a friend and colleague with whom I can discuss kinship, traditional law, and social practices in Aboriginal communities. Additional appreciation is extended to other colleagues and friends: Leslie McBain, Chris Andersen, Christi Belcourt, Signa Daum Shanks, Keith Thor Carlson, Heather

Devine, Gregory Scofield, Teresa Carlson, Janet Smylie, Kim Anderson, and Jean Barman.

To my good friends Michelle Robson, Larry Gautier and Judy Anderson, James and Cindy Froh, and Kim Kwas, and all the children in my life, but most especially Charlie, Jill, Cruz, Riel, Anthony, Samson, Wilson, and Star, each of you has provided me with welcome diversions that have permitted me to approach my work refreshed. There have also been several student researchers affiliated with the Matri-X group out of the University of Alberta, as well as my own students, whose abilities and insights have been critical to my own intellectual growth. Most notably, these include Anna Ryding, Clayton Leonard, Kevin McKlennan, Peter Dodson, Melanie McLean, Carmen Baker, Cheryl Troupe, and Kristina Duffee, as well as the many students from the Saskatchewan Urban Teacher Education Program, whose research into their own family histories illuminated the scope and nature of Metis families across western Canada.

In a study about the importance of family, I would be remiss if I did not thank my own family for all their support as I have pursued more education than was ever in my imagination. To all the Macdougalls, Irvings, Harrisons, Van Brienens, and Soiseths – the strength, support, and encouragement of family was critical at every stage of my life. To my late father, Jack Macdougall, and my late aunt, Ruth Shannon, my appreciation for your managing to convince me not to drop out of university and become a hairdresser is immeasurable – you knew what you were doing when I thought I knew better. Over the past several years, my sister Sandra and her partner, Steve, have given me their love and support and have unfailingly taken in all the strays that I've brought them. Your good humour and sense of life have been appreciated.

Finally, to the two most important intellectual mentors and friends in my life, my husband, Neil Soiseth, and my dear friend Maria Campbell. There are not enough words to thank either of you for the love, encouragement, skills, and knowledge that you have both so freely shared with me as I have struggled to understand what I was doing and finish writing this manuscript. Thank you, Maria, for all the long drives, conversations, and teachings about traditional Metis family life and society. I have enjoyed every kilometre that we have travelled together; I am all the richer for your friendship. And to Neil, you have been my best friend for too many years to count now. Thank you for reading and editing countless drafts of chapters and putting up with my ability to procrastinate.

Note on Methodology and Sources

Although a more detailed description of the methodology employed in this study is found in the Introduction, I thought it useful to provide additional information on the range of sources and the database approach used to organize an array of archival records. Dr. Frank Tough's research into the scrip claims of the Metis in northwestern Saskatchewan, work begun while he was at the University of Saskatchewan, inspired the doctoral work on which this book is based. Although my research focuses on the nature of Metis culture and society in northwestern Saskatchewan communities through an explication of historical genealogies, I adopted a database approach to records management in a manner encouraged by Dr. Tough. Reconstructing the genealogies for northwestern Saskatchewan's ancestral families required a large set of records from a variety of sources, including scrip applications; Hudson's Bay Company post records, such as journals, correspondence, censuses, post reports, and employment data; parish registries from Île à la Crosse, Portage La Loche (present-day La Loche), and Green Lake (also known as Lac Vert); and Canadian censuses from 1880, 1890, and 1901, and the 1906 prairie census. From his own research program, Dr. Tough graciously provided me access to the scrip applications and the 1880, 1890, and 1901 census records that he and a research team affiliated with the Matri-X project (Metis Aboriginal Title Research Initiative "X") gathered and databased. Both record groups are in the public record and available in a variety of locations, although the originals are housed at Library and Archives Canada (LAC) in Ottawa. I made several trips to LAC to view some of the original applications as well as the scrip ledger books, though I accessed most of these records via Dr. Tough's databases, which reduced some of the travel costs that often make research prohibitive. The Matri-X project transcribed verbatim 710 records for scrip applications, entering them into a Filemaker™ database labelled "AppiDB/8, FileMaker" (from 25 January 2002), while their Census Database contained 2,645 records (from 24 April 2001). These databases remain in the possession of Dr. Tough at the University of Alberta's Faculty of Native Studies.

Although the use of scrip applications and census data was integral to this research, the genealogies that frame the methodological core of the study would not have been produced had the Church of Jesus Christ of Latter-Day Saints not microfilmed the Roman Catholic Church registries for northwestern Saskatchewan in the 1970s, maintained them at their main facility in Salt Lake City, and made them accessible through the Mormon Family History Centre in Saskatoon. The diocese in The Pas, Manitoba, which owns the original records, was unable to make these records available at the time I was conducting this research. At the Mormon Family History Centre, I examined record groups for each of the three missions in northwestern Saskatchewan and photocopied in their entirety each of the three registries – baptismal, marital, and burial. Since the completion of the initial data-collection phase, the diocese has sent these records as well as other documentary sources for the region to the St. Boniface Historical Association (SBHA) in Winnipeg, where researchers are now able to access them. (The Mormon Family History Centre still makes its microfilmed records available to any of its branches located where there is a temple.) More recently, I accessed additional Oblate records, such as the *Liber Animarums,* Latin for "book of souls," through the SBHA. These books are genealogies that were created and maintained by priests to establish a basic historical record of each family in the community and their origins in the region. Technology such as microfilming and digitization have made many primary records more accessible, but this does not mean visits to archival repositories have become irrelevant. Between 1999 and 2008, I made several trips to Winnipeg and Ottawa to view original documents, including historical maps; scrip ledgers, coupons, and applications; journals; correspondence; censuses; and genealogies constructed by the Church.

After collecting all the necessary records, it was essential to locate a process by which order could be brought to the rich but voluminous evidence. The genealogical data in particular needed to be organized to render it readable, so a commercially available genealogical program,

Reunion 8.0™, was selected. For each individual identified in the historical record, I created a personalized profile based on the entire array of historical records available. Using Reunion™ made it possible to efficiently database the roughly five thousand individuals identified as belonging to the English River District between the late 1780s and mid-1900s. Personal information was recorded and linkages between people identified through the generation of family charts, many of which are reproduced throughout this book.

For any given person, we have an accounting of their full name (as well as nicknames and alternative spellings), date and place of birth, date and location of baptism, date of death and burial, location of grave, names of godparents, religious denomination(s), years and kind of education acquired, occupations, any racial or cultural identifiers provided (such as "Chipewyan Breed," "Scots Breed," "French Breed," or simply "Halfbreed"), numbers of and types of languages spoken, and any other pertinent, qualitative, personal information revealed in the various record groups (see Figure 0.1). Once the records for each individual were completed, they were connected genealogically to other individuals based on bio-

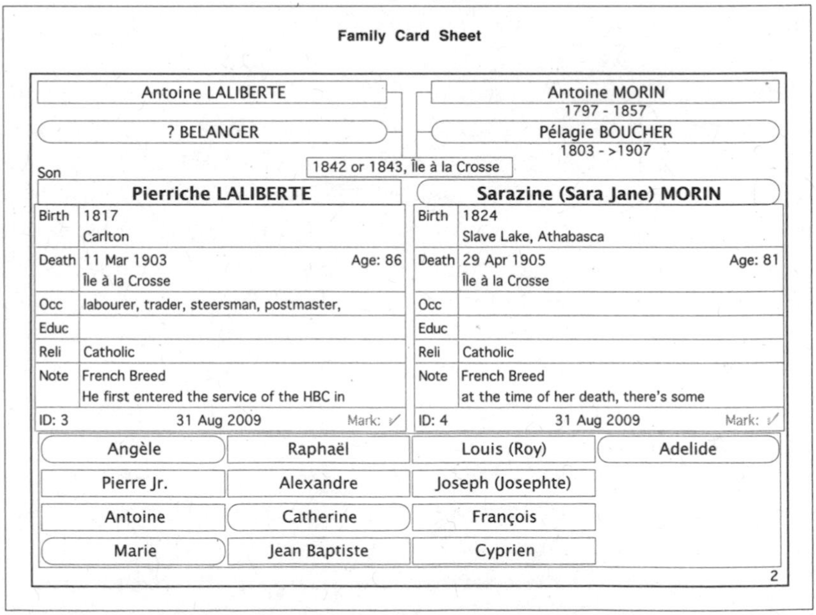

Family Card Sheet

	Antoine LALIBERTE		Antoine MORIN
			1797 - 1857
	? BELANGER		Pélagie BOUCHER
			1803 - >1907

Son — 1842 or 1843, Île à la Crosse

Pierriche LALIBERTE		**Sarazine (Sara Jane) MORIN**	
Birth	1817	Birth	1824
	Carlton		Slave Lake, Athabasca
Death	11 Mar 1903 — Age: 86	Death	29 Apr 1905 — Age: 81
	Île à la Crosse		Île à la Crosse
Occ	labourer, trader, steersman, postmaster,	Occ	
Educ		Educ	
Reli	Catholic	Reli	Catholic
Note	French Breed	Note	French Breed
	He first entered the service of the HBC in		at the time of her death, there's some
ID: 3	31 Aug 2009 — Mark: ✓	ID: 4	31 Aug 2009 — Mark: ✓

Angèle	Raphaël	Louis (Roy)	Adelide
Pierre Jr.	Alexandre	Joseph (Josephte)	
Antoine	Catherine	François	
Marie	Jean Baptiste	Cyprien	

FIGURE 0.1   Family card sheet

logical, marital, and fictive family relations, revealing a large web of interconnected Metis families living throughout the region.

The database made it easy to trace multiple marriages, adoptions, fictive relations, or any other complicated form(s) of familial or additional linkages, so any individual's personal history is easily connected to relatives and their own genealogies. These charts also provided the visual aids necessary to make sense of an otherwise rather large and unwieldy dataset. For instance, married couples were linked to one another with either the date and location of the wedding or the general time when they became married according to custom. Directly above the names of the couple are the names of both sets of parents, thus establishing a continuous link with the families of origin, while the names of any children appear below those of their parents and serve as links to the personalized record of each child. This means that for any individual and/or couple, up to three generations of a family are displayed by Reunion™, which, in turn, permitted me to search families for patterns of intergenerational behaviour. An important methodological decision was to list women under their maiden, rather than married, surnames, which made it easy to show broad interfamilial and intergenerational connections via extensive female networks.

Once completed, the genealogical database of the families from the northwest served as the methodological tool to organize, interpret, and analyze the wahkootowin, framing the region's socio-cultural world. Furthermore, the database has provided a means to generate additional charts based on an array of variables, such as surname, location, or occupation, and then cross-reference the data to other qualitative data sources, such as trade records, journal entries, correspondence, and employment records.

Note on Writing Conventions

Whenever possible, the French spelling of Christian or given names is used, based on verification against Church registries for Île à la Crosse, Green Lake, and Portage La Loche. As a result, given names that are often misspelled by English speakers/writers have been restored, so that Pilagie appears as Pélagie, Angel as Angèle, and John as Jean. We cannot know how the people in the community spelled their names because they did not leave any personally written documents. Therefore, historical spellings are used.

However, in order to ensure that the descendants of these families find value in this work, the spelling of surnames conforms to contemporary, often anglicized or indigenized conventions. So, for example, La Liberté becomes Laliberte, de la Ronde becomes Delaronde, Des Roches becomes Durocher, Kippling becomes Kyplain, and L'Esperance becomes Misponas. To preserve the original French, English, or Scottish surnames and/or establish a connection between contemporary and historical names, particularly where one is not obvious, alternative spellings are provided either in footnotes or parentheses after their first appearance in the text.

In many instances, people went by multiple names, which can be classed as nicknames or indigenous language names, and some people were even known by alternative or multiple surnames over the course of a lifetime.

It is, therefore, difficult to trace some individuals. In cases where alternative names are known, they are provided either in parenthesies or in a note, depending on the level of complication.

TOPONYMY

Choosing place names for the northwest has proven to be as complex a process as sorting through the genealogical connections among individuals and families. The northwest is layered with multiple place names for locations, beginning with those developed by indigenous peoples. Cree and Dene names for particular places – which are themselves often in conflict – have been overlayed with French, then English and, finally, Michif names. What we today call the Churchill River was once known in Cree as Missinipi and, to the traders of the St. Lawrence network, the English River. Île à la Crosse (the lake and the community) was known to the Cree and Metis as Sakitawak, and the name remains significant in the region.

In cases where multliple names are known, I have chosen one name over the others, and have based that choice on several criteria. For places that have a known indigenous place name (whether it be Cree, Dene, or Michif), the indigenous name is used. I have also chosen to privilege historical names over their contemporary variants. Because this book is about the Metis who made northwestern Saskatchewan their home, whenever the homeland, territory, or locations integral to their identity and history are referred to, they are identified by their Michif or Cree place names. For instance, when appropriate, Sakitawak and "the northwest" are privileged over Île à la Crosse or the English River District. Likewise, Missinipi and English River are privileged over Churchill River, which has a far more contemporary application. In cases where I have not been able to identify the indigenous name of a place – or if there is no known name in Cree, Michif, or any other Aboriginal language – then the most appropriate historical French or English place names are applied. Where Michif or Cree words appear, their spelling does not conform to the modern spelling established in the last several decades by languages scholars. Instead, the words are spelled phonetically. Because these two languages have only recently become a part of a written tradition, most speakers are not "literate" in the new written versions of their language but will recognize phonetic pronunciations.

Local place names	*Also known as*
Ala-Point du Trembles	Île aux Trembles, Poplar Point Island
Amisko-sipi	Beaver River
Belanger-kaki-wekit	Belanger Point
Bull's House	Riviere La Loche, Dillon
Big Buffalo Lake	Churchill Lake
Green Lake	Lac Vert
Lac au Serpent	Snake Lake, Pinehouse Lake
Lac Prairie	Meadow Lake
Little Buffalo Lake	Peter Pond Lake
Methy Lake	Lac La Loche
Missinipi or English River	Churchill River
Moostoos-sipi	Buffalo Narrows
Nehiyo-wahkasi	Sandy Point
Nehiyo-wapasi	Canoe Lake
Patsu-wana	Patuanak
Portage La Loche	La Loche
Sakitawak	Île à la Crosse
Sipisihk	Beauval, La Plonge
White Fish Lake	Garson Lake

In some instances, there are multiple locations with similar or even identical place names. For instance, there are references to a Deers Lake and a Grey Deer Lake. However, there is not enough information to determine whether these were the same lake or, in fact, two different lakes. Similarly, there are several Devils, Jackfish, and Fishing lakes spread throughout the fur trade districts. Because of the nature of fur trade writings, there is often no geographic reference point for readers to determine where these places are or whether they are the same place.

To establish a distinction between Aboriginal and Euro-Canadian spaces and landmarks, when specific posts or mission stations are mentioned, they are referred to by their English and French names (e.g., Green Lake/Saint-Julien, Île à la Crosse/Saint-Jean-Baptiste, and Portage La Loche/Mission de la Visitation). The purpose of this distinction is to establish a separation between the spaces occupied and used by these two groups. By using Michif and Cree place names, the Metis sense of self as grounded in their landscape is highlighted and privileged, while the use of English and French place names demonstrates the creation of new spaces by outsiders as represented by the institutions of the trade and missions.

One of the Family

Introduction

I'm one of the family, the family of those who grew up at Sandy Point.

When I walked up today after coming from across the lake, I saw many people that I hadn't seen for years. I started shaking hands and the smiles were there. They acknowledged me [as] a part of this family.

As I look out across the bay ... I see the house that I grew up in. It's not there any more, but *I* see the house I grew up in. I see my grandmother washing clothes. I see my grandfather building a boat. I see all that, because the work ethic was there. The need to survive, the connection with the land. That continued need with us, with our children, with our grandchildren, to show them the importance of what [was] here. If we don't do it, nobody else will. You have to have that connection to this particular place, in order to be able to do that.[1]

This description of community situated in a particular place conveys the idea that identity is encompassed in one's connection to home, which, in turn, is definable by land and family. While at a family reunion at Lake Île à la Crosse (Sákitawak) the narrator of the opening excerpt, Lawrence Ahenakew, references all three criteria for identity when he speaks of his grandparents, immediately establishing an ancestral connection to the other families of Nehiyo-wahkasi (Sandy Point) and their shared history.[2] Family is central to Ahenakew's sense of self, which he expresses in his simple yet eloquent statement, "I'm one of the family." He cites the values held by his grandparents as a foundation for personal growth and development, shaping both his sense of belonging to the community and his self-worth as an individual. Furthermore, he references an ongoing connection with the land on which he was raised as an integral part of his sense of self and family. Community is established through mutual responsibility, and Ahenakew articulates his responsibility for connecting his children and grandchildren to this shared cultural identity, this community, and the land or place from which he came. He acknowledges his duty to pass on values learned through family responsibility and obligation. Noting that his children and grandchildren will likely never live at Nehiyo-wahkasi, or even in nearby Sakitawak, memory and the maintenance of family relationships become even more vital for connecting future generations to their ancestral past.[3] Family and place are central elements in this examination of the historical processes that led to the emergence of the Metis and their socio-cultural development in northwestern Saskatchewan. Ahenakew further grounds us, the readers, in this shared understanding of identity: "I am a part of *this* family ... and what I do matters to the people [of] Sandy Point."[4]

At first glance, there is nothing remarkable about the history of either Sakitawak or "the northwest" (historically known as the English River District and today known as northwestern Saskatchewan).[5] Neither had a large population like the Red River Settlement, nor did the region figure prominently in any of the Metis nationalist movements of the nineteenth century. Because of its size and role in the nationalist movements, Red River has been the focal point of Metis historical discourse. Indeed, the disproportionate attention paid to it has led some scholars to note that Metis historiography has suffered from "Red River myopia."[6] The response in recent years has been a marked increase in our historical peripheral vision, with scholars recognizing that a Metis identity developed in many parts of North America, and concepts of nationalism could and did take many forms. This study of a subarctic Metis society contributes in some measure to this expanded vision and also represents an expansion of a Native Studies perspective that offers family, land, and identity as necessary tools for understanding an Aboriginal worldview. All three elements are essential in our conceptualization of relatedness and are embodied in the common invocation "all my relations." The stories that emerge from this region explain and articulate that worldview and, therefore, tell the history of the place and reveal the origins of the Metis. Because Metis ancestry draws from two distinct cultural heritages – European and Aboriginal – these stories are not told in one voice or by one group. Rather, the stories are layered, beginning with the traditions and values of the Cree and Dene, which are then overlapped by the story of the fur trade's expansion into that part of North America. From these first two layers, the story of the subarctic Metis of the northwest emerges, influenced socio-culturally by their grandmothers' and mothers' worldview. Then we begin to hear the voices of the Hudson's Bay Company, which dominated the region economically from 1821 until the early twentieth century and which is itself an enduring connection to Metis paternity. At the same time, the maternally derived spiritual connections to land and family became a part of the Roman Catholic mission that brought another framework for the Metis religious or spiritual sense of family and relatedness. By peeling back these layers of history and the multiple voices telling those stories, we begin to see what was remarkable about northwestern Saskatchewan's history and people.

What makes the northwest truly compelling is that it is home to one of the oldest, most culturally homogeneous Metis communities in western Canada, a community of people who grounded themselves in the lands of their Cree and Dene grandmothers by adhering to a way of being embodied in the protocols of *wahkootowin*. The Metis family structure that emerged in the northwest and at Sakitawak was rooted in the history and culture of Cree and Dene progenitors, and therefore in a worldview that privileged relatedness to land, people (living, ancestral, and those to come), the spirit world, and creatures inhabiting the space. In short, this worldview, wahkootowin, is predicated upon a specific Aboriginal notion and definition of family as a broadly conceived sense of relatedness with all beings, human and non-human, living and dead, physical and spiritual. Ahenakew references all these points of connection as he describes his sense of self as being tied to place, Nehiyo-wahkasi, and to the past, present, and future generations represented by his grandparents, himself, and his children and grandchildren. This layered structure represented by ancestral *(ni'amspsko chapanak)*, living *(ni'wakomakanak)*, and future *(ni'chapanak)* relationships extends beyond even his own relatives to include a sense of place and land as integral to how he understands himself and those around him. Identity, in this conceptualization, is inseparable from land, home, community, or family. They are all one and the same.

From the standpoint of Canadian historiography, the northwest is a place of note because of its role as one of the most important regions of the fur trade and Christian expansion into Rupert's Land. Indeed, the use of Sakitawak as a residential post predated the founding of the Red River settlement by almost forty years. Île à la Crosse rose to prominence as the central administrative depot of the English River District during the late eighteenth century, and the two most important and stable outposts were Portage La Loche and Green Lake. Portage La Loche served the Methy Portage, which took voyageurs farther north into the Athabasca and Mackenzie districts, while Green Lake operated at the southern limits of the English River District as a pemmican depot to fuel those northern brigades. After 1776 and the arrival of Thomas and Joseph Frobisher from the Montreal-based St. Lawrence trade network, additional French Canadian, English, and Scottish voyageurs and traders from the XY, North West, and Hudson's Bay companies, respectively, quickly followed. These men, as part of the trading experience, established intimate and often long-lasting relationships with local Cree and Dene women, and the result of these unions was the beginning of Metis people and communities in the northwest. It was in these initial relationships between indigenous women, who were grounded in the experiences and realities of the local environment, and men not indigenous to the region that the framework for Metis culture emerged, necessarily rooted in the homeland and worldview of maternal relatives rather than paternal ancestors. By virtue of place – where people were born, lived, and died – the Metis were themselves a part of the family. Over time, this region became home to a group of Metis people working for the fur trade within their own homeland as employees and on the trade's margins as freemen, free traders, and subsistence hunters and fishermen.

When the Oblates of Mary Immaculate, representing the Roman Catholic Church, arrived in the English River District in 1845 and established the first western mission outside Red River, they encountered a population infused with a spiritual understanding of the world similar to several of the Church's own doctrines. In particular, the Roman Catholic emphasis on the Holy Family – Jesus, Mary, and Joseph – as the spiritual embodiment of the living family was a concept Aboriginal people understood because it made a real connection between the living and spirit worlds. Furthermore, the mission was established in the mid-1800s among a populace that, to the missionaries' surprise, already understood and practised the blessings of the sacraments, observed the Sabbath regularly, and acknowledged the power of the saints over their lives. The presence of Catholic rituals in the district is attributable to the efforts of French Canadian voyageurs from the Catholic parishes in Lower Canada, in the employ, first, of the North West Company and then later the Hudson's

Bay Company (HBC), who adhered to these rituals in an effort to maintain but also recreate familiar socio-cultural values within this unfamiliar, foreign space. However, the acceptance of these rituals was the result of the Aboriginal people's respect for the manner in which new ceremonies were introduced and conceived of in this new landscape. According to historian Carolyn Podruchny, during the eighteenth century, novice voyageurs from the St. Lawrence area were ritually baptized by their brethren at several sites along the brigade route in order to mark their entrance into the West and, symbolically, their new lives. The final site of ritual baptisms performed by voyageurs was Portage La Loche, before the men crossed the watershed marking the height of land between the Athabasca and Mackenzie districts and the English River District and following the twelve-mile Methy Portage reputed to be the most difficult in Rupert's Land. The trip across the portage began with the men of the La Loche brigade carrying packs loaded with goods along an eight-mile trail to reach Rendezvous Lake, where they met the Mackenzie River brigade, which had just travelled southward and completed the remaining four miles of the portage to arrive at the meeting place. After a short rest, the La Loche brigade hauled the loaded fur packs back across the portage to begin the final trip south for the season.[7]

Podruchny concluded that the final baptismal site, at Portage La Loche on Methy Lake (also known as Lac La Loche), was particularly significant because for many voyageurs it marked a point of no return. A combination of hardship and potential loss of life while crossing the difficult portage, mixed with an understanding that many would remain employees in the subarctic trade for the duration of their lives, meant that this final baptismal site indeed marked their passage into a new life. Cree, Dene, and later Metis people would have understood and respected this ceremony of voyageurs, who had created for themselves a sacred site where they sought the protection of their relatives in the spirit world, represented by the holy family, while also linking themselves to one another as living relatives, as brothers of the portage. This emergent folk Catholicism practised by voyageur laypeople became an important tradition for their descendants in the English River District. Like the fur-trading companies before it, the Church worked to establish itself in this community throughout the latter half of the nineteenth century, acculturating to the demands of Metis cultural identity while striving to improve the rudimentary teachings of Catholicism held by residents. As a result, the Metis of the English River District developed a flourishing socio-religious life that incorporated both indigenous and Catholic religious traditions, establishing a yearly spiritual calendar marked by periods of intense revelry and religious piety in a celebration of land, home, life, and family. Significantly, the missionaries arrived in the region at the behest of the trade employees and their families, who, since the early part of the century, had incorporated aspects of Catholicism into their lives.

Against this backdrop of often competing interests and layered histories, the Metis people who lived around Sakitawak in the nineteenth century created for themselves a community defined by the values of social obligation to, and mutual responsibility among, family members, and they bequeathed this legacy to their descendants. This sense of self – defined by an ancestral legacy, living family relationships, and the land identified so eloquently by Lawrence Ahenakew – is not unique to Nehiyo-wahkasi but is observable throughout the history of those Metis who have lived for many generations in family bands around the perimeter of Sakitawak and in the many northwest communities to which they were connected genealogically. The families at Nehiyo-wahkasi, including the Morins and Gardiners to whom Ahenakew is related, were part of an extended, regional family system that shaped their cultural identity. All those who lived around the lake were connected in a chain of history and memory defined by acceptance of, and adherence to, their regional narrative. These combined elements were part of a Metis worldview that privileged family above all else and directed actions and behaviours in a manner that reflected the values, taboos, virtues, and ideals of this society, which, in turn, were the laws by which people lived. Family or wahkootowin was, to borrow an anthropological phrase, the "style of life" that reflected a shared cultural identity across northwestern Saskatchewan.[8] Understanding a society's culture is more than just identifying its outward expressions or obvious symbols. Rather, one must look to its relationships to the land and its inhabitants, from which ideas, values, laws and taboos, manners of independence and hospitality, and virtues emanate. It is all these things together that make up the specific concepts embedded in a people's connection or relationship to one another. The style of life, composed of tangible and intangible qualities, guides and influences people's daily behaviours, decisions, and actions.[9] The intangible aspects of culture, according to Clifford Geertz, are what require examination and explanation if we are to truly understand, and be able to engage with, a people on their terms.[10]

FAMILY AND LANGUAGE IN THE ENGLISH RIVER DISTRICT

Language both expresses and shapes a society's worldview, and the Cree language frames the notion of family as the binding fabric of society. As an expression of cultural identity, wahkootowin provides structure to society; infuses institutions with meaning; establishs protocols and frameworks for interaction and behaviour; is the foundation for pursuing any economic, political, social, or cultural activity; and is essential for the creation of an alliance. "Wahkootowin," a Cree word, best articulates the Sakitawak Metis style of life and, therefore, cultural identity.

Metis definitions of family in the northwest were historically based on a Cree concept largely because Cree was the dominant maternal ancestry to which the Metis of the region traced their lineage, and also because Cree represented the lingua franca (common language) that facilitated trade in this region during the nineteenth century. The dialect of Sakitawak and the northwest had a stronger Cree influence than was the case in other areas of the western plains where, linguistic scholars have argued, a more typical dialect of the Michif language developed.[11] The influence of the Cree language across the expanse of Rupert's Land and the trade was apparently related to the ease with which non-Cree speakers learned it. Fur trader and cartographer David Thompson, in his journeys throughout the various Indian territories, noted that the Cree language was "easy of pronunciation and is readily acquired by the white people for the purposes of trade, and common conversation."[12]

It is important to note that the term "wahkootowin" does not appear in any of the historical records used for this study, though it is not surprising that fur traders and missionaries did not record or use the term when they described the social or cultural customs of Aboriginal peoples among whom they lived and worked. Although outsiders knew Aboriginal languages, they learned those languages only to advance their own agendas – expansion of the fur trade or conversion to Christianity. These outsiders were not necessarily interested in the cultural dynamics of the community itself or in understanding the philosophical or religious meaning behind a people's actions or behaviours. So while men like David Thompson recorded in detail certain types of behaviours or characteristics he found most interesting about a people with whom he lived, he did not search for the underlying purpose or meaning behind those behaviours. And yet, "wahkootowin" is an ancient term that is still used in northwestern Saskatchewan by both Michif and Cree language speakers – particularly, but not exclusively, in spiritual invocations during ceremonies and during elder teachings about the importance of family – because wahkootowin was (and still is) the foundation for society in the region and an integral part of the Cree way of seeing the world, *nehiyaw tahp sinowin*. Because Cree was the maternal ancestral language of the Metis community, Cree terminology and concepts of family construction are privileged in this study over francophone, anglophone, and Dene phrases or concepts about family structures, even where similarities in practice may exist. This point is critical, for the story of the socio-cultural development of the Metis community in the northwest – the focus of this book – is best understood from the perspective of traditional Aboriginal family structures and their interaction with land and community.

"Wahkotoowin" has been translated by scholars of the Cree language as "relationship" or "relation," but such a translation misses much of the meaning and sentiment that the term and its various derivatives actually express.[13] As much as it is a worldview based on familial – especially interfamilial – connectedness, wahkootowin also conveys an idea about the virtues that an individual should personify as a family member. The values critical to family relationships – such as reciprocity, mutual support, decency, and order – in turn influenced the behaviours, actions, and decision-making processes that shaped all a community's economic and political interactions. Wahkootowin contextualizes how relationships were intended to work within Metis society by defining and classifying relationships, prescribing patterns of behaviour between relatives and non-relatives, and linking people and communities in a large, complex web of relationships. Just as wahkootowin mediated interactions between people, it also extended to the natural and spiritual worlds, regulating relationships between humans and non-humans, the living and the dead, and humans and the natural environment.

There is precedent for understanding the internal workings of an Aboriginal community through its conceptualization of family. In 1944, Sioux scholar Ella Cara Deloria wrote a path-breaking treatise on Sioux family life entitled *Speaking of Indians*. She described the Sioux *tiyospaye*, or extended family, which served as the social structure of the Sioux, calling it "the scheme of life that worked."[14] As an ethnologist, Deloria sought to explain the large and all-encompassing web of social obligation and responsibility that connected individuals and communities throughout their territory within an extended family matrix. Deloria argued that tiyospaye referred to a system of relationships that had historically regulated Sioux social, political, economic, cultural, and spiritual/religious behaviour and held everyone together by establishing peace, decency, and order among a communal people. According to Deloria, the Sioux defined humanity as being a part of a large family structure; without the struggle to both maintain and gain relatives, she explained, one's humanity was lost.[15] Deloria's was the first account of Indian family and social life explicating the philosophical underpinnings of an indigenous worldview and rebutting the dominant anthropological kinship methodology devised by Lewis Henry Morgan in the mid-nineteenth century. The rather mechanical nature of academic kinship methodology has obscured the humanity of indigenous people in its efforts to trace patterns of descent, marital practices, and concepts of inheritance and classify Aboriginal societies according to matrilineal, patrilineal, or bilateral structures.[16] Deloria's work, however, went largely ignored until anthropologist Raymond J. DeMallie observed in a 1998 article that kinship – that is, family – was the foundation of Native American (and, by extension, Native Canadian) society. DeMallie argued that "the family, culturally defined and embedded in a social system of greater or lesser structural complexity, is basic to understanding Native American peoples."[17]

In order to understand the subarctic Metis society of the northwest, a broader comprehension of Aboriginal familial conceptions generally, as well as a grasp of the linguistic traditions that expressed the philosophical underpinnings of their social structure is necessary. Tiyospaye in Sioux, *nkonegaana* in Anishnaabe, *etoline* in Dene, and wahkootowin in Cree are all terms that privilege the concept of family relationships that are manifest daily in behaviours, attitudes, and decisions made by individuals, families, and communities. The use of a Cree word, in this instance, reflects the dominance of that language in the region, not that the Metis of the English River District were more Cree than Dene or more French than Scottish in their cultural worldview. Whether expressed as wahkootowin, tiyospaye, nkonegaana, or etoline, their worldview was, and is, rooted in family relationships begun on the land, where the marriage of two individuals spread outward to encompass all their relatives (including ancestral relations), the children of that union and their spouses, and those naturalized through adoption and trade or military alliances, all of which informed their decision-making processes, economics, and, eventually, the socio-religious expression of Catholicism.

While all cultures regard blood and marriage as foundational to relationships, Aboriginal communities across North America had additional categories of social relationships that mimicked blood and marriage ties in order to transform strangers – potential enemies – into relatives. Family was easily defined as people encompassed by *ni'amspsko chapanak, ni'wakomakanak,* and *ni'chapanak* (ancestral, living, and future), but it was further extended to include clans and nations, as well as individuals and groups recruited into kinship through methods for naturalization such as adoption. In anthropological terminology, these additional social relationships are defined as fictive because they are "something made," as opposed to genetic connections.[18] The term "fictive," however, does not mean that the relationships are false or unreal.[19] Once established, these relationships were treated as true as any other, a reality that takes on considerable significance because nehiyaw tahp sinowin, like the worldviews of other Aboriginal people, required that relatives not harm one another, whether physically, economically, or politically. As a result, when strangers were acculturated into a community, protocols were in place to naturalize them as relatives, thereby forging deep and personal levels of trust and responsibility. No individual in a territory or community was to be without connections, so a place was made for everyone to belong.[20] Conversely, there were protocols and laws, such as banishment or refusal to accept them as family, to expel or repel those who violated the principles of wahkootowin.[21] Throughout trading territories across North America, the principles for creating family were applied to white fur traders when they arrived in Indian territories.

METHODOLOGICAL AND THEORETICAL PERSPECTIVES

Scholars of family life in colonial New France or British North America will surely find familiar the concepts and values embedded within wahkootowin, but this is not a comparative study.[22] Rather, it is an exploration of historical Metis family construction in a particular geographical location and under specific circumstances as a means to understand their origins, socio-cultural formation, and development as a people over time. It is important to remember that while wahkootowin was the ideal by which individuals and whole communities formed alliances with other individuals, communities, and institutions, the ideal was not always the achievable reality. Human frailty and the complexity of situations sometimes superseded the idealized Metis representation of wahkootowin and made it unattainable. In times of food shortages, for instance, families had to make life-and-death decisions about who most needed the available food. But as a social value grounded in religious and intellectual teachings about how to be a good relative – how to be human – wahkootowin helped people do their best with what was at hand. It is this act of being human within a prescribed societal framework like wahkootowin that merits close scrutiny and evaluation.

I examine the effects of wahkootowin on the economic, religious, and socio-cultural history of this region primarily through an analysis of the historical processes of the Metis emergence as a people and the subsequent formation and interaction of families in the community. The primary method was to reconstruct their genealogies, which were then cross-referenced with qualitative descriptions of the people, their economy, and their religion that were captured in trade and mission journals, correspondence, and employment records. Genealogical information for the region was available from a variety of sources, including the baptismal, marriage, and death registries from the missions of Saint-Jean-Baptiste at Île à la Crosse, Saint-Julien at Green Lake, and the Mission de la Visitation at Portage La Loche, dating from the mid- to late 1800s up until 1912, as well as the Arbre Généalogique for Île à la Crosse and Portage La Loche, recorded by the Oblates in the *Liber Animarum* for each community.[23] Additional genealogical and descriptive data were gathered from the Île à la Crosse, Green Lake, and Portage La Loche post records, dating from the late eighteenth century through to the early twentieth century; Canadian censuses from 1881, 1891, 1901, and 1906; and late-nineteenth- and early-twentieth-century Metis scrip applications. Tracing family genealogies reveals a community's origins and wahkootowin, which, in turn, provides insight into the region's cultural identity and its economic, socio-cultural, and religious history.

In many ways, this study borrows heavily from the techniques of the school of new social history. Methodologically, these techniques offer a means of examining individuals who were largely ignored in historical discourse, gathering all available quantitative records to better understand the lives of women, labouring classes, slaves, Aboriginal peoples, and others marginalized in a discourse dominated by elites. The research into Metis society and economy that most clearly drew from this methodological tradition was Gerhard Ens' work on the Red River parishes of St. Francois Xavier and St. Andrews. In *Homeland to Hinterland,* Ens used what he referred to as a family reconstitution model that relied on parish records to evaluate the chief demographic characteristics of his subjects.[24] By his reckoning, not all families could be fully reconstituted because of their movements in and out of these parishes. Ens' purpose, however, was not to trace family members over time but rather to record and evaluate changes in fertility, nuptuality, and mortality to assess the economies of these two very different parishes. While we gain a great deal of insight into the economy of these communities, we learn little about who these people were philosophically because we gain no insight into their worldview. My work, which is weighted more to qualitative than quantitative data, differs from that of both Ens and other social historians in terms of style more than method.

My purpose is not to quantify the demographic characteristics of this community, to reveal or analyze such things as birth rates, marital ages, or mortality. Instead, the methodology used here draws from the qualitative methodologies employed by such microhistorians as Natalie Zemon Davis and Carlo Ginzburg. In *The Return of Martin Guerre,* Davis noted that historians have learned a great deal about the European peasantry by using sources such as marriage contracts, parish registries, and accounts of courtship rituals, but she concluded that we still know little of the individuals' "hopes and feelings; the ways in which they experienced relations between husband and wife, parent and child; the ways in which they experienced the constraints and possibilities in their lives."[25] Davis sought to develop methods by which she could infer meaning and purpose in the types of choices, reactions, and decisions that her subjects made. Her account of Martin Guerre's story was part invention, "but held tightly in check by the voices of the past."[26] Focusing attention on the same types of populations the social historians studied, Davis and Ginzburg searched for the simple clues, the "inadvertent little gestures," embedded in historical evidence that would reveal much about the relationships between individuals and communities.[27] According to Ginzburg, we need to strive to gain insight from "apparently insignificant experiential data" that reveal "a complex reality that could not be experienced directly."[28] Instead of digging deeply on a narrow and confined topic, Davis and Ginzburg used smaller case studies to discern what might be suggested about the larger historical and intellectual processes of a people. This is where my study of family and community in the northwest is situated methodologically – what can the genealogical reconstruction of family structures tell us about larger historical issues of Metis identity across western Canada and the northern plains, and what can it tell us about the intellectual processes that went into the establishment of a new society? That does not mean this study is a microhistory. Rather, it should be clear this is a local and regional history that combines several methodological traditions in order to privilege an Aboriginal perspective of the role and place of family within a cultural worldview and social framework. By using genealogical records, we can ascertain how specific families formed alliances and whether those alliances were short-term or traceable intergenerationally; how newcomers to a region were acculturated into a society; how people were granted or denied acceptance within a community; and how a host of otherwise intangible aspects made up the Metis style of life.

Existing Literature on Metis Family Life

Tracing family connections, or even using genealogy as a primary methodological approach, is not new to Metis scholarship. There has been a long-standing recognition of the conceptual importance of family in the socio-economic history of the Metis, dating back to Marcel Giraud's two-volume study *The Metis in the Canadian West*. Giraud described Metis family as "swollen with friends or collaterals," whose influence over individual and community behaviour contributed to their poverty and disease by the 1930s.[29] Giraud further claimed that the personality deficiencies of individuals were a result of miscegenation, and he argued that this deficiency spawned a culture that hampered Metis social development. Family members were so reliant on one another that, according to Giraud, sons neglected their own tasks to assist their fathers and vice versa. This closeness did not just exist between parents, children, and close relatives, but "extended as much to the most distant relatives, to friends, or to their descendants."[30] Giraud's analysis of the Metis family was overwhelmingly negative and verged on the eugenic, but the research itself, when stripped of its overly moralizing commentary, reveals the priority that the Metis continue to place on family relationships in times of stress, famine, poverty, and infirmity, while also promoting a sense of shared responsibility among individuals.

There was little subsequent research on Metis family life and culture until the 1980s, when feminist scholars began to explore gender and family life in traditionally male-dominated spheres such as the fur trade. In their pioneering work, Sylvia Van Kirk and Jennifer S.H. Brown argued persuasively that family life in the fur trade was an important aspect of economic and political alliance formation, thereby offering a new means of analyzing Metis society and economy.[31] Diane Payment further focused on the social life of the Metis villages along the South Saskatchewan River valley, exploring religion, gender, and family as a means of evaluating the history of Batoche.[32] More recently, studies by Martha Harroun Foster, Susan Sleeper-Smith, Tanis C. Thorne, and Lucy Eldersveld Murphy continued the exploration of the interrelationship between family and community as both a personal and social construction among Metis in the United States.[33]

Despite such growth and sophistication (not to mention attention), one of the historiographical limitations of much of the scholarship on the Metis to date relates to a rather dogged thematic focus. While much of the new American scholarship is preoccupied with why there are no discernible Metis communities left in the United States, Canadian scholarship tends to focus on how best to classify the Metis – were they more white or Indian, more French or British? In short, Canadian scholars, like their American colleagues, have been overly preoccupied with race at the expense of culture. For instance, relying on evidence provided primarily by the Protestant clergy at Red River, Frits Pannekoek concluded that racial and religious differences between the English-speaking Protestant Halfbreeds and French-speaking Catholic Metis of Red River irrevocably divided the community on the eve of the 1869-70 Resistance.[34] Indeed, continued reliance on terms and categories such as French-speaking, English-speaking, mixed-blood, Métis, Halfbreed, country-born, Catholic Métis, or Protestant Halfbreeds by scholars of all intellectual bents fosters a notion that pulls the community apart rather than binds it together.

Conversely, Irene Spry refuted the existence of racial and/or cultural divisions along French and British lines by surveying non-clerical sources, which showed that "Métis and mixed-bloods" were linked in "ties of blood and long association on the hunt and trip."[35] Intermarriage between the so-called English- and French-speaking families at Red River was, according to Spry, fairly widespread, and so the emphasis on division was less useful for assessing the community's social makeup. The racial paradigm, however, is still with us today, and we need to move past this preoccupation with whether the Metis were more European than Indian or more French than British because it undermines the authenticity of their identity as Aboriginal people who established a culture intrinsically linked to their homeland. One of the ways we can transcend this preoccupation is by evaluating how Metis notions of family or relatedness shaped their participation in the fur trade, their interaction with religious institutions, and their relations with outsiders – Indian or white, Cree or French, Scottish or Dene. To this end, a genealogical reconstruction of the historical Metis families of the English River District and an analysis of the HBC records clarifies the relationship between social and economic realities. As a consequence, a cultural identity is brought into focus, and a people's origins are revealed.

My attention to genealogical reconstruction closely aligns this study methodologically with the work of Heather Devine, who also utilized genealogical research to study the socio-political alliances, migration patterns, economic status, and acculturative forces on several generations of the Desjarlais family. Devine focused on this one family and its collateral relatives over time as they operated within the milieu of the fur trade, radiating out from Quebec across the northern plains and to areas as far flung as St. Louis and New Mexico, to gain an understanding of how "privileges and obligations of kinship" operated in societal contexts.[36] Importantly, Devine expanded on the work of John Foster, whose article on the role of wintering outsider males in the creation of Metis culture on the Plains further entrenched the idea of the paternal organization of Metis family structures and emphasized the role of Canadian freemen *(l'homme libre)* in the ethnogenesis of the Metis.[37] The methodology employed in Devine's study was characteristic of that done by laypeople and professional genealogists alike, because the research began in the present and moved into the past, starting with surviving relatives, informants, and vital statistics to establish a documentary link between the living and historical generations.

These scholars have established a solid foundation upon which to draw. Throughout the course of this study, family is the central theme, with land and language taking strong supporting roles. The genealogical record is examined to contextualize individual or family experiences in relation to the two dominant institutions in the English River District represented by fur trade companies (primarily, although not exclusively, the Hudson's Bay Company) and the Roman Catholic Church. Metis history is generally posited in relation to fur trade or mission histories that conclude that these institutions had a significant impact on the Metis. As a result, within studies of the fur trade and missions, the Metis are often relegated to the margins of a larger narrative. It could be argued that neither form of historical inquiry is capable of truly addressing the role that the Metis had in their own creation. However, reading records in a way that allows us to glean insights from "apparently insignificant experiential data" may reveal that much more complex historical and intellectual processes were at work within Metis communities.[38] For instance, the trade records, the bulk of which were generated by the HBC, describe and identify groups of men and women working together, the perceptions and reactions of individuals and families to trade policies, the interaction of the labouring families with the trade elite (i.e., chief factors, traders, and sometimes clerks), and, perhaps most importantly, the individual families' social, economic, and spiritual calendars. Van Kirk and Brown pursued this type of qualitative research in their early work on the role of women and families in the fur trade. The distinction between that earlier scholarship and my research is that by cross-referencing the genealogical record of a specific, geographically bounded community with the existing HBC records, we can identify the random references to people – servants and their families – that appear in the records and determine whether they were related to others with whom they were working. This form of cross-referencing provides for a better understanding of the nature of labour at the margins of the fur trade economy and the ways in which family members mobilized themselves as a unit of production.

When we examine the relationships within and between families, and between families and representatives of fur trade companies and the Church, from the perspective of the northwest Metis, with their emphasis on family obligation and responsibility, we see that these institutions often had to adjust their expectations and values to accommodate the local worldview. In the northwest, Metis people and communities were not primarily united or created by external forces like the fur trade, the Church, or nineteenth-century nationalist movements that developed to the south and east of them, but rather by the relationships created and nurtured through wahkootowin, which shaped identity, community, and society that, in turn, forged their place within the fur trade and the Church. By using genealogical reconstruction to analyze the historical interplay between families and non-Metis-created institutions, Metis socio-cultural practices relating to naming practices, popular social and religious events, and living arrangements, we can observe and examine wahkootowin as it existed.

GENEALOGICAL RECONSTRUCTION OF THE ENGLISH RIVER DISTRICT

As the genealogies of families in the northwest were reconstructed and as this data was contextualized by information available in the trade records, my research revealed new insights into economic, social, and religious behaviours of the Metis community. In particular, the focus on a large intergenerationally connected and regionally based family system permitted a closer evaluation of gender relations, the nature and structure of various levels of Metis social organization, and the ways in which each generation responded to new issues or pressures. An otherwise large and unwieldy amount of information was synthesized into a database, and forty-three Metis family groupings were identified as the core of the region's society and culture in the nineteenth century. These forty-three core families were grouped by patronyms identified from several hundred surnames listed in the database. Each of these forty-three families ranged in size from a dozen individuals to well over a hundred as each generation grew or contracted over a century or more of existence. These families form the core of the data set for several important reasons: (1) they are traceable intergenerationally; (2) they were linked to one another through marriage, adoption, and socially constructed relationships (e.g., godparents); (3) they were closely linked to Cree and Dene bands in the region; (4) they operated in a variety of economic niches in the fur trade and its associated operations, such as hunting and fishing; and (5) they were Roman Catholics.[39]

Examination of the genealogies of the northwest reveals five generational cohorts between approximately 1800 and 1912. However, only the latter four cohorts will be examined in detail, partly because of the availability of sources, but more importantly because these four generations characterize Metis genesis and socio-cultural development in the northwest. Each of the latter four generations reinforced patterns established in the late eighteenth century by the initial generation, which comprised the first wave of outsider male fur trade employees who entered the region and established relationships with local Aboriginal women. In subsequent generations, female-centred family groups residing throughout the region were identified locally by the men's surnames, thereby establishing a trend of patronymic connections. The women indigenous to the region became the centripetal and centrifugal force that incorporated successive waves of outsider males. These men carried the surnames that came to mark the communities' spread across the northwest, while also identifying the families locally and patronymically. Metis women also influenced the local socio-cultural integrity of the region by maintaining connections to local Cree and Dene communities via intermarriage with local bands, a phenomenon that historian Nicole St-Onge suggests merits further study as we seek to understand the cultural and historical inheritance of Metis communities.[40]

The initial group of residents in the northwest is best understood as a proto-generation, in which the first ancestral men, not indigenous to the

TABLE 1.1   The emerging generations of Metis families in
the English River District (ERD)

Generation	Years	Nationality	Region of origin
Proto-generation	1780s–1810	Cree	ERD
		Dene	Quebec
		Indian	
		French Canadian	
First generation	1800–1830s	Metis	ERD
		Cree	Quebec
		Dene	Scotland
		French Canadian	
		Orkney	
Second generation	1830s–1850s	Metis	ERD
		Cree	Red River
		Dene	
		French Canadian	
Third generation	1860s–1880s	Metis	ERD
		Cree	Rupert's Land
		Dene	
Fourth generation	1890s–1910s	Metis	ERD
		Cree	Rupert's Land
		Dene	

region, arrived and married local Cree and Dene women. The proto-
generation was not characterized by mixed-ancestry people; its members
were the Aboriginal and non-Aboriginal individuals whose actions and
decisions sparked Metis ethnogenesis in the region (see Table 1.1). As non-
Aboriginal fur traders arrived in the English River District in the latter
part of the eighteenth century, their associations with Cree and Dene
women marked the first phase of trade relations and were characterized
by intermarriage and interpersonal alliances. While we often know the
names of these first traders and labourers in the region, the women's names
and even the locations or cultural groups of origin from which they came
are lost, making full genealogical reconstruction for that generation difficult. As a result, locating all the proto-generation's children is often
challenging, although there is a greater amount of documentation for these
offspring than for their parents. The real challenge is to properly link the
first generation to its proto-generation parents. In this task, the family

descriptions and genealogies contained in the Oblate's *Liber Animarum* are particularly useful. The Île à la Crosse and Portage La Loche missions, for instance, maintained local genealogical records that, besides outlining basic family trees of many different branches within a particular patronym, often provide a description of how or where the family originated, as well as descendants. These accountings of family origins have greatly clarified the link between the proto and first generation.

The first generation of Metis in the northwest, the first to demonstrate qualities of socio-cultural development distinct from either of their parents, was born in the late eighteenth century, matured and formed its own families by the 1820s and 1830s, and gave birth to the second generation between the 1820s and 1850s. In the scrip records, members of the first and second generations are often listed as the parents of the late-nineteenth- and early-twentieth-century scrip applicants, and our knowledge about them comes mostly from the recorded memories of their descendants. Mission, census, and HBC records further support the scrip evidence. It should be noted, however, that mission records are not available prior to 1867, so individuals of the first generation are not typically represented in either the birth or baptismal records except as parents and/or godparents. As it was for the proto-generation, the *Liber Animarum* was important in reconstructing this generation as completely as possible. Precise data about the marriages of first-generation Metis are not always available in the mission registries, so the details of their lives were compiled through statements made by their children (the second generation's base) in the scrip applications. Nineteen first-generation couples were identified through the available records. Typically, one half of any couple was born in either the northwest or the hinterlands of Rupert's Land. Based on available evidence, first-generation families began establishing themselves in the area around Lac Île à la Crosse and across the region between 1800 and 1830. It was this first group of married couples and their children who established a stable community to which other individuals and/or families attached themselves when they entered the region, typically as a result of trade demands.

Second-generation families – individuals born in the 1830s, 1840s, and 1850s – were made up of children from first-generation families who continued the pattern of intermarriage. Also like the first, the second generation also incorporated, through intermarriage, new arrivals to the region after the 1821 merger of the Hudson's Bay and North West companies. These newcomers were primarily men who joined the community by marrying daughters of local families and then integrated and acculturated themselves into the emergent Metis society. In a couple of isolated instances, second-generation families were characterized by newly arrived married couples or a son of the first generation returning from Red River with his bride. For instance, George Bekattla travelled to Red River with the HBC brigades and returned to the region with a wife, Nancy Kippling, in the late 1850s or early 1860s. Nancy's younger brother, John Thomas Kippling, eventually joined his sister at Île à la Crosse when he became an HBC servant a couple of decades later. In virtually all instances, these are the individuals who applied for scrip themselves at Lac Vert in 1886 and 1887 or at Île à la Crosse and Portage La Loche in 1906 and 1907, providing information about themselves, their parents (the first generation), and their children (the third generation).

The most comprehensive information exists for the third generation, born in the 1860s through to the 1880s, because the scrip and mission records most accurately correspond to this generation's life cycle, and because the first Canadian census for the area was taken in 1880. The third generation, like its second-generation predecessors, was formed first by another layer of interterritorial intermarriage among the children born toward the end of the child-bearing years of the first generation and from second-generation marriages. This generation further emerged from marriages between Metis women and local Cree or Dene men, Metis or Indian men arriving from other northern communities, or another wave of incoming males new to the region's fur trade economy. As with the second generation, the number of incoming traders included in this cohort's development decreased sharply after 1821, a pattern that intensified in the latter half of the nineteenth century. There are a number of possible reasons for this continued decline of outsider males marrying into the local community. The most likely is the ability of a growing Metis community to establish a stable population that could intermarry and reproduce itself. This Metis population formed a "home-grown" labour pool for the HBC, which no longer had to recruit French Canadian or British traders to the region. The decline may also be linked to a corresponding decline in fur returns for the English River District during this time, which, again, would have been a disincentive for the HBC to recruit new servants to the region.[41] Regardless of the cause, there was a significant reduction in the number of third-generation families with outsider-male heads of household and a concurrent expansion in the number of households headed by couples who were both born inland to Metis families.

.The numerically largest generation examined in this study is the fourth, born between the 1890s and 1910s. All three record sources – census, scrip, and church – coalesce in these decades. The fourth generation was made up of individuals born to the third generation, represented in mission records, and verifiable through census data. However, the records used in this study end at approximately 1912, leaving this generation's profile largely incomplete because their parents were still having children well past that date, and not all members of the third cohort were yet matched up to spouses. This fourth generation is currently the oldest living cohort in the northwest. One important feature of these four generational cohorts is their ever-increasing degree of intermarriage with one another, which established and reinforced community-based interfamilial and inter-generational relationships characterized by regionally based networks centred on females, but with strong patronymic connections.

Conclusion

This study of Metis culture and society did not begin in the present, with living descendants, in an attempt to connect an existing community with its ancestral past. Rather, the research methodology began with late-eighteenth-century records and their reconstruction, and then moved forward in time to fully appreciate the connection of the historical community – the families – to a specific place. Due in part to the nature of the qualitative evidence, this study constructs Metis family history in a thematic rather than chronological manner. As a result, there will be times when the narrative and the families fold back in on themselves as layers of their experiences are peeled back, analyzed, and relayered to build the story's strata. The other organizational choice was to examine a particular community – Sakitawak – in depth and to focus on the intergenerational development of a Metis community bounded by a specific territory in order to reach some conclusions about how Metis communities, made up of both the tangible and intangible qualities embedded in their style of life, interacted with their geography.

As the families of Sakitawak lived, worked, and socialized together, they cemented their responsibilities and obligations to one another, to their land, to their ancestors, and to their spiritual world through relationships defined by wahkootowin. For a historically and genealogically rich Metis community like Sakitawak, mapping family relationships is a means of entering the community and understanding who people were – and still are – and how they defined themselves in relation to all creation surrounding them. People created their culture through these relationships, defined here as an all-encompassing family. They were actively involved in becoming, rather than passively awaiting identity transmission through external forces and trauma. The Metis of Sakitawak and the northwest asserted and established themselves as culturally distinct through their interaction with their families, the economics of the district's fur trade, and the religious demands of the Roman Catholic Church.

"They are strongly attached to the country of rivers, lakes, and forests"

The Social Landscapes of the Northwest

T he local name for Île à la Crosse – the lake and the community – is Sakitawak, which translates as "big opening where the waters meet." Indeed, for several hundred years, travellers canoeing into Sakitawak have been struck by an overwhelming feeling of landlessness as the shoreline disappears on the horizon.[1] This sensation was articulated by Richard Hood, a midshipman in Sir John Franklin's expedition to the Arctic Ocean, which wintered at Île à la Crosse in 1820. Hood described reaching the opening of Sakitawak and travelling through a long succession of woody points until they were engulfed by the lake. Sakitawak was so large, Hood recorded, that he felt as though they had already reached the Polar Sea.[2] About fifty miles in length, Sakitawak is a long, narrow lake, and at any point across it is only two to two-and-a-half miles wide. While not one of the largest northern lakes, Sakitawak is sizable enough to be unpredictable and, therefore, dangerous. On seemingly calm days, the wind can come up quickly, funnelling down the length of the lake to create strong, peaking whitecaps capable of swamping and capsizing a boat. Yet despite the potential danger, this lake, a point on a map that many people passed through, stopped at, and visited between 1776 and 1907, came to be the staging area for a variety of associations marked by negotiated compromises, accommodation, and violence, as well as the site of lasting social relationships, as Metis people defined themselves in terms of their relation to the region.

Located in what many today regard as a remote and isolated region, Sakitawak in the eighteenth and nineteenth centuries was a critical junction

PHOTO I.I   This photograph was taken by surveyor Frank J.P. Crean in 1908 as he catalogued the region's culture and economy during a surveying expedition. The long dock leads to the main gates of the Hudson's Bay Company post, which included trade buildings, houses for servants, and the house of the chief factor (the darker building in the centre of the square). | *The Hudson's Bay Company post, Île à la Crosse, as seen from the waterfront on September 1908* | Frank J.P. Crean fonds, SAB, S-B8937

in the northern trade networks of, first, the independent Montreal traders, then the North West Company (NWC), and finally the Hudson's Bay Company (HBC). By 1821, Île à la Crosse was the HBC's administrative centre for the English River District, boasting a large fur depot that co-ordinated the transportation of furs, servants, and trade goods between York Factory, to the east on Hudson Bay, and the Athabasca and Mackenzie districts to the north and west (see Photo 1.1). The history of the fur trade at Sakitawak – this first point of contact with outsiders – is an important story to tell. But equally important is the story of how the people framed their humanity in relation to the geography in which they lived. This story of people and landscape will orient us as we move into the region's history, a "big opening" where a variety of cultures converged and negotiated their relationships with one another. In addition to being a physical description relating to the lake's size and centrality, "Sakitawak" serves as a metaphor for both the genesis and pervasiveness of the Metis community that, by the early nineteenth century, had developed on the lake's shorelines and throughout the northwest. It is vital to remember that the northwest was primarily an indigenous landscape, whose geography defined (and was defined by) Cree and Dene conceptions of humanity, worldviews that valued reciprocal relationships between family members.

The appearance of rival fur companies in the late eighteenth century did not displace this indigenous worldview; rather, the European and Canadian men who worked closely with Aboriginal trading partners became a part of it. Scholars generally agree that the fur trade's success depended on a trader's ability to establish meaningful social relationships with Indian peoples who refused to trade on purely economic grounds.[3] In his study of military and trade diplomacy from the late seventeenth to the early nineteenth century, Richard White asserts that Indians and traders each had culturally defined expectations regarding protocols for establishing and maintaining their relationships. He concludes that the ambiguous interaction between cultural groups resulted in the formation of a middle ground of accommodation.[4] Questions about how genuinely or authentically each group played out the roles expected of it are less relevant than the ritual of enacting social behaviours that sanctified the relationships. The northwest's fertile geographic positioning created a zone of interaction that was a middle ground economically, socially, and politically; it created a space for an emergent and unique family life. The northwest's physical expansiveness, ecological abundance, and natural connection to other regions ensured its importance to all who lived and worked there. Much like the old port cities of Europe, it served as a meeting space for various cultural groups whose extensive family networks – Cree, French, Dene, British, and Metis – created processes of economic and religious accommodation and acculturation based on mutual interest.

This big opening where people met was not an idyllic landscape – it was a region where food shortages, harsh climatic conditions, violent confrontation, and disease tested the resolve of the population to build their lives. Furthermore, as people met in this big opening, space for each had to be negotiated. The process of accommodating everyone was not always easily or peacefully accomplished, which is why it was so necessary to build alliances through the creation of familial relationships. Because alliances were fashioned under difficult circumstances and by peoples with often competing cultural values, an intellectualization of the possible connections between divergent groups was established based on the organization and conceptualization of family structures. And yet, in the midst of all this, trader and explorer David Thompson observed, "Notwithstanding the hardships the Natives sometimes suffer, they are strongly attached to the country of Rivers, Lakes, and Forests."[5] The Metis of the region emerged within a series of intellectual and physical borders that created space for their development – the geographic overlap of Dene and Cree territories, indigenous worldviews that created family among strangers, and a competitive trade that fostered a particular form of social interaction. This chapter, then, is an exploration of the historical and intellectual contexts within which Metis culture and society were established and the processes by which Metis family organizational structures emerged in this "big opening."

Sakitawak is situated south of the Canadian Shield in a low-lying area with narrow, stony beaches backed by bush made up mostly of aspen and some spruce. Sakitawak, Buffalo Lake, and Clear Lake are actually a single body of water joined by a series of narrows. Combined, these three lakes are identified as the headwaters of Missinipi, renamed the English (now Churchill) River system (see Map 1.1).[6] The low-lying land surrounding the lake is marshy and prone to spring flooding, which should have been reason enough to avoid establishing trade houses on its shores. But the location of the lake at the confluence of these waterways made it ideal for a centralized trade depot that directed the movement of goods, furs, and provisions between northern and southern districts. The lake was rich in fish and waterfowl and served as a summer gathering spot for local Cree and Dene people because the abundance of food could support large family assemblies for sustained periods. Throughout the area, mushrooms, blueberries, chokecherries, cranberries, rosehips, and other plants formed the basis of a local diet supplemented by large game. By the late eighteenth century, fur-bearing animals and natural hay meadows added to the region's economic wealth and desirability.

When Thomas and Joseph Frobisher, private entrepreneurs out of Montreal, in partnership with Alexander Henry the Elder, first reached the Missinipi and Sakitawak in 1775, they met a band of Dene hunters who supplied topographic and geographic information about Lake Athabasca, Peace River, Slave River, and Slave Lake and traded twelve thousand beaver and some otter and marten pelts.[7] Although the first people the Frobishers met were Dene, there has been speculation ever since as to whether they or the Cree were indigenous to the region or whether this region was located where traditional territories intersected and overlapped.

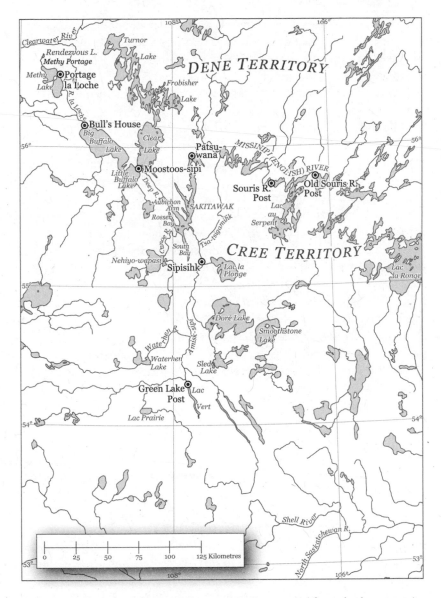

MAP 1.1 Eighteenth- and nineteenth-century indigenous and fur trade place names in the northwest

Despite a lack of firm data, archaeologists and anthropologists have endeavoured to trace the ethnohistorical record and material culture of the Woods Cree and Thi-lan-ottinè Dene to determine which people first occupied the Sakitawak region.

Ethnoarchaeologists Robert Jarvenpa and Hetty Jo Brumbach have shown that the earliest trade records establish Sakitawak as a Cree stronghold by the time Montreal traders arrived in the 1770s. Alexander Mackenzie, who came to the area in 1785, described the Cree as both the permanent and most numerous inhabitants of Sakitawak. He further believed that the Dene were strangers to the region, noting that they seldom stayed in the area more than three or four years before returning to their territories farther north.[8] Mackenzie thought that the boundaries demarcating Cree and Dene territories were roughly north of the Methy Portage for the Dene and south of the English River for the Cree.[9] (Perhaps the Dene were at Sakitawak in 1775 because it was part of their southernmost harvesting territory, or perhaps they were already aware that Montreal traders were travelling north to trade and came to the lake to meet them. The networks of Native people may have communicated news of the fur traders and their plans for expansion.) However, by 1793, Mackenzie identified Dene territory as encompassing both Portage La Loche and Sakitawak, with only a few Cree remaining in the Île à la Crosse region.

At about the same time that Mackenzie was in the English River District, David Thompson, whose wife Charlotte Small was born at Île à la Crosse, gave a more precise rendering of the boundary and recorded that the Cree (whom he called the Nahathaway) lived south of 56° latitude, while the Dene (or Dinnae) lived north of that line. The latitude Thompson was marking lies just north of Sakitawak and runs across Little and Big Buffalo lakes (now Peter Pond and Churchill lakes, respectively) (see Map 1.1).[10] Compared to the boundary description provided by Mackenzie, Thompson's boundary shortened the distance between Cree and Dene territories. Thompson elaborated that "from the rigorous clime of sixty one degrees north, [the Cree] went southward to fifty six degrees north; the Dinnae, or Chepawyans [sic], in like manner occupied the country down to the last named Latitude, and westward by the Peace River to the Rocky Mountains; and have thus quietly extended themselves from the arctic regions to their present boundary, and will continue to press to the southward as far as the Nahathaways will permit."[11] The region in between – Methy Lake, Moostoos-sipi (present-day Buffalo Narrows), south to the northern edge of Sakitawak – was a shared (or overlapping) region where both groups accessed resources on the edges of their respective territories.

According to anthropologist David W. Friesen, the southward shift of the Dene into the Île à la Crosse area occurred between 1789 and 1793. He postulates that a series of smallpox epidemics preceding the arrival of NWC traders in the 1781-82 trading season diminished the Cree population. Those traders reported that the Cree avoided contact with outsiders as they attempted to recover from the disease. Smallpox flared again in 1784 and 1786, and by 1790 the Cree were nearly decimated.[12] As the Cree population at Île à la Crosse declined, fur traders actively encouraged Dene to migrate into the region to serve as fur procurers. By the 1790s, Friesen concludes, the Dene had permanently relocated to the La Loche and Moostoos-sipi regions, which now served as their southern boundary, a theory that corresponds to Thompson's observations.[13]

An analysis of environmental adaptations and material culture led Jarvenpa to conclude that Missinipi was a natural dividing line between northern Thi-lan-ottinè Dene and southern Woods Cree. Within these two territories, Dene and Cree adaptation to significantly different environments fostered distinct cultural traditions. For example, while both the Cree and Dene depended on foot travel in the winter, the former used birchbark canoes during summer to travel long distances, whereas the latter continued to rely on walking as their main form of transportation. According to Jarvenpa and Brumbach, the different transportation methods indicate that the Dene had adapted to a region without large water transportation networks, such as the northern tundra. Furthermore, they note that until the end of the eighteenth century, the Dene constructed only small caribou skin or bark canoes, which they carried long distances until it was necessary to ferry across large waterways in pursuit of caribou herds. The Dene seemed to travel by water only out of necessity, even after they had moved into the Île à la Crosse region, with its plentiful lakes and rivers. Additionally, the Dene continued to rely on caribou for sustenance and as a supplier of all materials needed to sustain life (including hides, sinew, and bones), which indicated a recent adaptation to the Sakitawak environment. Caribou ranges were located farther north than Sakitawak, where moose and deer – both solitary, not herd, animals – were prevalent. In contrast, the Woods Cree relied on moose and deer for sustenance, as well as whitefish common to northern lakes and rivers.[14]

However, Jarvenpa and Brumbach may have overemphasized the role of diet as historical evidence that the Cree lived in a water-rich environment while the Dene lived farther north on the tundra. According to Thompson, Cree men loathed fishing: "Nothing but sad necessity can compel a Nahathaway hunter to carry away fish, and angle for them, this is too mean for a hunter; meat he carries with pleasure, but fish is a degradation."[15] On the other hand, "when the land is scarce of Deer ... [the Dene] take to Lakes to angle Trout or Pike at which they are very expert."[16] Another indication of this territorial divide can be found in HBC journals, which recorded the frustrations of Company servants at having to teach the Dene how to trap smaller fur-bearing animals, as well as how to skin them and stretch the hides. Jarvenpa concludes that the traders' frustration indicates these activities were not part of the eighteenth-century Dene economy.[17]

Evidence about the traditional geography of the Dene can also be derived from their own intellectual tradition, which reveals how they related to the lands in which they lived. Father Émile Petitot, an Oblate who lived in and ministered to the northernmost Dene territory in the mid-nineteenth century, noted that there were four branches of society: Etøen-eldili-dene (Caribou Eaters), T'atsanottine (Yellowknife), Kkpest'ayle-kke-ottine (Aspen Dwellers), and Thi-lan-ottinè (Those Who Dwell at the Head). The latter group resided in the area north of Sakitawak, at the southernmost edges of the Dene territory, and Petitot believed that the term "Thi-lan-ottinè" referred to the location of their traditional territories at the headwaters of the English River. He also recorded a traditional Dene narrative about a giant named "He Whose Head Sweeps the Sky," which details the connection between the Thi-lan-ottinè and the geography of northwestern Saskatchewan, and provides additional evidence of the term's English translation:

> In the time of the giants "He Whose Head Sweeps the Sky," Yakke-elt'ini, used to wander by the Arctic Ocean. One day he met another giant whose name was Bettsinuli and they engaged in a fierce fight. Bettsinuli was the stronger of the two and would surely have won, but "He Whose Head Sweeps the Sky" was saved by a Dene man, whom he was protecting, who cut the back of Bettsinuli's ankle with an axe made of a giant beaver's tooth. The bad giant fell backwards into the sea in such a manner that his feet lay in the West and his head rested in our own country. His head reached the area around Cold Lake and it is for this reason the Dene of these parts call themselves Thi-lan-ottine, "the people at the end of the head." The giant's body became a huge mountain, stretched out as it was and, in time, it became the natural route of migration for the caribou.[18]

How a people name themselves and insert their narrative into a landscape reveals a great deal about their self-conceptions. In this instance, the Dene of the subarctic have a term for themselves that identifies their homeland and how they came to live in the region, which is articulated by their story about the giants.

Despite the observations provided by early traders and the subsequent ethnoarchaeological research, there is no definitive conclusion about who can claim the immediate region around Sakitawak as their traditional territories. What seems clear from the range of evidence is that the region between Moostoos-sipi to just south of Sakitawak was a borderland between Cree and Dene territories. Whether the territory was initially Dene or Cree is, in many ways, inconsequential – these were peoples who came to be intertwined in complex systems of familial relatedness during the fur trade era and identified themselves as belonging to a particular landscape through a variety of means. And in these borderlands, their cultures and histories converged so that by the time fur traders arrived in the late eighteenth century, that new presence was easily integrated into the social landscape of the region. It is in this space and in the act of defining themselves that the borderland became a shared homeland.

This indigenous space underwent significant transformation when the northwestern fur trade economy was established. The history of late-eighteenth- and early-nineteenth-century northwestern Saskatchewan is characterized by exploration, competition, and a continuous search for access to ever-richer fur territories. The history of contact between the Cree, Dene, Scots, English, French, and Metis in the northwest began at Sakitawak and is a story recounted in journals kept by traders, cartographers, and explorers, who discussed how their own economic rivalries fuelled the race to control the regional fur trade, all of which is reflected in the names they gave to the landscape in their own languages. Based on the information and furs obtained in the first transaction with the Dene in 1775, Thomas Frobisher accompanied them to their northern hunting territories that year to see if he could access the Arctic Ocean from Lake Athabasca. While unsuccessful in that venture, Frobisher ascertained the region's advantage for trade.[19] He subsequently built the first trading post at Lac Île à la Crosse in the winter of 1776 on an isthmus at the southwest end of the lake, precipitating the residency of British and Canadian traders, their wives, and their children.[20] Montreal traders hoped that the region, as an opening to the Athabasca territory, would give them easy access to Deh Cho (known today in English as the Mackenzie River), which, in turn, would serve as a conduit to points farther west and, eventually, the Pacific Ocean. If they found such a route, they would no longer have to send furs to Montreal for shipping but could transport them directly to

Asian markets from Pacific posts.[21] When easy routes to the Pacific Ocean were not found, Sir John Franklin, Peter Fidler, and David Thompson (among others) launched exploratory missions to locate routes to the Arctic Ocean, and while these desired passages were never discovered either, their efforts mapped the English River, Mackenzie, and Athabasca districts and expanded the fur trade north.[22] After their foray inland, other Montreal traders followed and established the posts and depots of Lac La Ronge, Cumberland House, Île à la Crosse, Portage La Loche, Green Lake, Souris River, and on Lake Athabasca.

Lac Île à la Crosse became critical to the subarctic trade because of its location near the intersection of the continental divide and two major drainage systems – that of the Athabasca River in the north, which led to the Arctic Ocean, and the English River, which connected to the Hudson Bay drainage system. Methy Portage, at the northern edge of Methy Lake, crosses the height of land that divides two of North America's largest drainage basins – the Clearwater River to the north drains into the Arctic Ocean, while the La Loche River to the south drains into the English River. The English River District was a transitional zone, and as a result it was quickly populated by traders from rival companies competing for furs, trade allies, and prime locations on which to build their establishments.[23]

By the late eighteenth century, independent Scottish traders from the Montreal-based St. Lawrence trade were moving steadily into the English River District and competing actively with the HBC's lucrative York Factory trade on Hudson Bay. At this time, the Montreal traders were not formally aligned with any single company. Instead, between 1763 and 1783 they operated as independent entrepreneurs or in loose partnerships. (In 1783, the Frobisher brothers and Henry the Elder, among others, formalized their operations under the name the North West Company.)[24] As part of the British takeover of the French trade, these new, mostly Scottish, merchant traders relied on the experience and labour of the French Canadian voyageurs in their search for new trade territories in the western subarctic. The Montreal traders reached Lac Île à la Crosse by travelling from Grand Portage at the head of Lake Superior (after 1804 they went through Fort William) to Lake Winnipeg, where they accessed the English River, named for Joseph Frobisher, believed to be the first English-speaking man in the region (see Map 1.2). From there they travelled west to Cumberland House and then north to Île à la Crosse, covering, in total, approximately three thousand miles to reach these trading territories. The Montrealers soon established permanent inland posts and transportation networks to facilitate trade in these regions. The HBC

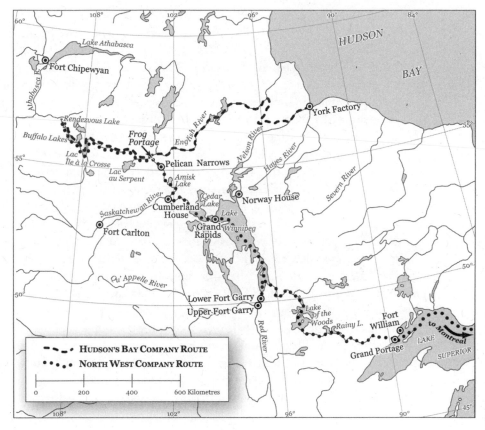

MAP 1.2   Transportation routes of the Hudson's Bay Company and the North West Company

traders, who quickly followed their Montreal competitors into the area, had to travel only about a thousand miles from their position on Hudson Bay to Methy Lake via the English River, passing through a series of lakes and portages.[25]

In 1777, the Frobishers sent Peter Pond inland to chart a route from Île à la Crosse to Athabasca.[26] After wintering at Île à la Crosse that year, Pond made his way north after the ice cleared, initiating a pattern that made Île à la Crosse a general resting place and organizational depot for traders heading farther north or south. Pond crossed the Methy Portage with five canoes in the summer of 1777 and reached the mouth of the Athabasca River.[27] When he returned to Grand Portage on Lake Superior in 1780, he reported on his success at crossing the continental divide and trading with the northern Dene for thousands of furs. Based on Pond's report, other pedlars from Quebec moved in to take advantage of the lucrative opportunities. The English River District quickly became a competitive space involving St. Lawrence-based Scottish/French Canadian interests and the British-owned HBC in an increasingly aggressive trade marked by the rapid construction of rival posts at Île à la Crosse in the 1790s.[28]

Throughout the 1780s and 1790s, smaller companies and established firms alike built competing posts at Île à la Crosse and smaller outposts throughout the district.[29] This eighteenth-century trade was marred by episodic violence, alternating with bursts of friendly interaction between rival trade companies and between traders and the local Aboriginal populations. In this big opening, all groups had to, at some level, mediate and negotiate their space. Trade records from the era often lack specificity about which cultural group of Indian peoples the companies were dealing with. In many respects, the Cree and Dene were essentialized as culturally indistinct "Indians," little more than procurers of furs, and many traders embarked on a path that could have resulted in erasure of the Cree and Dene intellectual space within the region. Yet there were instances when some traders, in the midst of their own battles for economic supremacy, attempted to record details about the people with whom they were trading and the families at their posts. It is in these details that we can see how incoming outsider males inserted themselves into the landscape and, for a brief period, transformed it into a fiercely contested space while paradoxically fostering an opening suited for social interaction predicated on establishing relationships, in particular family relationships.

It was in this socio-cultural context that the NWC sent Patrick Small inland in 1784 to become the company's first employee to live at Île à la Crosse year round. Small, like many of his contemporaries, entered into a relationship with at least one local Cree woman (although he may have been involved in polygamous relationships), and the resulting union produced at least three children: Patrick Jr., Charlotte, and Nancy. Like many of his competitors, Small also engaged in an intense struggle for trade in which he sought to destroy rivals and cultivate necessary relationships. A rival group out of Montreal, Gregory, MacLeod and Company, built a post at Lac Île à la Crosse in 1785 under Alexander Mackenzie's control, and for the next several years the various Montreal-based companies attempted to steal trade and clients from one another.[30] During those first decades of fur trade expansion, the HBC was often unable to compete effectively against its rivals. It was slow to entrench itself permanently at Île à la Crosse, establishing its first post there only in 1791 and not supporting its year-round occupation until 1799, because of the often hostile competition between the companies and, at the time, its disadvantage in manpower.[31]

In 1786, Mackenzie sent his cousin, Roderick McKenzie, to Lac au Serpent (also known as Snake Lake, present-day Pinehouse Lake) to build a post for Gregory, MacLeod and Company. The NWC countered and sent in William McGillivray that same year with specific orders to build a post alongside McKenzie's and monitor his activities. On arrival at Lac au Serpent, McGillivray, isolated from other NWC employees, became good friends with McKenzie and convinced his rival to move his post closer so as to have some companionship. The following season, McKenzie and McGillivray travelled east together as far as possible on the English River, which, according to McGillivray, was good for the morale of both crews. Clearly, in the early years of the trade in northwestern Saskatchewan, rivalry had its limits in isolated environments where adversaries were often each other's only companions throughout the long winter months.[32]

In the autumn of 1790, Peter Fidler, Malchom Ross, and Philip Turnor of the HBC arrived at Île à la Crosse on an exploratory expedition to the Athabasca country. Because of their arrival late in the season and the lack of adequate provisions for the trip, the three wintered that first year at Île à la Crosse under the care of Small and the NWC.[33] Small's hospitality was conditional on the HBC men's promise not to trade with local Indians. As a result, the party lived that winter entirely on fish because they could not obtain any other foodstuffs from Indian hunters or traders.[34] When Fidler built the first HBC post at Île à la Crosse in 1791, the once-friendly Small stationed a party of *battailleurs* (professional enforcers) to watch and intimidate any Indians who attempted to trade with him. Uncomfortable with this new, decidedly hostile relationship, Fidler and his men abandoned the post, which was promptly burned by the NWC.[35] The burning of rival posts became a common NWC tactic as it attempted to overwhelm its rivals throughout the early 1800s, and posts at Île à la Crosse and throughout the district were regularly razed.[36] This pattern of intimidation and destruction exemplifies the fiercely competitive nature of trade relations at the time, but, importantly, there were occasional breaks in hostility, as demonstrated by the relationship between McKenzie and McGillivray and by the initial goodwill of Small.

After the merger of the XY Company and the NWC in 1804, the newly reformed North West Company, the final incarnation of that company, became, for a time, the strongest organization operating in the English River District. From 1804 until 1821, when the NWC and HBC merged under the latter name, levels of violence not previously seen marred competition between the two and proved destructive to regional trade as a whole. In August 1804, William Linklater of the HBC reported to his superiors that two Indians had awaited his arrival at the Grey Deer River. They wanted to know if the information they had was correct – that the Canadians were now the most powerful traders after destroying Churchill Factory and killing all the English. In his report, Linklater assured his superiors that he had informed these two men that the English from Churchill Factory would always supply them with provisions and that the fortunes of the HBC had improved since the incident.[37] All was not well, however. Throughout the 1805 trading season, HBC men in the English River District had to be careful in their trade dealings so as not to cause the NWC to punish the Indians. According to Linklater, while the Dene expressed goodwill toward his men, the NWC and other Montrealers were intimidating them so they would not trade with the HBC. For instance, Linklater noted that on 22 September 1805, two large canoes of Canadians arrived at the HBC post and tried to intimidate the Indians gathered there to trade. Because of this, the Indians decided to trade with the NWC instead, explaining that they could not support themselves and their families near the HBC post. Furthermore, the Indians stated that the Canadians had a better inland trade network and were so numerous that they (the Indians) were afraid to disobey.[38]

This strategy of intimidation was not restricted to dealings with Indians. Tensions escalated in 1805 when NWC clerks, led by Joseph Laroque, kidnapped HBC servant Magnus Johnson Jr. near Lac Vert because he had plans to remain inland with the Cree during the winter. Laroque told Johnson that he was not welcome to stay inland with "their" (the NWC's) Indians. As a means of persuasion, Johnson was put on an island with no boat. Within a few hours, however, he was rescued by a Mr. Campbell and taken to Green Lake, where he took refuge at the HBC post under the care of Mr. Sutherland. Linklater confronted MacDonald of the NWC about these actions but received no satisfaction in the matter. In a similar incident in January 1811, the NWC sent Peter Skene Ogden, John Duncan Campbell, and a Mr. Black to intimidate Fidler into abandoning HBC posts at Île à la Crosse. The NWC men built a watch house overlooking the HBC's gates and manned it with battailleurs, whose job was to prevent the Cree and Dene from trading with the rival company. Ogden and Black then conducted a systematic campaign of violence and intimidation against the HBC, shooting at the post's weather vane and flags, carrying away firewood, scaring off geese, stealing fishing lines, and cutting fish nets in an attempt to either freeze or starve the company out of Île à la Crosse. According to Fidler, the NWC even forbade HBC men from leaving their establishment. The NWC's tactic of cutting off the HBC's food supply was so successful that Fidler was eventually forced to enter an agreement with Roderick McKenzie in which he promised to refrain from trading with the Indians in return for much-needed provisions.[39] Believing that they had defeated him, the NWC declared that Fidler lacked the aggressiveness and courage necessary to be successful in the English River District and declared him an unworthy competitor.[40]

From January until the spring thaw in 1811, the HBC men endured Canadian threats and intimidation.[41] While it is clear from the HBC records that they believed they were the aggrieved party in this dispute, the lack of surviving NWC records make it impossible to gain a balanced perspective. There are indications in the HBC's Île à la Crosse correspondence books, however, that such tactics as the destruction of fish nets were not restricted to the NWC. Throughout 1810 and 1811, NWC employees John Duncan Campbell and William Henry complained that the HBC was intimidating and bullying their employees and families. In a letter to Fidler dated 11 July 1810, Henry complained that the HBC's "request" for NWC men to remain inside their fort or else be regarded as hostile created a difficult situation. Henry asked, "If you allow us to neither walk or speak now, what's to be our situation when we move in with so many women and children."[42] Furthermore, Henry felt that the HBC's suspicions of NWC mischief were imaginary and that no actions had been taken except in retaliation.[43]

The hostile behaviour between the companies continued until the 1821 merger, after which Île à la Crosse became the headquarters and administrative centre for the entire English River District and, therefore, one of the most important posts in the HBC's northern department.[44] Because of its location at the intersection of distinct cultural and ecological zones, it became the main depot, administering all the outposts and ensuring that its northern and southern gateways operated as efficiently as possible. English River District posts varied from large permanent structures, such as Île à la Crosse, Portage La Loche, and Green Lake, to seasonal outposts, such as Bull's House, Souris River on the northern end of Lac au Serpent, and White Fish Lake (now Garson Lake).[45] While trade companies used these seasonal outposts irregularly, over time they became permanent sites of Metis communities.

Next in size and importance after the Île à la Crosse post were the two posts at the northern and southern access points to the district, Portage

La Loche and Green Lake. The northern post in the English River District was the southern entry point to Methy Portage, which separated the waters draining to Hudson Bay from those running into the Arctic Ocean and also connected the English River District to the Athabasca and, later, the Mackenzie districts. The initial route Pond took to the Athabasca District in 1778 remained relatively unchanged for the next hundred years. Those wanting to cross the Methy Portage first canoed north from Île à la Crosse through a twenty-mile arm into a strait of the English River, called Deep River, which led to Clear Lake before entering Buffalo Lake. From there, travellers canoed northwest for another thirty-six miles, to the spot where Buffalo Lake emptied into the La Loche River, which led to Methy Lake. At the northern end of Methy Lake, traders reached the Methy Portage and followed the first eight miles of the arduous twelve-mile portage, which took them to Rendezvous Lake. At the northern end of that lake was the final four miles of the portage, leading to the Clearwater River, which, in turn, led to the mouth of the Athabasca River and then Lake Athabasca (see Map 3.1). Men who worked this portion of the route never travelled into the Athabasca but rather exchanged cargo with the Athabasca brigade. References that describe the Methy Portage trail as hilly are not accurate. It was a trail over a low, broad ridge of land surrounded by spruce and jack pines. The final four miles, however, ascended a steep valley wall.[46] Although only twelve miles long, Methy Portage was one of the most difficult and dangerous portages in all Rupert's Land. The staging area of Rendezvous Lake, near the end of the portage, performed the same function as the NWC's Grand Portage (and later Fort William) at the western end of Lake Superior. These two locations, Rendezvous Lake and Grand Portage, were central points in transportation routes where goods were exchanged.[47]

William Cornwallis King, eventually an HBC chief trader who was stationed briefly at Île à la Crosse from 1885 to 1886, described the Methy Portage as the "separating point between ancient and modern freighting."[48] He further observed that at one time all Company freight went over this route. The annual journey of the southern branch of the La Loche brigade – the group of tripmen (see Glossary) who operated on the Methy Portage – began in Red River during the first week of June. The brigade's first stop was at Norway House to pick up supplies for the Mackenzie District. According to King, until 1848, the La Loche brigade was made up of two separate flotillas and fifteen York boats in total. The two flotillas were always separated by several days' travel. An additional flotilla and two more boats were added to the brigade in 1866.[49] From Red River, the brigade headed northwest across Lake Winnipeg through Cedar Lake, west along the Saskatchewan River to Cumberland House, and then north on the Sturgeon Weir River to the English River. From there, the men followed the English River system to Lac Île à la Crosse and then headed north to Little Buffalo Lake. Upon reaching Methy Portage after this long, already dangerous journey, the men from the southern brigade met the Athabasca brigade, which awaited their arrival at Rendezvous Lake with the proceeds of the winter trade and employees who planed to leave the district. The proceeds and personnel were exchanged for supplies, trade goods, and new servants. The season's journey was not yet complete, however. Each branch of the brigade then returned to its respective territory until the following summer's exchange. Leaving Rendezvous Lake, the Athabasca brigade followed both the Clearwater and Athabasca rivers to reach the southern tip of Lake Athabasca before heading northwest into the Arctic territories, while the southern brigade travelled east to York Factory. At Hudson Bay, the furs were loaded onto boats heading to England, and the La Loche brigade picked up supplies destined for Portage La Loche the next year. The brigade paused at Norway House only long enough to store its cargo before heading south to Red River, where the men spent the winter. In all, the southern brigade's journey took four months.[50]

The La Loche brigade was under the command of Alexis Bonami (or Bonamis) dit L'Esperance, while Baptiste Bruce was the guide and commander of the second flotilla.[51] When King travelled with the La Loche brigade to the Athabasca territory in the 1860s in order to take up a position as clerk, he was a passenger in Bruce's boat. King left a detailed description of Bruce's flotilla, and his account provides insight into the importance of the loads and the danger faced by men employed in this capacity:

Under his [Baptiste Bruce's] sharp, quick commands, the crew looked to their cargo. Bruce inspected it himself, examining the lashings carefully. The complement of each boat was seventy-five to one hundred packages of one hundred pounds each and the value estimated at five thousand dollars. The cargo load of the entire brigade, nine boats, was estimated at forty-five thousand to fifty thousand dollars.

All this cargo was entrusted to one man, Baptiste Bruce, for safe carriage over the treacherous waters to Methye [sic] Portage. I can still hear Bruce's commands. They came short and clear. At his word, when everything about the long, low, open boats had been made safe, the crew fell into their places.

We had a crew of eight men: a steersman, a bowman, and six middlemen. Although I was the officer in charge of the brigade, I took the place Bruce gave me with the men.

Suddenly, through the noise of the send-off, one word rang out: *embarque!* That call was more potent than any military reveille. With a shout the men grasped their oars. The boats shot out from their moorings. The men sang in time to their oars. In the bow of my boat Baptiste Bruce stood like a figure-head, calm, rigid. As we drew farther and farther away, the voices of the crowd, whose very existence depended upon the returns of the fur cargoes, grew fainter. I looked at the rowers. Beads of sweat stood round and silvery on their hairy breasts and between their powerful brown shoulders. The great voyage had begun! ...

The actual commander of the brigade was Baptiste Bruce. From the moment that he put his foot in the first boat of the brigade until the boat touched shore, no matter where, he was in complete command. No other officer of the Company, no matter what his rank – even the governor of the Company himself – dared interfere. There was wisdom in these rules as you will see.

King expressed the exhilaration he felt as fear gripped them all when waters were bad, followed by the joy at surviving the trip:

"Towich!" commanded Bruce. The crew came alive. The vigour of that command brought me to attention, too. The men dragging their starboard oars, swerved the boat and with long strokes steered straight out to open water.

"What does 'towich' mean?" I asked. But though I stood immediately above the oarsman, my voice came faint through the hoarse wind. "'Out into the open lake.' It is Cree," he answered. Then he roared a curse of defiance as an avalanche of water raked the boat from stem to stern. Without missing a stroke, the men got out of their wet jackets and, bare-bodied, doubled to their oars.

A long hour passed. The wind rose to a gale. Bruce moved to the steersman. Through the roar of wind and water, his orders came distinct. "The other boats," he commanded, "must not be allowed to catch up to us or come nearer than two hundred yards. They must not pass us!" He watched to see that when he hoisted or slackened sail, the men in the other boats did likewise.

Now Bruce took the steersman's place. The wind had grown dangerous. Bruce's voice, iron-cool, reached every man. Still his orders were distinct and unhurried. He said: "put the smoked moose tarpaulins (covering from fifteen to eighteen feet long and nine feet wide) over the boats. Nail them securely over the edges. Take all spare oars off the outside of the boats. Lash them right, lengthwise, down the middle of the cargo. Attend to the fastenings at bow and stern. All men to the pans and bail!"

I found myself with the men, bailing, bailing, bailing. Heavens! how the water found, and lodged in, the hollows. Despite the great seamanship of the men, I feared we would be swamped. Now I understood the wisdom of Bruce's command, "towich!" Out here on the open water, the waves were less treacherous than inshore. They were longer and heavier, more like sea waves. Nearer shore, the backwash would have swamped the boat.[52]

The crew survived that moment on their journey, and King's esteem for Bruce and the entire brigade crew grew. King's description makes it clear that the thousands of miles travelled by the brigade were both monotonous and unpredictable, and the life of a boatman in the La Loche brigade was a prized position for that class of servant. When King questioned Noel, his personal attendant on the journey, Noel, commented, "The life of a boatman – it is one big, full life. Me? I would rather be in this ... brigade than – than anything else. It is one big honour for a man to be picked for a boatman in Bruce's brigade."[53]

The brigade crew was made up of anywhere from thirty to sixty men (eight men to a York boat, each of which carried three to four tons of freight, although the capacity was six tons per boat). The real difficulty at the portage was the weight of goods, supplies, and furs that the men were expected to carry. Each York boat was loaded with twenty-five packs weighing seventy-two kilograms each – 1,800 kilograms in total – carried by teams of five men over the course of five days. After the 1840s, oxen and carts were put to work on the portage trail, moving goods back and forth between the portage's south end and the valley rim. In addition to the tripmen required to work on the bridage itself, the La Loche brigade depended heavily on the physical efforts of a substantial resident labour pool, based in the English River District, to maintain the portage, repair the necessary equipment, and care for the animals needed to haul the York boats across the portage. In the 1870s, when Chief Trader Henry J. Moberly built the Methy Portage switchbacks (bends in a road or trail at acute angles that give the trail a zigzag pattern and lessen the steepness of the descent), HBC labourers were assigned the task of physically transforming the portage. In 1875, Moberly again employed local labourers to re-contour the steep valley wall between Rendezvous Lake and the Clearwater River so that ox carts would be able to travel the entire distance of the trip, thereby eliminating the need for the men to carry such heavy cargoes.[54]

Although it had no comparable system of York boat brigades, the post at Lac Vert was another conduit for resources important to the overall operation of the English River District. The Green Lake post, located on Lac Vert's eastern shore, was the collection point for furs from several posts across the district, such as Canoe and Sled lakes. More importantly, however, the Green Lake post joined the English River District with the pemmican-producing forts of the Prairies via a transportation network connected to the southern waterways of the Saskatchewan, Big, and Beaver (Amisko-sipi) rivers. This post obtained a great deal of pemmican for the northern areas, supplying the La Loche and Athabasca brigades with the food necessary to undertake their trek successfully. Because pemmican was an important food staple for traders and trippers, the efforts of the Green Lake post helped ward off starvation in particularly lean years.[55] The Green Lake Road to Prince Albert (via Devil's Lake, Shell River, and Big River) connected to the Carlton Trail, which connected to Red River and points across the western plains. Consequently, the Green Lake Road was a critical junction that linked the northern and southern transportation systems (see Map 3.1).[56] And just as it altered the physical terrain of Methy Portage in the late nineteenth century to meet the needs of the trade, the HBC also made alterations to the Lac Vert transportation corridor: first by introducing steamboats in the mid-nineteenth century to transport the pemmican and then by having servants construct the Green Lake Road. Notoriously wet and muddy, portions of the road actually took the form of a corduroy road, constructed annually with logs harvested by Company servants. Corduroy roads were made by placing logs perpendicular to the direction of travel over a low or swampy area. While such a road improves transportation over impassable mud or dirt trails, it produces a bumpy ride and needs to be continuously maintained as the logs shift or decay. The Green Lake Road along the southern edge of the boreal forest and the northern range of the parkland required constant maintenance, so a supply of labourers was needed to ensure its upkeep.

Many of the men employed along the transportation corridors of the English River, whether as trippers or labourers, left their mark on the district by entering short- and long-term relationships with local Cree, Dene, and eventually Metis women. The presence of these men, whether lengthy or brief, was felt throughout the region as their children became part of the regional family structure and worked in the fur trade economy. Alexis L'Esperance, for instance, the leader of the La Loche brigade, entered into a relationship with a woman named Mary Petawchamwistewin (also known as Ee-Ya-Nis) in the English River District. Alexis and Mary had a son, Samuel, born in the 1840s at Île à la Crosse. Although L'Esperance was a resident of Red River, having been granted an HBC land allotment near Upper Fort Garry in 1835, he made his reputation as commander of the La Loche brigade, navigating the routes to and from the Methy Portage each year. Samuel L'Esperance, conversely, was raised, worked, and married inland in the northwest. Raised in the northwest by Mary and her husband, Abraham Lariviere, Samuel was known to be L'Esperance's son and identified himself as such in 1907 when he applied for scrip.[57] At that time, Samuel explained that he was a boatman for the HBC in the summer and a hunter during the winter. (Because of his job as a boatman, he had been away when the 1906 scrip commission visited Île à la Crosse.) In 1862, Samuel L'Esperance married Veronique Durocher, also of Sakitawak, and their descendants remained in the northwest with a surname that, by the end of the nineteenth century, had evolved from L'Esperance to Misponas. Similarly, there were families at Lac Vert, like the Lalibertes, who worked along the Green Lake Road and whose association with that portion of the region dated to the mid-nineteenth century.

As happened in other fur trade communities, outsider males entered the district as traders, boatmen, fishermen, and skilled tradesmen to set up the infrastructure necessary to exploit the rich fur potential of the subarctic. These men, the progenitors of the local Metis community, established themselves both as workmen within an extremely large and lucrative economic system and as family men, marrying into local Cree and Dene communities beginning in the late eighteenth century and becoming the proto-generation. Information about this initial generation is derived largely from the early trade journals or the testimony of their children recorded in scrip records for the English River District. As a result, the region's documentary record lacks precise detail about the male lineages of the proto-generation.[58] As well, the surnames of many of these initial male progenitors, such as Small, have not had a lasting impact on the region. The men often left the district after completing their contracts, ending the unions they formed.

Many of the children resulting from these unions remained in the northwest with their maternal relatives, but their future depended largely on their gender. Male children were often incorporated into the trade economy when they reached maturity and were typically stationed elsewhere. Females appear to have remained in the region and married the next wave of incoming outsider males in the early 1800s, thereby

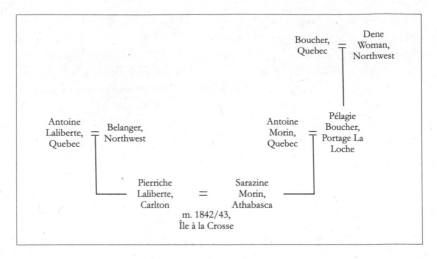

FIGURE 1.1   Emergence of a Metis family in the northwest, ca. 1800

establishing the first generation of Metis families. This is especially significant because it meant that Metis society and culture in Sakitawak
became characterized by a female-centred or matrilocal residency pattern
at the regional level. The family structure that emerged at Sakitawak was
rooted culturally in the history and in the local landscape and worldview
of Aboriginal women. For instance, in the late eighteenth century, a male
trader named Belanger entered the English River District and, by the end
of his contract, left behind a daughter known in the historical records
only as "the Belanger woman." Like her mother before her, this woman
married an outsider male, Antoine Laliberte from Quebec. The Belanger/
Laliberte union resulted in the birth of one of Sakitawak's first-generation
males, Pierriche Laliberte, who married Sarazine Morin, the eldest daughter of Pierriche's colleague Antoine Morin and his wife, Pélagie Boucher,
herself the daughter of a French Canadian trader and a Dene woman (see
Figure 1.1).

    As the English River District became home to Metis children like
Pélagie Morin and Samuel L'Esperance, Metis society emerged and gained
strength because of its connection to indigenous worldviews that were
predicated on the children's ancestral connection to the lands of their
female relations. Over time, the region itself was transformed into a Metis
homeland not only by virtue of the children's occupation of the territory,
but also through their relationships with the Cree and Dene women and

fur trader men from whom they were descended. The Metis, like their Indian and fur trader relations, lived in a social world based on reciprocal sharing, respectful behaviour between family members, and an understanding of the differences between themselves and outsiders. The Metis of the area were part of the economic structure of the fur trade, facilitating its success by embodying the principles of family loyalty, accountability, and responsibility.

In the eighteenth century, David Thompson recorded a number of details about the social values of the Cree and Dene that were explained to him by male elders or that he observed himself. Thompson's observations about Cree and Dene societies are significant because they reveal elements of wahkootowin that came to play a central role in shaping Metis society in the northwest, laying a foundation for the Metis social reality. For instance, according to Thompson, the Cree "are all separated into many tribes or extended families, under different names, but all speaking dialects of the same language, which extends over this stony region." Of Dene hospitality, he observed, "They are as charitable and humane to those in want, as circumstances will allow them."[59] Thompson provided detailed ethnographic information about how family relationships shaped the social and geographic landscape of Cree society and, in turn, how that landscape shaped the region's social geography.[60] About extended family relations among the Cree, Thompson noted that "after a long separation the nearest relations meet each other with the same seeming indifference, as if they had constantly lived in the same tent, but they have not the less affection for each other ... Those acts pass between man and man for generous charity and kind compassion in civilized society, are no more than what is every day practiced by these [people]; as acts of common duty; is any one unsuccessful in the chase, has he lost his little all by some accident, he is sure to be relieved by the others to the utmost of their power, in sickness they carefully attend each other to the latest breath decently."[61]

Although these general ethnographic descriptions about the Cree and Dene are informative, Thompson's observations of people's behaviour and beliefs in the afterlife and the Witigo spirit reveal much about how subarctic people ordered their world and understood humanity. Encountering a Dene woman who had just lost her six-year-old son, her only child, Thompson observed that she mourned for the boy a full twelve months, as was the custom of her people. But after several months passed, he noticed that her grieving was not quite as strong as before, and he asked her why. The woman responded,

When my little son went to the other world, there was none to receive him, even his Grandfather is yet alive; he was friendless, he wandered alone in the pitching track of the tents, (here she shed tears) there was none to take care of him no one to give him a bit of meat. More than two moons ago, his father died, I sorrowed for him, and still sadly regret him but he is gone to my son, his father will take great care of him. He will no longer wander alone, his father will always be with him, and when I die, I shall go to them.[62]

Thompson was struck by how this belief in the afterlife comforted the woman and, in particular, how people maintained and acknowledged the importance of their family connections even in death. He attempted to impart to the woman something of his own Christian beliefs, telling her that to achieve happiness in the afterlife, people must remember to lead good lives on earth. Yet life in the physical world was not at the heart of her story. Family, whether living or dead, cared for one another, and so this young boy needed relatives in the afterlife so that he would not be alone, without family.

Likewise, there were terrible circumstances in the living world that people faced as they strove to survive in a harsh environment and retain their humanity. Witigo, the cannibal spirit, was familiar to all people of the boreal forests. Although the spirit normally inhabited the forests, during times of famine or extreme hardship it could take over a human. According to Thompson, "The word Weetego [sic] is one of the names of the Evil Spirit and when he gets possession of any Man, (Women are wholly exempt from it) he becomes a Man Eater, and if he succeeds; he no longer keeps company with his relations and friends, but roams all alone through the Forests ... preying upon whom he can, and as such is dreaded by the Natives."[63] Thompson provided two rather long stories about Cree Witigo with which he was familiar. In the first tale, a man is killed after informing his people that he is possessed by the Witigo spirit; in the second story, another man is saved from imminent death after becoming Witigo because people feel that he has been favoured by the Creator. The man killed in the first story, Wiskahoo, had gone for a long time without being able to catch any animals and was unable to feed his wife and children. Wiskahoo was twice so close to starvation that he considered eating one of his children to save the others. Fortunately, they were all found before such a horrible act could be completed, and his family's hunger was relieved by the kindness of others. But according to Thompson, "these sufferings had, at times, unhinged his mind."[64] Because of his misfortune and the suffering of his family, Wiskahoo grew melancholy and fearful of being left alone. After a time, he told the others around him, "nee weet to go," which Thompson translated as "I must be a Man eater" and understood as Wiskahoo's declaration that he was possessed by the spirit that craved human flesh. After hearing this declaration, the men of the community tied Wiskahoo up and took him to his tent. Although Wiskahoo did not actually devour anyone, his troubling behaviour continued for several years, and the sadness he felt was never released. After three years, feeling that there were no other options, the men "shot him, and burnt his body to ashes, to prevent his ghost remaining in this world."[65]

In the second tale, another beaver trapper, Apistawahshish, was saved from such a fate. While attempting to dislodge some beaver from their lodge, Apistawahshish so damaged his tools that he could no longer cut firewood or chisel the ice. Because the lakes were frozen, he and his family had no means to seek help or repair their tools. According to Thompson,

> Distressing times came, and they were reduced to use as food the youngest child to save the others. They were so weak they could barely get a little wood for the fire; sitting in sorrow and despair looking at the child next to lose it's life, a Rein Deer came and stood a few yards from the tent door; he shot it and [it] became the means of saving them, and recovering their strength; and for the winter he was a fortunate hunter. Both himself, his family, and the Natives believed that this Deer was sent by the Manito in pity to himself and family.[66]

So why was one man saved and the other killed for the same crime of being Witigo? One man recognized the gift of humanity that he had been granted, while the other was unable to see past his sorrow and continue on with his life despite tragic circumstances. According to Thompson, Apistawahshish was not held responsible because

> the Indians ... felt they were all liable to the same sad affliction; and the Manito sending him a Deer, showed a mark of favor. As the strong affections of an Indian is centered in his children, for they may be said to be all he has to depend upon, they believe the dreadful distressed state of mind which necessity forces on them to take the life of one of their children to preserve the others, leaves such sad indelible impressions that the parents are never again the same [as] they were before, and are liable to aberrations of mind. It is only on this Region and the Lakes westward to near the great plains, where there are Horses, that the Natives are subject to this distress

of hunger, their Dogs are starved and do them very little good. If the country contained but half the Deer and other animals some writers speak of, the Natives would not suffer as they do.[67]

The humanity of these northern peoples was in wahkootowin, which, in turn, framed their sense of family and home as embodied by their landscape. It was in the context of this universal worldview that the proto-generation established relationships that laid the foundation for their children to create a society that reconciled this space into their own worldview, predicated on extended family connections as the basis of their humanity.

Just as an understanding of Cree or Dene conceptions of family can be understood in relation to often-tragic oral narratives that show the darkest possibilities of the human condition, one of the best pre-1821 sources of evidence about family activity are the HBC's tales of intense conflict with their competitors. In the 1810-11 trading season, when the level of hostility between companies greatly increased, one particular incident involving a marital conflict profoundly affected both the trade and human relationships. According to the Île à la Crosse post journal entry for 6 July 1810, HBC fisherman Andrew Kirkness and his wife got into an argument, and she left him to "go over to the French House [a NWC post] last Saturday."[68] A full week after her departure, two HBC men went to the Canadian house to appeal to the woman to return to her husband, but they subsequently reported that she was afraid to return because the Canadians had threatened to cut off her ears. The Canadians apparently believed that Mrs. Kirkness, not her husband, was the actual HBC fisher and that her absence from the post would hasten the Company's demise that season. Kirkness, deeply distraught that his wife had left him, also went over to the NWC post to convince her to return to the HBC with him.[69]

When Mrs. Kirkness refused his pleas, Andrew deserted the HBC sometime between four and five o'clock on the morning of 4 August 1810 and went over to the NWC house to work as their fisherman.[70] Peter Fidler wrote to John Duncan Campbell of the NWC house at Île à la Crosse, angrily demanding "that you no longer detain, but, allow them both [Kirkness and his wife] to return to us now, unmolested. – The term of his last Contract with the Hudson Bay Company being unexpired; consequently he is still [our] lawful servant."[71] Campbell replied that because Kirkness was already inclined to do so, he would permit him to return to the HBC when the Company was ready to leave for Churchill Factory in the fall. In the meantime, however, Campbell warned Fidler that the Company should not interfere with either Kirkness or his wife while they were at the NWC post.

The HBC men, dependent on Kirkness and his wife for daily sustenance, were angry that both these valuable workers were gone. Although Kirkness was the contracted servant, it seems clear that he relied upon his wife's assistance at the fishery. Officials of both companies acknowledged that Mrs. Kirkness, although not herself a contracted servant, was a valuable contributor to the post's subsistence, and that without her the HBC's fisheries would collapse. Because Kirkness and his wife supplied the HBC post with its most reliable source of food, the loss of their services and skills was an enormous blow. None of the other men employed by the HBC were skilled fishermen, so the Company employed Fidler's wife, Mary, a Swampy Cree woman from York Factory, in that position for almost two months until a skilled man arrived from Churchill Factory with the following season's outfit.[72] In a journal entry written years earlier, Fidler ruminated on how important Aboriginal women, with their knowledge of the land and environment, were at these isolated outposts, noting that Malchom Ross was travelling with his wife and two children because "an Indian woman at a House is particularly useful in making shoes, cutting line, netting snowshoes and cleaning and stretching beaver skins and that the Europeans are not acquainted with."[73] His assessment of women had changed little in the ensuing years, and he attempted to convince Mrs. Kirkness to return to the HBC with her husband. Kirkness eventually did return to the employ of the Company, but without his wife, who, according to Fidler, remained a "captive" of their rivals. It is unclear what occurred between the couple, but the outcome for the two companies is certain. As a result of ongoing conflict, of which the Kirkness incident was but one example, the HBC's London Committee ordered the abandonment of the post at Île à la Crosse in the spring of 1811.

There were no Kirknesses in Île à la Crosse after this incident, so it seems that the family made no discernible patronymic imprint on the English River District. However, the dynamics of family life and labour experienced by the Kirknesses' relationship set a long-lasting pattern for the Metis people of Sakitawak. At the start, a marital dispute caused Mrs. Kirkness to leave her husband and move to the other establishment. Motivated by love or by an instinct for survival, Andrew Kirkness likewise abandoned the HBC for its rivals so he could be reunited with his wife. Life hinged on women's ability to draw to them individuals who would become integral to their family, as well as on women's skills as articulated by Fidler, who attempted several times to secure the return of Mrs. Kirkness before employing his own wife as the post fisher. Furthermore, residence patterns in Sakitawak were regionally matrilocal. In the case of the Kirknesses, Andrew followed his wife over to the NWC's employ.[74] There is no other data on Mrs. Kirkness, so we do not know if she was Cree or Dene or if she was even from the region, but the decision to leave her husband after a quarrel indicates a particular self-assurance and possibly a connection to the lands and people of the region. Mrs. Kirkness had enough confidence in her knowledge of the area to leave her husband and move over to the NWC post alone. The HBC representatives rationalized the incident by blaming the NWC for what occurred, claiming that she was a captive rather than acknowledging that, as an Aboriginal woman, she had other choices about where and with whom she would live and work. This family-based self-interest was instrumental in shaping the form and content of Metis cultural life in Sakitawak over the next four generations.

At these geographic locations and moments, Metis communities were established and thrived in an environment that needed their labour. Metis emergence in the region occurred within a series of intellectual and physical borders that created space for their development – the geographic overlap of Dene and Cree territories, an indigenous worldview that created family among strangers, and a competitive trade that fostered a particular form of social interaction. The role of Cree and Dene cultures in creating a sense of humanity within the landscape is as important as the way the terrain directed people's interactions with the physical ecology of the region. The introduction of white traders into this social and physical landscape was the final crucial piece. From these key antecedents, we will now turn to more specific aspects of the Metis community that developed in the northwest.

2

"The bond that connected one human being to another"

Social Construction of the Metis Family

In 1907, Hudson's Bay Company officer R.H. Hall of Prince Albert wrote to Chief Trader Angus McKay at Île à la Crosse regarding Charles Eugêne Belanger's intention to wed Marie Béatrix Maurice, a young woman from a well-established local family. The young couple had met at the Île à la Crosse post, where Béatrix was employed as personal maid to Chief Factor A.A. McDonald's wife and Charles was a newly arrived servant. Both Charles and Béatrix came from families with long histories of employment with the HBC. Béatrix was the daughter of Philomène Lariviere and Magloire Maurice. Magloire was the son of a French Canadian HBC servant, François Maurice, who began his career in the English River District as postmaster of Portage La Loche, a job held by his son in the late 1890s. After arriving in the district, François married Angèle Laliberte, a local woman who was the daughter of HBC servant Pierriche Laliberte and his wife Sarazine Morin, who was the daughter of proto-generation parents (see Figure 2.1).

Béatrix's maternal relatives, the Larivieres, were equally connected to the HBC. Philomène's father was Abraham Lariviere, a Company fisher-man, while her brothers were general labourers and her sisters married Company men. Furthermore, through both her maternal and paternal relatives, Béatrix was not only connected to men employed by the HBC (father, grandfathers, brothers, brothers-in-law, and uncles), but was also related to a long line of women whose uncontracted, casual, seasonal labour was an important part of the English River economy.[1] Béatrix herself became an employee, working as a domestic for Mrs. McDonald. Béatrix's

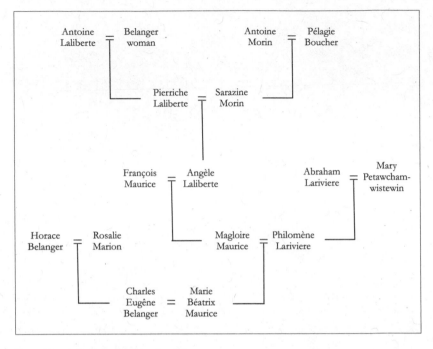

FIGURE 2.1   Béatrix Maurice family

lineage in the region and with the Company, it is clear, dated to the late eighteenth century.

In contrast, Charles Belanger had only been stationed at Île à la Crosse that year. However, because of his family's reputation and his first five years of service at Lac du Brochet, he was seen as a promising young servant and well suited to this new environment. Within five years of signing on with the Company in 1902 as an apprentice clerk, Charles had attained the rank of outpost manager at Buffalo River in the English River District.[2] According to Hall, Charles possessed many of the same abilities as his brother, Horace Belanger Jr., who was regarded as a shrewd and capable trader with "considerable tact dealing with Cree Indians and Halfbreeds."[3] Charles was being groomed for a career with the Company, but Hall felt that his impending marriage to Béatrix placed that career in jeopardy. Hall reasoned that marriage to Béatrix would pull Belanger "down to the level of his wife's relations."[4] Hall was determined to save Charles from himself and declared his intention to help the young man choose a better path. Still, he feared that it was too late, lamenting that young men such as Charles often believed they knew better than their elders.[5]

The same day that Hall wrote to McKay, he also wrote directly to Belanger, reminding him that Horace had come to regard his marriage to a "Native" woman as a mistake that he was stuck with for the rest of his life. Hall further noted that while many men who married into northern Aboriginal families were useful HBC servants, they were socially handicapped because the "native Indians and Halfbreeds of the north" were "raised in low moral surroundings and in homes where the wages and habits of civilization [were] not practiced."[6] While Hall obviously felt that Belanger was marrying below his station, he nevertheless allowed for the slim possibility that working for Mrs. McDonald might enable Béatrix to learn the necessary skills to become a fit wife and rise above her low moral background. Hall concluded his letter with the following assessment of the northern Metis: "I have always believed that the Halfbreeds would make as good men or women as other people if properly brought up and we know that there are no better or purer women than some of the Halfbreeds who grew up in proper surroundings in Manitoba."[7]

Despite Hall's strong opinion and fatherly intent, on 1 April 1907, twenty-six-year-old Charles Eugêne Belanger and seventeen-year-old Marie Béatrix Maurice were married at the Île à la Crosse mission. Sixteen days later, Belanger resigned from the Company.

Four months later, the saga of Charles and Béatrix resumed in the HBC correspondence records. Hall wrote to McKay at Île à la Crosse, reminding him of Charles' mistake in marrying Béatrix. Hall further outlined what he believed were the young man's deficiencies as a Company servant. For one, as an outpost manager Belanger had proven, in Hall's view, incapable of earning a profit. Furthermore, Belanger's commitment to his employer was also seen to be lacking. Within days of resigning in April, Belanger re-engaged, then resigned again in September 1907 to enter the service of Revillon Frères, a Paris-based trade company now competing with the HBC in the English River District.[8] However, Belanger quickly broke his contract with Revillon and returned to the HBC. Belanger's waffling between these two competitors, Hall argued, proved that he lacked the "ballast" and personal qualities required to be a successful HBC employee. (Nevertheless, and rather curiously, even though he had resigned twice within a matter of five months, the Company rehired him.) Belanger's inability to commit to an employer, Hall concluded, was directly linked to his choice of wife, and Hall lamented that he had not done more to secure Belanger's future, concluding that, for the sake of Belanger's family, the young man should have been sent to another district earlier "in order to prevent his marrying one of the half-civilized Natives."[9] Belanger, a

once-promising employee with many of the same qualities as his brother
and father, was no longer trustworthy. As such, Hall advised that he be
placed on the temporary employee list.[10]

The marriage of Béatrix and Charles reproduced two long-standing
patterns that had emerged a century earlier and became common to families in the northwest. These two patterns were a broadly defined matrilocal
residency, where women drew men into the region and grounded them
in the values, beliefs, and behaviours of the local culture, and a counter-
balancing reliance on patronymic connections, or the association of
specific family surnames with particular locations. In both these patterns,
wahkootowin provided the structure and values important to the creation
and spread of a Metis cultural identity in the region. Like her female relatives – specifically her mother Philomène, grandmother Angèle Laliberte
Maurice, great-grandmother Sarazine Morin Laliberte, and great-great-
grandmother Pélagie Boucher Morin – Béatrix incorporated an outsider
male trader into the maternal heritage of the district and the broader
regional Metis community. By doing so, she created for her husband a
space within the family-defined cultural system that provided him with
relations on whom he would be able to rely as a trader in her family's
homeland. In turn, the Belanger surname was incorporated into the
familial-based community at Île à la Crosse and was associated with that
specific community and geography during the first decade of the twentieth
century. The issue of place – the land of Béatrix's mother and grandmothers
– is a central part of the family narrative and history of the district, but so,
too, is the emergent patronymic legacy of surnames such as "Belanger,"
which took its place alongside other, more established surnames in the
region.

Taken at face value, it is possible that Hall's criticism of Belanger was
simply based on racist and classist ideas about Aboriginal people and what
constituted civilization. It may also have been an employer's response to
an employee's determination to work for a competitor. When the story of
the Belanger/Maurice marriage is deconstructed, however, it reveals a great
deal about Metis family life and its relationship to the HBC. As he expressed
concern for Belanger's future and life choices, Hall's approach was to first
criticize Béatrix and then denigrate her family, her homeland, and her
community. By extension, Hall criticized the local community's values, or
what he regarded as a lack thereof, as evidence of its incivility. The Company's attitude toward families was paradoxical. On the one hand, wives
and children of employees contributed positively to the economy by providing additional labour, such as fishing, tending gardens, and caring for

livestock. But these families were, at best, unpredictable. At worst they placed their interests, relationships, and personal obligations above all other considerations, including the Company's profit margins. Judging the people of the northwest by his own standards of civility and gentility, Hall revealed his ignorance of how civility manifested itself in the north-west. He did not devalue the centrality of family, as embodied in the worldview of wahkootowin; it was invisible to him. To comprehend fully how wahkootowin functioned in the northwest, we have to go back to its beginnings among the Metis of this place. We must use the methods of genealogical reconstruction to piece together the region's social patterns and dissect the clues that they provide. By doing so, we can chart and evaluate the kinds of structures that brought coherence and unity to this Metis community over time and in a specific place.

Genealogy is a methodological tool that in and of itself says little more than who is related to whom. For genealogies to mean anything – for them to speak to a culture's social organization, beliefs, or values – we must apply an analytical framework that allows us to interpret the reasons behind a people's behaviours. Understanding genealogies as a reflection of social organization can reveal, as Herbert G. Gutman, a historian of the black family in America, observed, whether a people's beliefs are congruent with their behaviours.[11] While the two chief types of historiographic traditions in which the Metis are discussed – fur trade and mission studies – may use a genealogical method, they have nevertheless only told us what those institutions have done to shape or influence Metis behaviour and cul-tural development; they do not reveal how Metis beliefs shaped either of those institutions or reflected their own worldview. That is, they treat the Metis as objects being affected by institutions, not as subjects in their own right. The reason for this focus on behaviour as opposed to beliefs is, in part, a reflection of the analytical frameworks that have previously been used to interpret Metis genealogies. Metis culture and, by implication, the people themselves still tend to be described solely as an amalgam of First Nations and European cultures and institutions. How many parts Cree to Scottish does it take to make a Metis? How many parts French to Saul-teaux? Which is more important in the mix – European or Indian ances-try? When is one too Indian or too European to be considered Metis? Questions such as these handcuff meaningful investigation. Related to this, one of the limitations of traditional genealogical analysis is that it focuses on the individual, not the family or community, as an integrated system. As a result, a single person can be removed from his or her fam-ilial and social context, and the individual's actions can be evaluated as a single moment in time rather than as a series of behaviours influenced by beliefs. As such, the individual's ancestry, rather than his or her cultural identity, becomes the focus of the inquiry.

Because of this emphasis on ancestry, Metis scholarship has developed categories of "Metisness" to describe individuals, family groups, or communities as either French-speaking Métis or English-speaking Halfbreeds, as HBC country-born or NWC Métis, as Catholic Métis or Protestant Halfbreeds, or, finally, as Métis or metis. Each of these reference points establishes a binary between types of Metisness that, in essence, privileges an ongoing Canadian discourse that pits the English against the French Canadian experience. These labels, however, have done little to explore Metisness as either an Aboriginal phenomenon or a dynamic process of metissage, a cultural force that has continued to grow and evolve with the people since the eighteenth century. Concepts of time and space have been regarded as less relevant than which paternal heritages have had the greatest influence on Metis socio-cultural contexts. This lack of attention to the emergence of Metisness as an expression of Aboriginality is the result of scholars focusing their gaze on the process of becoming, rather than exploring what it is to be a new people.

For this work, I constructed genealogies using records created by church, state, or economic institutions, but the analytical framework I applied is Aboriginal – specifically a Cree or, more broadly, an Algonquian one that also resonates with Dene and other indigenous nations' conceptions of relatedness. Applying the principles of wahkootowin to the genealogies provides insight into beliefs regarding family relatedness. Furthermore, when the genealogies are read alongside, and within the context of, the textual records of the HBC, such as correspondence, journals, and narratives, we gain greater insight into how behaviours are influenced by those principles. In the context of wahkootowin, individuals were taught that who they were could only be understood in relation to others in their family and community, as well as in relation to the environment, the sacred world, and outsiders. According to Saskatchewan Cree elders, family systems were "the bond that connected one human being to another [and] ... the Creator," holding everyone together in a web of interpersonal relationships that involved both great rewards and sacrifice.[12] Importantly, wahkootowin socialized an individual to the proper way of behaving toward all people (oneself included), the land itself, and all realms of existence. Family relationships were the social institution and cultural essence that regulated both internal and external community relations. Within Metis society of the northwest, family served as the foundation for all other relationships – economic, religious, social, and political – and had an enormous impact on how non-Metis relationships were structured and interpreted throughout the region.

The question, then, is how does a philosophical belief become operationalized on a daily basis? One of the means by which this interior landscape of Metis cultural identity and social formation can be evaluated is by first reconstructing, and then deconstructing, the community's genealogies through an explication of the clues to the behaviours and beliefs of the people that are embodied in such decisions as naming, marriage, and adoptions.

Regionally, the Metis community was centred on matrilocal residence patterns. Anthropologically, matrilocality refers to household residency. In a matrilocal culture, women remain in their mother's household after marriage, along with her husband and children. Sons move out of their mother's household after marriage to join the household of their wife's family. Matrilocal residency takes a number of forms, including bride service, in which a man moves in with his wife's family but sets up his own household after he has met his obligations to repay the family for the loss of a daughter. Brief periods of matrilocality might also occur to permit the wife a period of adjustment as she makes the transition from child to married woman. However, in this study the term "matrilocal" is used in a much broader context, applying to the regional, rather than household, marital systems of northwestern Saskatchewan and assuming that the arrangement is permanent rather than a transitional stage in a marriage's life cycle (see Table 2.1). Couples may have lived anywhere in the region, including apart from the wife's immediate or birth family, while still adhering to the pattern of matrilocal residency. If the region as a whole is regarded as a Metis homeland (although not necessarily exclusively so, as seen in Chapter 1), then all outsider male traders who entered the region and subsequently married into one of the northwest's families also married into a society marked by a regionally defined matrilocal residency. Men joined a community that had, as part of its maternal ancestral legacy, a strong relationship to the land that was defined by the presence of women born on that land.

The community, family-band, or household level was the second pattern evident in the region. Families were marked by strong patronymic connections, and their branches became identifiable with specific locations in the region. In *Metis of the Mackenzie District,* Richard Slobodin argues that a widespread feature of Metis family and social life was the development of a cultural identity centred on a patronymic connection, which

TABLE 2.1 Family matriarchs of the northwest, 1800–1850

Name	Birth date	Place of birth	Nationality	Married	Husband
Margaret Bear (L'Ours)	1830s/1840s	?	Halfbreed	1850s	Jean Baptiste Jourdain
Marie Betkkaye	1846	Île à la Crosse	Chipewyan breed	24 May 1869	John Catfish
Pélagie Boucher	1803	Portage La Loche	Montagnais Metis	1818	Antoine Morin
Agathe	1836	NWT	?	?	Baptiste Montgrand
Thérèse	ca. 1800	?	?	1820s	Old Montgrand
Julie Desjarlais	ca. 1811–1815	NWT	French breed	1. 1830s 2. 1830s	1. Louison Roy 2. Michael Bouvier Sr.
Marguerite Bouvier	1842	Île à la Crosse	Halfbreed	1866	Vincent Daigneault
Mary (or Marianne) Catara	1850s	Île à la Crosse	Chipewyan French breed	1. ? 2. 1896	1. François Magloire Touslesjour/ Herman 2. Baptiste Charlot Lafleur
Marie Durocher	1826	Green Lake	French breed	1865	David Lariviere
Véronique Durocher	1846	Île à la Crosse	Cree breed	1862	Samuel Misponas/L'Esperance
Eliza Durocher	1843	?	Cree breed	1860s	Baptiste Natomagan
Louise (or LaLouise) Herman	1846	Portage La Loche	French breed	1. 1860s 2. 1870s	1. Baptiste Sylvestre 2. Baptiste LeMaigre
Marguerite Ikkeilzik	1832	?	Dene/Montagnais	1850s	Pierre Malboeuf
Elizabeth Janvier	1814	Portage La Loche	Chipewyan breed	1840s	Louison Janvier
Angèle Laliberte	1830s/1840s	Portage La Loche	Metis	1850s/1860s	François Maurice

Name	Birth	Location	Ethnicity	Marriage	Spouse
? Belanger	1790s/1800	NWT	Halfbreed	1810s	Antoine Laliberte
Sarazine Morin	1824	Athabasca	French breed	1840s	Pierriche Laliberte
Marie Morin	1830s/1840s	Île à la Crosse	French breed	1850s	Peter Linklater
Sophie Morin	1840s/1850s	Île à la Crosse	French breed	1. 1861 2. 1870s	1. William Linklater 2. Paul Delaronde Sr.
Géneviève Lapouce	1850s	Portage La Loche	French breed	1903	Louison Velner
Marie Ann Janvier	?	Portage La Loche	?	1840s/1850s	? Velner
Angélique Lariviere	1849	Île à la Crosse	Halfbreed	1870s/1880s	William Iron
Marie Lariviere	1839/1840	Green Lake	French breed	1852	François Roy
Marie dite Marissis Lariviere	1849/1850	Île à la Crosse	French breed	1867	James McCallum
Marguerite Montgrand	1826	NWT	?	1830s	Old Sylvestre
"Hay Sister"	1800	?	?	1830s	Baptiste Herman

SOURCES: Parish registers from Mission de Saint-Jean-Baptiste (1867–1912), Île à la Crosse, Saskatchewan; Saint-Julien (1875–1912), Green Lake, Saskatchewan; Mission de la Visitation (1890–1912), Portage La Loche, Saskatchewan; Scrip Applications, 1886–1906, volumes 1333 to 1371, Library and Archives Canada (LAC), RG15, Series DII 8c; and Canadian census returns, 1881, 1891, 1901, for Île à la Crosse, Green Lake, and Portage La Loche, LAC.

he describes as the carrying of, and emphasis on, family surnames as a means of inspiring and creating social and cultural unity. He attributes the central role of patronymic connection to the vastness of the region(s) in which they lived, coupled with the relatively small populations, as well as the range of economic activities in which they participated.[13] This feature of the socio-cultural makeup was evident when the genealogy of the district's families was reconstructed. The western European practice of adopting and perpetuating male lines through the use of patronymic surnames was a useful means of distinguishing between families in the district, particularly as they grew in size in subsequent generations. Furthermore, trade companies' need to track their employees in the accounting system necessitated the use of these surnames in the context of the trade (see Table 2.2).

This new Metis society did not, as some have mused, emerge just nine months after the arrival of the first trader, and Metis self-consciousness as a people was not the result of a pitched battle against the HBC or the state.[14] The origin of a people is a process, not an event. In the northwest, Metis identity emerged slowly after the initial marital and sexual unions in the proto-generation of the late eighteenth and early nineteenth century. The numbers of proto-generation couples and the size of their families are hard to calculate because of a lack of documentation, so evidence for them is derived from their descendants' scrip applications, occasionally from burial records of the late nineteenth century, and from Company records that make reference to employees and their families. For instance, the textual evidence suggests a growing presence of families at HBC posts in the district, particularly after 1821. Post journals and employment registers reveal the importance of family life to male traders over the years as Company officials began to record their numbers regularly. At the request of HBC governor George Simpson, who visited Île à la Crosse during the 1822-23 trading season, George Keith enumerated the number of women and children attached to the posts in the English River District, providing the first post-merger accounting of families. Keith recorded that there were sixty-one women and children (the latter defined as those under fourteen years of age) at Cold Lake, twenty at Lac La Ronge, and nineteen at Île à la Crosse – a total of one hundred dependants at district posts.[15] Two years later, Keith recorded that the Île à la Crosse post families consisted of five adult males, four married women, two widows, and a total of twenty-four children, which was, he stated, a decrease from the 1823 total of four adult males, four women, and thirteen children.[16]

In January 1825, Keith recorded that he was permitted to have two Company officers, two experienced clerks or traders, one guide, three

TABLE 2.2 Patronyms and residency, 1800–1850s

Name	Date of birth, location	Nationality	Spouse	Residence
Jean Baptiste Aubichon	1838–1840, St. Vital	French breed	Philomene Girard	Green Lake
Michel Bouvier Sr.	1801–1811, NWT	French breed	Julie Desjarlais	Île à la Crosse
Michel Bouvier Jr.	1838, Île à la Crosse	French breed	Julie Marie Morin	Île à la Crosse
Charles Caisse	1827–1830, Montreal	French Canadian	Mary (Pilon) Sinclair	Île à la Crosse
John Catfish	1848, Red River	Saulteaux French breed	Marie Betkkaye	Île à la Crosse
Vincent Daigneault	1835, Montreal	French Canadian	Marguerite Bouvier	Île à la Crosse
Paul Delaronde Sr.	1834–1836, Red River	French breed	Sophie Morin	Green Lake/Shell River
Pascal Janvier	1813, Portage La Loche	Chipewyan breed	Françoise Tssitanui/LeMaigre	Portage La Loche
Joseph dit La Corde Janvier	1846, NWT	Chipewyan breed	1. Adeline Maurice 2. Sophie Testawitch 3. Isabelle Velner	Portage La Loche
Pierre Jolibois	1820s, NWT	?	Louise Janvier	Portage La Loche
Jean Baptiste Jourdain	1800s, Montreal	French Canadian	Margaret Bear (L'Ours)	Île à la Crosse
Baptiste Jourdain Jr.	1840s, Green Lake	French breed	Ann (Nanette) Bekattla	Île à la Crosse
Charles Lafleur	1830s, ?	Metis	Louise Vadney	Île à la Crosse
Antoine Laliberte	1840s, ?	French breed	Mathilda Collings	Île à la Crosse
Louis (Roy) Laliberte	1850s, Portage La Loche	French breed	Virginie Merasty	Portage La Loche
Pierre Laliberte Jr.	1840s, Île à la Crosse	French breed	Géneviève Jourdain	Île à la Crosse
Pierriche Laliberte	1817, Carlton	French breed	Sarazine Morin	Portage La Loche/ Île à la Crosse/Green Lake

▼ TABLE 2.2

Name	Date of birth, location	Nationality	Spouse	Residence
Abraham Lariviere	1831, Île à la Crosse	French breed	Mary Petawchamwistewin	Île à la Crosse
Baptiste Lariviere	1847, Green Lake	French breed	Josephte Chatelain (or Petit Chassour)	Green Lake
David Lariviere	1821, Souris River	French breed	Marie Durocher	Green Lake
Thomas (or Thomy) Lariviere	1842, Souris River	French breed	Véronique Bouvier	Île à la Crosse
Baptiste LeMaigre	1841, Portage La Loche	French breed	Louise (or LaLouise) Herman	Île à la Crosse
Peter Linklater	1835, Red River	?	Marie Morin	Lac la Caribou
Pierre Malboeuf	1828, Saint-Hyacinthe, Quebec	French Canadian	Marguerite Ikkeilzik	Île à la Crosse
Pierriche Malboeuf	1850s, Île à la Crosse	French breed	Pélagie Morin	Green Lake
François Maurice	1831, Montreal	French Canadian	Angèle Laliberte	Portage La Loche
James McCallum	1847, English River	French breed	Marie dite Marissis Lariviere	Green Lake
Magnus McCallum	1849, Île à la Crosse	Cree French breed	Mary (Ida) Charles	Green Lake
Bazile Merasty	1848, NWT	?	Josephte Durocher	Green Lake
Samuel Misponas/ L'Esperance	1840, Île à la Crosse	Cree breed	Véronique Durocher	Île à la Crosse
Henry John Moberly	1835, Penetanguishene, Ontario	English	Philomene Rat	Île à la Crosse
François Montgrand	1840s–1850s, La Loche Mission	French breed	Angelique Jolibois	La Loche Mission
Baptiste Montgrand	1831, NWT	?	Agathé	Portage La Loche
Fleaur Montgrand	1836, NWT	?	Charlotte	Portage La Loche
Joachim Montgrand	1836, NWT	Halfbreed	Marie	Portage La Loche

Name	Birth	Ethnicity	Spouse(s)	Location
Joseph Montgrand	1830s–1840s, Portage La Loche	French breed	Josephine Dzuizki	Portage La Loche
Louison Montgrand	1840s, La Loche Mission	French breed	Julie Ratt	La Loche Mission
Paulet Montgrand	1845, NWT?	?	Madeleine	?
Stanislas Montgrand	1831, Île à la Crosse	Chipewyan breed	1. Charlotte 2. Isabelle Tssekewiyele 3. Marie Philomène Testawitch	Portage La Loche
William Montgrand	1840s, Portage La Loche	French breed	Suzanne Zach	Portage La Loche
Antoine Morin Jr.	1826, Athabasca River	French breed	1. Suzette Dion 2. Véronique Merasty	1. Île à la Crosse 2. Cumberland House
Antoine Morin Sr.	1797, Montreal	French Canadian	Pélagie Boucher	Île à la Crosse
Cyprien Morin	1836, Athabasca	French breed	Marie Cook	Île à la Crosse/Lac Prairie
Louis Morin	1848, Île à la Crosse	French breed	Marguerite Jourdain	Green Lake
Pierre Morin	1834, Athabasca	French breed	?	Green Lake
Raphaël Morin	1830, Athabasca	French breed	Betsy (or Elizabeth) Cook	Île à la Crosse/Devil's Lake
Zéphrin dit Catholique Morin	1838, Athabasca	French breed	1. Madeleine Girard 2. Marie Elizabeth Jourdain	Green Lake/Île à la Crosse
Baptiste Natomagan	Pre–1846, Île à la Crosse	Cree breed	1. Eliza Durocher 2. Marie Ann Fisher	Île à la Crosse
François Roy	1836, Île à la Crosse	French breed	Marie Lariviere	Île à la Crosse
James Nicol Sinclair	1843, Fort Frances	English breed	Josephte Durocher	Green Lake
Alexis Sylvestre	1843, NWT	French breed	Marie Anne Fisher (or Daldonille)	Portage La Loche

SOURCES: Parish registers, Mission de Saint-Jean-Baptiste (1867–1912), Île à la Crosse, Saskatchewan; parish registers, Saint-Julien (1875–1912), Green Lake, Saskatchewan; parish registers, Mission de la Visitation (1890–1912), Portage La Loche, Saskatchewan; Scrip Applications, 1886–1906, volumes 1333-1371, Library and Archives Canada (LAC) RG15, Series DII 8c; and Canadian census returns, 1881, 1891, 1901, for Île à la Crosse, Green Lake, and Portage La Loche, LAC.

interpreters, one blacksmith, and sixteen canoemen and/or labourers at the Île à la Crosse post. Additionally, three deserters from the New Caledonia brigade – Pierre Guillaume Sayer, Peter Grant, and Ignace McDonald – were working there in late 1824, although they were preparing to depart soon for Athabasca, and a large number of women also lived at the post. The total complement of servants and families in the English River District, which at the time comprised the Île à la Crosse, Green Lake, Lac La Ronge, and Grey Deer Lake posts, was twenty-seven men, twenty-two women, and fifty-seven children. Keith attributed the large number of employees divided between the four posts to the fact that, at the time of the HBC-NWC merger, a number of men in the district were in debt to the Company, and it had been advisable to keep them on to ensure repayment.[17]

Keith further noted that the number of Dene who traded at Île à la Crosse and Deer's Lake in 1824 totalled 87 adult males, 106 adult females, 136 young men and boys, and 140 girls, while the Cree, who traded primarily at Green Lake and Lac La Ronge, totalled 64 adult males, 76 adult women, 45 young men or boys, and 50 girls. There were also a number of freemen with families in the district, but they were so few in number that Keith felt it was unnecessary to enumerate them (although he noted they were expensive and burdensome to the Company).[18] The only reason for not getting rid of the women at the post, according to Keith, was that their presence sustained an excellent set of labourers who were essential to the Company. In this sense, not much had changed since Peter Fidler made a similar observation back in 1790. Keith was happy to report that several of the more experienced men were set to retire soon and that the contracts of several others would expire in 1826, thereby giving the Company an opportunity to rid itself of some of the women.[19] A great deal of the expense associated with the women, and by extension their families, arose from the expectation that the Company would supplement the families' incomes by providing food rations in the winter months and housing for permanently contracted servants.

The relief that the Company expected from ridding itself of some families did not come to pass in any meaningful sense. In 1826, Keith noted that Chief Trader John Spencer had been charged with building a large canoe at his post to accommodate the transportation of families destined to leave the district. However, Spencer did not have the canoe built, so the families would not be leaving as planned. Regardless of the chief trader's inability to carry out these orders, Keith informed Spencer and other men that the Company would not be responsible for providing the same amount of provisions to families as it had in previous years.[20] The number of posts in the district rose and fell over the years depending on need and profitability, and the movement of families between posts within the region likewise fluctuated. In 1844, the enumeration of families at Île à la Crosse totalled thirty-four "souls in all within the fort," which broke down to two men, three young men, ten women, and twelve children. This figure included the report's author, Thomas Hodgson of Green Lake, in addition to an Indian man and his wife and two children, and a blind Indian who normally resided there.[21]

If used alone, without corroboration of the vast genealogical sources for this community, these figures would seem insignificant. Based on HBC accounting, the population of the district included only the Company's suitably contracted servants and their dependants. What is missing in these reports is evidence that many of these families were, by the early to mid-nineteenth century, permanent residents in the district. However, what is captured in these scant references is the fact that the proto-, first, and second generations were establishing a solid presence in the region.

By the early nineteenth century, outsider males found entry to, and gained acceptance within, the region's socio-cultural structure by marrying local, first-generation Metis women who were themselves the daughters of proto-generation couples (see Table 2.3). These young women lived their whole lives in the region, establishing for their fathers, nephews, brothers, and sons a web of social alliances through their marriages. Young men of this era, sons of the proto-generation, had greater mobility and opportunities to leave the region of their birth to work and trade in other districts. By the 1820s, however, a sufficiently mature, indigenous, mixed-ancestry population was settled at Sakitawak, supporting the coalescence of a distinct Metis community that encouraged continuation of a pattern of district-wide intercommunity intermarriage. When the second generation of Metis children in Sakitawak reached maturity and began to marry, regionally defined patterns of matrilocal residence were well established.

As the region came to be characterized by this matrilocal residency pattern, families established an enduring identification with the surnames of their Euro-Canadian trading ancestors at the local or community level. These patronymic connections were a means of organizing and identifying specific families within the community, thus establishing another social pattern. In the only prior in-depth study of Metis society in northwestern Saskatchewan, anthropologist Philip T. Spaulding conducted fieldwork to assess Metis cultural traditions by examining contemporary social structures.[22] While focusing on contemporary Metis life, Spaulding's study

TABLE 2.3 First-generation couples, 1810s–1830s

Husband	Nationality or place of birth	Wife	Nationality or place of birth
Michel Bouvier Sr.	French halfbreed	Julie Desjarlais	French halfbreed
Joseph Girard	French Canadian	Marguerite Jackson	Halfbreed
Baptiste Herman	Halfbreed or German	"Hay Sister"	Indian
Charlot Herman	Fort Chipewyan/unknown	Marie Montgrand	Halfbreed
Samuel Herman	NWT/unknown	Julie Montgrand	English halfbreed
Baptiste Iron	Cree halfbreed	Thérèse Durocher	Cree halfbreed
Raphaël Iron	Cree	Euphemie LaChance/Opikokew	NWT/unknown
Louison Janvier	Chipewyan halfbreed	Elizabeth Janvier	Chipewyan halfbreed
Pascal Janvier	Chipewyan halfbreed	Françoise Tssitanui/LeMaigre	Indian/halfbreed
Pierre Jolibois	Unknown	Louise Janvier	French halfbreed
Jean Baptiste Jourdain	French Canadian	Margaret Bear (L'Ours)	Halfbreed
Baptiste Charlot Lafleur	French halfbreed	Angélique Jourdain	French halfbreed
Pierriche Laliberte	French halfbreed	Sarazine Morin	French halfbreed
Abraham Lariviere	French halfbreed	Mary Petawchamwistewin	Cree/French halfbreed
David Lariviere	French halfbreed	Marie Durocher	French halfbreed
Old Montgrand	French Canadian	Thérèse	Unknown
Stanislas Montgrand	Chipewyan halfbreed	1. Charlotte 2. Isabelle Tssekewiyele 3. Marie Philomène Testawitch	1. Chipewyan halfbreed 2. Unknown 3. French halfbreed
Antoine Morin	French Canadian	Pélagie Boucher	Montagnais Metis
Sylvestre	Unknown	Marguerite Montgrand	Unknown

SOURCE: Canadian census returns, 1881, 1891, 1901, for Île à la Crosse, Green Lake, Portage La Loche, Library and Archives Canada (LAC); Scrip Applications, 1886–1906, volumes 1333–1371, LAC, RG15, Series DII 8c; North-West Half-Breeds and Original White Settlers, Registers and Indexes, 1877–1927, volumes 1425–1555, LAC, RG15, Series DII 8m.

provided historical contextualization that the Metis of Île à la Crosse had lived as family-based residential groups, whether in the bush or near posts. According to Spaulding, these family-based residential groups were structured around a male relative (the patriarch), although the household itself belonged to the wife or eldest female in the group.[23]

Examining the patterns of surnames within communities and naming practices within families is an important means of understanding both Metis relationships to their homeland and the connections of a living population with its ancestral past. For instance, Belanger-kaki-wekit (or Belanger Point), home to Charles and Béatrix Belanger and their descendants, is on the northeast side of Sakitawak. The Belanger surname first appeared in the community records in the late eighteenth century, but no other Belangers lived in the region until Charles arrived in the first decade of the twentieth century.[24] Because of the initial foray of the British-owned, Montreal-based trade companies, which transported large numbers of French Canadian voyageurs into the region in the late 1700s, it would seem likely that French surnames would dominate the region. The voyageurs' influence certainly seems to be evident in the number of their patronyms in the region, but closer inspection suggests that the surnames actually represent the multiculturalism (not biculturalism) of the area's Metis society. In addition to French surnames, there are names of British and Indian origin in the region, and the relationship between all these types of names reflects the same phenomenon described by Irene Spry when she examined the intermarriage between Catholic and Protestant, French- and English-speaking Metis in Red River.[25] As at Red River, specific surnames in the English River District were connected with one and sometimes two communities and were divided between the northern and southern regions of the district in a manner reflecting the historical divisions between Cree and Dene territories, not the divisions of French and English Canada.

As a natural dividing line between Cree and Dene territories, Sakitawak served as the central community for this Metis society. Families located in the more northerly regions, from the area around Portage La Loche (including Turnor and Descharme lakes) down to Sakitawak, and touching all points in between, were primarily associated with the Dene and can be broadly characterized as Metis with Dene ancestry. Surnames such as Herman, Touslesjour, Montgrand, Sylvestre, Piche, Bekattla, Jolibois, Janvier, Deltess, and Velner were associated with the communities north of Sakitawak, while surnames such as Sinclair, McCallum, Roy, Lariviere, Durocher, Merasty, and Desjarlais became associated with the Metis and

Cree communities at Lac Vert, Nehiyo-wapasi (present-day Canoe Lake), Lac Prairie (present-day Meadow Lake), and Waterhen Lake, as well as Doré Lake, Sled Lake, and Lac au Serpent farther south. In some instances, the degree of intermarriage and movement between northern and southern communities in the northwest was such that families had both Dene and Cree ancestry. The Morins and Lalibertes, for example, are two of the oldest and largest families of the forty-three core families found in the historical records, and people with that surname are found in virtually every community across the district. They, consequently, married into both Cree and Dene communities. More typically, however, the Metis surnames in the district can be divided geographically in the same manner that Cree and Dene traditional territories were divided.

The *Liber Animarum,* maintained by the Oblates, provides additional insight into the geographic and cultural origins of these surnames in the northwest. For instance, the Herman family was described as originating with a Metis man who was said to have lived like an Indian, taking many wives. Furthermore, because he had many wives, it was difficult for the priests to tell which child belonged to which mother. In all, Old Herman had at least twelve children; there was never an official count of his wives.[26] Likewise, it was noted of the Montgrand family that "cette Famille une des plus nombreuses est originaire d'Athabaska Montagnais s'etables [sic] au Portage La Loche" (this large family was originally in the Athabasca region before coming to reside in Portage La Loche).[27] The first Montgrands, according to scrip records, were Old Montgrand and his wife, Therese, who had at least nine children living in the La Loche region. Old Montgrand was either a French Canadian or Metis voyageur with the Canadian trade in the Athabasca area before becoming an HBC servant, posted with his family to the English River District. By the nineteenth and early twentieth centuries, the Montgrands were identified in census records as "Chipewyan Halfbreeds."[28]

The division of the Metis into different groups culturally, geographically, matrilocally, and patronymically frames broad, rather than specific, patterns. It is significant, however, that these patterns correspond to historical cultural and territorial divisions of their maternal Cree and Dene ancestors, and so perhaps an examination of the family structures of these two peoples is warranted. While there are some fundamental differences between the Cree and Dene, they share a similar worldview that places families at the centre of community existence. Consequently, the closest comparisons to Metis socio-cultural development are case studies of Cree and Dene societies, both of which were made up of small, family-based hunting communities within relatively fixed geographical domains that were linked regionally by an intricate web of intercommunity and inter-generational alliances.[29] According to anthropologist Regina Flannery, northern Cree socio-political structures "consist[ed] mainly of the single family or very close kin in such small groups bound together by blood and marriage ties."[30] Similarly, anthropologist Henry Sharp concluded that Dene communities were organized around the eldest man of a hunt-ing group, usually a father, working with his grown sons and possibly sons-in-law. In this arrangement, the entire family lived in a system of co-residence and economic cooperation.[31]

These Cree and Dene familial styles were eventually reflected in the matrilocal and patronymic ordering of the Metis community. Men and women at Sakitawak, for instance, established relationships with others of their own gender and generational cohort that mimicked genealogical relationships based on blood or family relationships. For example, to sig-nify their relationship or partnership, men or women who worked together could agree to treat one other as siblings or according to the values that defined other types of familial relationships. For instance, men assigned to collect furs, work on the brigades, man the fisheries, or perform other shared tasks often forged a relationship as brothers if they were the same age or as father-uncle and son-nephew if their ages differed signifi-cantly. The reasons for establishing such relationships varied from preserv-ing bonds between lifelong friends who wanted to work together to seeking mutual economic advantage within the trade when the individuals involved had no real personal sentiment for one another. Spaulding, who described these relationships in his study, argued that this type of social structure had important implications for cultural identity and solidarity of action through daily behaviour, although what, exactly, those significant social implications were in practice remains unclear. Presumably, creating familial relationships where none existed was a strategy to establish socio-cultural bonds among people with shared interests and to unite them against anyone or thing that challenged those interests.[32]

People of the northwest maintained their links to one another, and cre-ated a unified social whole, through marriage, which formed the basis of family organization. Marriage into a Cree or Dene hunting group or a patronymically defined band like the Metis provided newcomers with the alliances necessary for social integration into a new community.[33] Marriages between already related bands were encouraged to maintain intergenera-tional relationships throughout Cree, Dene, and, eventually, Metis territory. Social taboos forbade young people marrying within their own, immediate, hunting group. Both these directives ensured that each hunting group was connected by marriage to a wide range of other groups, which also prevented incest within the hunting group of origin. Preferably, however, marriage partners were selected from families already allied with one another. Anthropologists have categorized Cree, Dene, and Metis marital patterns as cross-cousin alliances, which means that parents encouraged marriages between the children of their siblings of the opposite sex: men encouraged their children to marry their sisters' (i.e., paternal aunts) children, while women encouraged their children to marry their brothers' (i.e., maternal uncles) children. Within this cross-cousin arrangement, the best possible arranged marriages were those between two brothers from one family and two sisters from another because this would confirm a close social bond between each married couple and their hunting groups.[34] For example, within the Morin family, two sisters, Sophie and Marie, married two Linklaters – William and Peter. The family connection between William and Peter is not clear, but they were relatives, and their marriage to two sisters forged a bond that strengthened both families according to the principles promoted through cross-cousin marriages.

One of the chief differences between the Metis and their Indian relatives, however, was the pattern of residence. Patrilocal residency was the end result of Cree and Dene living arrangements after marriage, although there may have been a temporary period of matrilocality. In Cree and Dene communities, the eldest sons were likely to become the leaders of their own hunting groups, which incorporated one or two brothers and eventually sons and sons-in-law. Brothers often ended up living and working together, bonding to each other intimately. As a result, the children of these brothers grew up with one another and were raised to regard each other more as siblings than distant relatives. Conversely, brothers and sisters had a more distant relationship after they reached maturity, married, and lived in separate hunting groups. Their respective children regarded one another as distant relatives, if they considered themselves related at all. However, when two sisters married two brothers, they were able to remain close physically and emotionally, with their children raised as siblings.[35] This basis for local Cree and Dene hunting bands was translated into Metis social organization as established, intermarried groups of families came to be linked to particular geographic locations. As well, an extended family structure occupied definable territories and connected other groups in the region through economic, political, and social alliances.

It was from these two maternal societies and cultures of the land that the Metis forged their own society, formulated a worldview, and established a unique cultural identity in the northwest. However, Metis culture in the northwest was more than just an amalgamation of Indian (or even Euro-Canadian) cultural practices. It was a coherent organization or system of practices with an underlying conscious, conceptual order manifested because of wahkootowin, which, in turn, supported and sustained their economic and religious needs. Perhaps less obvious are the ways in which family and culture relate to each other. According to Gutman, "to focus on the 'family' also means to focus on 'culture.' Socialization nearly always occurs first in families, and it is through families that historically derived beliefs usually pass from generation to generation."[36] But what is the link between socialization into a worldview or cultural system and a cultural identity? What are the beliefs that shape behaviours?

In the northwest, the complexity of the relationship between beliefs and behaviours is revealed in the regional matrilocal social organization, with its emphasis on patronymic connections. As such, the Metis community can be represented as being either Metis Cree or Metis Dene. This is not an attempt to establish a new binary of Metis identity based on Indian ancestry, but rather an acknowledgment that there is a great deal of overlap between Metis, Cree, and/or Dene culture, particularly as those groups continued to intermarry throughout the nineteenth century. These divisions simply represented a significant part of their ancestral legacy and connection to land and language, just as French, Scottish, and English ancestries shaped a significant portion of their sense of self. For instance, in 1885, Raphaël Laliberte, a Metis man with Dene, Cree, and French ancestry from Portage La Loche, married Eliza (or Aloïsa) Bekattla, a Metis woman with Dene and English ancestry from Île à la Crosse. In the 1901 Canadian census, Eliza was listed as a "Chipewyan Breed," while Raphaël and Augustine, his daughter with his first wife, were listed as "French Breeds." Of course, these labels are problematic – they were generated by the census takers, and we cannot know whether they were terms used within the communities or by the people themselves. However, if we assume that the census takers were attempting to reflect accurately the "ethnicity" or "race" of those being enumerated, these terms have some value to us now as we attempt to understand the cultural configuration of regions such as the English River District. Raphaël, son of Pierriche Laliberte and Sarazine Morin, was a hunter, fisherman, and seasonal labourer with the HBC. This branch of the Laliberte family lived north of Sakitawak at Portage La Loche, while Raphaël's brothers and sisters lived throughout the district in communities like Sakitawak, Lac Vert, Nehiyo-wapasi, Sipisihk (known historically as Beauval, now known as

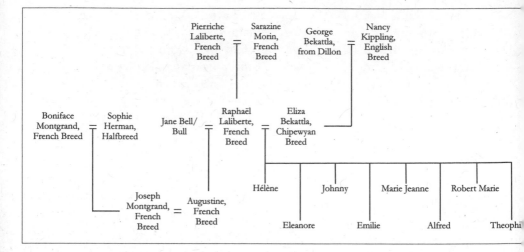

FIGURE 2.2   Cultural genealogy of R. Laliberte and E. Bekattla's immediate family

La Plonge), and others. Additionally, many of Raphaël and Eliza's children came to reside in the Moostoos-sipi region (see Figure 2.2).[37] Furthermore, in 1901 Raphaël and his family were listed in the Chipewyan section of the Île à la Crosse census.[38] Raphaël had an opportunity to articulate an emotional connection to his ancestral lands in his 1906 scrip application when he stated that, but for the two years he had lived with his brothers and sisters at Lac Vert, he had always lived in the La Loche region because "the country had always been [his] home."[39] In 1903, his daughter Augustine married Joseph Montgrand, who was born at the La Loche mission site but was identified as a French Breed. Joseph was the son of Boniface Montgrand and his first wife, Sophie Herman, both from the northern reaches of the region – Portage La Loche, La Loche River, and the La Loche mission site – areas associated with the Dene. Boniface Montgrand (b. 1856, La Loche mission) apparently lived at Bull's House with his family, which was also where several of Eliza Bekattla's relatives came to reside.[40]

Not all surnames that appear in the historical records became embedded in the region's social or physical landscape. There are surnames from the nineteenth century that today have no resonance in northwestern Saskatchewan, including Small, Dreaver, Thompson, and Keith. In other cases, the names themselves may not have established a patronymic connection but nevertheless became a part of the ancestral legacy of district families. For instance, the surname Catfish originated in Red River and belonged to a Metis man of Saulteaux and French ancestry named John, who came

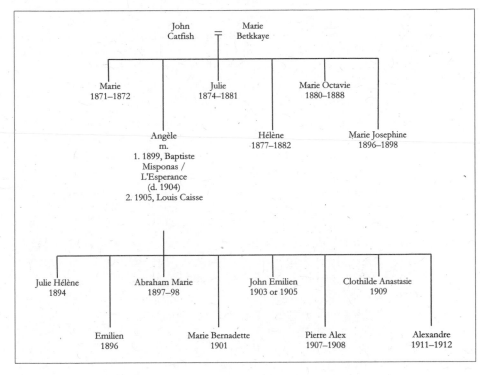

FIGURE 2.3   Catfish family

to Île à la Crosse in the 1860s as a voyageur and servant of the HBC. John Catfish married a local woman, Marie Betkkaye, who was born in 1846 at Île à la Crosse to a mother named Biskay, the widow of a man named Laviolette (perhaps François Laviolette, who was employed by the NWC at Athabasca in the late eighteenth century).[41] Like Laviolette, the Catfish name did not survive in the region beyond John because he and Marie had six daughters, only one of whom lived to marry. Because of the adoption of male surnames and establishment of those patronymic connections at the time of marriage, the Catfish name disappeared from visible representation in the community's genealogies and the patronymically identifiable family bands. Angèle Catfish, John and Marie's only surviving daughter, first married Baptiste Misponas/L'Esperance, with whom she had four or five children, and then married Louis Caisse, with whom she had three or four more children, thus ensuring the perpetuation of the Misponas and Caisse surnames in the northwest (see Figure 2.3).[42] The adoption of male surnames at the time of marriage clearly had a notable impact on the legacy of names existing in and, in some instances, dominating communities. However, the lack of some surnames (such as Catfish) also tells us an important story about the cultural identity of the region in terms of its social organization.

Although French, Scottish, and English surnames became the core of the region's patronymic legacy – thirty-four of the forty-three core family surnames were French or British in origin, mostly the former – in several instances there were surnames with apparent links to Cree or Dene languages, such as Ikkeilzik and Natomagan.[43] These surnames were often listed in records in their language of origin and with literal English or French translations provided. For instance, Bear was Petit Ours (or just Ours) in French, Iron was Pewabiskussa in Cree and Petit Fer or La Cendre in French. Today these surnames are more likely to be associated with First Nations communities in northwestern Saskatchewan, such as Canoe Lake First Nation, rather than Metis communities. In some instances, surnames appear to have no obvious meaning in any language, and there is no clear sense of what the translations meant. This is apparent in the case of the surname Misponas, which was an indigenization of L'Esperance (French), or Bekattla, which was known alternatively as Percateler (language or origin unknown, although it is likely a phoenetic misspelling of Bekattla) and Sargent (English). According to local understanding, "Bekattla" may have actually been a Blackfoot name or word, although it came to be associated with Dene and Metis families north of Sakitawak.[44] The continued presence of surnames of Indian origin suggests a pattern of marriages between Metis women and Indian men within the northwest. As noted by Nicole St-Onge, scholars have ignored marital connections between Metis women and Indian men by focusing exclusively on intermarriages with white, European or Euro-Canadian, male fur traders as the primary alliance formation that gave shape to Metis cultural identity.[45] However, we need to begin to contemplate the idea that Metis people maintained and supported their relationships with their maternal relatives by ensuring that some of their daughters married Indian men.

Because of the nature of certain surnames, some families were more difficult to track intergenerationally. However, more often than not the difficulty arose from a number of shortcomings related to the records rather than from idiosyncrasies of Metis culture or nineteenth-century naming practices. Families such as the Bekattlas and Misponas, as already noted, were also known as Percatlers and/or Sargents and L'Esperances, respectively, and were therefore difficult to track through the records. These inconsistencies in naming are revealed only when attempting to reconstruct the genealogical record by using all available evidence and comparing data such as dates, names of children and spouses, and locations of birth, residence, and death. In some instances, it required conversations with descendants who had insight into names and naming practices.

Other names were irregularly spelled, but because they were similar, they were more easily linked in the documentation, such as Kippling/Kyplain, De La Ronde/Delaronde, Durocher/Des Roches, Caisse/Caix, Merasty/Meraste, Aubichon/Obichon, and Halcrow/Alcrow. Had only one or two of the record groups been used for the genealogical reconstruction, making connections would have been quite difficult. Instead, genealogies were not constructed until all the available records were collected and then carefully compared. However, documentation for some families was insufficient to make connections to alternative names or spellings, and so, in a few cases, genealogical reconstruction was less successful. In some of these instances, the *Liber Animarums* maintained at each of the three main mission sites in the region provided useful additional information on the families and made it possible to identify some otherwise difficult connections in the first or second generations. For instance, the head of the Lariviere family was Abraham Lariviere, whose first son, Thomas, was adopted (Thomas' natural family is not identified). Furthermore, Abraham's second son was actually the son of Abraham's wife, Mary Petawchamwistewin (Ee-Ya-Nis), who had had an earlier relationship with the famed leader of the La Loche brigade, Alexis Bonami dit L'Esperance. In time, Samuel ceased to use the name L'Esperance, becoming known as Samuel Misponas or Samuel Lariviere. Without the *Liber Animarum,* this connection between the Misponas and Lariviere families, the origins of the Misponas name, or details of how children were integrated into families would remain unknown.[46]

Once families were reconstructed satisfactorily, it was possible to assess their patterns of marriage and residency, naming legacies and cultural ties, and economic opportunities over four to five generations (from the early nineteenth century to about 1912). However, in a few cases it was not possible to reconstruct the genealogy fully because the range of available data proved unreliable or was insufficiently maintained from one generation to the next. Two particularly difficult family arrangements to trace intergenerationally were those of the Herman and Touslesjour (alternative spellings are Toutlejour and Torisleyous) families. Indeed, it is difficult to ascertain whether this is one or two families because of the overlap and convergence of various given names over the years. A connection between the two names was made as a result of scrip applications that made reference to François Magloire Herman, whose name also appeared as Legyour, Legyour Touslesjour, and Gregoire Herman, while his son François was known as François Herman and Touslesjour. Touslesjour appears to be phonetically similar to Gregoire and Magloire and may have been linked in that manner.[47] However, the *Liber Animarum* indicates that these may have been two separate families, with the Touslesjours' origins being unknown save for the fact that the first man of that name married Marie Montgrand. The Herman family originated from a Metis man who "lived like an Indian," having taken many wives, in the Indian tradition.[48]

Tracking names intergenerationally through the record groups was often made difficult by the record keepers' lack of consistency. They frequently switched between French, Cree, Dene, or English names, creating confounding irregularities. For instance, Iron, Pewabiskussa, Petit Fer, and La Cendre were used interchangeably in the mission records, with no clear indication of whether the individuals with these names were related to one another; whether it was, in fact, one person; or whether the surnames were being used interchangeably at the whim (or lack of knowledge) of the record keeper.[49] For instance, at least one Raphaël Iron was recorded at Île à la Crosse, but whereas in one record he was married to Marguerite Marie Couillonneur, in another he was married to Euphémie Opikokew.[50] It is certainly possible that there was only one Raphaël Iron who married twice, but with only limited data that conclusion is little more than conjecture. From the archival documentation available, we know a Raphaël Iron was chief of Nehiyo-wapasi (Canoe Lake Cree) in the late nineteenth century. But we do not know if two Raphaël Irons existed, if it was a name passed on from father to son to grandson, or if only one man with that name ever lived in the region. Adding to the confusion is the fact that Raphaël's surname is listed throughout the records as Iron, Pewabiskussa, and Petit Fer, with no attempt at consistency.

Despite difficulties in tracking some names, most surnames were clearly identifiable over time and across the generations, which helped establish the multiple ancestral heritages of the people. These surnames formed localized patronymic connections that identified family groups by community and also reflected a strong matrilocal residency pattern. Equally important, however, was the intergenerational transmission of given names within particular families, which provided additional information regarding the form and structure of wahkootowin and the maintenance of an ancestral memory between generations. In the Metis society of this region, specific first names were used repeatedly within the immediate family, within different branches of the same family sharing a patronymic connection, and intergenerationally across large extended families. As with surnames, the given names in Metis communities in this region were, by and large, both French and Catholic in origin, although there were, of course, exceptions. French names, especially those associated with Catholic saints came to dominate the region regardless of paternal or maternal cultural ties. For instance, the names Jean Baptiste, Jean Marie, Baptiste, Alexandre, Pierre, Prosper, Joseph, and François for men and Marie (with many possible combinations, such as Marie Philomène, Marie Agnès, or Marie Elizabeth), Marguerite, Philomène, Pélagie, and Angèle for women were common to all Metis families in the region.

Heather Devine convincingly argues that Metis naming practices were an amalgam of French Catholic and First Nations spiritual traditions. Roman Catholic doctrine required parents to select given names for children from the names of male and female saints, while in Dene and Cree practice, elders endowed with specific spiritual abilities were given offerings of tobacco and cloth and asked to pray for an appropriate name. In both instances, providing children with spiritual names – be they shared with saints or divined through prayer – ensured that this new life was given spiritual protection.[51] The repetitive use of given or Christian names could be attributed to a lack of imagination by parents, a limited pool of names from which to choose, or an insistence by the clergy that children have Catholic saint names. Or it could be that such choices are an important clue to the method by which families maintained connections to long-dead or geographically distant relatives.

Certainly, names such as Jean Baptiste and Marguerite had spiritual properties, as evidenced by their connection to the French Catholic tradition of giving children names of saints. However, the power of these names in the district went beyond endowing children with these spiritual properties. Conferring familial first names on children was also, perhaps, a means to symbolically maintain the ancestral ties to French or British relatives in eastern Canada or Europe. Naming became a practical way to establish an ancestral memory of a people and a place that most northwestern Saskatchewan Metis would never see or experience. They were a people who lived in the lands and socio-religious landscape of their maternal relations, but their paternal heritage was equally relevant to shaping their cultural identity. When he analyzed naming practices among American slaves, Gutman was able to demonstrate that, between 1820 and 1849, African American slaves historically and culturally worked to infuse their families with a memory of both their West African heritage and their living parents. A tradition existed, for instance, of naming at least one child in a marriage after a father or grandparent, a practice that, Gutman concluded, "reveal[s] an attachment to a familial 'line' and suggest[s] the symbolic renewal in birth of intimate familial experiences identified with a parent or grandparent."[52]

In the northwest, long before the arrival of missionaries in the 1840s, the practice of giving children names that linked them to their ancestors was, like ritual baptisms on the portage, a well-established pattern of behaviour supported by a local belief system. For instance, of Antoine Morin and Pélagie Boucher's female grandchildren and great-grandchildren, five and two of them, respectively, were named Pélagie after their grandmother, while one son, two grandsons, and a great-grandson born between the 1830s and 1884 were named Antoine after the patriarch. In the Laliberte family, six Jean Baptistes (the saint for whom the mission station at Île à la Crosse was named) were born between 1858 and 1908, and seventeen Maries or women with a name prefaced with Marie were born between 1850 and 1909. Nineteen Marie Montgrands were born between 1831 and 1910.[53] While these names are, by and large, French and Catholic in origin, not all the given names bestowed on Metis children had that cultural root, just as not all the families were French or Catholic in origin. Such names, however, represented a desire to pass on ancestral names. In the John Thomas Kippling and Angèle Lariviere family, one son and three grandsons were named John, while one granddaughter was named for Angèle. Another grandchild was named for Angèle's father, Abraham Lariviere, and one daughter was named for Angèle's mother, Mary (see Figure 2.4). Clearly, the social power of naming was as great as its obvious spiritual significance. The spiritual power in names emanated from a pattern that endowed and established children as living links to an ancestral memory for long-distant (geographically and deceased) relatives.

The repetitive use of ancestral British, French, or Catholic names created genealogical tracking problems. Within the Lariviere family alone, at least eleven Josephs were born between 1846 and 1904, and not all had enough basic genealogical data, such as years of birth, names of parents, dates of death, and/or marital records, to confirm their identity and place them within the Lariviere family genealogy.[54] As a result, multiple entries for single Joseph Larivieres may have been created in the process of reconstructing the Lariviere family tree, and there may be fewer than eleven Josephs in the family. Compounding the problem is a general lack of specific genealogical information for the Lariviere family, so all Josephs may not be linked to their proper branch because those branches are difficult to delineate.

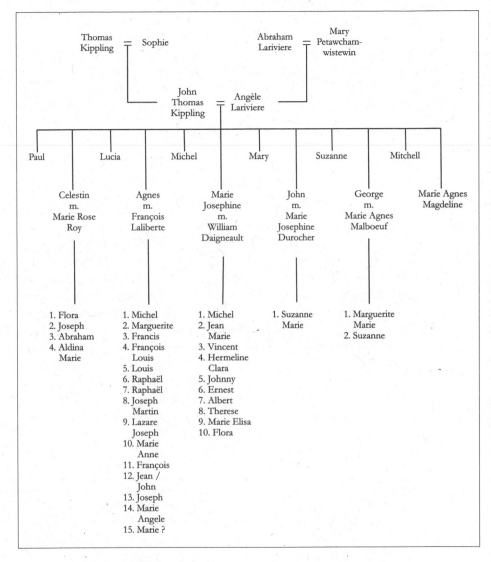

FIGURE 2.4   Naming practice in John Thomas Kippling and Angèle Lariviere's family

Even in less genealogically complicated families, recycling Christian names within the same immediate family was a common practice. For instance, when children died young, their given names were often reused when another child of the appropriate gender was born. Between 1889 and 1911, four sons in the family of Charles Maurice and Julie dite Canadienne Bouvier were given the names William and/or Alfred as either single names

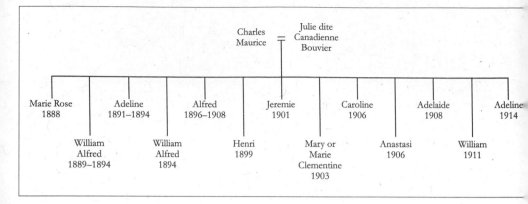

FIGURE 2.5   Charles Maurice and Julie Bouvier's family

or in combination (see Figure 2.5). The first son, named William Alfred, was born on 16 July 1889 and died in January 1894. In that year, a second son was born and also given the name William Alfred. Although there was no record of the death of the second William Alfred, a third son, born in 1896, was given the name Alfred. This third son died in 1908, and in 1911 a fourth son was born and given the name William.[55] Because it is apparent that the first three of these sons died, there was no difficulty determining how living descendants connect to these William Alfreds.

Because of this repetitive use of given names intergenerationally among the Metis of the northwest, nicknames were a means of distinguishing between people with the same names in a particular family, as well as those in separate branches of a family sharing the same surname. Devine explained the role of nicknames or "dit/dite" names in Metis society in her study of the Desjarlais family.[56] However, as many of the nicknames in the northwest were Cree or Dene in origin, rather than French or Catholic, their socio-cultural relevance should be evaluated from an indigenous perspective. For instance, names such as Marie dite Pakama Desjarlais, Victoran dite Tsi Buck Laliberte, André dit Piyettasiw Durocher, and Baptiste dit Napew Durocher were all represented in the records as were names such as Assiny, Louis dit Wahskway Morin, Jeffery dit Tsoo loo Morin, and François dit Paskwawewiyimiw Lariviere. Cree and Dene names were as integral to an individual's or family's identity as French, British, or Catholic names. There was a William Archie from Moostoossipi who was also known as William Shazhounen because his father was called both Old Shazhounen and Antoine Archie. According to the *Liber Animarum* from Portage La Loche, this family originated in Île à la Crosse and settled in the Portage La Loche region by the end of the nineteenth century. Old Shazhounen had children with two sisters, and the clergy deemed one to be the legitimate wife and the other a "concubine." With the first, legitimate wife, Old Shazhounen had a son, Jean; with the other wife he had three more children, William, Suzanne, and Louise.[57] William, known for his knowledge of traditional medicines, married Marie Angèle Maurice around 1895. While William eventually came to be known (for unexplained reasons) as William Archie, his brother Jean and sister, Suzanne, maintained Shazhounen as their surname.[58]

There were also people who, according to the records, carried Indian given names. Pierre Cyprien Morin's wife, Véronique Chatelain, was known in the community as Miyamow and also known by the maiden surname Siyakikwaniw. Véronique's mother was Pa-ya-ta-skit Chatelain, and her father was See-a-kee-ka-noo, which may be a phonetic representation of "Siyakikwaniw."[59] This endurance of Cree and Dene names in the northwest and other regions where Metis communities flourished was common. While travelling with the northern Alberta scrip commission in the late 1890s, Charles Mair noted that the Metis he encountered in the Mackenzie Basin had public Christian names, used with outsiders, and private Cree names that were used at home among a person's relations. Mair concluded that because Christian or baptismal names had not entirely displaced older Indian naming practices, Metis communities were demonstrating their maternal cultural influence.[60] The complexity of naming practices in northwestern Saskatchewan may make genealogical reconstruction challenging, but, more importantly, it reflects subtle nuances that established connections to their religious faith and paternal relations as they lived in a region defined by the history and culture(s) of their maternal ancestors.

Just as voyageur baptisms and Metis socio-religious naming practices emerged and developed in the district long before the arrival of Catholic missionaries, social rituals or protocols existed for creating, acknowledging, and facilitating familial relationships that were otherwise tenuous or non-existent. It was critical for wahkootowin to expand the boundaries of family by bringing additional people into the group, thereby increasing as much as possible the total number of relatives an individual could look to for support, an ethos essential to survival in this harsh subarctic environment. For example, marriage not only united individuals but also brought together entire families, thereby serving as a protocol for creating alliances between family groups. A less obvious means of establishing (or re-establishing) family ties in Metis families was through the ceremony and

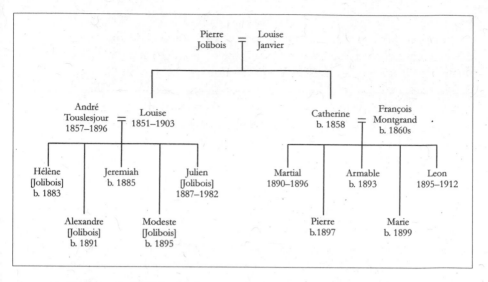

FIGURE 2.6 Jolibois adoption

act of adoption, which created new family members and established roles that were modelled on, and mimicked, biological relationships. Adoption of young children by other family members, particularly after the death of their biological parents, was an important social institution that ensured the perpetuation of wahkootowin because it allowed a family to survive death. Children remained integral to the family because of their role as inheritors and continuers of Metis cultural identity in the region.[61]

Adoptions within the region were public and private displays of familial behaviours and beliefs. Because many adoptions occurred simply as a matter of cultural practice according to custom, they can be difficult to locate in written records. However, instances of interfamily adoptions were recorded in the scrip applications of the English River District. In virtually all available recorded examples of these types of adoptions, maternal relatives took the children and raised them. For example, Hélène, Julien, Alexandre, and Modeste Jolibois, the children of André Touslesjour and Louise Jolibois, were raised by their maternal aunt and uncle, Catherine Jolibois (Louise's younger sister) and François Montgrand, after the death of their parents in 1896 and 1903, respectively (see Figure 2.6). After the death of their father in 1896, the children assumed their mother's surname, Jolibois, perhaps to strengthen their connection to their maternal relatives.[62]

George Bekattla adopted his grandson, Barthelémy Girard (who eventually came to be known as Ross Cummings), a child by his daughter, Jeanne

Bekattla. Barthelémy's mother was alive at the time of his adoption by George, although his father's whereabouts were unknown.[63] Likewise, Adélaide Lafleur, daughter of Catherine Laliberte and Charles Pierre Lafleur, was adopted and raised by her maternal grandparents, Pierriche Laliberte and Sarazine Morin; George Murray, son of Jack Murray and Marie Elizabeth Jourdain, was adopted and raised by his maternal grandparents, Baptiste Jourdain Jr. and Nanette Bekattla; and the two sons of Marie Clara McKay and Alexandre McCallum were adopted and raised by their maternal grandmother, Angèle Lariviere, wife of Henry McKay.[64] As a cultural practice, the adoption of grandchildren served two goals. Children raised by the old people learned the histories and experiences of the preceding generations, an education that bridged generations and served as a conduit for cultural transmission. The young person was also a benefit to the older people – he or she could physically assist elders as they aged and keep them connected to the wahkootowin by sharing memories, protocols, and lifeways with children.

Naming in all forms – surnames, given names, saint names, Indian names – established linkages between ancestors and their descendants, thus ensuring a continuity of family memory through this generational bridging mechanism. Family systems formed discrete and stable communities that persisted beyond the life and death of individuals. As a result, these large, extended Metis family systems were flexible enough, in composition and structure, to permit the addition of genealogical points of reference even as others were subtracted over many generations. However, the fluidity of familial boundaries or allegiances should not be mistaken for casualness or informality within wahkootowin. Because Aboriginal societies often lacked clearly identifiable institutions demarcating and enforcing social and cultural boundaries, it is assumed that interpersonal relations were devoid of structure or clear organization. Rather, the structure and organization of wahkootowin is visible within the family structures that are revealed by a community's genealogical configuration and its members' behaviour toward one another, which in turn provide clues to evaluate local beliefs. Wahkootowin in the northwest was not restricted or closed to particular individuals because of their culture, race, or religion if they were willing to adjust their own expectations of family life. Rather, wahkootowin was an inclusive, holistic philosophy, predicated upon one real stricture – being a good relative – which required adherence to the values, protocols, and behaviours expected of family members. After 1821, as HBC families engaged in a pattern of intergenerational and intercommunity intermarriage, wives and daughters worked at Company tasks in support of their male relations, and male relatives worked together to complete their assigned duties, much as Cree and Dene family would have supported one another within the hunting bands. The continual connecting and reconnecting of HBC servants' families to one another economically, socially, and culturally served as a means of strengthening wahkootowin.

However, just as some outsiders became a part of the regional family, others remained separate from the socio-cultural organization of the Metis community and were never members of the family (a concept dealt with more fully in Chapters 4 and 5). Arrival in the northwest did not mean automatic admission; citizenship required an active process, such as the establishment of marriage alliances. The quickest and simplest means to formulate a relationship with the local and regional family structure was through marriage, and yet there were outsider males who never married into the matrilocal regional group and, therefore, never established a patronymic connection in the region. For instance, there were HBC servants and officers throughout the English River District who maintained a social and cultural distance from the Metis community by remaining outside the family. In fur trade historiography, these same individuals may have had an impact on the region's social and cultural history when they passed through as traders. The decision not to become part of the local family was based on a variety of factors, including religion, cultural heritage, and notions of social hierarchy and what constituted a well-ordered society.

A survey of the available genealogical records reveals how the Metis organized themselves in relation to one another in localized settings. Inferences can be made about how they understood themselves in relation to others. In the English River District, the Metis came to be a distinct people, sharing a collective history that formed their sense of tradition and rationalized their existence, landholdings, cultural identity, shared lifeways, and social organization.[65] While concepts of kinship have formed the basis of anthropological studies of Aboriginal societies to date, there is still little articulation of how family is the manifestation of a particular indigenous worldview.[66] Wahkootowin is a system of values, beliefs, and attitudes, but it is manifested through behaviours that can be mapped genealogically. Typically, genealogies are a linear rendering of an individual's relatives for the purpose of identifying ancestors and descendants. But they can be expanded to become an interpretive tool that helps develop an understanding of how the beliefs embedded in a worldview shape familial behaviours.

Genealogies ground a culturally determined family system (in this instance, wahkootowin) and provide a visual representation of intangible lifeways and cultural identity. Those placed within a genealogical matrix are understood to be relatives and are, therefore, family members regardless of biological connectedness because genealogies encompass social relationships that ritually mimic biological relatedness. In short, genealogies are a social blueprint for the larger cultural processes that make people relatives. As a foundation for understanding how specific groups became associated with particular local communities, Chapter 3 will look at how families moved about the district, the land of their maternal ancestors, at the behest of the Company, while Chapter 5 will address the economic symbiosis developed by the servants, their families, and the HBC in the nineteenth century. Trade records from the latter half of the nineteenth century, a time when families became firmly established throughout the region, serve as a lens for observing how matrilocal residency and patronymic connections took shape across the northwest and how families entwined with one another across successive generations.

3

"To live in the land of my mother"

Residency and Patronymic Connections across the Northwest

When asked by scrip commissioners at Green Lake in 1887, "How long have you lived there and where have you lived previously?" fifty-seven-year-old Raphaël Morin responded in a way that frames several important concepts about homeland, residency, and identity. Raphaël stated that he had moved to Devil's Lake on the Shell River because he wanted "to live in the land of my mother who was originally from the lands of [her] parents [because] we most of the time were in the said lands of her relatives as we had no interest in the lands ... where my father and myself" were born and raised.[1] Raphaël Morin privileged his maternal ancestry as the source and definition of his homeland, but he further suggested that the conception of territory or space for his family was broadly conceived to include the entirety of the northwest. However, and just as importantly, Raphaël also very clearly declared that his identity was not French Canadian and that he was not from Quebec, because there was no sense of connection to the land of his father or, by extension, his paternal relatives. Raphaël provided insight into the connection between homeland and labour by indicating that he took his family to Devil's Lake after working his entire adult life for the Hudson's Bay Company. In the latter half of the century, Raphaël and several close relatives who had worked much of their adult lives in various aspects of the trade deliberately positioned themselves at Devil's Lake, a point on the Green Lake Road, an important artery in the English River District's supply route, at the southernmost edge of the region (see Map 3.1). Establishing himself on this trail suggests that Raphaël had not, despite his retirement,

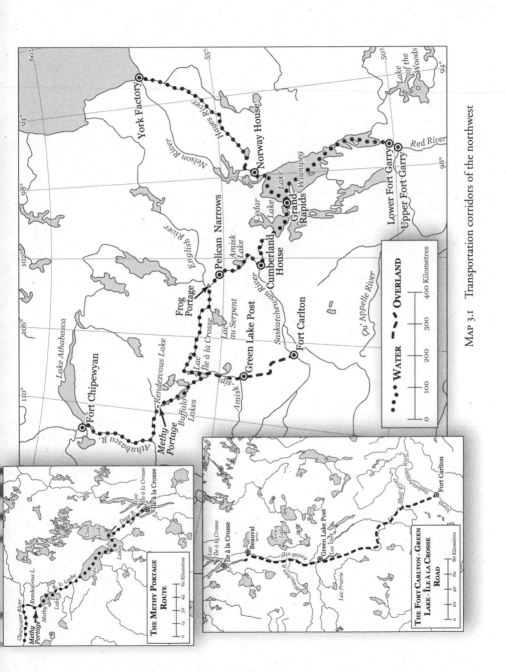

MAP 3.1 Transportation corridors of the northwest

entirely divorced himself from the district's trade economy, but rather ensured that he was still living in a landscape shaped by his mother's heritage and a trade economy that dated to the late eighteenth century.

Raphaël's assertions of homeland and territorial expanse were echoed two years later by his sister Marie in her scrip application. After her husband's death in 1880, Marie likewise took her three youngest children to the Shell River area to live in the "country of her mother."[2] Raphaël and Marie's sister Sophie similarly moved to Devil's Lake, presumably to be nearer to her brother and sister, thus ensuring that she was close to her family.[3] Also living in the Lac Vert–Shell River region was the family matriarch, Pélagie Boucher Morin, who, after her husband's death in 1873 at Sakitawak, lived with several of her children and grandchildren, moving from house to house over the years.[4] In 1881, according to census records, Pélagie was living with her grandson, Pierre Marie, but by 1887, according to her scrip application, she was with her son Louis, on the east side of Lac Vert. Louis, like his sisters, was born at Sakitawak, but by 1870 he was living at Lac Vert, where he worked for the HBC. By the time of the 1901 Canadian census, Pélagie was living south of Lac Vert with her daughter Sophie and Sophie's second husband, Paul Delaronde Sr.[5]

The Metis families of the northwest shared with their maternal relatives a worldview that privileged family above all other relationships, but they also grew up in an environment framed by the trade economy. This meant that while they were grounded in a geographic space infused with the beliefs and behaviours of their maternal relatives, their continued connection to one another was facilitated by their long association with the trade. Metis families coalesced in the region, residing at these particular locations, for reasons very much intertwined with the trade. In the proto-generation, outsider male employees of various fur trade companies entered the region to work and, in the process, helped lay a foundation for the emergence of the Metis. In subsequent generations, this connection between land and economy was further entrenched as people maintained their employment in the trade while living in the homeland opened to them by their maternal connection to the land. Although the relationship of the Metis to their homeland was shaped by their maternal heritage, it was also strengthened by travelling and working on the land in occupations that supported the trade economy, which was an important aspect of their paternal heritage.

In a sense, the scope of this study resembles a strawberry plant, which spreads out from its centre through the extension of low, arching stems or runners. Sakitawak is at the centre, drawing people into the area because of its abundant resources and access to other regions. As the Metis emerged

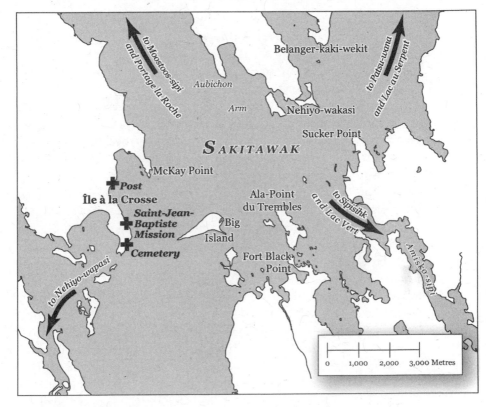

MAP 3.2   Historical and contemporary Cree and Michif place names on Sakitawak

and took root on the shores of Sakitawak, and as the demands of the economy were exerted, these families began to radiate outward from the lake, establishing themselves throughout the region in new communities, including outposts, fishing stations, and wintering camps, near Cree and Dene bands and key transportation routes. If the full length of the family connections were traced across western Canada into areas beyond the scope of this study, they would easily be linked to families in Alberta, Northwest Territories, Manitoba, Ontario, Quebec, British Columbia, and even Montana, North Dakota, and other American states.

In the immediate vicinity of Sakitawak, the HBC post and the Roman Catholic mission were, in the mid-nineteenth century, located on the lake's west side on a peninsula between Aubichon Arm, named for the Aubichon family, and Rosser Bay (see Map 3.2). Some families in the region, such as the Bouvier, Daigneault, and Lariviere families, lived near the end of the peninsula, close to where the Roman Catholic mission was established.

Because of the Bouvier family's lengthy association with the peninsula, the area came to be known as Bouvierville. However, it was more typical for families to live around the lake in smaller, family-based settlements, coming into Île à la Crosse only to trade, attend religious services, or participate in festivities at Christmas and New Year's.

Rising out of the lake, covered in aspen and spruce trees, Big Island was just across from the mission site. No families lived permanently on Big Island, but it was a place where people – particularly the Dene – socialized during the summer months. Aubichon Arm stretched northward and served as the entryway to the Deep River (in actuality a channel of the English River that connects Lac Île à la Crosse to Big Buffalo Lake), which led to Big and Little Buffalo (present-day Churchill and Peter Pond) lakes. The community of Moostoos-sipi was situated at the junction of Big and Little Buffalo lakes, and it was here that the Ikkeilzik (now Keizie) family lived. From here, one continued north to Bull's House (also known as Riviere La Loche or, today, Dillon), where Bekattlas lived, and then north to Portage La Loche, where the Maurice, Montgrand, and Janvier families were located.

Across from Big Island on Sakitawak was Fort Black, the site of the old North West Company post and another family settlement, where the Deschambeaults, Daigneaults, and Desjarlais lived. To the north of Fort Black was Ala-Point du Trembles (also known as Île aux Trembles or Poplar Point Island), a large island where the Kippling (now spelled Kyplain) families lived. A half mile east of Ala-Point du Trembles was the mouth of the Amisko-sipi (present-day Beaver River), which connected Sakitawak to the more southern Metis community of Sipisihk (also called La Plonge, now Beauval) on Lac La Plonge, where branches of the Laliberte family lived near the Durochers and Maurices. Sipisihk was established in the late nineteenth century as an outpost of the Île à la Crosse mission. At the southern end of Amisko-sipi, families such as the Durochers, Aubichons, Morins, and Lalibertes, along with the Merastys and Sinclairs, lived on Lac Vert. West of Lac Vert was Lac Prairie, where Cyprien Morin and several of his sons established ranches in the late nineteenth century before being joined by other Metis families from Lac Vert and Sakitawak. Farther south and east, branches of the Morin family, along with their relatives the Delarondes, lived at another Company outpost at Devil's Lake near the Shell River.

North of the mouth of Amisko-sipi is Sucker Point, which today is part of the English River Dene Nation's reserve. In the nineteenth century, it was one of many Metis family settlements, home to, among others, the

Natomagan and Misponas families (see Photo 3.1). Directly across the lake from Sucker Point was Nehiyo-wahkasi (Sandy Point), the location of the 1999 family reunion mentioned by Lawrence Ahenakew in the Introduction and also believed to be the site of an HBC post under William Linklater (possibly the father of Sophie Morin's husband, also William Linklater) in the late 1700s/early 1800s.[6] Morin, Lariviere, and Gardiner families lived at Nehiyo-wahkasi, and according to one descendant, the Morins and Gardiners inherited the use of the area from the Larivieres after two Lariviere sisters married a Morin and a Gardiner.[7] North of Sandy Point was Belanger-kaki-wekit, home to the Belangers.[8] North of this main body of family-based settlements, Sakitawak stretched northeast toward the Missinipi, the main artery into the region from the east. At the northernmost tip of this part of Sakitawak was Patsu-wana (now Patuanak), which is now part of the English River Dene Nation but was historically home to many Metis families, such as the Larivieres.

This list of names associated with particular communities and locales is not exhaustive but merely demonstrates how families clustered around Lac Île à la Crosse, the initial site of congregation, because of the trade and then moved outward in ever-widening circles throughout the nineteenth century, even as they remained connected to Cree and Dene communities and worked for the HBC.

The relationship between where families lived and where they worked was not lost on the HBC. In 1889, a chief factor commented, "[Where] the Halfbreeds move or live depend[s] on the HB Company for a living – as a rule they have large families."[9] This suggestion that the Company dictated Metis movements is obviously a one-sided interpretation of the HBC's influence on the lives of its employees. The Company official was not asserting a statement of identity framed by landscape, such as that found in the Morin siblings' scrip applications, but his observation about the size of families reflects a significant part of Metis culture that surely impacted how and why they moved and lived where they did, as well as their relationship with the Company. Of the forty-three core families, twenty-six were traceable specifically because of their historical association with the trade economy in all its employment capacities. As a result, employment in the trade was an integral part of nineteenth-century residency patterns. Large, extended, intergenerationally intertwined Metis families spread outward across the district as employees of the trade, and over time their patronyms became associated with specific locations. The purpose of this chapter, then, is to analyze and discuss the regional genealogical record of Metis families in the northwest in relation to their residency in

PHOTO 3.1   This is a photograph of Baptiste dit Mistikechak
Natomagan and his second wife, Marie Anne Daldonille (or Fisher).
Daldonille was significantly younger than Natomagan. Natomagan
was a fisherman who sold his catch to the Hudson's Bay Company.
Described in the *Liber Animarum* for Île à la Crosse as the son of an old
Cree, Natomagan had been born in the early nineteenth century and
had previously been married to Eliza Durocher. Daldonille was born in
the 1870s near Buffalo Narrows and, upon being orphaned, was raised
at the mission school. She was married to Baptiste Charbois and Alexis
Sylvestre before she married Natomagan. | *Baptiste Natomagan (or
Nawtomaugan) and his wife, Anne Daldonille, Île à la Crosse, 1920* |
LAC/Dept. of Mines and Technical Surveys collection, PA 18349

the region as influenced by employment with the HBC, exploring the nature of their association with one another, the Company, and, consequently, the places where they lived.

The connection between the Metis and the fur trade has been well documented since the earliest days of the trade, so much so that it has become a part of our national mythology. Popular depictions of the Metis are typically romanticized, with overtones of machismo, perhaps a consequence of the vigorous physical demands of fur trading, voyageuring, and buffalo hunting – important sectors of Metis economies writ large.[10] Notions of Metis culture have relied on highly descriptive narratives and images, full of the *joie de vivre* of voyageurs and hunters singing and fiddling as they paddled over dangerous rivers or roamed the open plains in search of buffalo herds. These masculine representations of Metis life showed a society perpetually in motion – hunting furs, transporting goods, chasing buffalo – and originated largely from the accounts of nineteenth-century writers and artists who spent time travelling in the *pays d'en haut*. Contemporaries, such as traders Daniel Williams Harmon and Alexander Ross, provided detailed descriptions of the Metis that shaped these popular representations. In 1815, Harmon described voyageurs – perhaps French Canadian, perhaps Metis – as "ficle [sic] and changeable as the wind, and of a gay and lively disposition ... they make Gods of their bellies, yet when necessity obliges them ... they will endure all the fatigue and misery of hard labour and cold weather and for several days without complaining."[11] Ross, noted as Red River's first historian, wrote of the Metis:

> Half-breeds, or as they are more generally styled, brules, from the peculiar colour of their skin, being of a swarthy hue, as if sunburnt, as they grow up resemble, almost in every respect, the pure Indian. With this difference that they are more designing, more daring, and more dissolute. They are indolent, thoughtless, and improvident. Licentious in their habits, unbounded in their desires, sullen in their disposition. Proud, restless, and clannish, fond of flattery. They alternately associated with the whites and the Indians, and thus became fatally enlightened. They form a composition of all the bad qualities of both.[12]

Filling out these detailed descriptions of the character and physical appearance of traders and Metis men were accounts of camps, wintering sites, parishes, and villages filled with women and children, raucous dances with wild fiddling, and fancily dressed women who had a love for European manufactured goods such as dresses, ribbons, and china. Ross again had occasion to write about the Metis, but this time reflected on what he clearly regarded as the odd juxtaposition of Aboriginality and femininity found in the women: "Exceedingly well-featured and comely – many even handsome; and those who have means are tidy about their persons and dress. They are fond of show, and invariably attire themselves in gaudy prints, and shawls, chiefly of the tartan kind ... [B]ut, like Indian women, they are very tenacious of the habits and customs of their native country."[13] While these characteristics may have contributed to the development of an archetypal Metis culture, they were not necessarily the foundational structures of a Metis identity grounded in familial alliances within a broadly defined regional landscape.

Many stereotypes or myths, however, are founded on the smallest glimmer of truth. In the 1850s, Johann George Kohl, a German travel writer and geographer, travelled through the United States to map coastlines. In that decade, at L'Anse on the shore of Lake Superior in Wisconsin, he met a Metis voyageur who expressed the ties between his occupation and his identity: "Where I stay? I cannot tell you. I am a voyageur – I am a *chicot*. My grandfather was a voyageur – he died during a trip. My father was a voyageur – he died during a trip. I will also die on a trip and another chicot will take my place. Such is our course of life."[14]

Interpretations of the relationship between Metis culture and the trade economy have been dominated by notions of transience – a form of nomadism that discouraged permanent settlement in favour of following animals and goods between distant posts. This style of life in all its configurations, whether on the lakes and rivers of the subarctic or the Plains, encouraged a male-centric approach to living. Women, when they are a part of this narrative, are the assistants processing buffalo hides or helping the male trade economy, but otherwise they are absent from the path that men travelled. In western Canada, the Red River settlement became the home or base from which men moved – all other places were merely stopovers in this narrative of perpetual motion or seasonal movement. These descriptions of Metis life do little to explain how the relationship between culture and economy was operationalized within landscapes such as the northwest. Jennifer S.H. Brown's research into the structures of the North West Company and Hudson's Bay Company, Jacqueline Peterson's exploration of the different types of trading posts in the southern Great Lakes trade, and John Foster's analysis of Metis communities as reflections of different cultural expressions all provide insight into how trade cultures and company hierarchies could (and did) shape the types of Metis communities.[15] Nobody, however, has yet linked the nature of Metis trade communities to the cultural landscapes or socio-economic geographies in which they existed. These concepts – homeland, residency, and the trade – were all necessary to spark and/or foster the emergence of the Metis as a people. Prior to 1821, the often vicious competition between the fur companies destabilized areas such as the English River District enough that a proto-generation became key to fostering positive economic and social relationships between Indian and Euro-Canadian societies. As seen in Chapter 1, such violence receded in the decades immediately after the merger, and as the northwest stabilized, those who were born to the proto-generation took the next step to shape home and family life.

Large-scale genealogical reconstruction of families across the region in the post-1840s era of the fur trade, when the northwest was at its most socially, politically, and economically stable, reveals how families became associated with specific locations and how the needs of the economy served to encourage the establishment of branches of families in those locations. Employment in the fur trade, in short, influenced the emergence of strong local or community-based patronymic connections. By the mid-nineteenth century, the two key features of subarctic Metis society, matrilocal residency and patronymic connections, were an established way of life. But how did these maternal and paternal realities actually frame a new people? Analysis of regional genealogies over time, and as framed within trade experiences, permits an evaluation of how people lived within the lands of their mothers and how the trade economy of their fathers created locally defined communities or family-based residency patterns at specific geographic points in the matrilocally defined region. Raphaël, Sophie, and Marie Morin, as individuals and family members with long associations with the trade, provide a succinct expression of these two legacies. They continued to "live in the lands of [their] mother who was originally from the lands of [her] parents," while also using that homeland's economy as a means to move throughout the northwest and define its geography by patronyms. It was within this larger context that the Metis families in the northwest engaged with the Company and formed a socio-economic symbiosis that permitted the growth and extension of these two cultural institutions across the region.

Raphaël Morin was the third child of a proto-generation couple, French Canadian Antoine Morin and Pélagie Boucher, a woman known "by the HalfBreeds and Indians generally as a halfbreed, the child of a French

Canadian and an Indian [Montagnais] woman."[16] After entering the district in the early nineteenth century, Antoine abandoned his connections to French Canada and was fully absorbed by the economic, social, and physical landscape in which he spent the remainder of his life, working, raising his children, and consolidating his place in the extended family network. Antoine Morin's genealogy is certainly traceable to Quebec, and back to France, but for this study it is only important that he acculturated to the local socio-cultural norms after entering into a marriage with a local Aboriginal woman. Pélagie and Antoine's experience, however, diverged sharply from that of her parents. Pélagie's father was likely Louis Boucher of Berthierville, Quebec, a voyageur who had worked for the NWC at Île à la Crosse in the late eighteenth century. Boucher, like other voyageurs, took a country wife, a Dene woman from the northwest, but, unlike his son-in-law, he was not one of the family and did not integrate himself into the region's state of being. Instead, by 1811, Louis Boucher had returned home to Lower Canada, leaving behind his wife, daughter Pélagie, and possibly other children.[17] In contrast, Antoine remained with his family in the district and raised his fifteen children, seven of whom were born at Athabasca or Portage La Loche and the remainder at Île à la Crosse (see Figure 3.1). Of those children, ten left clearly traceable genealogical imprints in the region and are known to have married and lived throughout northwestern Saskatchewan, from Portage La Loche in the north to Devil's Lake in the south and as far west as Lac Prairie. The Morin surname is today found throughout the region in Metis and First Nations communities, and all of those who carry it can be traced to this nineteenth-century beginning.

Once they were old enough, Raphaël and his brothers became HBC servants and were stationed in various sectors of the district.[18] Raphaël, for instance, worked at Île à la Crosse and Green Lake, and upon his retirement around 1881 he became a farmer and rancher at Devil's Lake.[19] Within a few years, he was joined by some members of his extended family. In addition to a number of brothers and sisters, several sons took up ranching/farming around Lac Vert, Devil's Lake, and Lac Prairie, and as a family they cared for the now-widowed Pélagie, who was in her eighties. At the same time, there were Morins at Sakitawak, Pelican Lake, Portage La Loche, Sipisihk, and Bull's House, to name a few. What is interesting about the scrip applications of these three particular Morin siblings, however, is that they all indicated they had moved nearer to Lac Vert, which they identified as being part of the lands of their mother and maternal

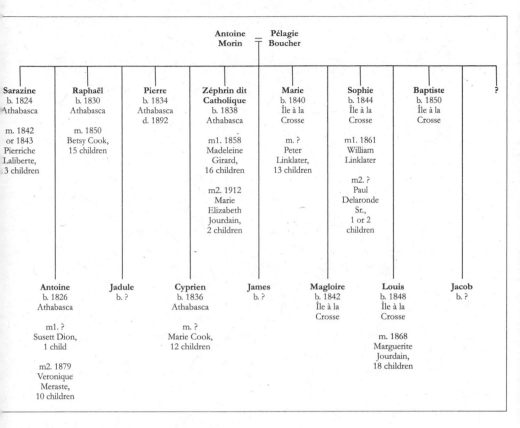

FIGURE 3.1   Antoine Morin and Pélagie Boucher family

grandparents. It has already been noted that Pélagie was identified as a Montagnais Metis ("Montagnais" is a term the Oblates used to refer to the Dene) born in the Portage La Loche region, which is considerably farther north than either Devil's Lake or Lac Vert. The Morins' identification of a broad geographic landscape as homeland indicates, perhaps, a disjuncture between how the Dene (and even the Cree), as Indian people, and their Metis relatives defined and identified their territories, a reality that may have been driven by differing relationships to the trade economy. At the very least, based on declaratory statements included on their scrip applications, all three adult Morin children regarded the territory around Devil's Lake and Shell River as the southern boundary of their mother's homeland. They clearly indicated that they believed their territory to be defined broadly and included much of the northwest, rather than just

Athabasca, where their father had worked as an HBC servant for the first several years of his employment; Portage La Loche, where their mother was born; or even Sakitawak, where many of them had been born, were married, and worked. For the nineteenth-century Metis, the notion of homeland encompassed the vast territory where the people worked and travelled, but it also included specific locations or communities within that territory.

Throughout the nineteenth century, the number of posts in the district expanded and contracted depending on need and profitability, so the movement of men and their families between the various posts likewise fluctuated. The HBC district reports provide post descriptions that include locations, infrastructure evaluations, and servant complements. For instance, the 1862 report for the English River District notes that there were six posts that employed a total of forty men. Île à la Crosse employed one officer and fifteen men; Rapids River employed one clerk and four men; Deer's Lake and Portage La Loche each employed a postmaster, although the former had four men and the latter employed five; and, finally, Jackfish Creek and Lac Vert each employed one interpreter and three men.[20] These reports, however, tell us little about the families connected with these men or the socio-cultural milieu in which they lived.

Similarly, the 1871 Company census, which recorded the number of women and children at its posts, gave a total for Île à la Crosse alone of fifty-one women (two of whom were widows) and 106 children. Clearly, the number of children was growing and becoming a significant part of the Company's responsibilities. (As early as 1853, Chief Trader George Deschambeault had written that "the number of Families at this place is surprising."[21]) It is important to note that the families recorded in these reports were only those with male heads of households under contract with the HBC, not families of men employed on either a seasonal or temporary basis, the freeman families, or those who lived a subsistence lifestyle and were not employed by the Company. The district reports submitted a year later by Samuel McKenzie listed four posts (rather than the six that existed a decade earlier) in operation in English River: Île à la Crosse, with one commissioned officer, one senior clerk, one interpreter, one farmer, one cowherder, four fishermen, two guides, and eleven canoemen/labourers; Portage La Loche, with one senior clerk; Bull's House, with one postmaster, one interpreter, two fishermen, and six canoemen/labourers; and Lac Vert, with one senior clerk, one postmaster, one interpreter, two fishermen, and five canoemen/labourers (see Photo 3.2).[22]

PHOTO 3.2   This photo was taken in the early 1900s, likely at Bull's House in the region of Buffalo Narrows, where the Hudson's Bay Company kept oxen. This representation of women and children gives us a sense of the types of cabins some families lived in and a sense of outposts as places of residence for families. The large number of dogs reflects the transportation needs of the outpost. Sled dogs were used to transport goods and supplies between outposts during the winter. | *Group of Native people, Buffalo Narrows, SK* | LAC/Department of the Interior fonds, PA 44538

Six months later, William McMurray's descriptions of three posts provide perhaps the greatest insight into family life and the reasons families congregated in specific locales. Portage La Loche, McMurray recorded, was located on the west side of Methy Lake, about six miles from the store at the south end of Methy Portage. At the time, McMurray felt that Portage La Loche should be abandoned and rebuilt near that store because the soil in the original location was not productive except for growing potatoes. However, there was a small but important winter fishery at the original location, plus a reliable moose and caribou population. Both Dene and "descendants of French Canadian Halfbreeds" frequented the post (McMurray noted that he preferred the character of the latter), and several families had built houses or huts at certain points around the lake, supporting themselves with small gardens and hunting. What McMurray was identifying were family-based settlements typical of Metis residency across the northwest. These types of family-based communities were identifiable by their patronyms.[23] McMurray noted that Bull's House was located on the north end of Little Buffalo Lake, forty-five miles from the store at the south end of Methy Lake and seventy miles from Île à la Crosse. The purpose of this post was to winter the oxen required for the summer transportation system at the portage. These animals could graze the natural hay meadows at Bull's House. When water levels were too high, hay was obtained from Little Buffalo Lake, three miles from the post. Bull's House also apparently had the best winter fishery in the district, supplying both Portage La Loche and Île à la Crosse when their own fisheries failed.[24]

McMurray further recorded that the post at Île à la Crosse was located on Lac Île à la Crosse's border and had always served as a winter residence for the officers in charge of the district. Whitefish was the main source of food, supplemented by moose, reindeer, and deer meat. While the soil at Île à la Crosse was not especially arable, he felt that with proper management it could yield a fair return of wheat, barley, potatoes, and other hardy vegetables. There was also a herd of forty head of cattle at the Île à la Crosse post, as well as a small grist mill to process wheat.[25] The descriptions of these posts and their labour needs related to food production and consumption (for both humans and animals) are important because they are strong indicators that the men and their families were located in areas deemed essential for the trade and its support, an activity that demanded detailed planning and scheduling. In turn, these locations became associated with specific branches of interrelated families over time.

Perhaps the single best visual representation of the relationship between HBC servants and the local residency driven by the trade's needs is a map officially titled "Sketch Map of the English River District and Outposts and also Winter Trading Stations and Indian Hunting Lodges" (see Map 3.3). Commissioned in about 1895 by Chief Trader William Cornwallis King when he was at Île à la Crosse, the sketch map contains no topographical data that would orient the reader to the physical geography of the district and the Company's posts or other habitation sites.[26] Rather, the map demonstrates the strawberry plant metaphor by highlighting the relationship between the Île à la Crosse post, located at the centre of the map, and its subsidiary posts, outposts, winter stations, and Indian camps spread across the region. The distances (via land or water) between the main depot and the outer locations are recorded, suggesting that the map's primary use was as a blueprint for planning the movement of men, goods, and furs. It is an expression of the economic geography of the HBC in the English River District. The broader geography of the district is noted in the handwritten comments at the map's corners and

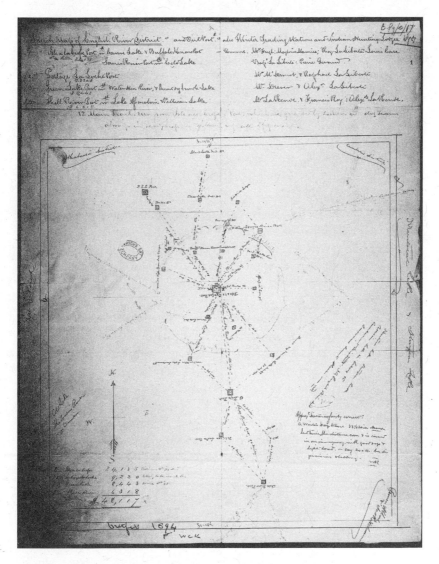

MAP 3.3   Sketch map of the English River District | HBCA/PAM, B.89/e/17

along the sides, which indicate the location of Battleford, Prince Albert, Lac La Biche, and Cumberland House in relation to Île à la Crosse. Additionally, and most importantly for this study, a list at the top right hand side of the sketch map identifies thirteen men who worked as runners (see Glossary) and the region for which they were responsible, giving us clues about how certain locales became associated with specific families.

The sketch map reveals a great deal about the relationships between the HBC and its employees as well as the spatial and temporal orientation of the men and, by extension, their families within the district. The legend at the top of the map lists twelve posts, outposts, winter-trading stations, and Indian camps on the left and thirteen runners on the right. Île à la Crosse is associated with the posts at Canoe Lake, Buffalo Narrows, Souris River, and Cold Lake. Portage La Loche is listed seperately, while the Green Lake post is associated with the Waterhen River and Burnt Dog Bundle Lake posts. Finally, the Shell River post is associated with Lake Assiniboine and Pelican Lake posts. Like Raphaël Morin's articulation of the relationship between his cultural identity and his homeland, and the Metis voyageur who articulated that his identity and job were synonymous expressions, the runners identified by location on King's map provide an important revelation about the connection between land, masculinity, and identity.

Of the thirteen men identified as runners on the sketch map, ten were integral to the HBC servant class in the latter half of the nineteenth century and, significantly, were all related to one another either through birth or marriage. Reading the regional genealogies together with the sketch map gives a sense of the social and economic interactions between the region's posts, communities, and families. Some relationships are more apparent than others because of easily identified patronymic connections between families. The list includes two sets of brothers – Roy (actually Louis Roy), Baptiste (Jean Baptiste), Raphaël, and Alexandre (Alex) Laliberte, all born in the district between 1851 and 1860; and Alexandre and William La Ronde (Delaronde), who were born, respectively, in Manitoba in 1868 and near the Waterhen River by Lac Prairie in 1874. Genealogical reconstruction adds considerable detail and reveals intriguing patterns of relatedness. These two sets of brothers were, in fact, related to each other because their mothers, Sarazine Morin Laliberte and Sophie Morin Delaronde, were sisters.

Four additional men listed were closely related to the Laliberte and Delaronde men: Pierre Girard was a brother-in-law to Sarazine Morin, mother of the Laliberte brothers; François Roy was the husband of Caroline Morin; Magloire Maurice was a nephew of the Labertes; and Louis Caisse was Magloire's brother-in-law through their respective marriages to sisters Philomène and Sophie Lariviere (see Figure 3.2).

Three names on the list of runners – William Dreaver, William McDermott, and Alfred Fugl – have no patronymic legacy in the English River District. These three men all worked for periods of time within the region, but none married local women or left any imprint on the region's

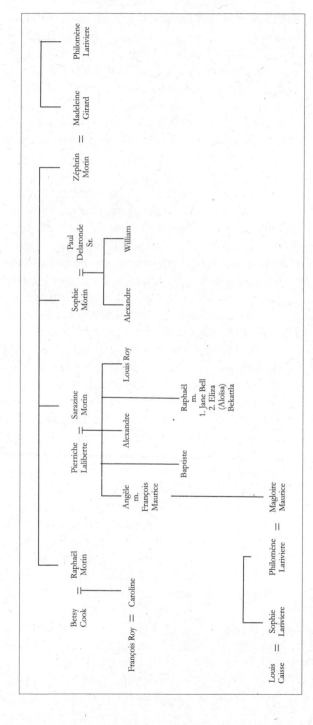

FIGURE 3.2   Family relationships between men on King's map

familial landscape. They were not, however, the only men who were not connected to the families of the region. While employment alone was not enough to establish a lasting place in the families or the history of the northwest (see Chapter 4, which assesses the importance of Catholicism within wahkootowin), the focus here is on how each of the ten related men were organized in relation to King's map and how the territory to which they were assigned as runners related to the development of local communities and the establishment of patronymic connections in communities throughout the English River District.

The level of detail on the sketch map is far greater than the information applied in the legend. According to the sketch map itself, the English River District was divided into sections of activity, and the six main runners out of Île à la Crosse – Fugl, Maurice, two of the Laliberte brothers, Caisse, and Girard – were each assigned one of the four sections of the region. The map was marked with their names to indicate the trade territory for which each was responsible. Maurice, Fugl, and Baptiste Laliberte were assigned trade territories within traditional Dene lands north of the English River. Maurice was assigned the area encompassing the Portage La Loche post, Bull's House, Buffalo Lake House, the Buffalo Narrows post, Clear Lake Indian House, and Island Lake Indian House, along with the White Fish River Indian camp to the northwest. Fugl was assigned Campbell House, Bernard House, and an Indian winter lodge site that traded at the Souris River post. Baptiste Laliberte was assigned the Souris River and Cold Lake posts in the northeast. Caisse's zone was to the east, covering a series of encampments in both Cree and Dene territories. Roy Laliberte operated in the southwest, covering McCallum House, Waterhen Lake, and Green Lake, along with a number of Cree lodges/camps. In the centre, between Caisse and Roy Laliberte's territorial zones, was Burnt Dog Bundle Lake Indian post, although it appears this was in the latter's purview. Finally, the last of the six runners, Pierre Girard, is not represented in a specific area, although it is possible he took the western zone, which, like the eastern side, encompassed an area that straddled Cree and Dene territories. However, the writing on the map is faint and largely illegible, so we cannot be certain which was Girard's site of responsibility.

Baptiste Laliberte, identified in both the 1881 and 1901 censuses as a French Breed,[27] began his career with the HBC as a voyageur before apprenticing to become a clerk like his father, Pierriche Laliberte, at Portage La Loche. After a total of eight years in the Company's service, Baptiste was appointed clerk for Portage La Loche and eventually succeeded his father as postmaster in 1889-90.[28] Although a long-time servant, Baptiste's relationship with the Company was not always amicable. In an 1877 letter from Walter West, clerk at Île à la Crosse, Baptiste was criticized for arriving at Île à la Crosse nine days ahead of schedule despite clear instructions about when he was expected. Although West did not explain in the letter why this early arrival was problematic, he made it clear that Baptiste was unable to get things right and concluded that the Company would do better without him, so he was "no longer considered [to be] in the service – He can look out for himself some other way."[29] It is unclear when the Company rehired Baptiste (or even if he was actually released from service), but in 1888 he was described as "a careful post manager" who was "more likely to err on the side of excessive caution and economy ... not the reverse."[30] Four years later, in 1892, Baptiste requested a promotion to the rank of clerk along with a wage increase, stating that he would otherwise leave the service entirely. Île à la Crosse chief trader Henry J. Moberly supported Baptiste's request, noting that he had provided more than satisfactory service as postmaster and that Moberly expected there would be no drop in his performance if promoted. However, Company officials in Winnipeg chose not to promote Baptiste, although they did increase his wages and extend his contract for an additional three years.[31] By 1895, when the sketch map was drawn, Baptiste was still a postmaster at Portage La Loche and was responsible for the trade returns at the Souris River and Cold Lake posts within that northern section.

Baptiste laboured on the northern edge of the English River District alongside several male relatives, including his brother Raphaël Laliberte and nephew Magloire Maurice, who were both identified on the sketch map as working in that area. Indeed, several branches of the extended Laliberte family lived in this part of the district, beginning with the birth of family matriarch Sarazine Morin in about 1824 and the subsequent arrival of family patriarch Pierriche Laliberte early in the century. Their son Raphaël, whose family life was discussed in detail in Chapter 2, entered the service of the Company while a young man, like his brothers. Initially serving in the Portage La Loche region, by the closing years of the nineteenth century he was living at Lac Vert and working as a hunter and fisherman.[32] In all, Raphaël and his two spouses, Jane Bell/Bull and Eliza Bekattla, had ten children, all of whom were born in the Portage La Loche region. Two of his daughters, Augustine and Eleanore, married men from Portage La Loche and remained in that part of the district.[33] Similarly, nephew Magloire Maurice, the eldest son of Raphaël's and Baptiste's sister Angèle Laliberte and her first husband, François Maurice, was born at

Portage La Loche. By the time of François' death during the 1885-86 trading season, Magloire was already engaged as an HBC servant and working in the Portage La Loche region. By 1888 he was in charge of the Pine River (Tsa-tsigamihk) outpost, and in 1892 he was put in charge of the Cree Lake (otherwise known as Sandy Lake) winter post, which serviced mostly Dene peoples. One of his duties at Cree Lake was to act as interpreter for dealings with the Dene. Although his maternal grandmother, Sarazine, was Metis with Dene maternal ancestry, Magloire was identified in the 1901 census as a French Breed, and his primary language was French.[34]

Another of the six main runners out of Île à la Crosse was Louis Caisse, Magloire's brother-in-law. Louis was a long-term servant of the Company, working as a general labourer, fisherman, and tripper. In 1882, Louis married Sophie Lariviere, the sister of Magloire's wife, Philomène, at the Saint-Jean-Baptiste mission.[35] (The Larivieres are another family discussed in greater detail in the previous chapter.)

Finally, of the six related men from this initial group, Pierre Girard was born in Athabasca circa 1852 and worked for the Company in the English River District as a trader and postmaster for much of his adult life.[36] Pierre's sister, Madeleine Girard, was married to Zéphrin dit Catholique Morin, brother to Sarazine Morin Laliberte. Pierre was therefore uncle by marriage to the Laliberte brothers and great-uncle to Magloire Maurice.[37] Pierre entered the English River District's economy when he became a trader with the HBC in the mid-nineteenth century, and he became a member of the community with his 1869 marriage to his first wife, Sophie Lulie, the daughter of a Dene couple. This connection to the district was reinforced in 1890 when Girard married his second local wife, Eliza Misponas of Île à la Crosse, at Lac Vert's Saint-Julien mission.[38] Eventually, the Girards became associated with the southern communities around Lac Vert and Shell River. Although not visible on the sketch map, as his five counterparts were, Girard would have been useful in several sectors of the district, including Souris River, where he is listed as a runner in 1895.

Rounding out the remainder of the interrelated men are Roy and Alexandre Laliberte, William and Alexandre Delaronde, and François Roy. Named Louis Roy at birth, the first of these two Laliberte brothers preferred to be known as Roy and was called "Petit Roi" by others in the HBC. He was born in either 1856 or 1860 at Portage La Loche and married Virginie Merasty from Lac Vert in 1881 after being briefly posted in the south.[39] Roy and his family are listed in the Lac Vert census for 1891 and 1901, which indicates that after beginning his career at Portage La Loche, but before the sketch map was drafted, Roy was relocated to the southern portion of the district. Little else is known about him except that he was an HBC servant for his entire adult life and he fathered thirteen children.

At the district's southern end, the final Laliberte brother, Alexandre, served as Green Lake postmaster in 1892, an appointment that came after he had operated' the outpost at Canoe Lake from 1888 to 1890. Significantly, Alexandre's wife, Mary Isabelle (or Elizabeth) Iron, was the daughter of Chief Raphaël Iron of Nehiyo-wapasi.[40] This familial connection to the Canoe Lake Cree band made Alexandre an invaluable HBC servant on the southern edges of the district. In 1899 he retired from the HBC and took a job with a fur buyer out of Prince Albert, although he returned to the HBC for another contract before retiring again in 1902. Alexandre's entire career in the trade was based in these southern communities, and in 1895 he was operating as a runner at the Green Lake post for the communities of Waterhen River and Burnt Dog Bundle Lake. From 1902 until 1931 he ran the Revillon Frères store at Sipisihk (see Photos 3.3 and 3.4).[41]

Farther south was the Shell River post, which since the early 1890s had been controlled by the Delaronde family. Paul Delaronde Sr. came from Manitoba with several children by his first wife, Marguerite Sinclair.[42] Delaronde married Sophie Morin, the aunt of Roy, Baptiste, and Alexandre Laliberte. There is no record of a marriage in either the Saint-Jean-Baptiste mission or Saint-Laurent church, so we could assume that the marriage was formalized according to the custom of the country. The Delaronde brothers listed on the sketch map were not Sophie's biological sons. Both Alexandre and William engaged with the HBC in the English River District as soon as they became old enough to handle trading responsibilities, and this established for them an important economic link to their stepmother's territory. Alexandre Delaronde was an "Indian trader" who worked for the HBC. While it is known that William was also a servant, little other information about him has survived except that he died in a fire around 1909. What is evident is that these two brothers worked with several male members of their stepmother's family and were based in the southern part of the district, where Sophie Morin had gone to live to be near her brother, Raphaël Morin. Furthermore, Alexandre and William each married young women from the Morin family – cousins who were both named Marie Agnès – which further rooted them in the region.

The sketch map notes that Alexandre and William Delaronde were working with François Roy, a third runner in the district, who married Caroline Morin at Lac Vert in 1876. François was the son of François Roy Sr. and Marie Lariviere, while Caroline was the child of Raphaël Morin

PHOTO 3.3   Alexandre Laliberte *(left)* was the Hudson's Bay Company's postmaster at Canoe Lake before he ran the Revillon Frères store at Sipisihk, where this photograph of himself, his son François *(middle)*, and his uncle Raphaël Morin (or Ralph Morin) *(right)* was taken. Although Laliberte was known as one of the first permanent residents in the Sipisihk region, François actually moved there in 1909, one year before his father, mother, and the rest of his brothers and sisters took up residence. Raphaël Morin told the scrip commissioners in 1887 that he lived in the lands of his mother. | *Alexandre Laliberte, François Laliberte, and Raphaël Morin, St. Louis School, Beauval, ca. 1890s* | SAB, S-B1146

PHOTO 3.4 The children in the photograph are those of Alexandre Laliberte and Mary Isabelle (Elizabeth) Iron, daughter of Raphaël Iron, chief of the Canoe Lake Cree (according to the photo caption, they are, from left to right: Victor, Marie Adelle, Adolphe, Margaret Marie, and Alexandre). The photograph was taken at Sipisihk in the Île à la Crosse district. Although the photograph is dated 1890, based on the ages of the children – Joseph (full name Joseph Victor) (b. 1900) and Adolphe (b. 1903) – it was taken in 1906. Joseph Victor operated a tow-line ferry on Lac La Plonge from 1923 until 1942 and owned the local pool hall. He married three times. He had four children with Suzanne Kyplain, a son with Victoria Roy, and four children with Rosa McCallum, whom he married in 1930. Marie Adelle (or Marie Adel) would have been about twenty-one and had either just married or was about to marry François Maurice, while her sister, Marguerite Marie (Margaret), would eventually marry Frank Fidler. Marguerite Marie was known in the region for being a cook in her father's store. Alexandre (Alexander) was born in September 1898 and would eventually marry Albertine Belanger, daughter of Marie Beatrix Maurice and Charles Eugêne Belanger. Adolphe (Adolph) eventually married Flora Corrigal. | *Laliberte family, Île à la Crosse, old Revillon Frères residence, ca. 1890.* | SAB, S-B1153

and Betsy Cook, which made her the niece of Sophie Morin. François and Caroline were both baptized at Île à la Crosse, but they were living at Lac Vert by 1874 because of François' employment with the HBC. After working at Green Lake, François was posted to Devil's Lake, close to his wife's relatives.

To understand familial roles in northwestern Saskatchewan Metis society, with special attention to the emergence of a cultural identity, we must locate patterns within the genealogical data for each of the district's forty-three core families and assess the four generations of Metis people. Using this analytical framework, we can trace the life cycles of generations of people as they were born, married, began their families, and moved throughout the region. Each generational cohort represents a period of between twenty and thirty years, the time from birth to marriage and the establishment of their own families. These families had a significant degree of geographical mobility throughout the northwest, and because of the large geographic range in which they lived and worked, they had an impact on other Metis and Indian families in the region.

Aspects of the Laliberte family's early foundation have been discussed in previous chapters, and their economic role in the district will be more completely addressed in Chapter 7. At this juncture, however, a description of the ways different branches of the families became associated with various locations and intermarried with the Morins and Delarondes will show how one family could spread itself across the district through work, but especially through intermarriage. The Laliberte family traces its paternal ancestors to Quebec; its ties to the northwest are rooted in the Cree and Dene cultures of the wives' families. Patriarch Antoine Laliberte was born in the late 1700s in Quebec. It was his marriage to a woman named Belanger, a "Halfbreed" from the northwest, that ensured their sons' future in Rupert's Land.[43] Little is known about Antoine Laliberte or his wife except that Antoine was an HBC trader and in 1817 he and his wife had a son, born at Carlton, named Pierre (who came to be known as Pierriche). According to the Île à la Crosse post journal, an HBC servant named Antoine Laliberte was buried at the post on 4 June 1889.[44] There was no record of this event in the Catholic Church records, but we can presume that this Antoine was the patriarch of the Laliberte family in northwestern Saskatchewan, as there was no other Antoine Laliberte to whom this event could be matched.

Pierriche became a servant in the trade and married a local woman, Sarazine Morin, at Sakitawak. This first union of the Laliberte and Morin families in the district is a central act that affected many of the families subsequently associated with the region. The linkages between the Morins and Labertes were reinforced with each successive generation well into the early twentieth century.[45] Sarazine's father, Antoine Morin, was much like Antoine Laliberte – both men remained in the district, where they worked, married local women, and raised large families in this maternally demarcated homeland. Indeed, the life cycles of both Sarazine and Pierriche and Antoine and Pélagie are nearly identical in terms of the socio-cultural and economic foundation they laid for their descendants. Throughout his lifetime, Pierriche worked at posts in Île à la Crosse, Green Lake, and Portage La Loche as a labourer, trader, steersman, and postmaster and eventually became a private freighter and farmer in the Lac Vert region. However, he and Serazine did not live their entire adult lives in the northwest.[46] In 1849, Pierriche briefly retired from the Company and moved with his family to Red River, but in 1851 he re-engaged as a steersman and returned to the northwest, the land of his wife's birth, where they remained.[47] After the family's return to the region in 1851, Pierriche worked for the HBC as postmaster at Portage La Loche, where he was in charge of the trade and transport business, and then later at Green Lake in the same capacity.

Pierriche and Sarazine were one of the first-generation couples of the northwest, and because of Pierriche's association with so many communities through his work, the Laliberte children and their descendants were well represented throughout the territory. After the first generation of families was firmly established at Sakitawak, they moved outward into the other communities, perhaps pursuing alternative economic opportunities in new locales or perhaps assigned to specific regions by the Company, as indicated by the sketch map. The Laliberte and Morin families lived throughout the district, working as traders, hunters, trappers, and fishermen. With each generation, Euro-Canadian, Metis, and Indian men married the daughters of local families, and each cohort's development hinged on the stability of women as keepers and shapers of family life. For instance, several daughters of both Pierriche Laliberte and Antoine Morin married incoming outsider males, such as Paul Delaronde Sr., drawing them into the ever-expanding geographical influence of their parents' families and simultaneously establishing extended family relationships for their own newly formed immediate families while creating new patronymic connections in specific locations.

It seems that young women rarely, if ever, left the region but rather remained to marry incoming traders sent by the HBC or young Metis men from their generation who also remained behind. As was already mentioned, Pierriche Laliberte and Serazine Morin's eldest daughter, Angèle Laliberte, married her first husband, François Maurice of Montreal, in the late 1850s or early 1860s. Over the course of their marriage, Angèle Laliberte and François Maurice had six sons and six daughters (see Figure 3.3).[48] Three of those daughters married HBC employees working at the Île à la Crosse, Portage La Loche, and Souris River posts, while four of their sons were HBC employees who married into the Sakitawak and Portage La Loche families of Lariviere, Couillonneur, Bouvier, and Natomagan. When François died at forty-nine years of age, Angèle married Raphaël Souris, a fisherman in the Portage La Loche region who adopted two of her grandsons.[49] Of Serazine Morin's two other daughters, Marie and Catherine, genealogical data was available only for the latter. Catherine married Charles Pierre Lafleur, and their daughter, Adélaide, was raised by Serazine and Pierriche after Catherine's death in 1873. Like her daughter Angèle, Serazine raised a grandchild and ensured that Adélaide was raised among her mother's relatives in the homeland of their birth.

This pattern of female-centric cultural development and outsider male acculturation through marriage occurred because of the demands of the trading lifestyle. Unlike their female relatives, men had greater potential to travel to other districts for education or employment opportunities. Some of the first generation's sons became traders and left the region to join posts in other districts. Antoine Morin Jr. (b. 1826, Athabasca), the eldest son of Antoine Morin and Pélagie Boucher, left the English River District and ended up in northeastern Saskatchewan, taking scrip at Cumberland House in 1886. Several of Pierriche and Serazine's eldest sons were formally educated, including Alexandre, who attended school at Red River.[50] Overwhelmingly, however, sons born to the first-generation couples remained behind. By the second generation, these men were like their female relatives, indigenous to the region, and they marked that landscape with their surnames. As men worked throughout the district, and created new places of residence, women moved with them. The basic principle, however, remained unchanged. Women framed the regional pattern as matrilocal, while men lent their patronyms to specific locales organized around family-based settlements. Over time, an intricate nexus of families linked to the trade economy was established throughout the English River District.

In the Morin family, second-generation sons followed their fathers into the trade in various capacities and forged marital alliances that positively affected both individual and familial opportunities within the region. Of Antoine Morin and Pélagie Boucher's thirteen children, only eleven had

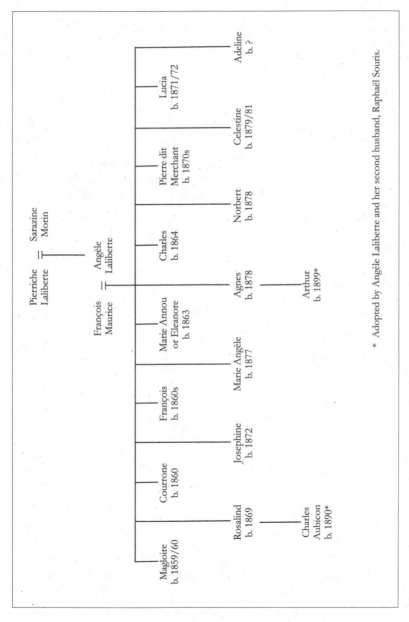

FIGURE 3.3   Angèle Laliberte and François Maurice family

Pierriche Laliberte = Sarazine Morin

François Maurice = Angèle Laliberte

Magloire b. 1859/60
Courrone b. 1860
François b. 1860s
Marie Annou or Eleanore b. 1863
Charles b. 1864
Pierre dit Merchant b. 1870s
Lucia b. 1871/72

Rosalind b. 1869
Josephine b. 1872
Marie Angèle b. 1877
Agnes b. 1878
Norbert b. 1878
Celestine b. 1879/81
Adeline b. ?

Charles Aubicon b. 1890*
Arthur b. 1899*

* Adopted by Angèle Laliberte and her second husband, Raphaël Souris.

enough genealogical data available to evaluate their lives over time. Of those eleven, only five had a significant impact on the culture and society that emerged in the trade district. There were four daughters, although significant genealogical information exists only for Sarazine, Sophie, and Marie.[51] The fourth daughter, Jadule, reportedly married Louis Lalonde and received scrip in Manitoba, but there is no other information available on her or her descendents.[52]

Marie Morin, meanwhile, married Peter Linklater, who in 1855 arrived at the Île à la Crosse post from Manitoba as a servant of the HBC. They ultimately had thirteen children. By 1870, Peter and Marie were living at Lac la Caribou (Reindeer Lake) in the English River District. Peter died there in 1880 while still in the service of the HBC. As noted at the beginning of this chapter, after her husband's death, Marie resided at Shell River with her children. As a widow, living near her relatives was an appropriate decision, for she would need economic support from her extended family. Interestingly, there is no indication that Marie was unable to care for her children.

Several of the nine Morin sons made a lasting imprint on the history of the district (see Table 3.1). No biographical information exists beyond the birth years for four of the Morin sons – James (b. 1840), Magloire (b. 1842), Baptiste (b. 1850), and Jacob (b. ?). As already noted, Antoine Jr. relocated to Cumberland House, while Pierre (b. 1834) entered the service in 1857 and worked around the district at posts such as Lac du Brochet, Cold Lake, and Green Lake. However, who Pierre married and how many children (if any) he had is unknown. Of the remaining four – Raphaël, Cyprien, James, Zéphrin dit Catholique, and Louis – all worked for the HBC and spread out across northwestern Saskatchewan into several communities, where they raised large families. In 1834, Raphaël Morin married Elizabeth (Betsy) Cook of La Ronge, an area that was originally part of the English River District.[53] As previously mentioned, Raphaël lived throughout the northwest and worked for the HBC until his retirement around 1887, when he moved to Devil's Lake and became a farmer.[54]

Cyprien was one of the best remembered people in the entire region because he was a founder of Lac Prairie and a devoted Catholic who built the church there on his own land. Born in 1836 near the Athabasca River, Cyprien lived to be ninety-six, dying in 1932 at Lac Prairie. After moving to this southern part of the district in 1873 with his family, Cyprien became a farmer and rancher on the lake's west side at Island Hill on the Meadow River. Like his brother Raphaël, Cyprien was a freighter for the Company and served as postmaster at Meadow Lake in 1873. Cyprien married Marie

TABLE 3.1   Locations associated with Pierriche Laliberte and Sarazine Morin's children

Name	Positions	Residency	Spouse	Number of children
Sarazine	n/a	Île à la Crosse Green Lake Portage La Loche	Pierriche Laliberte	13
Antoine	postmaster middleman labourer steersman guide freeman	Portage La Loche Pelican Lake	1. Susette Dion 2. Véronique Merasty	1 10
Raphaël	freighter farmer	Île à la Crosse Shell Lake Devil's Lake	Betsy (Elizabeth) Cook	15
Judile(?)	n/a	n/a	Louis Lalonde	n/a
Pierre	interpreter postmaster	Lac du Brochet Cold Lake Green Lake	n/a	n/a
Cyprien	bowsman steersman freighter farmer postmaster middleman interpreter	Île à la Crosse Cold Lake Meadow Lake	Marie Cook	12
Zépherin dit Catholique	freighter farmer	Île à la Crosse Green Lake	1. Madeleine Girard 2. Marie Elizabeth Jourdain	16 2
James	n/a	n/a	n/a	n/a
Marie	n/a	Île à la Crosse Caribou (Reindeer) Lake Shell River/Lake	Peter Linklater	
Magloire	servant	Île à la Crosse Fort á la Corne	n/a	n/a
Sophie	n/a	Île à la Crosse Lake Manitoba Waterhen River Shell River Devil's Lake	1. William Linklater 2. Paul Delaronde Sr.	1 0

▶

◄ TABLE 3.1

Name	Positions	Residency	Spouse	Number of children
Louis	cattlekeeper labourer farmer freighter freeman	Île à la Crosse Green Lake	Marguerite Jourdain	15
Baptiste	n/a	Île à la Crosse	n/a	n/a
Jacob	n/a	n/a	n/a	n/a

Cook, and together they had twelve natural children and an adopted son, George Desjarlais.[55]

Zéphrin dit Catholique, a freighter and farmer, was also employed as a fisherman and carpenter, working for both the Île à la Crosse and, by 1887, Green Lake posts. Zéphrin also worked for periods as an independent trader. In 1858 he married Madeleine Girard from Red River, sister of Pierre Girard and the daughter of Joseph Girard and Marguerite Jackson, with whom he had fifteen children (thirteen lived to adulthood). Although born in Red River, Madeleine arrived in Île à la Crosse with her parents after the HBC sent her father to the English River District. (It should be noted that in a few isolated instances, young men from Sakitawak and other northwest communities married women from outside the region, bringing them back and acculturating them into the community. Besides the example of Madeleine Girard, this occurred with George Bekattla and Nancy Kippling/Kyplain of Red River and, in the third generation, Hélène Lafonde from Muskeg Lake, who married Pierre Marie Morin, son of Raphaël Morin and Betsy Cook. However, on the whole, far fewer women acculturated into the region than men.)

By 1887, Zéphrin and his family had left Île à la Crosse and were living at the HBC post on the east side of Lac Vert. In 1912, after Madeleine's death the previous year at the age of sixty-seven, seventy-four-year-old Zéphrin married Marie Elizabeth Jourdain, daughter of Baptiste Jourdain Jr. and Nanette Bekattla, a woman thirty-five years his junior.[56]

Finally, Louis Morin, like his older brothers, was a freighter and farmer, as well as a general labourer for the HBC. In 1853, Louis married Marguerite Jourdain, the daughter of Jean Baptiste Jourdain and Margaret

Bear and sister to Baptiste Jourdain Jr., which made her the aunt of Marie Elizabeth Jourdain, the second wife of Louis' brother Zéphrin.[57]

Sophie Morin's story is particularly illustrative of how home and economics in the northwest affected a family's movement and, as a result, shaped the region's socio-cultural residency patterns. In 1861, Sophie married William Linklater – possibly the brother of her sister Marie's husband, Peter – and the couple lived at Île à la Crosse until 1868, when they moved to Lake Manitoba because of Linklater's contractual obligations with the HBC.[58] In 1869, Sophie and William moved to Waterhen River, again for his employment, and lived there until 1874, when they moved to Shell River near Devil's Lake, which was on the way to Lac Vert. Although not well documented, it appears that by the late 1870s/early 1880s William and Sophie again left the district, returning to the Lake Manitoba region of his family. Sophie had returned to her homeland by 1881, when she was living at Lac Vert with Paul Delaronde Sr., the son of a woman from the North-West Territories and a French Canadian.[59]

Paul Delaronde Sr. first appears in the Île à la Crosse post records in the 1870s. Over the next two decades, while a permanent resident of the region, he attempted to establish various commercial enterprises throughout the English River District.[60] Delaronde Sr., himself a former resident of the Lake Manitoba area, was well known to the clergy of Red River, who considered him one of Saint-Laurent's better-educated citizens. By the middle of the 1870s, however, Delaronde was, in the opinion of the clergy, making questionable decisions. In an 1874 letter, Father Taché at Red River expressed disappointment in Delaronde's living arrangements. According to Taché, Sophie Morin had been brought to Red River by her first husband, William Linklater, who "gave her" to Paul, who then left with Sophie for the "prairies or somewhere north."[61] Sophie's first husband, William, had gone to Duck Bay to find himself another wife.[62] On the surface, it would be simple to condemn William Linklater for "giving" his wife to Paul Delaronde, and clearly Father Taché had that inclination. However, another way to interpret what occurred was that Sophie Morin found a means by which she could return home to the lands of her mother when her first husband decided to remain in Manitoba near his own family. She and her second husband went to an area where she had lived previously with her first husband and where, presumably, she had some connection with and knowledge of the area. Furthermore, by now Sophie's mother, several siblings, and other extended family were living nearby. The Morin and Delaronde names figured prominently in this part

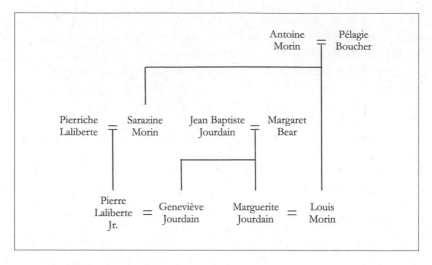

FIGURE 3.4   Morin-Jourdain family connection

of the district and created a significant family-based settlement with a complex genealogical connection.

Within each generation, old marriage patterns were reinforced between families that had already forged alliances with one another, or new alliances were created with other families, expanding outward in ever larger concentric circles and encompassing more communities and territory. Based on the patterns in which they were living and the manner in which they connected to one another economically as well as socially, the worldview of wahkootowin was very much a part of the Morin-Laliberte family's style of life. Beginning in the second generation and escalating in the third, a pattern of familial intermarriage continuously reintroduced specific surnames into one or more of the core forty-three families. For example, two daughters of Antoine Morin and Pélagie Boucher – Marie and Sophie – married Linklaters. Additionally, Sarazine Morin's granddaughter, Eleanore (or Marie Annou) Maurice, daughter of François Maurice and Angèle Laliberte, married Archibald David Linklater of Red River in the early 1880s. While there is not enough genealogical data on any of these men to prove a familial connection, the unusual nature of this name in the region hints that they were related. Also within the second generation, Pierre Laliberte Jr. married Géneviève Jourdain, sister of Marguerite Jourdain, who was married to Louis Morin, son of Antoine Morin and Pélagie Boucher, and therefore brother to Sarazine Morin Laliberte (see Figure 3.4). In short, Sarazine's son and brother married sisters.

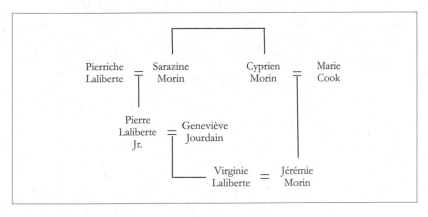

FIGURE 3.5   Laliberte-Morin cross-generation marriage (1)

While there were "crossover" marriages, such as those between families in the second generation that reinforced familial alliances, in the third and fourth generations, intermarriages between Morins and Labertes, as well as with additional families to which they were previously connected, highlighted a clear pattern of decision making. Although these crossover marriages reinforced familial alliances, they are complicated and difficult to trace genealogically. Like a spider's web, the fabric of family connections revealed through the genealogies was intricately woven. For example, Virginie Laliberte, daughter of Pierre Laliberte Jr. and Géneviève Jourdain, married Jérémie Morin, son of Cyprien Morin and Marie Cook. Pierre Laliberte Jr. was the son of Sarazine Morin and Pierriche Laliberte, making Virginie and Jérémie second cousins (see Figure 3.5).

Similarly, three children of Antoine Laliberte and Mathilda Collings (also known by the surnames Fraser and/or Clement) – Clement, Pierre Goodwin Marchand, and Marguerite Marie – married Morins (see Figure 3.6). Clement married Aldina and Marguerite Marie married Placide Morin, respectively, the daughter and son of Pierre Marie Morin and Hélène Lafonde. Pierre Goodwin Marchand married Rose Meraste, the daughter of Célestin Meraste and Pélagie Morin (the daughter of Louis Morin and Marguerite Jourdain). Rose's mother, Pélagie, was the cousin of Aldina and Placide Morin.

To further add to the complicated interconnectedness of the Morins and Labertes, four of Angèle Laliberte and François Maurice's grandchildren married into either Laliberte or Morin families, keeping the connections between them active through the Maurice/Laliberte branch of the family that came to reside in the Portage La Loche region. Once again,

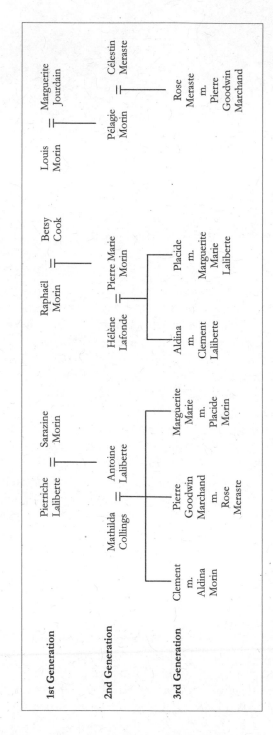

1st Generation

Pierriche Laliberte = Sarazine Morin

Raphaël Morin = Betsy Cook

Louis Morin = Marguerite Jourdain

2nd Generation

Mathilda Collings = Antoine Laliberte

Hélène Lafonde = Pierre Marie Morin

Pélagie Morin = Célestin Meraste

3rd Generation

Clement m. Aldina Morin

Pierre Goodwin Marchand m. Rose Meraste

Marguerite Marie m. Placide Morin

Aldina m. Clement Laliberte

Placide m. Marguerite Marie Laliberte

Rose Meraste m. Pierre Goodwin Marchand

FIGURE 3.6   Laliberte-Morin cross-generation marriage (2)

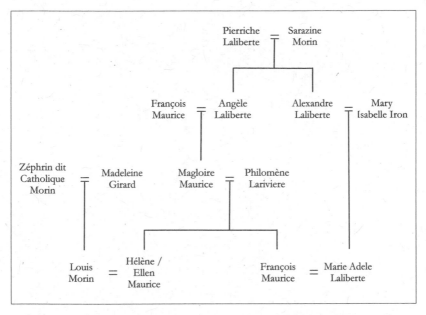

FIGURE 3.7   Maurice-Laliberte-Morin cross-generation marriages

wahkootowin was central to this behavioural pattern. François Maurice, son of Magloire Maurice and Philomène Lariviere, married Marie Adele Laliberte, daughter of Alexandre Laliberte and Mary Isabelle Iron. Alexandre was the son of Sarazine Morin, and therefore brother to Angèle Laliberte, uncle to Magloire Maurice, and great-uncle to his new son-in-law. François' sister, Hélène (Ellen) Maurice, married Louis Morin, the son of Zéphrin dit Catholique Morin, who was also the brother of Sarazine Morin and therefore was the great-great-uncle of his new daughter-in-law (see Figure 3.7).

Similar, although less obvious, was the marriage between Isadore Roy and Adélaide Malboeuf. This couple appeared to be unrelated prior to their marriage because of their different surnames. Isadore Roy was the son of Courrone Maurice, granddaughter of Sarazine Morin Laliberte. Adélaide was the granddaughter of Cyprien Morin, Sarazine's brother. Meanwhile, Adélaide's parents were Pierriche Malboeuf and Pélagie Morin, the daughter of Cyprien Morin and Marie Cook. Therefore, Pélagie was Sarazine Morin's niece and Angèle Laliberte's cousin. Similar, although less obvious, was the marriage between Isadore Roy and Adélaide Malboeuf. This couple appeared to be unrelated prior to their marriage because of their different surnames. Isadore was also the cousin of François and Hélène

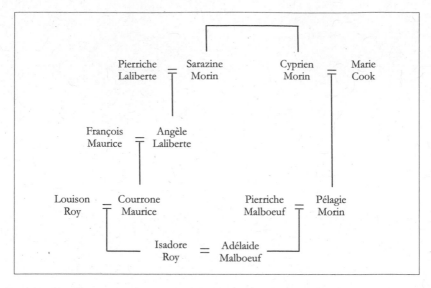

FIGURE 3.8   Maurice-Roy-Morin cross-generation marriages

(Ellen) Maurice, the children of Magloire Maurice and Philomène Lariviere, while Adélaide was a distant cousin of Marie Adele Laliberte and Louis Morin. Therefore, Isadore and Adélaide were related through their great-grandparents and grandparents, respectively (see Figure 3.8).

One could spend considerable time puzzling out the biological relatedness in the unions between Morins, Labertes, and Maurices, trying to determine if the marriages were between cousins, second cousins, or third cousins twice removed. Earlier kinship studies often focused on the degrees of relatedness rather than the social meanings and cultural values of such marriages.[63] However, the greater point to consider is that, early in the nineteenth century, the Morins, Labertes, and Maurices established a connection that actively worked to maintain and perpetuate itself intergenerationally as sons, daughters, nieces, nephews, and grandchildren came of age and sought suitable marriage partners and then linked their families across the northwest. Because of the frequency of intermarriage between these families, it would be difficult to consider these unions accidental or even random. Clearly, these are choices that were deliberately and methodically undertaken because, on the whole, none of the marriages described are between individuals of close biological relatedness. Each marriage demonstrates enough biological distance to indicate that there were rules regarding appropriate marital arrangements and that care was

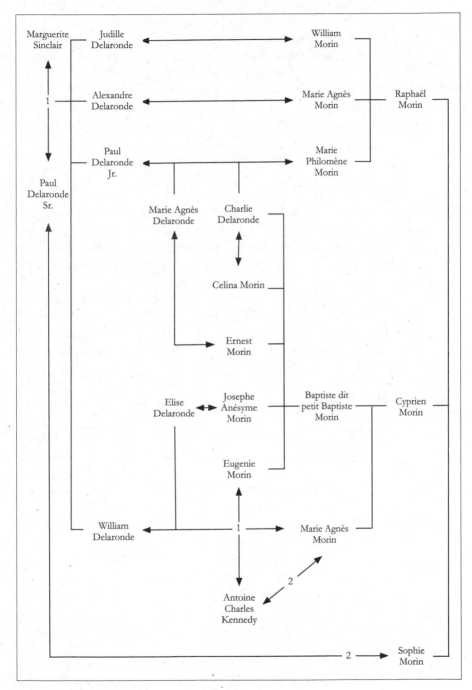

FIGURE 3.9   Intergenerational intermarriage between Morins and Delarondes

taken to ensure that only the most "distant" of relatives married. It could further be argued that intergenerational, interfamilial marriages were so prevalent because of the limited opportunities to find partners from outside the region. However, young men and women sometimes located spouses from as far afield as Muskeg Lake near Carlton, Lac La Ronge, and Red River.

While there were obvious, albeit subtle, continued associations between them, the Morin and Laliberte families also sought out marital alliances with other Metis and Indian families from the region. Alliances with such families as the Delarondes illustrate how intricately interwoven particular families were – especially those associated with the fur trade – over the four generations identified in this study. Paul Delaronde Sr.'s children with Marguerite Sinclair, who became Sophie Morin's stepchildren, married the latter woman's nieces and nephews (see Figure 3.9). William Morin married Judille Delaronde; William's sister, Marie Agnès Morin, married Alexandre Delaronde. Another Marie Agnès Morin, cousin to William and Marie Agnès, the daughter of Cyprien Morin and Marie Cook, had as her first husband William Delaronde. Meanwhile, Paul Delaronde Jr. married Marie Philomène Morin, daughter of Raphaël Morin and Betsy Cook and, therefore, sister of William and Marie Agnes. A generation later, Marie Agnès Delaronde, the daughter of Paul Delaronde Jr. and Marie Philomène Morin, married Ernest Morin, son of Baptiste dit petit Baptiste Morin and Marie dite Pakama Desjarlais. To further complicate matters, Ernest's sister Eugenie was, prior to her death, married to Antoine Charles Kennedy, who, upon being widowed, married his deceased wife's aunt, Marie Agnès Morin, who had previously been married to William Delaronde. Furthermore, Marie Agnès Morin's daughter with William Delaronde, Elise Delaronde, married Joseph Anésyme (Onisine) Morin, son of Baptiste dit petit Baptiste Morin and his second wife, Marguerite Marie Aubichon. Joseph was the half-brother of Ernest and Eugenie Morin. Drawing to a close the complicated extended family structure of the Morins and Delarondes, Charlie Delaronde, son of Paul Delaronde Jr. and Marie Philomène Morin, married Celina Morin, daughter of Baptiste dit petit Baptiste Morin and Marguerite Marie Aubichon. As already mentioned, Sophie Morin, aunt of Baptiste dit petit Baptiste Morin, had a relationship with Paul Delaronde Sr. that produced one child, Marie, who was, as a result, aunt to her cousins.

Perhaps one of the overriding purposes behind such crossover marriages between families or, more precisely, interfamilial intergenerational marriages, was to build community loyalty and regional unity among this new people. From his research on the Metis in the Northwest Territories, Richard Slobodin concluded that extended family loyalty overrode community loyalty despite the fact that "every Metis household [was] embedded in a far flung network of relationships."[64] Yet after reconstructing the genealogies of the northwestern Metis, it is difficult to see how family – extended or otherwise – was distinct from community. Branches of families exist across the region, which means that as people travelled from their own community, they would be sure to locate relatives in other parts of the district on whom they could rely for support or assistance. Specific locations in the region did become associated with particular patronyms, but the complexity of the region's far-flung relationships is embedded in the connections these particular families forged with one another in a regionally defined extended family system. The intergenerational, interregional marriages were a definite strategy to unite people across a large geographical domain that allowed only limited communication between families as they travelled to hunt, fish, or work for the Company. At the same time, the strategy concentrated specific families in specific locales. In a similar study of the Metis community at Batoche, Diane Payment asserted, "the 19th-century French Canadian/Metis family was guided by the principle of unity, the need to maintain tradition and valued the primacy of collectivity over the individual."[65] Of course, there was a concept of individuality, but it was quite a different notion than that expressed in the western European tradition. Metis society, according to Payment, placed obligations and responsibilities on individuals to ensure that the well-being of the collective was a primary cultural value. Mutual aid and support extended throughout Metis communities between large family collectivities, and the localized patronymic connections were one means by which relatives could locate one another.[66]

The complex interweaving of the genealogies demonstrates the reinforcement of ideals and values emphasized within the worldview of wahkootowin intergenerationally as families connected and reconnected to one another through male and female lines across the district. The Morin, Laliberte, Maurice, and Delaronde extended family began as incoming, outsider males forged alliances with females known to have been born in the northwest. Men helped define the community of Sakitawak specifically, and the northwest more generally, as their surnames became central to the organization of family units, came to be associated with specific familial alliances, and were linked to economic activities in well-defined areas that became local communities. Meanwhile, the grandmothers, mothers, wives, and sisters of men established the foundational base from which intercommunity and interfamily socio-cultural, religious, and economic alliances were formed. The records make clear that the four generations formed the most stable and trackable core of the community over time and were, by and large, part of a significant and dominant HBC servant class within the fur trade. In addition to the Lalibertes and Morins, the surnames Aubichon, Bekattla, Bouvier, Caisse, Catfish, Corrigal, Daigneault, Delaronde, Girard, Halcrow, Kippling, Lafleur, Malboeuf, Maurice, Moberly, Roy, and Sinclair were all linked to the HBC through servants' records and post journals dating to the early nineteenth century. Some of these surnames spread out of Sakitawak, as illustrated by the sketch map, into other communities in the district, such as Portage La Loche and Lac Vert.

The Metis social foundation of the northwest was very much framed within the maternal legacy of homeland, an idea succinctly described by Raphaël Morin in 1887. But just as the Metis families of the region identified their association to the homeland as the lands of their mothers and other maternal relatives, they also shared an economic connection to a trade that influenced (at least initially) where each family would eventually reside. The patronymic connections of family-based settlements to communities such as Bull's House, Portage La Loche, Devil's Lake, Lac Vert, and, of course, Sakitawak framed the traditional lands of specific branches of a large, extended family system, reliant on the philosophy underpinning wahkootowin, that spread out across the district. Residency and employment in the trade were both significant framers of Metis identity in the nineteenth century. These were not a people in perpetual motion – they lived and worked in the northwest or English River District, and their movements, as associated with their employment, were very much tied to a well-defined and regionally bounded geography.

4

"After a man has tasted of the comforts of married life this living alone comes pretty tough"

Family, Acculturation, and Roman Catholicism

In October 1893, Green Lake clerk George Dreaver wrote to his superior at Île à la Crosse, Chief Trader Henry J. Moberly, to express his deep loneliness and his hope that "a poor lonely Begger [sic] like me may have the pleasure of seeing you soon." At the time, Dreaver was living without his wife Elizabeth and two young daughters, and he clearly felt isolated. He wrote, "After a man has tasted of the Comforts of Married life this living alone comes pretty tough."[1] Dreaver had not been alone long; his family had been with him just a few months earlier when he had written to Île à la Crosse asking for a bottle of "lung balsam" because his "Little Ones" had colds.[2] By October, however, his family was gone from the district, and Dreaver faced a long winter with only the other post servants for companionship. Unlike the families discussed in earlier chapters, the Dreavers are not represented in district genealogies because they were not members of the local Metis community. According to the records, none of the Dreavers married locally, none served as godparents for children in the community, and none remained in the district past the end of the nineteenth century. That the Dreavers were also Presbyterian, not Roman Catholic, ensured a substantial social distance between them and the rest of the forty-three core Metis families of the northwest and the values of wahkootowin.[3] As much as any other factor, a family's religion determined its connection to others and whether there were relatives to whom family members could turn in times of need.

Metis interaction with the Roman Catholic missions of Saint-Jean-Baptiste (established at Île à la Crosse in 1846), Saint-Julien (Green Lake,

1875), and Mission de la Visitation (Portage La Loche, 1890) was integral
to their cultural identity. The Church, of course, had considerable influence on the spiritual life and socio-cultural identity of the Metis, but this
chapter is not primarily an evaluation of the Church or its history in the
region. Just as previous chapters focused on how the Metis adapted their
Indian relatives' social order, grounded in a spiritual and philosophical
worldview that framed their experiences within the landscape and economy
of the region, this chapter will explore how Roman Catholicism appealed
to the people in the district within their existing knowledge and interpretive systems. After 1846, the significant events in most individuals' lives
were formally marked by socio-religious expression and personal adherence
to, and acceptance of, the Roman Catholic Church's ritual calendar, as
well as secular public celebrations. In the English River District, the value
of the sacraments as a form of initiation and community building; the
adoption of the concept of godparents as a means to maintain relationships
between Hudson's Bay Company employees and the extended families
intergenerationally; the Sabbath and Mass as central rites of the faith; and
the conversion of Protestant outsider males in order to marry locally, all
became important signifiers of who was – and who was not – a member
of the Metis regional family. In turn, when these Catholic traditions supported the values of wahkootowin, they were incorporated into that worldview and became integral to the maintenance and expression of self, family,
and community identities.

Nineteenth-century missionaries and contemporary scholars alike have
accepted the idea that the European paternity of the Metis made them
more "naturally" Christian or, at the very least, that their mixed ancestry
made it easier to instruct them in proper Christian values and behaviours.[4]
Part of this image derives from Île à la Crosse's reputation as a "Cradle of
Christianity" in western Canada because it was home to the first Catholic
mission west of Red River and four of its first priests later became bishops.[5]
In 1915, a lawyer from the town of Battleford, Rufus Redmond Earle,
travelled to northwestern Saskatchewan. He later published an account
of his trip in Battleford's newspaper, *The Press*, in which he commented
on the relationship between the Church and the people of the region:

> The thing that impressed me the most, however, was the devotion and
> energy of the Roman Catholic missionaries in this part of the country. It
> certainly requires, it seems to me, great devotion to live the lives that these
> people are. There is no doubt of the beneficial influence that has been exerted

over the natives through these missions; in fact apparently the only civilizing and refining influence of work in this country, practically speaking, is the Roman Catholic missions, and the effect is very noticeable throughout the whole country, in the manners and modes of living of the Halfbreeds and Indians.[6]

Earle's report implies that it was the missionaries' devotion to the lives of the people in the region that civilized the Aboriginal people, and there continues to be a popular belief that the Metis easily accepted and embraced Catholic doctrine and theology. Fuelling this popular image of Metis people as devout, natural Catholics was their connection to French Canadian voyageurs and their mixed ancestry. Such ideas about "natural" Christian experiences within Metis communities require some investigation, however.

The social foundations of the Metis worldview in the northwest were grounded in the social philosophy of Cree cultural experiences and spiritual knowledge. David Thompson's late-eighteenth-century ethnographies about Witigos and belief in the afterlife (see Chapter 1) cover ideas that would have been shared with subsequent generations because they were important foundational concepts of wahkootowin that addressed the meaning and importance of family. Father Marius Rossignol, a priest at Saint-Jean-Baptiste in Île à la Crosse for much of the first half of the twentieth century, travelled and lived with the Cree and the Metis across northern Saskatchewan and Manitoba, but his observations were derived from his position as a missionary whose job it was to train those people to be good Catholics. Rossignol recorded some of his experiences within this society in two ethnographical articles published in the 1930s. On one occasion, Rossignol asked an elderly man about "the ancient Cree thought about God before the evangelization of the country." The old man replied,

I could not tell you all that they knew or thought, but certainly they knew that God exists. They had the custom of telling the Children: "Here, you young people, destroy nothing. Take good care of everything and do not waste anything, because it is God who is the master. Do not insult the wind, God has Made it. Do not have contempt for water, God has created it. Accept rain with-out murmuring, for God sends it to us. Do not abuse the trees or anything else, because God has provided these things for our use." These sayings of the old men which they would repeat to us over and over again have remained quite distinct in my memory.[7]

Although not specifically an explicit statement that spiritual beings were family, what the old man recounted was a theological concept and belief in a supreme being who created the world and permitted humans to use its resources. In return, people had to protect and not mistreat what they were given. Many years later, after he had been converted, the old man recalled this memory of a spiritual teaching that was also an important economic, social, and political concept about resource use. Indeed, it is difficult to separate spiritual from cultural values, even after conversion to a new faith. Over the years, many scholars have asked whether indigenous people's conversion to Christianity was authentic, whether Aboriginal people fully understood and embraced Christian theological concepts, or whether they converted because it was a convenient means of accessing trade goods. These are the wrong questions, however, because they obscure the complexity of Christianity's interaction with the theologies developed by Aboriginal societies. What shaped the stories recorded by Thompson and Rossignol represented an intellectual canon and spiritualized system of familial relationships.

Mission and religious scholars have not been able to articulate convincingly why Christianity broadly, or Roman Catholicism specifically, appealed to Metis or Indian people. This is largely a problem of focus. Canadian mission studies are preoccupied with the actions of clergy and the growth of missions rather than the theological messages and intellectual interaction of distinct socio-religious systems. These types of studies, therefore, are often more concerned with chronicling stories of privation, hardship, and suffering experienced by missionaries as they struggled to carve out Christian havens in harsh climates and among often hostile audiences. Studies of Dene Catholicism, for instance, describe their conversion as occurring soon after the arrival of priests in the mid-nineteenth century, but the question of why it was so quick goes unasked.[8] Similar studies of the northern Cree during the same time period indicate that their conversion was slower and harder to achieve, but, again, no one asks why this was the case.[9] While there is a general, popular belief that, regardless of the pace of conversion, First Nations people simply gave up an older religion to become Christian, it is likewise accepted without much analysis that the Metis had no conversion experience. Instead, it is assumed that within households headed by parents of different races, an uneasy compromise occurred between First Nations mothers and European fathers, one that favoured the latter's cultural sensibilities and aspirations for their children's educational and religious instruction. The foundation of this assumption, however, runs counter to prevailing understandings that mothers have greater influence over the socio-religious development of their children – a reality surely heightened when the family unit is living in (or surrounded by) the mother's community and an extended family system derived from a specific socio-cultural worldview that values the gathering or collection of relatives. What is relevant about missions in the English River District, then, is how the Metis of the northwest internalized and adapted their Christian ideas to an existing spiritual worldview centred on familial relationships.

Historians John Foster and Keith Widder suggest that a form of "folk Catholicism" developed within Metis communities well before Roman Catholic and Protestant missionaries arrived in Rupert's Land or the Great Lakes. Foster, for instance, notes that missionaries found Plains Metis buffalo hunters in the 1840s practising infant baptism and holding prayer services, even though many had never been to church.[10] But we are left wondering: What did such a concept mean in the daily lives of people? How were the rituals of baptism or prayer understood? How was a new theology of the Plains fashioned? That the people of the northwest, like Plains Metis, were practising rituals associated with Christianity prior to 1846 is not in question. Indeed, upon their arrival at Île à la Crosse, Catholic missionaries quickly recognized that there was enough understanding to attempt to perform the appropriate rituals, though they were unable to assess the full extent of Metis knowledge about the faith.[11] Voyageur ritual baptisms at Portage La Loche and local performance of other Christian ceremonies such as baptisms and burial rites were a part of life in the district long before the missionaries arrived, and such practices continued even after their arrival when clergy were unavailable.[12] And yet, we should not assume that acceptance of Christianity in any form was either natural or complete for the Metis of the northwest.

What are harder to see are signs that Metis people adhered to the beliefs and rituals of what Rossignol referred to as "ancient Cree thought." Even Thompson, who lived and travelled with Cree and Metis people, admitted that his ability to discern their beliefs was hampered by Aboriginal cultural traits:

I have always found it very difficult to learn their real opinion on what may be termed religious subjects. Asking them questions on this head, is to no purpose, they will give the answer best adapted to avoid other questions, and please the enquirer. My knowledge has been gained when living and travelling with them and in times of distress and danger in their prayers to invisible powers, and their view of a future state of themselves and others, and like most of mankind, those in youth and in the prime of life think only of the present but declining manhood, and escapes from danger[,] turn their thoughts on futurity.[13]

Even as he stated that he found it hard to know Aboriginal spiritual beliefs, however, Thompson further described how the Cree of the subarctic infused their landscape, and therefore existence, with spiritual power:

> They believe in the self existence of the Keeche Keeche Manito (The Great, Great Spirit) they appear to derive their belief from tradition, and [believe] that the visible world, with all it's [sic] inhabitants must have been made by some powerful being ... [H]e is the master of life, and all things are at his disposal; he is always kind to the human race, and hates to see the blood of mankind on the ground, and sends heavy rain to wash it away. He leaves the human race to their own conduct, but has placed all other living creatures under the care of Manitos (or inferior Angels) all of whom are responsible to Him; but all this belief is obscure and confused, especially on the Manitos, the guardians and guides of every genus of Birds and Beasts; each Manito has a separate command and care, as one has the Bison, another the Deer; and thus the whole animal creation is divided amongst them ... The Forests, the ledges and hills of Rock, the Lakes and Rivers have all something of the Manito about them, especially the Falls in the Rivers, and those to which the fish come to spawn ... They believe in the immortality of the soul, and that death is only a change of existence which takes place directly after death. The good find themselves in a happy country, where they rejoin their friends and relations, the Sun is always bright, and the animals plenty; and most of them carry this belief so far, that they believe whatever creatures the great Spirit has made must continue to exist somewhere, and under some form.[14]

The idea that land and creatures were infused with spiritual life in this world and the next was an intellectual and theological concept embedded within the very essence of wahkootowin. As such, the social and the religious, the material or living and the spiritual realms, cannot be separated. Wahkootowin was not simply a way to organize people socially in family units – it was also part of a religious system that drew the land, creatures, and people together as spiritual relatives with all creation and, therefore, included spirit beings as a part of the extended family. In this context, memories such as the one shared with Rossignol and the types of spirits in the land and animals that Thompson noted were part of living socioreligious systems that influenced all activities. As the Metis learned about wahkootowin – all my relations – from their Cree maternal lineage, they came to understand that this system did not simply relate to living (or real) family members but included the land, animals, winds, birds, water, rocks, trees, and every other object around them. This relationship was so real that Thompson noted the Dene believed that the "Great Spirit descended on a rock, took a Dog, tore it to small pieces and scattered it, that these pieces became a Man, or a woman, and that these Men and Women are their original parents, from whom they have all come; and thus the Dog is their common origin; On this account they have very few dogs; frequently several tents have not a Dog among them; and they abhor the Dog Feasts of the Nahathaway's [Cree] and of the French Canadians."[15] The Cree, meanwhile, were religiously observant hunters who "at the death of each animal [gave] thanks to the Manito of the species for being permitted to kill it ... If [these acknowledgments were] not made the Manito would drive away the animals from the hunter."[16] The Dene and the Cree both invoked spiritual relationships to animals as a theological construct that influenced the manner in which they hunted and treated particular animals.

Historian Allan Greer's recent biography of the Mohawk convert and near-saint Kateri, or Catherine, Tekakwitha addresses some of the complex issues regarding Aboriginal adaptation of Catholic beliefs and structures into an indigenous worldview.[17] Greer evaluates Tekakwitha, who is often described in terms of Catholic hagiographical metaphors, within the context of the world in which she lived, a multifaceted contact zone in which Mohawk subjectivity was hybrid, shifting, and unstable. Tekakwitha's social context was both Iroquoian and Canadian, a place where the "'natives' were also 'newcomers,'" and therefore had to "find ways of adjusting to the expectations of the ambient society without melting into it."[18] According to Greer, Mohawks like Tekakwitha added or modified Catholic rites to indigenous practices so that their Iroquoian lifestyle, which was historically dominated by a world of women, female work routines, and a matriarchal culture, was substantially unaltered even as they converted to Catholicism. Notably, they produced expressions of devoutness unmatched by many born into the faith. This attempt to understand Tekakwitha as a Mohawk first and a Catholic second, and, just as important, to understand Catholicism as an expression of Mohawkness, has added immeasurably to our understanding of how Christianity was modified to fit the needs of Aboriginal societies and serves as a useful framework for understanding how Catholicism was integrated into the Metis wahkootowin in the northwest.

It is clear that Roman Catholicism played a role in northwestern Metis society from its earliest beginnings. Catholic rituals were a means of demonstrating socio-religious unity and facilitating cultural identity at the posts. With its monopoly over Rupert's Land, and its knowledge and control of the transportation systems, the HBC could have hindered access to the West for missionaries of any denomination. Indeed, Christianity had no formal role in the trade prior to 1818, when the first Roman Catholic mission was built at the Red River settlement. For almost another quarter century, mission activity was restricted and access to the western and northern posts was tightly controlled by the HBC. Nevertheless, in the early nineteenth century, individual and communal, private and public expressions of socio-religious activities across the northwest reinforced wahkootowin by placing family within the context of a religious and spiritual environment, and, beginning with the proto-generation, this environment melded indigenous and French Canadian beliefs.

Missionaries' success in converting and instructing depended on their ability to fashion a message that indigenous people found appealing and that did not clash with their existing values. According to mission historian Terrance L. Craig, missionaries, regardless of denomination, sermonized about the concept of home, framing the ideal of home as a strong immediate family. Missionaries were responsible for modelling a home life that exemplified Christianity – a haven of health, security, contentment, and education. Furthermore, "home was the larder" of the immediate family or community that had not only produced the missionary but also incubated his beliefs and shaped his religious experience. So missionaries preached and disseminated messages about home, of which religion was a part and which religion celebrated.[19]

Protestant missionaries easily modelled the ideal home and family life – they were able to marry and have their wives and children with them in their missions. Indeed, within Protestant missions, wives and daughters often took central roles in educating children and working directly with female parishioners.[20] Catholic clergy, conversely, with their vows of celibacy and prohibitions of marriage, had to deliver this message through proper behaviour and fellowship and by using symbols of domesticity. Without families of their own, the Catholic clergy became living representations of the Holy Family (defined as Jesus, Mary, and Joseph). The use of familial titles – Father, Brother, Mother, and Sister – to refer to clergy by rank and gender established individuals as a symbolic or spiritual family within the Catholic faith.[21]

The emphasis on both natural and spiritual families in Catholic theology resonated with Aboriginal people in the northwest, just as it did with many other Aboriginal societies. The Cree tradition of wahkootowin, imparted to the Metis by their maternal ancestors, was based on a belief that spiritual entities were members of the human family and vice versa. The clearest example of this cultural belief was Wisakejak, an important spirit being and cultural figure whose actions taught people the social laws governing moral and ethical behaviour.[22] Wisakejak was only referred to by name during the winter months, the season for telling stories; for the rest of the year, the people referred to him as "elder brother." The relational term "elder brother" suggests that Wisakejak was regarded as an actual once-living relative of the Cree who, significantly, remained a spiritual relative. Likewise, both Cree and Dene spiritual practice invoked personified and relational terms for elements in nature, including "mother" for the land, "grandmother" for the eldest of the female spirits, and "grandfather" for the eldest male spirit invoked within religious ceremonies.[23]

Exploring similar ideas among the Sioux, anthropologist Raymond J. DeMallie analyzes that nation's family system as both a genealogical and social phenomenon by focusing on their belief that everyone was directly related to the spirit world. The invocation of an ancestral relationship with their deities established a theology that determined all Sioux, regardless of tribe or community affiliation, were members of one large culturally sanctioned family or *tiyospaye*.[24]

Similarly, when he first arrived in Île à la Crosse, Rossignol was present at a ceremony where an old man chanted and drummed to invite spirits into the ritual. According to Rossignol,

Four [spirits] came at his call and talked. The first, Sawan (south wind), said: "My little children, a bad epidemic is approaching. Take precautions to escape it, I warn you." The second one, Awasapiskokimaw ('Master of the other side of the Rockies'), said: "My little children, there are whites not far from here who are trying to do you harm. Do not trust them, I warn you." The third, kiwatin ("North Wind"), said: "My little children, be glad. The lynx are traveling toward us. You will kill many, I predict." The fourth and last, Kiwatcawasis ("Orphan Child"), said: "My little children, good weather is coming to an end. Tomorrow it will snow. The cold will be felt. Take heed, I warn you." All the above was of course said in Cree, and was heard by me as well as by the Pagan Cree around me. The four spirits had no other will, it seems, but to do good to those who had invoked them to give them good advice.[25]

Rossignol did not attempt to interpret this prophecy, but his description shows that the four spirits each addressed the people at the ceremony using a relational term and, like a parent, advised the listeners to make themselves ready and safe because the future was uncertain.

The Metis of the northwest had a similar understanding of their relationship to the spirit world and saw little separation between material and spiritual realms of existence. In this context, the idealized holy family of the universal church was not incompatible with wahkootowin, which made it possible and, indeed, fairly straightforward to accept two seemingly alien systems. Both religious systems were present in the values of the proto-generation beginning in the late 1700s. Whether the Metis accepted and followed the religious traditions of their Indian relatives or were more Catholic in outlook is not especially pertinent. What is important is the basic compatibility between many of the Indian and Catholic religious concepts. Furthermore, indigenous people of the subarctic openly engaged in theological discussions with the clergy, indicating a willingness to explore new ideas. When he visited Cree camps to preach, Rossignol noted that he often had a difficult time persuading the men to listen to him. When he finally got their attention, Rossignol observed that the old men were "real orators," who often rose at the conclusion of his sermons to discuss the teachings he had introduced.[26] The priest noted further that the old people at Sakitawak had been subject to Catholicism for so long that it was difficult for him to determine what "pagan" beliefs and rituals predated missionary influence. He did, however, believe that many of these beliefs were still present. At about the same time, scrip commissioner J.A.J. McKenna likewise observed that the Saint-Jean-Baptiste mission at Île à la Crosse was the "common gathering place of the Indians and half-breeds, who sit and smoke with an ease that seemed born of a long habit of free intercourse with those who have undertaken the cure of their souls."[27] This easy willingness to engage in discussions with the missionaries about religious ideas, and their sense of comfort at the mission, denotes a level of confidence and an awareness of the Aboriginal sense of self or place in this system and within the mission itself. Unfortunately, we do not know the details that clergy and congregants discussed. As with other aspects of Metis life, we must dig deeply to locate the clues in their behaviours and beliefs in order to interpret how they responded to and interpreted Catholicism. If we look more closely at how the Metis behaved toward one another publicly and privately, and toward this institution within their community, we can evaluate how both the clergy – priests, nuns, brothers – and their beliefs became an important element of the extended family system.

The arrival of Catholic missionaries in the English River District was neither accidental nor unexpected. Largely because of the insistent demands of people in the region for a priest, Chief Factor Roderick McKenzie wrote to Bishop Joseph-Norbert Provencher of St. Boniface, Red River, in 1845 to request that a mission be established at Île à la Crosse. From both the Company's and McKenzie's perspective, the adherence of the district's primary labour force (Metis, along with some French Canadians) to the Catholic faith was critical to their socio-religious well-being, which, in turn, would improve their economic productivity. McKenzie further felt that a local mission site would guarantee the population's satisfaction with its living arrangements, and a missionary presence would incline the Cree and Dene to remain attached to the post. By the mid-1840s, the Cree and Dene were being enticed onto the southern plains by lucrative opportunities in buffalo hunting and the pemmican trade. It is unclear whether there was an actual exodus of northern Cree and Dene, but McKenzie believed there was a real possibility the resident Aboriginal population would leave to take advantage of such opportunities and that the presence of missionaries would stem the flow of Indian people from the region.[28] At roughly the same time as McKenzie's request, Father Jean-Baptiste Thibault was touring Rupert's Land, travelling as far north as Portage La Loche and as far west as Lac Ste. Anne, to assess the viability of establishing western missions outside Red River. On his return to Red River, Thibault was able to convince Bishop Provencher that establishment of permanent missions throughout the subarctic was necessary and would be welcomed by the indigenous people.[29]

With the support of HBC governor George Simpson, Provencher arranged for canoes to transport the first two priests, Fathers Louis-François Laflèche and Antoine Taché, from the Order of Mary Immaculate (OMI, or the Oblates) to the English River District. Simpson further assured Provencher that the HBC would provide the priests with free lodging and support at Île à la Crosse until the mission was built, and he authorized McKenzie to assign Company servants to construct the mission if the diocese paid for their food rations.[30] This intersection of Church and Company interests is an important theme in the socio-economic relationships of the district. Both institutions were key participants in the lives of district residents, but neither held the upper hand. For the forty-three core families, HBC employment and membership in the Church were both necessary features, as was the creation of links to other people through marriage, adoption, and other socially constructed relationships, as well as the maintenance of close connections to Cree and Dene communities in the region. Together, these features determined who was and who was not a member of the community. It was within this environment, and with these arrangements in place, that Laflèche and Taché departed in July 1846 for Île à la Crosse to build the first Roman Catholic mission west of Red River and the first in the subarctic.[31] The OMI was considered the ideal religious order for such an assignment because of its dedication to service and its determination, according to the motto adopted by the order's founder, Father Eugene Mazenod, "to preach the Gospel to the poor."[32] The Oblates annually travelled hundreds of miles in the district to find converts, conduct pastoral visits, continue missionary work among those already converted, and establish new mission stations.

During that first winter in the English River District, the priests lived at the Île à la Crosse post under McKenzie's care and spent their time learning Cree and Dene so they would be able to minister effectively to the people of the region. In the spring of 1847, construction began on the first mission building that was separate from the HBC facilities; initially called Chateau St. Jean, the Île à la Crosse mission was named for the patron saint of Quebec. It also served as the priests' residence.[33] Just as the trade companies had done before it, the Catholic Church used Île à la Crosse as an administrative centre from which the OMI coordinated all mission activity for the district. Although the Oblates travelled throughout the region to establish themselves, the Île à la Crosse mission attracted Aboriginal people from across the northwest who sought baptism and burial services or who wished to solemnize their marriages at the Church. In 1853-54, Taché recorded that there were seventy-five to eighty people living permanently at or near the mission.[34] As well as ministering to the people of Île à la Crosse, by the late 1840s the missionaries had established outposts at Portage La Loche, Lac Vert, Cold Lake, Lac La Ronge, Lac la Caribou, Fort Chipewyan, and Lac La Biche in much the same fashion as the HBC established outposts.[35]

Although charged with the daunting task of ministering to small populations spread over hundreds of square miles, the Oblates worked among the Metis of the region to ensure that they faithfully followed Church rules, observed the sacraments, attended Mass regularly, and contributed financial and physical support to the mission. These demands were made, in part, because the Metis were expected to serve as Catholic role models for the Dene and Cree, whom the Oblates were attempting to convert and who were believed to have no previous (or innate) knowledge of the faith.[36] By 1853, Chief Trader George Deschambeault of Île à la Crosse noted that the mission was doing well and that the clergy deserved great praise for their efforts to bring Christianity to the region. Deschambeault noted that most Indians at the post were now Christian, paying attention to their religious obligations and behaving morally.[37]

Taché recorded the success of the mission's activities a few years later (see Table 4.1), further noting that five Protestants lived at the post, making a clear distinction between "Christians" – i.e., Catholics – and Protestants, who, while not heathen, were nevertheless outside the Christian faith in the clergy's estimation. These categories provide insight into how the Church defined the people of Île à la Crosse, as well as giving an idea of how the missionizing process was progressing. Christians, of course, were those who already believed in the God of the Bible and were baptized. In this particular census, Christian meant Catholic. Catechumens referred to unbaptized believers who had committed themselves to preparing for baptism through study and prayer, a process that could take several days or even years. Heathens were irreligious and unconverted people who did not acknowledge the God of the Bible as the supreme spiritual being. Unlike Protestants, heathens were included in the survey's matrix because there was perhaps a hope that they would yet convert. The final category, "souls," indicated the total population at Sakitawak, those living in and around the post and mission, and also likely those living around the lake in family-based communities.

There are a number of problems with Taché's census that need to be addressed. We cannot be sure that the numbers of Christians, catechumens, and heathens actually equal the total number of "souls" in the region around Sakitawak, nor do we know the proximity of those souls to the

TABLE 4.1   Religious population at Île à la Crosse, 1856–57

	Christians	Catechumens	Heathens	Souls
Dene	350	22	47	419
Cree	100	30	100	230
Halfbreed	78	1	1	80
French Canadian	6	0	0	6
Total	534	53	148	735

SOURCE: Reproduced from A.G. Morice, OMI, *History of the Catholic Church in Western Canada: From Lake Superior to the Pacific* (Toronto: Masson, 1910), 1:260.

clergy or the frequency of contact that any particular group had with the mission. For people living in family communities around the lake, for instance, we cannot know how frequently they saw the priests or accessed the mission, or, indeed, if they avoided contact with the clergy by heading into the bush when they appeared. Furthermore, we do not have any indication of the number of other people with European or Euro-Canadian ancestry besides the six French Canadians. The five Protestants living in the district were not identified by nationality, so we are left to assume that they were British, although they could have been Metis or non-British HBC servants, such as Alfred Fugl (see Chapter 3). So while these figures reveal the prevalence of Catholicism among specific populations in the district, they are not an accurate count of the region's population or reflective of the general population's religious leanings.

Several clear and useful distinctions are evident in Taché's census, however. First, it distinguishes the Metis population from everyone else in the region, indicating that by the 1850s some obvious socio-cultural boundaries existed between communities. Interestingly, with the exception of one individual, all the Metis and French Canadians were identified as Catholic or catechumens, which indicates a significant representation of that faith within Île à la Crosse's families and perhaps across the district. The "heathen" aspects of the Metis population are an indication that the ancient religion Rossignol and Thompson spoke of still had a presence among them. What we cannot know, though, is how many Metis were regarded as heathen prior to this 1856-57 census. We also do not know what standard of Catholic knowledge was required to be considered sufficiently Christian under these conversion conditions. Other studies of conversion and Aboriginal people have suggested that the necessary level of Christian theological knowledge was lower than that for people with prior understanding of Church teachings.[38] By their own acknowledgment, the first priests at Île à la Crosse had a difficult time assessing how much the Metis actually understood about the Catholic theology underlying their participation in the rituals of the faith, notwithstanding the prior Metis experience with Christian rituals. Finally, the five Protestants from the Île à la Crosse general population were outside the region's social landscape – they are not even included in Taché's chart – and, as we will see, this separation took on very tangible qualities as people lived their lives in the district.

Fourteen years after the establishment of missions in the English River District, the Oblates requested that a female religious order join them to assist with the main mission's responsibilities. In 1860 the Sisters of Charity, more commonly known as the Grey Nuns because of the colour of their habits, arrived at Île à la Crosse and built their first northern mission, known as the "Mother mission."[39] On 6 October 1860, the day the Grey Nuns arrived, a celebratory Mass and feast consecrated their arrival and divine mission. Mass was, of all the Church's rituals, the most sacred because the Holy Eucharist – the blood and body of Christ – is both the source and pinnacle of all Catholic life. The Mass incorporates scripture, prayer, sacrifice, sacred food, and direction on how to live a Catholic life, making it the supreme act of worship. Central to the Mass is the establishment of relationships – first with God and second with the community – and on the day the Grey Nuns arrived at Île à la Crosse, the relationship with God was affirmed, while the community relationship was reaffirmed. On the same day, Île à la Crosse welcomed back Father (now Bishop) Vital Grandin, who escorted the sisters to the region. This celebratory welcome was attended by the community, which symbolically embraced the sisters as new members of both the real and the spiritual family.

As the sisters travelled from the southern edge of Lac Île à la Crosse toward the mission at the edge of the peninsula, they saw the church of Saint-Jean-Baptiste, with its high steeple and cross. Gathered on the shoreline, the people of the area, along with the Oblate fathers and brothers of the OMI already in Île à la Crosse, awaited their arrival. Upon disembarking, Grandin escorted the sisters to the church, blessed those gathered, and offered thanks for their safe arrival. He then performed the Mass to begin the day of religious celebrations and connect the community to the sisters. After the service, lunch was hosted at the priests' residence and the sisters were shown their new home, a two-storey structure complete with a classroom, kitchen, small rectory, and, on the second floor, five bedrooms and a community room where people could gather and visit with the nuns.[40] On one of his trips to France, Grandin had secured funds to build this structure, which included a hospital and a school, from a donation made by a monastery under the patronage of St. Bruno. As a result, the sisters' house was blessed and given the name Hôpital Saint-Bruno, a name kept until 1874, when a new building was constructed and consecrated under the patronage of St. Joseph.[41]

The Grey Nuns' work and spiritual union with the community began on the day of their arrival, when a sick nine-year-old boy, Phillipe Bekattla, became their first patient. There is no indication who Phillipe's parents were, although George Bekattla Sr. was likely his father, based on their respective ages. George was married to Nancy Kippling at Red River in the late 1850s or early 1860s, but he was also associated with a woman named Suzette, with whom he had a daughter in the late 1880s. However, its unlikely that either of these women was Phillipe's mother. Phillipe was with the sisters for several months, spending his days in the kitchen and sleeping in the second-floor community room. The nature of Phillipe's illness was not disclosed, but when his health showed no signs of improving, he was sent home, where he died.[42] Philippe was not alone at the hospital; by 15 October 1860, there were two orphans living at the mission, Gabriel and Marie-Thérèse Lafleur, along with two elderly women, Josephte Rougette and Mélanie Sathene.[43] There is not enough information to identify any of these people or their relations, so they cannot be genealogically connected at this time. The role of the mission and the sisters quickly became incorporated into the family system. The resources of the Church were used to care for those in need by providing shelter and medical care. The district's families used the opportunities offered by the mission in the same manner they relied on one another. Because the Church was both the symbolic embodiment of family and was consecrated within a social relationship with the community, what families expected from one another they now expected from the clergy. Wahkootowin not only required that people gather relatives but also dictated that family members had a responsibility to care for and support one another in times of need and behave reciprocally. Within this sociocultural construct, the Roman Catholic mission and its clergy became integral to the Metis conception of ethical behaviour.

From the mission's perspective, the sisters helped fulfill several important components central to the ideal of "Homeness." As part of a religious order, the sisters could model for female converts proper decorum, civility, and femininity. For the community they could fill the role of being a haven of education and health. They also performed this role by assuming, as the women of the house, responsibility for housekeeping at the mission. The sisters laundered and mended clothes for the priests and brothers and cooked all the meals to feed the mission's population, which included students, patients, and the elderly and infirm.[44] Wasting no time in spreading the message of home, less than a month after their arrival, on 26 November 1860, the sisters opened a boarding school in their residence, École Sainte Famille, and held classes for the first cohort of children to be educated at Île à la Crosse. There were fifteen students (eight boys and seven girls) in that first class, and they also boarded at the mission. The male students slept at the priests' residence, while the girls lived at the sisters' house.[45] Wahkootowin was not undermined by the operation of the hospital, orphanage, or the school. On the contrary, these institutions

– evidence of Homeness – became avenues for Metis families to access both new resources and another family system by which they extended their connections to others. The behaviour of the clergy supported the idea of the family's centrality in all things, a basic principle that the district's population understood, embraced, and then mobilized to access for themselves. As the Church and the clergy became incorporated into the district as family members, the Church's institutions – hospital, orphanage, school – became part of the family institutions and a larger nexus on which people drew in order to continue caring for their relatives as best they could.

From 1860 onward, the Oblates, with the assistance of OMI lay brothers and the Grey Nuns, laboured to expand the English River District missions, which by the end of the century came to include houses, chapels, churches, schools, farms, sawmills, fisheries, and independent transportation networks of roads and boats.[46] The growth of the mission infrastructure not only illustrates the Church's success in establishing itself among the local population, but it is also an indication of the types of resources on which families relied. In the northwest, local people contributed to the growth of the missions with their labour. Within the Catholic Church, "the maries" referred to a category of young women, usually drawn from local populations, who served as helpers to the sisters. As of 1875, the Île à la Crosse mission had three young local women working with the five sisters.[47] According to Canadian surveyor Frank P. Crean's 1908 assessment of the region, the Île à la Crosse mission had, in addition to the church and residence, a barn and three acres of ploughed garden.[48] According to Sara Riel, a Grey Nun stationed at the Île à la Crosse mission in the mid-nineteenth century, the church garden averaged 800 barrels of potatoes and 100 barrels of barley per year, as well as crops of turnips, onions, carrots, beets, and pumpkins. Furthermore, the clergy and those under their care or working at the mission alone ate 2,880 pounds of fish per year, which worked out to about 130 fish per day to meet the basic food needs of the station and its growing residential population.[49]

As it became a formal part of Metis tradition, the Roman Catholic Church provided an outlet for personal religious expression through its spiritual calendar of weekly Sunday Mass and, more generally, feasts, such as that held to welcome the sisters.[50] The regularized performance of ceremonies marking and celebrating the stages of life were likewise woven into the cultural traditions of the Sakitawak Metis community. All Catholic congregants or converts were expected to participate in the sacraments, although those most closely related to the principles of wahkootowin were baptism, confirmation (after abjuration) of adult converts into the faith, marriage, and extreme unction (or anointing of the sick) – rituals experienced by Christ and the Holy Family. As such, the sacraments performed in the Roman Catholic Church became important rituals for the maintenance of wahkootowin at Sakitawak in the latter half of the nineteenth century.[51]

Because the sacraments experienced by people at Saint-Jean-Batiste, Saint-Julien, and the Mission de la Visitation mimicked the events of Christ's life cycle, they were meant to provide congregants – His family of faithful – an opportunity to share their faith within the universal congregation locally, regionally, and, indeed, globally. The clearest representation of individuals and families within the Catholic system was the sacramental registries that recorded the baptisms, marriages, and burials at the three main stations of Île à la Crosse, Green Lake, and Portage La Loche. The statistics kept by these three missions include data for everyone – Metis, Cree, Dene, Euro-Canadian – who participated in the sacraments at the Mission de Saint-Jean-Baptiste (1867-1912), Saint-Julien (1875-1911), and the Mission de la Visitation (1890-1912).[52] Because the Cree and Dene visited the same parishes as the Metis, the mission did not provide a record of the stages of life for the Metis only. Nevertheless, even a superficial reading of the data reveals the Church's function in the region. Over the forty-year period for which records exist for Île à la Crosse, 1,898 people were baptized, 558 burials were observed, and 446 marriages were performed. The figures for the other two mission sites are considerably smaller, in part because the years of record keeping were shorter. At Green Lake, during thirty-seven years of record keeping, 555 baptisms were performed, along with 76 burials and 85 marriages. During a twenty-two-year period at Portage La Loche, 456 baptisms, 197 burials, and 99 marriages took place.[53] These numbers suggest the mission had a high degree of involvement in the lives of its parishioners, who accepted the sacraments in their lives.

Some of the most significant data on the importance of the sacraments describe the conversions of a number of Protestant HBC servants to Roman Catholicism just prior to their marriages to local women. The Church at that time did not sanction or acknowledge interfaith marriages as lawful or legitimate, so in order for non-Catholic outsider males to become socially acceptable as spouses and join the local community through marriage, they were required to undergo the lengthy conversion process. It began with catechism, in which the unbaptized learned Catholic theology through study and prayer. The second step was abjuration – the formal renunciation of apostasy, heresy, and/or schism – in which converts were required to abjure former doctrinal errors and positively profess their acceptance and belief in the Catholic faith. Next, the initiate was confirmed, promising to renounce Satan and believe in God. This rite completed an individual's initiation into the Church. Finally, the person was baptized, a rite in which the individual was born again by water and spirit so that he or she could be adopted into God's Holy Family. Baptism, the first sacrament of initiation into the Church, was typically performed at birth, but in the case of adult converts it took place after they had performed the first three stages of conversion. As early as 1869, then, the first formal conversions of these men – servants of the HBC – began so that they could marry local women.

The first recorded conversion of an outsider male Protestant HBC servant was that of John Catfish, a Saulteaux French Metis from Red River, who married Marie Betkkaye of Île à la Crosse in 1869. Similarly, HBC employees Robert (Robbie) Gardiner and John Thomas Corrigal, both Halfbreeds from Red River, abjured, were confirmed, and then baptized shortly after their arrival in Île à la Crosse as they prepared to marry the Daigneault sisters, Eliza and Sophie. Eliza Daigneault married Robbie Gardiner in 1884 at Saint-Jean-Baptiste shortly after his conversion, which followed an example set two years earlier when Corrigal converted to Catholicism to marry his first wife, Sophie, the youngest daughter of Vincent Daigneault and Marguerite Bouvier. Along with Catfish, Gardiner, and Corrigal, the mission records contain data on conversions through baptism for six additional HBC men who married local women: Frederick Kennedy, a Halfbreed from St. Peter's parish at Red River, married Joséphine Jourdain of Lac Vert; Archibald David Linklater, an English-speaking Halfbreed from Red River, married Eleanore (or Marie Annou) Maurice, daughter of François Maurice and Angèle Laliberte of Portage La Loche; James Nicol Sinclair of Fort Frances (Ontario) married Josephte Durocher of Jackfish Lake; John Thomas Kippling (now Kyplain) of Red River married Angèle Lariviere, daughter of Abraham Lariviere and Mary or Marie Petawcahmwistewin of Sakitawak; Archie Park, an English Halfbreed from Red River, married Adeline Janvier, daughter of François dit La Bosse Janvier and Marie Montgrand; and John James Beads married Célina Morin, daughter of Raphaël Morin and Betsy Cook (see Table 4.2). In each instance, in the days leading up to their marriages in the Catholic Church, these men were first initiated as members of the spiritual family

TABLE 4.2 Converts in Île à la Crosse

Convert	Date of conversion	Godfather	Godmother	Spouse
Catfish, John	7 February 1869	Illegible	Illegible	Marie Betkkaye
Kennedy, Frederick	24 September 1877	Louis Jourdain	Therese Grand Couteau	Joséphine Jourdain
Kippling, John Thomas	17 May 1878	Vincent Daigneault	Julie Bouvier	Angèle Lariviere
Linklater, Archibald David	6 June 1880	Father André Landry	Marie Lariviere	Eleanore (Marie Annou) Maurice
Kippling, Nancy	27 June 1881		Françoise Abiluakuhin	George Bekattla
Corrigal, John Thomas	15 January 1882	Michel Bouvier Jr.		Sophie Daigneault (1) Augustine Bouvier (2)
Gardiner, Robert (Robbie)	2 November 1884	Father L. Dauphin	Sophie St. Nandow	Eliza (Lucia) Daigneault
Sinclair, James Nicol	by 1901			Josephte Durocher
Park, Archie	2 November 1905	François Montgrand		Sophie Piche (1) Adeline Janvier (2)
Beads, John James	October 1906			Célina Morin

SOURCES: Parish registers, Mission de Saint-Jean-Baptiste (1867–1912), Île à la Crosse, Saskatchewan.

of the northwest and then became true members by taking the fourth sacrament, a ritual performed to both create and reflect community. The marriage was often performed one or two days following the newcomer's official conversion.

In addition to these outsider male converts, one woman, Nancy Kippling (Kyplain), like her brother John Thomas, travelled from Red River as an adult and converted to Catholicism upon arrival. George Bekattla Sr., a local hunter and trapper, had apparently travelled with an HBC brigade to Red River, where he met and married Nancy.[54] There is no indication in which church the two were married, or even if they were married in a church at all. What is clear, however, is that Nancy converted to Catholicism when she entered the English River District, indicating that her marriage to George Bekattla occurred prior to her entry into the region and, significantly, to her conversion. This would seem to suggest that her conversion to Roman Catholicism was an important part of her acceptance into the northwest, more so than her marriage.

While ten conversions to Catholicism between 1869 and 1905 is not a large number, it suggests a level of acculturation and accommodation by Protestants to the dominant socio-religious structure that characterized the region and opened opportunities for those individuals to transform socially.[55] At the very least, the conversion to Catholicism indicated a willingness to join/belong to a community as defined by wahkootowin. In the nineteenth century, the renunciation of the religion into which one was born was a significant act – it symbolized a break with one's past, family, and history in favour of an alternative cultural identity. That the core forty-three Metis families in Île à la Crosse consistently declared themselves Catholic on the Canadian censuses of 1881, 1891, and 1901 demonstrates just how important this religion and its rituals were to the community and its families.

The Roman Catholic Church in the English River District established a calendar of religious observances that represented a cycle of weekly, monthly, and yearly ceremonial activities. Most important, perhaps, were the daily or weekly religious observances of the Catholic Church, which were a regularized means of supporting and nourishing social cohesion in the northwest, becoming, in turn, a large part of the Metis cultural identity. Alongside observances of the sacraments, regular attendance was expected at Sunday services, an expectation that predated the missionaries' arrival. Company records for the region reveal that in the 1820s the people of the district were attending Sunday services held at the chief factor's house in Île à la Crosse.[56] These services were apparently well attended, and Company families were often given rations of fish and potatoes after the service, in keeping with an established HBC practice of issuing food rations to its employees.[57] Ration distribution after Sunday services reinforced an important element of the relationship between people's employment and their religious experiences. Chief Factor George Keith further reported that Sunday services on 31 October 1824 were conducted in French, rather than English, for the first time. According to Keith, the people of the English River District were pleased to attend and hear the services in French, which were read to them by a Mr. James Douglas, apparently a fluent French speaker.[58] References in Île à la Crosse post records to attendance at religious services echoed the manner in which the Company referred to the post and district population generally. There are vague references to "all the people" attending church or "people of the establishment attend[ing] mass."[59] Presumably, these were the families specifically associated with the post, because there are other references, such as "the people and Indians," when more than the local community was involved.[60]

As the HBC had done with James Douglas in the 1820s, the Oblate clergy attempted to appeal to their congregants by delivering the Sabbath sermon and Mass in languages other than Latin and by providing religious instruction in indigenous languages in the mission's early years. This was a way to protect Aboriginal communities from assimilation into the elite English-speaking, Protestant community at the posts.[61] French-speaking Catholic missionaries in Canada also sought to protect their own language, culture, and religion from being dominated by British Protestant society, and they regarded Native people as a means, in part, to protect francophone culture. As the post records make evident, it had become commonplace for services to be held in French, but there were occasions when Sunday Mass at the mission was spoken in Cree or Dene. On 17 September 1865, for instance, the people of the post attended a mass delivered in Cree. The priests were apparently responding to a rumour that Catholic missionaries might be responsible for a number of deaths in Indian communities, and, according to Chief Trader Samuel McKenzie, they may have decided to perform a service in Cree in order to remind local Halfbreed and Indian people of the mission's purpose of spreading the gospel and word of God, a message best heard in the northwest's dominant languages.[62] At that Mass, according to McKenzie, the priest, likely Grandin, detailed how the mission was first established at Sakitawak to save people and preach both repentance and forgiveness of their sins, not to cause their deaths. Furthermore, the priest declared that the Oblates' purpose was a divine mission, received directly from the "Apostles in all their power and glory."[63] A week later, Grandin repeated the same sermon again, once in the morning in both French and Dene, and then in the evening in Cree.[64]

Perhaps the rumour that priests were responsible for deaths in the region convinced them that they had to work harder to gain the confidence of the people, and so they preached in the local and dominant languages rather than Latin or English. However, this incident also reflected a greater effort to appeal to the community by performing rituals in Aboriginal languages. This made the sermons more accessible to a greater number of people, but it also demonstrated a certain desire for fraternity with the Metis of Sakitawak by sharing the faith with them in their language. Using Latin in church might have reinforced social separation because it was not the community's language. The subtext of conducting a sermon in Cree, Dene, or French could be an acknowledgment of a shared sensibility with the community, a shared religious identity.

Mass, the most central of all Catholic rituals, intended to connect all members of the faith as a family, was performed throughout the year at a variety of services to bring the community together. When Grandin visited the English River District in 1875, he kept a personal journal of his tour. These reminiscences are one of the few available records left by the clergy that focused on their activities and dealings with the people rather than exalting their divine mission or reflecting on their own religiosity. In particular, Grandin kept a record of religious events, such as the masses he presided over at Lac Vert and Île à la Crosse, which had the effect of drawing people together to participate in ceremonies during the spring and summer – a time when the need to prepare their families for the long winter would have been a competing priority. Throughout May and June, Grandin travelled through the southern portion of the district, performing Mass, visiting with congregants and HBC posts, and bestowing the sacraments of baptism, catechism, and marriage in various locations to initiate neophytes into the faith and forge community connections.[65]

In early June, Grandin conducted High Mass in Île à la Crosse, where he praised the Metis for how well they raised their children, stating that he was impressed with how respectfully they behaved toward the sisters and elderly of the community. Two days later, on 8 June, Grandin heard the catechism of the village's children. On 20 June, the Metis from across the northwest gathered at the mission for Mass to witness new members being confirmed into the congregation, which was followed by the procession, erection, and blessing of the mission's new cross. The following day, Grandin performed the sacraments of baptism and marriage for a few adults and young couples, respectively, before singing services for the dead at the Île à la Crosse cemetery. Throughout his visit, Grandin engaged in these types of religious ceremonies, which were intended to strengthen and reify the faith in the congregation as well as to draw the community together at a time when the annual subsistence and commercial economic activities meant that people were more dispersed than usual as they moved throughout the district in search of game and furs.[66] These ceremonies, for the living, the dead, and the Church itself, all centred on aspects of family and community, whether they involved natural members being baptized or married or newcomers joining the faith.

While Catholic missionaries oversaw the sacraments and assisted Metis families as they established connections with one another, their vows of celibacy obviously precluded their physical participation in the creation and maintenance of real family ties within the community. The Oblates and Grey Nuns were nevertheless often acculturated into the space carved out by family life and expectations in the northwest in a variety of creative ways. Perhaps the most significant sign that missionaries were accepted as a part of the community and integrated into the worldview was the frequency with which they served as godparents for district children. Over 1,800 baptisms were performed at the Île à la Crosse mission between 1846 and 1912, and close examination of the baptismal records reveals some distinctive patterns regarding the selection of godparents.[67] Godparents were an aspect of Catholic symbolism that established a spiritual family responsible for ensuring that a child or adult initiate received proper religious training, but it was not typical for clergy to serve in this capacity. In the northwest, however, missionaries were drawn into and connected with the values and expectations integral to wahkootowin in the most tangible ways. Of Véronique Bouvier and Thomas Lariviere's twelve children, for instance, two had members of religious orders as godparents. Their son Louis Joseph's godmother was Sister Sara Riel and his brother Joseph's godfather was Father Rapet, who served as godfather for more Metis children – seventeen in all between 1867 and 1911 – than any of the other male clergy who served in Île à la Crosse during this study's time frame. Conversely, the sisters were selected to stand as godmother far more evenly, averaging about two per Grey Nun throughout the latter half of the nineteenth and the early twentieth century. Perhaps the most interesting case of a member of a religious order serving as a godparent was that of Sister Sara Riel (renamed Marguerite Marie), whose father was born at Île à la Crosse to a fur trader father and Dene mother. When Sara Riel arrived at Île à la Crosse in 1871, she became integral to the family structure and served as godmother four times between 1876 and 1880 to local Metis

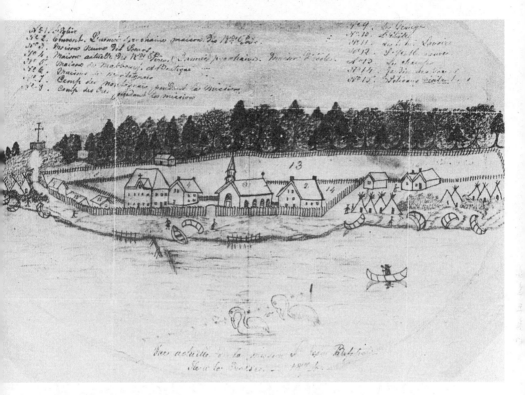

PHOTO 4.1   This image of Île à la Crosse is described as being etched on onion skin, but it was more likely drawn on birch bark. It depicts Saint-Jean-Baptiste mission on the lakeshore and, in the far left corner, the cemetery at the tip of the peninsula. The teepees and houses reflect the residential nature of the mission station. The view of the mission is the same one that visitors, paddling to the shore on the lake, would have seen. The pelicans on the lake are a common site on Lac Île à la Crosse even today. | *Sketch of Île à la Crosse mission, ca. 1874, by Sara Riel* | HBCA/PAM, Ile-a-la-Crosse 1, N3964

and/or HBC families. In at least one instance she served as godmother to a distant relative, her namesake Marguerite Marie, daughter of Charles Lafleur and Josette Lagimodière, on 8 June 1876 (see Photo 4.1).[68]

The role of godparents became a significant feature of Metis family life in the northwest as Catholicism was integrated into people's understanding and interpretation of wahkootowin. Apart from their spiritual responsibilities, godparents were also, historically, guardians of children if their parents should die, thereby establishing an additional form of extended family. The notion of spiritual guardians was a concept easily adapted to wahkootowin, with its emphasis on a holistic notion of family that involved the spirit world. Father Marius Rossignol observed in the early twentieth century that there remained a strong belief in what he referred to as the "cult of guardian spirits."[69] Every person in the Cree spiritual tradition had a guardian spirit or spirits that they honoured and invoked with offerings. These spirits, called "pawaganak," were protectors that helped the living when required in return for the offerings.[70] They were also similar in function to godparents, instructing and caring for children to protect them from harmful influences or divine consequences.

Baptism, whether it celebrated a new life or incorporated an outsider adult into the family and, by extension, the greater community of relatives, signalled a renewal of the immediate family, drawing members together with both the real or natural extended family and the spiritual family represented by godparents. However, while godparents had a clearly defined role within the Catholic Church as spiritual guardians, the niche they filled in the traditional family structures of wahkootowin also reinforced traditional indigenous values by providing children with multiple parents upon whom they could rely.

At this point, another intersection between economy and religion occurred, as Catholic rites and rituals influenced, and were influenced by, people's associations with one another via the HBC. Between 1867 and 1912, for instance, Bouvier women stood as godmothers seventy-seven times for members of their own families and others, Metis and Indian alike. Similarly, Morin women served sixty-nine times between 1868 and 1912, Morin men served as godfathers sixty-two times between 1867 and 1912, and Daigneault men served fifty-one times between 1881 and 1912. These family names appeared in the godparent category more frequently than any other surname, and all these families had strong associations with both the HBC and the Roman Catholic mission. In the lives of community people, the intersection of economy and religion was evident as they used the ceremonies of Catholicism to solidify intergenerational relationships between Company families. In particular, the Bouviers and Daigneaults often worked for the mission even while they were contracted with the HBC.[71] In the case of the Bouviers, first-generation Michel Bouvier Sr. and his wife Julie Desjarlais had a small family with three children – Michel Jr., Marguerite, and Véronique – who all married into large HBC families that were devoted to the Church and had strong social ties to others throughout the northwest. The interconnection between these families who worked for both the mission and the HBC became increasingly important as they and their spouses contributed to the establishment of second-generation families through connections to families like the Morins, Daigneaults, and Larivieres.

Because close family relatives typically served as godparents for grand-children, nieces, or nephews, Michel Bouvier Jr. and his wife Julie Marie Morin selected from maternal and paternal grandparents, uncles, and aunts to serve as godparents for their children and permitted one daughter to be adopted by Michel's parents, Michel Bouvier Sr. and Julie Desjarlais. People also selected godparents from families to which they were socially or economically close, or which they wanted to integrate into their world as defined by wahkootowin (see Appendix). By serving as godparents to these children and adults – all associated with the HBC in some way – families like the Bouviers extended wahkootowin to encompass an eco-nomic realm. In the northwest, this ritualized means of establishing familial relationships served to establish intracommunity social cohesion for people who might otherwise have no reason to support one another. A similar pattern of intrafamily support was repeated in other HBC fam-ilies of the northwest. For instance, Pierriche Laliberte and Sarazine Morin were godparents to at least four grandchildren and two great-grandchildren, as well as to several nieces and nephews within the Morin branch of their family.[72] Just as they carefully selected marital partners from one another's families intergenerationally, they engaged in a similar pattern of intra-familial, intergenerational alliance building through the Roman Catholic mechanism of godparent selection.

When we examine those who were excluded from the social network, we gain valuable insight into how social cohesion was initiated and main-tained. Attesting to their separation from the larger Metis community's cultural and social structure, certain HBC men, despite long years of service with the Company, are wholly absent from Roman Catholic mis-sion records. The Dreaver family at Green Lake illustrates this point well. George Dreaver had a background similar to that of other HBC men in the region. Although he was a clerk and not well educated, he made up for this deficiency, according to HBC inspector E.K. Beeston, with com-mon sense, ability as a "remarkable linguist," and "considerable influence with the Natives."[73] In the 1891 Green Lake census, the only genealogical information available for him and his small family, Dreaver was listed as a forty-year-old Scottish Presbyterian HBC clerk.[74] Additionally, the cen-sus tells us that he was married to Elizabeth, also Scottish Presbyterian, and that they had two daughters, Helen Dunlop and Elizabeth, both born in the North-West Territories.[75] Just as there is no patronymic imprint of the Dreaver family left in the region, neither is there any evidence that their Presbyterian daughters married into the local Catholic Metis families. Other non-French Canadians, such as Catfish, McCallum, Kippling (Kyplain), Iron, and Bekattla, successfully married into the northwest families despite their decidedly non-francophone heritages. That the Presbyterian Dreavers did not intermarry was possibly as much about holding to their original faith as it was about avoiding conforming to this particular community. The Dreavers' decisions excluded them from the social and economic networks that would have created a familial support system.

George Dreaver contributed to his social isolation by his attitude toward the Catholic Church. In his position as clerk at Green Lake, Dreaver openly displayed his disdain for the clergy. In a postscript to an 1892 letter, he remarked, "Bishop Pascal seems a nice sort of Fellow not a bit like the couple of Vipers you have down at Île à la Crosse."[76] He again commented on the local Catholic clergy in 1893, criticizing them for contributing to the immoral behaviour of the Metis. In describing a social scandal regarding a man named Merasty who had abandoned his wife, Dreaver voiced his distaste for Roman Catholicism. It was Dreaver's opinion that Mrs. Merasty, a woman he deemed as immoral as the husband who had abandoned her, should have been hired on immediately by the priests at the Saint-Julien mission to protect the rest of the community from her bad influence. According to Dreaver, Mrs. Merasty's problem was that she no longer had a man to camouflage her faults and provide her with a façade of morality. As a Presbyterian, Dreaver believed that what was more scandalous than the woman's faults was the Catholic clergy's inability to provide their parishioners with a positive influence.[77] Dreaver was not the only HBC official in the English River District who believed that the Roman Catholic clergy were less than genuine or beneficial in their mission. In 1849, Eden Colvile, a Company director visiting Île à la Crosse, described one of the priests who visited the post from the mission in this way: "That thief that did nothing but grin and rub his hands at Norway House last year [and] has got as fat as a pig on white fish."[78]

The Dreavers were unconnected to the regional Metis family system, not because they were culturally British, but rather because they were Protestant and, more specifically, because they did not connect to the community spiritually or religiously. Similarly, Samuel McKenzie, a Protestant chief trader at Île à la Crosse for nearly a decade in the latter half of the nineteenth century, kept a social distance between himself and his employees, choosing not to attend services at the Catholic mission, even though he was a religious man and it was the only church available. Instead,

McKenzie held private services for his family in the great hall of the factor's house, inviting other Protestant men, most of whom were junior officers, and their families to attend.[79] Surviving Company and census records contain the surnames of Protestant English and/or Scottish Company servants who likewise were never incorporated into the complex socio-cultural network. Names like West, McPhail, Daniel, Spence, Powers, Budge, McIntyre, Francklyn (likely Francklin), Moore, and Bethune were all present at HBC posts in the district during the nineteenth century yet have no resonance in those communities today and are not part of the regional genealogical reconstruction.[80]

By and large, local Company officers were Anglo-Protestant, of a different socio-economic class than their servants, and they had little direct influence on the creation or internalization of wahkootowin as a system of values guiding the people of the northwest, although they obviously affected the economic lives of families. (The officer class and its separation from the families and their worldview is discussed in greater detail in Chapter 5.) French Canadian George Deschambeault was the only Catholic officer in the English River District, and while he sympathized with his Catholic servants and was supportive of the Church, he also remained outside the familial support system because he did not marry into the region's families. Throughout its history, the post at Île à la Crosse was typically administered by English or Scottish white or Halfbreed men who were Protestant (Anglican or Presbyterian), with a personal religious ethnocentrism that was disdainful of Catholicism. The Company permitted the Roman Catholic clergy into the district because it wanted the Church's support in providing a Christian sensibility to a commercially oriented work ethic, a sense of individual responsibility, and a morality that would supplant the traditional Indian worldview.[81] The men in charge of the district had limited contact with the region because their time there was mostly limited to periods of three to four years. Although they often had families, they aspired to see their sons and daughters maintain their family's position as an HBC elite, which perhaps necessitated their social separation from the local community (recall, from Chapter 2, R.H. Hall's attempts to prevent Charles Eugène Belanger from falling below his station). Just below the officer class, skilled and semi-skilled servants – clerks, postmasters, interpreters, runners, and Indian traders – were a part of the family structure. They were often born in the district and most were married to local women. However, there were opportunities to leave the region. And so, while children like Alexexandre Laliberte and his brothers were sent to school at Red River, or women like Sophie Morin moved with their husbands to posts outside the region because they were entwined with local families there, they continued to hope they would return to be with their family. The expectation for the children of most senior Company officials who lived locally, however, was that they would rise socially through marriage or receive better postings than their parents, increasing or at least maintaining the family's status.[82]

It is clear that HBC officers or skilled servants who remained outsiders were, by choice, socially isolated from the community in which they lived. Without family connections to the region, they were far more likely to be reassigned to other fur districts or to retire outside the English River District. It was not just religion that formed the division between the HBC elite and the servant categories of employees within any given fur district, however. In the English River District, for example, elite Company men at the district headquarters – chief factors and traders in particular, but also some of the skilled servants such as interpreters – were separated from the general servant class of semi-skilled and unskilled labourers, whether these latter were employed at the headquarters or in charge of more distant outposts. Part of this division was based on the latter employees' willingness to integrate themselves in the local populace's worldview predicated on familial relationships, use their positions within the Company to support those families, and/or remain inland, thus adding their names to the local patronymic structure.

The tensions between the local community and non-Catholic HBC men can be seen in the response of local HBC officers in charge to Metis displays of faith. In July 1855, less than a decade after the mission was founded, the Île à la Crosse post clerk under Deschambeault reported that two Company servants planned to pay ten shillings each to the priest to have him perform Mass and pray to God to rid the district of potato worms that threatened that year's crop. Fearing a winter without enough food, the people of Île à la Crosse were willing to take extra measures to protect themselves. Later that day, the clerk added that he was happy to see people sacrifice their money, especially if the gesture worked. However, he was more skeptical about the religiosity of the cure, worrying that people would believe an actual miracle had occurred. Although Deschambeault was Catholic, his clerk was not and ruminated about Catholic superstitions, pausing to wonder if the men wasting their money did not remember what "our Reformers suffered for opposing Popery? the loss of estates, lives, liberties?"[83] Interestingly, the clerk did not see this act as a traditional form of offering made to the spirit world, as would have been required under the indigenous religion. Yet the similarity should not be dismissed. Almost fifty years later, another chief factor, A.A. McDonald, lamented that the spirit of superstition was alive and well in Île à la Crosse, adding that he believed people went to the church as much to gossip as for religion.[84]

The Church's role in setting social parameters and establishing who was a member of the community cannot be underestimated. Indeed, the Metis interacted with the mission and the clergy to set those boundaries. The acculturation of new people into the community coincided with the people's acculturation of the Church and its theology of Homeness into their existing values and belief system about family. Of greatest significance here is the personal decision individuals had to make about whether they would or would not be open to the opportunities afforded because of wahkootowin. In turn, openness to Roman Catholicism was one of the clearest paths to belonging. This emphasis on religion as a route to community acceptance was not a small issue in the relative geographical and cultural isolation of the English River District in the late nineteenth century. Wahkootowin's values promoted the creation of extended family structures and were, in turn, supported by Catholic ideals of familial relations, responsibilities, and obligations. In turn, Roman Catholicism became another vehicle transmitting the traditional cultural attributes that encouraged interfamilial connections and contributed to an individual's sense of identity. As a part of the community, the Church served as an instrument of accountability, setting and enforcing standards for behaviour and interpersonal interaction, as well as helping maintain the wholeness of the group through the blessings of the sacraments.

5

"The only men obtainable who know the country and Indians are all married"

Family, Labour, and the HBC

On the afternoon of 31 July 1889, Julie Bouvier, her daughter Augustine Mary Desjarlais, and her granddaughter Eliza, as well as Angela Catfish, Véronique Daigneault, and Caroline and Margaret Lafleur began weeding the Hudson's Bay Company's potato field at Île à la Crosse, a task that took almost four days to complete. Company families annually planted, sowed, and harvested a variety of root crops between May and October, contributing to a winter diet of fish and root vegetables.[1] What was unusual about the 1889 activity was not that women were working at Company jobs, but rather that they were all identified by name. Usually Company records simply referred to the "women of the establishment" or "all the women belonging to the post" working or social-izing.[2] On the surface, other than the stated familial relationships between the Bouvier/Desjarlais women in the potato field that day, there is no obvious connection between any of the other women – they shared no patronyms that make it possible for us to identify family relationships. But a fuller reading of the evidence reveals a complex family nexus linking male HBC employees to local, female, and family labour networks. The HBC, by now integral to Metis family structure in the northwest, was a conduit that drew families together so they could fulfill their reciprocal responsibilities to one another by sharing their employment, a loyalty to a common economic purpose at the posts, and a traditional sense of obli-gation toward one another. HBC families, established by outsider Metis and Euro-Canadian males and locally born women, created a long-term pattern of integrating men into the established family nexus marked by the regional matrilocal residency. In turn, these women supported both their husbands and the trade with their labour (see Photo 5.1).

Women's and children's labour received scant attention in the English River District post records. They were not formally contracted servants, but the Company depended heavily on their labour to sustain its posts. Although women worked year round, the months between May and September were the busiest in the district. Post journals reveal that during

PHOTO 5.1   *Front row, left to right:* Beatrice Belanger, Clementine Daigneault, Marie Rose McCallum, Flora Bouvier, and Catherine Daigneault. *Back row, left to right:* Victoria Daigneault, Marie Rose Desjarlais, Evangeline Daigneault, and Eva Hoffman. This photograph, even though it was taken in 1962, illustrates the types of family connections that women experienced in an earlier era. If we pay attention only to the surnames, we miss the nexus of family relationships among the women. These women are of the fourth generation and community elders. Beatrice Belanger (née Marie Béatrix Maurice) is the aunt of Catherine Daigneault (née Iron) by marriage. Clementine Daigneault (née Malboeuf) is the aunt of Marie Rose Desjarlais (née Daigneault), Catherine Daigneault (née Iron), Flora Bouvier (née Gardiner), and Evangeline Daigneault (née Desjarlais). Marie Rose Desjarlais and Catherine Daigneault are sisters-in-law. The family history of Victoria Daigneault is not known, nor is the connection between Catherine Daigneault and Marie Rose McCallum (née Couillonneur), although we do know that Marie Rose's mother was Rosalie Iron. Eva Hoffman was the wife of the doctor assigned to Île à la Crosse and, as in earlier eras, was not connected to the local family structure. | *Women at Île à la Crosse, 1962* | SAB, R-A22856

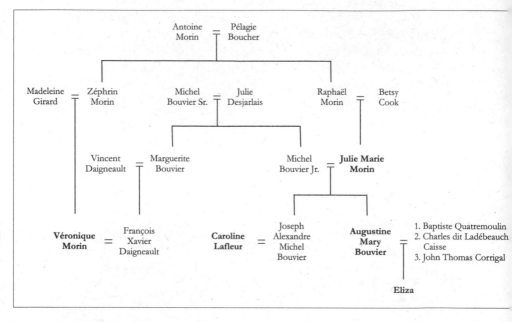

Antoine — Pélagie
Morin   Boucher

Madeleine — Zéphrin   Michel — Julie   Raphaël — Betsy
Girard   Morin   Bouvier Sr. Desjarlais   Morin   Cook

          Vincent — Marguerite   Michel — **Julie Marie**
          Daigneault Bouvier   Bouvier Jr. **Morin**

                                                        Joseph   1. Baptiste Quatremoulin
Véronique _ François   **Caroline** _ Alexandre **Augustine** _ 2. Charles dit Ladébeauch
Morin   Xavier   **Lafleur**   Michel   **Mary**   Caisse
               Daigneault   Bouvier   **Bouvier**   3. John Thomas Corrigal

                                                                        Eliza

FIGURE 5.1   The women in the potato field, 1889

those months they picked varieties of berries, mushrooms, and other ed-
ible wild plants in the surrounding bush, planted and tended to gardens,
cut and stacked the hay that grew in the island meadows, and hunted large
and small game.[3] From late May to early June the potato gardens were
planted, and by the end of June the women, girls, and boys were busy
hoeing the gardens, a task that could take several weeks.[4] Women also
worked in the local fisheries, a year-round job that helped feed post employees and families, the men working on the northern brigades and
southern transportation trails, and the winter dog teams. During the
winter, or when weather turned bad, women were reassigned to clean
inside buildings.[5]

   Like the men named on the sketch map (see Chapter 3), most of the
women named in the 1889 post record were related to one another through
either birth or marriage. Julie Bouvier was Julie Marie Morin, the daughter of HBC freighter Raphaël Morin and Betsy Cook. In 1868, Julie Marie
married Michel Bouvier Jr., son of Michel Bouvier Sr. and Julie Desjarlais,
at Île à la Crosse (see Figure 5.1). Within the mission records, there is no
record of a relationship between Julie Marie's daughter, Augustine Mary,
and a male Desjarlais at this time, although there could have been an

unrecorded relationship that transpired prior to her known marriage to Charles dit Ladébeauch Caisse in 1891. After Charles' death, Augustine married another HBC employee, John Thomas Corrigal, who arrived in Île à la Crosse around 1869.[6] If Augustine Mary did have a marriage with a Desjarlais man, it was likely according to custom because no marriage is recorded in any of the Church registries. Véronique Daigneault was the daughter of Zéphrin dit Catholique Morin and Madeleine Girard and was, therefore, Julie Marie's cousin. Caroline and Marguerite Lafleur were also cousins. Caroline was born at Île à la Crosse in 1872 to HBC fisherman Baptiste Charlot Lafleur and Angèlique Jourdain. Marguerite Lafleur was born three years after Caroline and was the daughter of Charles Pierre Lafleur, the brother of Baptiste Charlot, and Josette Lagimodière.[7] Angela or Angèle was the daughter of HBC servant John Catfish and Marie Betkkaye of Île à la Crosse. John and Marie had six daughters, but only Angèle lived to adulthood and had children of her own. Through her second husband, Louis Caisse, whom she would marry in 1905, Angèle would become a sister-in-law to Charles dit Ladébeauch Caisse and Augustine Bouvier.

Just as important, all the women working in the potato field shared a connection, through their male relatives, to the HBC as primary employer in the commercial economy of the English River District. Even if some were not directly related to one another, all were daughters of and/ or married or eventually married to men employed by the HBC, and so they came to make up a core, informal, uncontracted labour force. Julie Marie Morin's husband, Michel Jr., was occasionally employed as a Company tripper and freighter, and he worked intermittently at one of the region's many fish stations. Michel Jr.'s paternal grandfather was likely Jean Baptiste Bouvier, one of the early NWC fishermen at Île à la Crosse in the early 1800s. After the 1821 merger, both Jean Baptiste and Michel Sr. were employed by the HBC in the English River District.[8] Augustine's two known husbands were likewise HBC employees. Charles dit Ladébeauch Caisse was a Company fisherman and the son of Charles Caisse, who entered the service in 1853 as a boatman and fisherman in the English River District. John Thomas Corrigal was one of a long line of outsider males who converted to Catholicism in order to marry his first wife, Sophie Daigneault, in 1882. Corrigal entered the district as a carpenter and labourer for the HBC. Through their mother and father, respectively, John Thomas' two wives, Sophie Daigneault and Augustine Bouvier, were related.[9] Sophie's mother, Véronique Morin, was married in 1885 at Saint-Julien at Green Lake to François Xavier Daigneault, another Company fisherman and the son of Vincent Daigneault and Marguerite Bouvier. Vincent was an HBC carpenter who arrived at Île à la Crosse in the early 1860s, while Marguerite was the sister of Michel Bouvier Jr., and, therefore, the daughter of Michel Sr.[10] Caroline Lafleur's HBC connection came from both her father and husband, as well as her maternal grandfather and Company servant, Jean Baptiste Jourdain. In 1891, Caroline married Joseph Alexandre Michel Bouvier, another fisherman and the son of Michel Bouvier Jr. and Julie Marie Morin, making her the future daughter-in-law of the Julie Bouvier with whom she was working. Finally, Angèle Catfish's first relationship was with Baptiste Misponas (originally L'Esperance) in the 1890s before she married Louis Caisse at the Saint-Jean-Baptiste mission in 1905.[11] Baptiste Misponas' father was Samuel Misponas, the son of Alexis Bonami dit L'Esperance, chief of the Portage La Loche brigade. Baptiste and his father were both hunters. Louis Caisse was a Company tripman and fisherman.[12]

This chapter explores how wahkootowin in the northwest was reinforced by the integration of the HBC's structures into the reciprocal values held by local families. Particular attention will be paid to how Company families supported one another through intermarriage, group labour (regardless of age or gender), and the sharing of their lives with one another, all of which reinforced a greater sense of family, community, and home within this economy. According to Sioux anthropologist Beatrice Medicine, the Aboriginal conceptual model that guided such social and economic interaction is best described as a "reciprocity family model," which established familial alliances by providing a broader network for group social and cultural interaction through a web of flexible support systems.[13] Although Medicine's work speaks to her own Sioux cultural experience, this notion of family resonates with Plains Cree and Plains Metis, Woodlands Cree and Dene, and subarctic Metis. In each of these indigenous cultural groups, family relationships were broadly conceived, and all relatives, no matter how far removed from direct biological relatedness, were recognized as family members. As such, they were obliged to provide assistance and hospitality to one another as dictated by the reciprocal family model.

Father Marius Rossignol noted that the Cree frequently gave support and assistance to their relatives, expecting nothing in return. What was remarkable, Rossignol found, was that they did so even though "they trace[d] their relationships very far."[14] The social organization of subarctic peoples was integral to their economic behaviour, and those who have studied northern, subarctic societies have strongly developed this theme of support. Robert Brightman notes that the Cree practice of arranged marriages was integral to establishing these notions of support, concluding that "the consequences of these marriages are a strict alliance between the husband and the wife's relations and reciprocally between the wife's and the relations of the husband, as to their assisting each other."[15] Of the eastern Cree, anthropologist Richard J. Preston observes that it was normal for two or three groups of relatives or close friends to share a common residence, travel together, and coordinate their hunting activities. Waswanipi Cree social organization similarly centred on immediate and extended family members all producing and consuming together.[16] The similarities among Cree peoples across northern Canada, and a basic commonality of the reciprocal family model throughout Aboriginal societies, support the notion that this connection between social and economic organization was likewise central to the socio-economic organization of the people of the northwest. Ethnoarchaeologist Robert Jarvenpa concludes that, by the early nineteenth century, the Dene in the northwest began to resemble their Cree neighbours in terms of social and territorial organization as they moved farther south into the region around Sakitawak. The Dene, like the Cree, lived in hunting groups marked by "etnakwi," or brothers cooperating and working together, which signalled the importance of familial relationships in these forms of economic activities.[17] Living in the lands of their mothers and being raised within the worldview of wahkootowin ensured that the Metis understood the economic lifestyle and incorporated the reciprocal family model into their cultural identity, just as they did with many other aspects of this indigenous style of life.

In his research on Île à la Crosse, Philip Spaulding concludes that Metis people traditionally placed such a high value on family that individuals without relatives were non-persons in Metis society, making them objects of pity. Spaulding determines that, from a Metis perspective, large families were highly valued and a source of esteem. Family members were bound to one another by ties of loyalty, with obligations to speak and act on a relative's behalf when required, as well as to support them materially and emotionally.[18] This value placed on family and familial loyalty shaped the Metis community's relationship with the HBC. This is not to suggest that these families controlled either the trade or the Company. By and large, these were loyal HBC families with patriarchs who had good relationships with their superiors and the institution itself. However, the familial loyalty integral to wahkootowin created an unavoidable tension in the HBC hierarchy whenever large families asserted cultural solidarity within their workspace, which at times was at odds with Company interests.

Of the approximately forty-three core Metis families identified in the northwest, twenty-six families, including the Bouviers, Daigneaults, and Caisses, had long histories of employment in the fur trade. Some began with the North West Company, but all were connected to the HBC after the merger. This association of Metis families with the Company was not simply because they were an available resident labour pool. The Company deliberately hired these men with large families because, as stated in an Île à la Crosse post report from 1888, "the only men obtainable [for service] who know the country and Indians are all married."[19] The fur companies relied on wahkootowin as lived by male employees to facilitate the expansion of operations in the English River District prior to 1821. The HBC relied on those same families to stabilize the region following the merger. In turn, the trade economy provided a venue in which social solidarity, familial loyalty, and cultural identity were reinforced through informal, unpaid, and often unrecorded labour. Evaluating the genealogies of the women at work, such as the Bouvier/Desjarlais connection of mother, daughter, and granddaughter in the potato field, allows us to draw more connections between the families and the fur trade generally and to understand the complex relationship between the Company and the people of the northwest.

Much has been written regarding the HBC's policies and sentiment toward the families of its servants at the posts prior to and after the 1821 merger.[20] Throughout its long history, the Company often displayed ambivalence about the social activities of its servant class that, over time, came to manifest itself in a subtle but complex web of attitudes, behaviours, and contradictory policies. In its early years, the Company was uncomfortable with its employees marrying into local Aboriginal communities and enacted a formal policy banning marriage between its servants and Indian women, although it was never able to enforce this policy effectively. White women were banned from HBC posts until about 1820 because the Company felt that men would otherwise be too distracted from their work.[21] While a few women, such as Marie-Anne Gaboury, Louis Riel's maternal grandmother, entered those districts by 1803, white wives were not present until 1830, after Governor George Simpson married his English cousin, Frances, and brought her to Red River.[22] Although white women were in Rupert's Land after 1870, there is no evidence that there were any in the English River District, with the exception of the Grey Nuns, until possibly the early twentieth century. Despite these policies, almost from the beginning HBC servants (like NWC employees) made personal and professional choices to create families within the fur districts where they were employed, making family life central to the Company's informal trade practice.

By the early nineteenth century in the English River District, the Company recognized the economic benefit of those personal choices and so permitted families to be a part of the Company structure. It was, therefore, no accident that the wives, daughters, nieces, and sisters of HBC employees were working in the Company potato field in 1889. They did so because the job needed to be done and because their husbands, fathers, and brothers were otherwise engaged. Just as importantly, these women would have expected to receive a portion of what they harvested to support their large households in return for their labour, as well as an assurance of Company support during times of personal hardship, food shortages, or other kinds of stress. Rations, typically in the form of basic food staples, were advanced to Company servants based on the number of dependants a servant had, as well as his rank. Well into the mid-nineteenth century, apportioning food rations appears to have been a fairly standard and expected Company practice. As noted in Chapter 4, following Sunday services, the HBC often provided servants and their families with rations of fish and potatoes. During Christmas Day celebrations at the chief factor's house, the officer in charge of the district supplied the men and women of the establishment with alcoholic beverages and food such as cake and pemmican. When they left for their own homes, these families were provided with rations of barley and dried meat.[23] Rations were not simply for daily use but were also given as gifts as a means to curry favour with local people. On 31 December 1892, Chief Trader Henry J. Moberly received a letter of thanks from the Grey Nuns on behalf of the children at the hospice for his note and gift of flour and candies. According to the sisters, the children were delighted by the candy, and everyone was excited about the possibility of making cakes with the flour. The sisters extended their own thanks to Moberly for his kindness and charity, hoping that he would accept their best wishes for his health and prosperity and for that of his entire family.[24] On another occasion, Sister Agnès at St. Joseph's hospital sent a thank-you card to Moberly on Easter Sunday for the oatmeal and syrup that he had sent to the children. The sister further acknowledged Mrs. Moberly's earlier visit and her generous distribution of sweets to the children.[25] This gift of foodstuffs by the HBC fits the local conception of how families were expected to behave toward one another and would have been understood within that framework of support and obligation. Moberly made a special effort to extend the post's custom of offering rations to the children at St. Joseph's, perhaps because they were citizens of the district and their adult relatives were in some fashion engaged with the trade. By being kind to these children and the Roman Catholic mission, the Moberlys, although they were not members of the local family themselves, demonstrated their acceptance of the socio-economic ordering of the region. Such an act would have ensured a certain reciprocal generosity for the Moberly family.

By and large, women of HBC families, along with their children, tended to engage in group work, much as they would have done in a more traditional subarctic Aboriginal family setting that revolved around the seasonal activities associated with natural resources harvesting.[26] The 1889 example of women weeding the potato field was not an isolated event in the history of women, labour, and the HBC in the English River District. This instance of group labour by women and children at district trading posts followed older Cree and Dene cultural patterns, in which Aboriginal women worked with their children as a means of educating or training young people and preparing them for their role in the society. Furthermore, group labour fulfilled a cultural ideal of solidarity through shared socio-economic activities, with people engaging in daily activities that underscored the lived experience of wahkootowin. Through occasional references similar to the 1889 potato patch observation, we can see wahkootowin manifested in daily behaviours and activities.

One of the most important Company tasks in which women participated was the full-time, year-round operation of the post's fisheries. Fish was a food staple for people as well as the dogs used in the winter transport system. Officially, fishing was a job reserved for skilled male servants. The Company contracted male servants specifically as fishermen, from Andrew Kirkness in the early 1800s to Pierre Lafleur in the late nineteenth century, to supply Île à la Crosse with daily food supplies as well as prepare surplus for winter storage.[27] Yet, wives and daughters of HBC men, especially fishermen, found their services required to provide support for the Company fisheries. Women were often assigned the task of checking nets scattered at different points along Lac Île à la Crosse, at the mouths of rivers, and at nearby lakes, as well as producing and maintaining nets.[28] In the early-nineteenth-century example of Andrew Kirkness (see Chapter 1), his wife assisted him at his job, and when she left him and went over to the NWC post, the HBC feared that her loss would mean the abandonment of the Île à la Crosse post because they would be unable to withstand further aggression by the NWC or trade effectively without a steady food supply. Several days later, when Kirkness likewise abandoned the HBC post in order to be with his wife, the Company hired Peter Fidler's wife, an unnamed Swampy Cree woman, to operate the fisheries.[29]

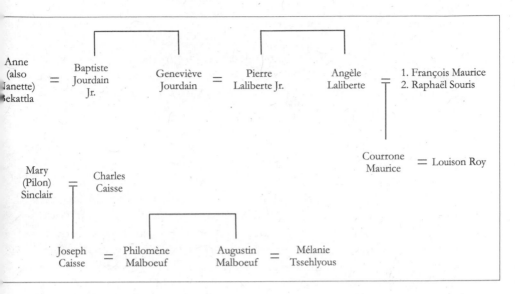

FIGURE 5.2   The women at the fishery, 1890

Because the fisheries operated year round and fish were a dietary staple at the English River posts, the tasks associated with their maintenance never ceased. After fish were caught, they needed to be cleaned, dried, and frozen, duties largely delegated to women. In early April 1890, nine women – Véronique Bouvier, Meline Malbeuaf, Widow Case, Widow McKay, Ann Jourdain, Corinne Roy, Mary Desjarlais, Angela Souris, and Mary Case – along with Old Souris were at work hanging fish, a task that took four days and eventually required the assistance of four boys and a couple of male servants to complete.[30] Not surprisingly, all these women were married to, or were daughters of, Company servants, and several were related to one another either through their birth families or through inter-generational intermarriage of HBC families (see Figure 5.2).

At this stage, it is hard to pinpoint Véronique Bouvier's family. Michel Bouvier Sr. and Julie Marie Desjarlais had a daughter named Véronique who married Thomas Lariviere, but it is puzzling why she was not referred to by her married name, as were the other women. However, the records contain no other Véronique who would be the right age, and Thomas Lariviere was a Company fisherman, as was his adopted father, Abraham Lariviere. Meline Malbeuaf was Mélanie Tssehlyous, wife of Augustin Malboeuf, an HBC fisherman who was the son of one of the first-generation couples, Pierre Malboeuf (another fisherman) and Marguerite Ikkeilzik, a Dene woman. The Widow Case was likely Philomène Caisse (née Malboeuf), daughter of Pierre Malboeuf and Marguerite Ikkeilzik, and therefore Mélanie Malboeuf's sister-in-law. Philomène had been married to Joseph Caisse, son of Charles Caisse and Mary (Pilon) Sinclair. Joseph had died two months earlier, in February 1890, and left Philomène with four young children. The Widow McKay may have been Angèle Lariviere, the wife of Henry McKay, who died in March 1890, a month before the women were at work hanging fish. Anne Jourdain was likely Anne (Nanette) Bekattla, the wife of Baptiste Jourdain Jr., an HBC fisherman whom she wed in 1879 at Green Lake. Based on the information currently available, Marie Desjarlais is unidentifiable in the genealogical record. Courrone Roy (née Maurice) married Louison Roy, an HBC tripman, in 1877. Courrone was the daughter of Angèle Souris (née Laliberte) and her first husband François Maurice. Angèle was, therefore, Courrone's mother and was remarried by 1890 to local fisherman Raphaël Souris, the Old Souris (actually thirty-nine years old at the time) who was working with the women that day.[31] Finally, Mary Caisse, another of the ten women working, was Mary (Pilon) Sinclair and, therefore, Philomène's mother-in-law. Mary's husband, Charles Caisse, was an occasional fisherman for the HBC.[32]

Just as groups of interrelated women worked informally for the HBC, when a group of contracted male labourers was required for a task, the men also tended to be related. The interconnections of male Company servants were, unsurprisingly, as complex as those found in the women's groups. Throughout February 1892, one particular group of closely related men often worked together. However, the familial connections between these men are not apparent unless their maternal lineage is examined. On 10 February 1892, for instance, Charles Maurice, son of François Maurice and Angèle Laliberte, went with his stepfather, Raphaël Souris, and an in-law, François Xavier Daigneault, to Waterhen River with eight horses to pick up freight.[33] François Xavier was the son of Vincent Daigneault and Marguerite Bouvier, while Charles Maurice was married to Julie dite Canadienne Bouvier, the daughter of Michel Bouvier Jr. and Julie Marie Morin. Marguerite and Michel Bouvier Jr. were siblings, which means that Charles and François Xavier were cousins-in-law. Five days later, the post journal recorded that Joseph Bouvier, Marcial Desjarlais, François Bouvier, and "Vincent Daigneault's son" had left Île à la Crosse for Buffalo Narrows with a load of flour destined for Portage La Loche.[34] While Daigneault's son was unidentified in the journal entry, he was likely François Xavier, the only son old enough at the time to be formally

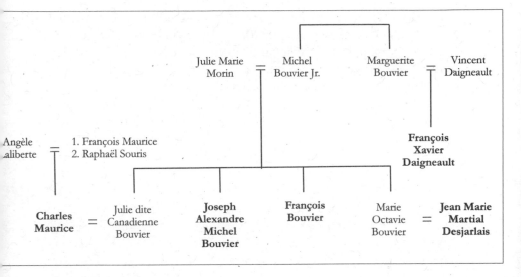

FIGURE 5.3 The Portage La Loche party, 1892

employed by the Company (in 1892 he was a contracted HBC fisherman). Furthermore, François Xavier's mother, as already stated, was the sister of Michel Jr. and therefore the aunt of Michel's sons Joseph and François Bouvier. "Marcial" Desjarlais was actually Jean Marie Martial Desjarlais, husband of Marie Octavie Bouvier, who was the sister of Joseph and François. So travelling together to Portage La Loche were two brothers, Joseph and François Bouvier, their brother-in-law, Jean Marie Martial Desjarlais, and their cousin François Xavier Daigneault (see Figure 5.3).[35]

The familial linkages between the women and men working together can be genealogically reconstructed and placed in a chart, but the meaning of those relationships was reinforced through socio-economic activities and transformed family into community. The demands of reciprocal familial commitments created by this web of interfamily marriages supported the Company by establishing a chain of connection upon which it could call for additional labourers. However, as early as the 1850s, the Company was consciously balancing the benefits of this "unpaid" labour force against the added costs associated with supporting large Metis families at their posts.

The Company's economic policies toward First Nations and Metis communities have been described as paternalistic, and in many ways this is true. But the interaction of families and communities throughout the English River District, as well as the Company's response to local demands, suggests that a more appropriate description may be "ambivalent benefactor."[36] In his study of the northern Manitoba fur trade, Frank Tough states that "the Company's 'kindness' and 'indebtedness' were basic to the relations between the Company and Native people."[37] While HBC officials in Winnipeg and Company elite in the district did what they could to minimize the costs associated with families at its posts, they nevertheless had to call on those same families for their support with tangential occupations associated with food production. Women and children were uncontracted labour, but the Company paid a price for this unpaid family labour because it became their benefactor in much the same way as godparents were expected to assume responsibility for children and adult male converts. Viewing the HBC as a godparent, Company servants used the Company to anchor the responsibility, rights, and obligations among their families, and so it became the repository of wills, distributor of pensions, transportation system, advisor for retirement, supporter of alternative economic ventures, dispenser of rations (food and goods), and landlord, determining who did and did not have a right to Company housing. As early as 1821, the Company recognized a need for a benefactor in the English River District. Chief factors and chief traders recognized that familial harmony improved the Company's economic viability. According to Tough, the HBC assumed the "overhead or social cost of production" as essential to maintaining the labour force in the face of economic fluctuations and the uncertainty of hunting.[38] Even if they did not themselves live according to the expectations embodied within wahkootowin, local chief factors and chief traders firmly placed themselves and the Company within the reciprocal family model, cultivating the loyalty of servants by supporting their family life.

One of the clearest manifestations of the HBC's role as benefactor for the Metis of the English River District can be observed in its response to the deaths of Company servants and the subsequent interaction with widows. There were occasional references in the post records to "old widows," or just widows, living at district posts, because they either continued to serve an economic role or were a financial burden.[39] However, the example of the group of women working in the fisheries in April 1890 shows that widowhood often meant continuing on as before. Of the ten women working in the fisheries, two were recently widowed and a third had been widowed several years earlier, although she had since remarried. While the consequence of losing a servant in the social milieu of the English River District affected both the post's economic health and wahkootowin within the northwest, there were additional, perhaps less obvious, ramifications. From a Company perspective, the death of a servant meant that it was faced with a widow and her dependent children who required support and looked to the Company for that aid. Chief factors and chief traders feared scenarios in which the Company would be left with the responsibility of caring for widows and children who had no alternative means of support. Company representatives' concerns were entirely economically driven – they feared taking on the costs associated with the care of families unsupported by male heads of household. In his study, Tough notes that in the late nineteenth century, low fur prices caused the Company to reduce operating costs, change the post system, and alter the mode of transportation, thereby reducing the demands for local labour and resources. Tough concludes that, "over time, this functioned to tear apart what had been a closely linked economy."[40]

While there were, at various times, widows such as Philomène Caisse and Angèle Lariviere living in or near the posts and selling the produce of their hunting, fishing, and gathering, or more simply working in fields or fisheries, the Company regarded and described widows as draining what it felt were already strained post resources. On the one hand, widows most likely still possessed important skills for the post's daily operation, but because they had no husband to support them, it often fell on the Company to cover their expenses. In the mid-1880s, Pierriche Laliberte had occasion to write that an unidentified "Old Widow" at his post had provided many furs for the Company in her younger days but now required its assistance to live because "Poor old wife, she was maken [sic] wooden traps [and then] got a blow on her Eyes" – she was now blind and had no relations to care for her. While Laliberte indicated that he planned to give the woman some of his own goods, he believed that the Company should support her in recognition of her long service and therefore recommended that she receive a pension as a retired servant would.[41] An elderly woman without family needed to locate relatives in the form of the Company or face serious hardship, and so Laliberte acted as required – he assumed responsibility for this woman who had worked hard for him at his post by supplying her from his own personal stock and advocating for her as a member of the regional family.

In addition to dealing with widows, there was also the matter of dispensing the deceased servant's estate and settling debts that the Company felt it was owed. One of the more troubling local incidents – at least from the Company's perspective – was the death of Benjamin Bruce. On the morning of 19 April 1823, "Old" Benjamin, a Company interpreter, left the Île à la Crosse post alone to hunt waterfowl. While out in the bush, a tree branch apparently fell, fracturing his skull and killing him. When Bruce did not return that evening, his son and Patrick Cunningham, his son-in-law, went out to search for him. These two relatives brought Old Bruce's body back to the post. The rest of the family began preparations for the funeral rites and burial that would take place the following day at Landsman Point. According to Company records, the elder Bruce's children were inconsolable at the sudden loss of their father. The men of the establishment took turns sitting with Bruce's remains all night as part of a pre-burial funeral ritual. At the funeral, the men in attendance were given two drams of rum to toast the deceased, one at the Company's expense and the other at Cunningham's.[42] The Company may have had an informal policy to supply rum at funerals, and the people of Île à la Crosse might have interpreted it as the act of a good relation, a benefactor. Patrick Cunningham's motive was clearly to honour his wife's father, a man to whom he was economically allied as a fellow employee of the Company, and likely to demonstrate the family's generosity at this significant moment. There is no reason to believe that the Company's actions were viewed any differently – it was behaving as required according to the expectations of the local populace. Death set the stage for funerals, which like so many other rituals, whether secular or religious in nature, were central to helping a collection of individuals coalesce as a community, as a socially cohesive group governed by similar values and sharing a common identity. In Sakitawak and throughout the northwest, such rituals were a tangible representation of wahkootowin. Whether local officials fully understood or accepted the values of wahkootowin or the responsibilities and obligations associated with the reciprocal family model is not really at issue. By extending rations to servants and non-servants, offering rum for toasts at family events, managing and dispensing wills and finances associated with savings, or simply giving needed work to female relatives of servants, the HBC became an integral part of the family structure in the English River District.

Benjamin Bruce was listed in the 1821 HBC census of servants at Île à la Crosse and was, at that time, fifty-five years of age. Bruce was originally from Walls, a parish in the southern part of the Orkney Islands, and served for thirty-two years as an interpreter. The son who went in search of him may have been Pierre Bruce, who was listed in the same census as an employee of the Canadian (or NWC) establishment, rather than the HBC. Pierre, like Benjamin, was an interpreter, and by 1821 he had spent sixteen years in the service. That a father and son were both in the English River District but with different employers was perhaps not unusual given the intense competition between the two companies leading up to the

1821 merger. Situating family members in different Companies could be interpreted as a way to maximize the family's economic options, hedging their bets by association with competitors. However, there were two Patrick Cunninghams listed in that 1821 census, one at the "European" or HBC establishment and one at the Canadian, which appears odd but can perhaps be explained as a consequence of the purpose of the censuses. Shortly after the 1821 merger, the HBC took a census of employees at its own establishments and at the NWC or Canadian establishments. There are a number of duplicate names in the census, listed as both NWC and HBC employees.[43]

Benjamin Bruce left a will stipulating the distribution of his property, but according to the Company – the administrator of both the will and his assets – Bruce had nothing to leave. Île à la Crosse chief factor George Keith observed that Bruce had invested £300 to £400 ($1,500 to $2,000) with an Orkney speculator who went bankrupt, leaving the Bruce family destitute and the Company to determine their fate in the English River District.[44] The details of the Company's decision are not revealed in the records, but because there are no substantial records for a Bruce family in the English River District after this time, it might be surmised that the widow and her underage children were relocated to Red River or some other district, or that the family was small enough, or lacked males to carry on the family name, that it was absorbed into larger families with stronger patronymic connections. There was, however, a reference to another "Old Bruce" in an 1850 letter from Chief Factor Roderick McKenzie to Winnipeg. Perhaps this man was one of Benjamin Bruce's sons who remained inland for a time. In that letter, McKenzie noted that this Old Bruce and his sons were expected at the Deer's Lake outpost to trade that winter, but there had been no word of their arrival.[45] There is also a record of Aloisa Bruce's marriage to Joseph Jourdain at the Roman Catholic mission on 8 November 1870.[46] Aloisa was apparently the daughter of Louison Bruce and Rosalie Delorme. Perhaps Louison Bruce was the Old Bruce of Mackenzie's 1850 letter and/or the son of Benjamin Bruce.[47] Otherwise, the only substantial record of the Bruce family in Île à la Crosse is that of Old Benjamin's accidental death and his family's destitution because of a failed investment.

In a similar incident in 1893, an HBC servant named John Harper died, and his daughter sent the Company a request for assistance in securing her family's future. Charlotte Harper personally wrote to ask for Chief Trader Henry J. Moberly's assistance in applying for scrip as her father's heir. Charlotte asked Moberly to write the commissioners in Ottawa with

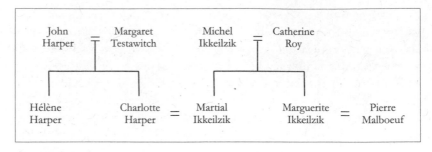

FIGURE 5.4   Charlotte Harper's family

details about her father's life, as required for the application. Moberly described John Harper as having come from Kildonan, Manitoba, before entering the HBC's service. Prior to being stationed at the English River District, he was employed in Athabasca. Moberly stated that Harper was legally married in 1872 to Margaret Tastawitch, a Chipewyan woman from the Fort Chipewyan area, whom he likely met in his earlier posting.[48] John and Margaret had at least two daughters, Charlotte and Hélène.[49] Accordinging to Moberly, by 1893 Charlotte was married in the English River District and "living in very poor circumstances."[50]

Charlotte had remained in the northwest after her father's death and in 1891 married Martial Ikkeilzik, with whom she had nine children between 1894 and 1912. Martial was the son of Michel Ikkeilzik and Catherine Roy and was probably the brother of Marguerite Ikkeilzik, wife of HBC servant Pierre Malboeuf (see Figure 5.4).[51] Pierre Malboeuf was an outsider male who arrived in the English River District by 1851, either from Sorel or St. Hyacinthe, Quebec. In the Abstracts of Servants Accounts of 1851, Pierre was listed as being twenty-six years of age and with five years of service in the Company as a midman before working as a fisherman in the English River District.[52] In the case of Charlotte and her family, it was Moberly's opinion that scrip would greatly assist them because of their poverty. Although not explicitly stated in the letter, Moberly may have also felt that if her application were successful, Charlotte and her husband would not request the HBC's help in the future.

When it came to old widows specifically, and families of deceased servants more generally, the HBC had an obligation toward them beyond what was required of a typical employee-employer relationship. As we have seen, the widows Caisse and McKay continued to work in the fisheries despite the deaths of their husbands.[53] Arguably, these women continued to work at Company jobs because the Metis of the northwest believed that the HBC was in some measure a part of the reciprocal family model, and by working for it, they could continue to access HBC resources. Their male relatives all had contact in some fashion with the Company, be it long-term or seasonal in nature, in the upper or lower strata of the HBC hierarchy. Angèle Souris, for example, was the daughter of Pierriche Laliberte, who had served as postmaster for Portage La Loche and Green Lake, and several of her younger brothers had likewise been well positioned as postmasters in those locations. Angèle's first husband had been in charge at Portage La Loche at the time of his death, after which her eldest son, Magloire, was employed by the HBC. Eventually another son, Charles, became a Company servant as well. It would not be difficult to imagine that Angèle, despite never having personally held a Company contract, regarded herself as part of that institution's structure and economic success. Furthermore, regardless of her male relatives' jobs, Angèle would have been fully within her rights to request that they protect and support her and her children by providing them with opportunities to support themselves, such as working in the fisheries or potato fields.

Just as it faced having to deal with the costs of supporting widows, throughout the latter half of the nineteenth century the Company was confronted more generally with rising costs and low fur prices. In 1872, William McMurray, the officer in charge of the English River District, received a memo stating that the families of HBC servants would receive their usual ration allowances for that season, but "no allowances will be made to the Families of any employees after this date."[54] Furthermore, he was to inform anyone entering the service from 1872 onward, particularly in the English River District, that their families were not entitled to maintenance from the Company.[55] McMurray was also told that servant contracts were no longer to exceed three-year terms except in the most exceptional circumstances.[56] By the late nineteenth century, the HBC no longer wanted families to feel they had a claim on the Company based simply on service. The Company clearly expected that the old system of paternalism, benefactorship, stewardship, and debt peonage would give way to a new era devoid of familial and/or social obligation.

The Company's refusal to continue with the long-standing practice of apportioning rations flew in the face of Metis expectations of their employer and benefactor, and despite the Company's attempts to scale back the use of rations, this 1872 edict was not faithfully implemented throughout the district. In 1885, HBC clerk James Nicol Sinclair of Green Lake wrote to Joseph Fortescue at Île à la Crosse, expressing concern that Green Lake might not be able to provide surplus fish to the district that year.

Any surplus from the fishery, he wrote, would have to feed the Green Lake HBC families so as to prevent a repeat of the previous year's events, when Sinclair had had to provide families with bacon and flour rations after the Green Lake fisheries failed and left them without enough food.[57] Almost a decade later, in April 1892, Charles Lafleur was advised by Moberly to give goods in the amount of ten Made Beaver and some fish rations to a woman who was married to a man named Martial so that she would have food until her husband returned.[58] There is not enough information to determine who either Martial or his wife were, but the record shows that local Company representatives continued to feel and act on an obligation to ensure that the families of its servants did not starve.

While Company officials in Winnipeg may have resented supporting the families of HBC servants that laboured for them, locally the Company continued to demonstrate a degree of responsibility and obligation because the families' support was not only required at particular times but also benefited the Company in the long run. The need to support families was often unavoidable because of natural resource strain or failure in any given year. Fish was the main diet at Île à la Crosse, so when the fisheries failed, everyone suffered. In 1873, the Île à la Crosse fisheries were doing well, so William McMurray decided the post would not require additional fish from the Bull's House fisheries to supplement its supplies. McMurray had intended to send a couple of men to help Company fisherman Joseph Vadnoit at the Bull's House fishery but learned that François Maurice had already sent John Thomas Kippling (Kyplain) from Portage La Loche to assist the operation, presumably because that post required additional fish supplies. It was McMurray's opinion that if Vadnoit worked hard and was productive, he and his small family at Bull's House would have enough fish to last them until spring and would not have to depend on Île à la Crosse.[59]

Over a decade later, in the 1888 district report, the chief trader at Île à la Crosse, Joseph Fortescue, lamented that the post was in serious jeopardy because of an almost universal failure of the district fisheries that year. As a result, they would have to purchase food from Prince Albert or Winnipeg to ensure that there were enough rations for the families and the dogs that winter.[60] According to the report, there were no more than three unmarried adult males in the entire English River District, and these were the only men the Company could employ to provision the post because servants were supplied food rations. If Fortescue employed married men, he would have to add additional people to the rations list and raise the cost of feeding the district.[61] But in the chief trader's estimation, it would be foolish not to hire married men or to discharge them early to minimize expenses, because men from outside the district would know "neither the trade, language, Indians nor country."[62]

In *The Canadian Fur Trade in the Industrial Age*, Arthur J. Ray explores the Company's continued use of rations or relief well into the twentieth century, despite efforts to cease the practice. To explain the continuation of this practice, Ray highlights two factors. First, he notes a widening division within the HBC between Company officials in the administrative centres such as Winnipeg and the officials and servants in the field, who dealt with local economic realities. This pattern of administrative centres being out of touch with the realities of a region were clearly evident in the English River District, particularly when it came to officers' attitudes toward Catholicism (see Chapter 4). Second, and more important, Ray points to the HBC's recognition that "Indians who remained loyal believed that the Company still had an obligation to look after them even though the legal responsibility [for them] may have rested [with other agencies]."[63] For the families who had long worked with, and for, the HBC, the Company fit into the worldview of wahkootowin – it was part of the reciprocal family model that provided support and connections.

The notion of the Company, the institution, serving as an overall benefactor extended into all branches of the HBC employment spectrum, and at each level men asked their superiors for special consideration for their families. Like George Dreaver at Green Lake, who lamented being without his family (see Chapter 4), Roderick McKenzie recorded his feelings of loneliness and his desire to be reunited with his family – a desire that could not be fulfilled without Company support and approval. In 1844, McKenzie had broken his leg and spent the winter bedridden at Île à la Crosse. With plenty of free time, his thoughts quickly turned to his absent family. He wrote to Governor George Simpson in Winnipeg, requesting that his eleven-year old son be removed from school at Red River and brought to assist his father with personal tasks. Furthermore, McKenzie, looking to the future and fearing that his health would not improve, requested permission to settle at Norway House when he retired so that he could be closer to Red River and among his old friends. In the summer of 1843, McKenzie's family was with him at Île à la Crosse, as Dreaver's family was with him for a period of time. McKenzie and his wife, Angèlique (an Ojibwa from Lake Nipagon), had five daughters and seven sons.

Furthermore, company officers such as McKenzie, men with no known connections to the region or its community or even men who had connections but did not appear to be part of the local Metis community's family structure, often made requests to their superiors on behalf of their sons to ensure that their immediate families remained connected and employed. By the mid-nineteenth century, McKenzie's sons were scattered throughout the world – Ferdinand was in Edinburgh, Scotland; Samuel was at a post at Rapid River; Patrick was in the Edmonton area, serving under Chief Factor John Rowand – but all seven were eventually employed by the HBC, and four daughters went on to marry Company men (the fifth died before she reached a marriageable age).[64] This family exhibited two important features common to the core families – an intergenerational connection to the region and a connection to the HBC – yet the McKenzies were not part of the socio-economic structure created by the district's families, and they were outside the Catholic Church. As an officer in the Company, Roderick McKenzie was one of a group of men across western Canada or based in Red River who associated with one another as an elite HBC cohort, who groomed and apprenticed their sons for good positions within the Company or sent them to schools in Great Britain, and who located appropriately placed officers for their daughters to marry. McKenzie ensured that his children were all well placed and cared for within the larger Company system, but as a result his family was spread out across Rupert's Land. Like his Metis workforce, McKenzie relied on the Company to take care of his family's needs, even as it physically separated family members.

In George Simpson's Character Book, McKenzie is described as an honest and well-meaning servant but also "irritable and short tempered to such a degree that it [was] unpleasant to do business with him."[65] More importantly, McKenzie's problem, according to Simpson, was that

> His Health and constitution [was] broken down and worn out so that his useful Days are over, and it is full time that he should retire from Service altho' he has not held his present situation exceeding two years; indeed he never was pocessed [sic] of abilities which could qualify him to fill such a situation with advantage, and he owed his late promotion entirely to the circumstances of his being senior of two Gentlemen who were in Nomination with him and being less objectionable in many points of view, the company having had the choice of three very indifferent and in some respects unfit men from among whom it was necessary to fill the vacancy to which he succeeded.[66]

The notion that McKenzie never had the ability or qualifications to fill such a role is an important point to examine. Roderick was the cousin of

Alexander Mackenzie, one of the first independent traders in the English River District in the late eighteenth century after the arrival of the Frobisher brothers. The McKenzie family had once been well placed in the NWC, had served as part of the transitional fur trader presence after the merger, and had actually established an historical presence in the English River District, yet they left no patronymic legacy. By the 1840s, Simpson, a man notorious for downgrading his officers' abilities, was suggesting that McKenzie, despite his marriage to an Aboriginal woman, had no effectiveness in this Metis territory. Within the northwest, McKenzie was severely disadvantaged socially because he was outside the community circle. Furthermore, the McKenzie family name no longer carried the weight it once had, and that, coupled with the lack of connection to the northwest's cultural identity, made Mackenzie a liability despite his family legacy or his own history in the trade. It was clearly not McKenzie's intention to live out his final days at Sakitawak (or even in the northwest), so his usefulness as an experienced chief factor was rapidly drawing to a close as his health deteriorated.

McKenzie's health improved, however, and in 1850, still at Île à la Crosse, he wrote again to Simpson about his family. He related that his youngest son, who had been attending school for the previous ten years, was now ready to begin his apprenticeship with the Company. McKenzie feared that if the Company did not hire the young man, the family would have to send him to California to earn a living, and if this were to happen, the family as a whole would be adversely affected. Although McKenzie's sons were dispersed across western Canada, they were all within the HBC system and still fairly close to their father and mother in the sense that they were connected economically and socially to close friends and relatives at other posts. However, a son in California, outside the HBC system, would have created a fissure in the family that had not previously existed. Three years later, McKenzie's son Samuel, who may well have been the young man at the centre of so many letters to Simpson, was in the Company's service at Île à la Crosse, and Roderick had retired to Red River.[67] McKenzie's letters over several decades in the nineteenth century express the importance of family and a father's wish that his sons will obtain employment with the Company nearby so that the family could be together, even for a short time.

What is clear in the case of both the Dreavers and McKenzies is that the families were close and concerned about the time they had to spend apart. It is also clear that these HBC officers, even as they lamented their absent wives and children, were socially isolated from the community in which they lived. Chief factors and traders like Roderick and Samuel McKenzie or even clerks like George Dreaver were far more likely than those at lower levels to be reassigned to other fur districts or to retire outside the English River District. A combination of culture and socio-economic organization divided the HBC elite in any given fur district from the servant categories of employees. Within the English River District, there was a separation between elite Company men at the district head-quarters – chief factors and traders in particular, but also some of the skilled servants such as interpreters – from the general servant class, but also from those in charge of more distant outposts such as Portage La Loche, Green Lake, Souris River, and Bull's House. This separation was largely based on the ease with which individuals integrated into the local family structure and the expectations of the reciprocal family model, using their positions within the Company to support the family or remain inland, thus adding their names to the local patronymic structure. Both groups – the officer and servant class – used Company resources or connections within the work sphere to benefit their families, but in different zones. McKenzie called upon his connections in Red River to try and get his son an apprenticeship, while district men and women worked locally to access foodstuffs and establish labour cohorts with relatives in their homeland.

Chief factors and traders, as much as the servant class, felt that the Company's role was to ensure their own and their families' socio-cultural and economic well-being. In an 1848 letter to George Simpson, Thomas Hodgson, Green Lake's postmaster from 1839 to 1853, and another Company man with no discernible familial connection to the English River District, requested that his son be hired at Île à la Crosse as a boat builder and rough carpenter for the upcoming winter. The young man had recently injured himself while working as a voyageur in the district on the Company's boats and was now unfit for physically demanding employment.[68] He was mar-ried with a small child and faced destitution, so his father asked Roderick McKenzie, his own district superior, to hire the young man. McKenzie's employment roster was full for the summer, and he could not hire Hodg-son's son without Governor Simpson's permission, so less than a month later, McKenzie also wrote to Simpson on the matter, stating that the young man had a wife and family and that he should therefore not be permitted to remain at Île à la Crosse unless he was able to support him-self. McKenzie further noted that the younger Hodgson was already a "good man and a good rough carpenter" and that in a year or two he would be able to build boats for the district. Perhaps more importantly,

McKenzie surmised that Thomas Hodgson was getting old and his son should be groomed as his replacement. While McKenzie did not directly ask permission to hire young Hodgson, he alluded to the long-term benefits to the Company of employing Thomas' son in the short term as a favour.[69] Presumably, McKenzie was thinking that, if the senior Hodgson were preparing to retire, it would be a mistake for the district not to begin planning for his replacement. Hodgson's skill was essential to this subarctic fur district, and the role of the boat builder would have been critical to the district's operation. However, McKenzie may have also been alluding to the importance of keeping men like Hodgson satisfied. By ensuring that the son was properly groomed and trained in the Company system, and by hiring the junior Hodgson, the father would be content. As a result, there would be a feeling of goodwill between such a skilled and valued servant and the officials of the district in which he was employed.

The notion of the Company, the institution, serving as an overall benefactor extended to all branches of the HBC employment spectrum, and at each level men asked their superiors for special consideration for their families. Officers and skilled tradesmen without familial connections to the local populace sought assistance for their families from the officials at Red River, whereas local families dealt directly with the posts within their homelands. The local HBC and its officers were representatives of the Company and, from the point of view of those in the district, were responsible for supporting the Company's relationships with its servants and ensuring that the families were satisfied economically. In this way, however unwillingly, the institution and its resources were often drawn into the reciprocal family model at the district level. By the late nineteenth century, HBC families in the northwest looked to the Company for such basic familial support as ensuring that widows had employment or that sons were hired, just as they required occasional rations when the district fisheries failed. The relationship of the Company to its various types of employees, the relationship of the Company officials in each of the fur districts, or the relationship of the Metis to the Company was a multilayered and complex narrative that was predicated upon individuals within an institution fulfilling roles and expectations. The role of the HBC locally was to ensure that it had a contented and satisfied workforce to ensure the larger entity's economic success. The people of the district, by and large, remained loyal to the HBC as their employer and worked within that system to care for and extend their families, though they often placed the needs and interests of family members first.

The HBC's role in the lives of Metis people facilitated a connection between the communities that developed at the posts and shaped the region's socio-cultural identity. The fur trade was more than just an occupation. Entire families were drawn into the economy, and fur posts became institutions integral to the socio-economic system of the families themselves. Just how relevant the HBC, and by extension the fur trade, was to the development of Metis communities in the northwest is underscored by a conversation held at Red River in 1870 during the first Riel Resistance. At a meeting of the Convention of Forty, Louis Riel called the HBC "A Company of strangers living across the ocean," accusing it of selling out the Metis just as it sold Rupert's Land to the Canadian state.[70] However, Riel's subsequent motion to the convention – to nullify all the arrangements and stipulations made by the HBC in the Rupert's Land transfer and assert that any future arrangements by Canada be made only with the people of Red River – was defeated in a vote of 22 to 17. In opposing Riel's motion, both convention chairman Judge John Black and representative Charles Nolin stated that it was important for the Metis to remember the Company's assistance and kindness to them on more than one occasion. Specifically, Nolin stated that while the Company could not be exculpated entirely, some acknowledgment of its contributions to communities in times of need was only proper. Riel's accusation may have been correct in a larger sense, but within the communities throughout the northwest, and even within Red River itself, the notion that the HBC was "a Company of strangers" with no relationship to the people did not ring true.[71] In each community, and throughout the region in which they were located, the HBC was made up of relatives and, as a result, was a fundamental part of Metis cultural identity in the nineteenth century. Just as individuals were incorporated into the reciprocal family model, so too was the HBC, which, in turn, fulfilled its role by adopting the behaviours that symbolized how families were to behave. Local HBC officials granted rations, provided housing, supplied alcohol for toasting, wrote letters and maintained financial accounts on behalf of its servants and their families, and ensured that women and young people were able to work at Company tasks in return for supplies. The HBC was integral to the development of a Metis cultural identity in the district because it provided a place where families coalesced and shaped a communal self-determination grounded in intergenerational family labour.

6

"The HalfBreeds of this place always did and always will dance"

Competition, Freemen, and Contested Spaces

I n 1892, Reverend Father Rapet accused ChiefTrader Henry J. Moberly of placing Metis socio-cultural traditions and, by extension, the HBC's relationship with the Metis ahead of the Church's attempt to cultivate proper moral behaviour. The priest charged that the HBC was, if not promoting immorality, permitting it to occur. In a letter to HBC inspecting officer J. Macdougal, Moberly answered Rapet's charges on this and a number of other issues that highlighted the growing tension between the HBC, the Roman Catholic mission, and the value that the Metis community placed on wahkootowin. According to Rapet, Moberly interfered with the Church's missionizing efforts by encouraging the Metis of the English River District in acts of excessive drinking and merriment through the hosting of local dances at the post.[1] Moberly regarded the priest's accusation as an absurd personal attack. Regardless of who was in charge, Moberly wrote, "the HalfBreeds of this place always did and always will dance in spite of the Priests orders."[2] He further noted that it was the Company's practice to host a few dances for the people of the district throughout the year, but he had actually reduced the number of people invited to those dances in response to the concerns of local missionaries.

Moberly firmly asserted that he believed the dances, accompanied by fiddle music and toasting with liquor, were important customary cultural practices that united Metis communities across the district. These particular Metis socio-cultural traditions were not at odds with the HBC's treatment of its servant class. As Moberly further explained, he was in the "habit of giving some of the servants and sometimes the HalfBreeds" a

183

drink after a trip or a good day's work was complete.[3] Like food rations, the Company's offer of alcohol to its servants fostered a social bond and also, more importantly, functioned as an extension of the reciprocal family relationship between the HBC and its employees. Since the early days of the fur trade, the distribution of gifts at the commencement of a financial transaction was a ceremony central to the establishment of a trade relationship. While the HBC in the English River District was not attempting to cultivate a more intimate relationship with its servants, the practice of gift giving had become an integral part of the Company's obligations and was expected by both Metis and Indian people. Moberly's hosting of dances and distribution of alcohol were important to the district's economic well-being and its social cohesion.

Gifts of food and alcohol were a Company tradition, and Moberly extended this custom to include the mission on several occasions. As noted in Chapter 5, Moberly and his wife, despite being Anglican, had provided candies, flour, oatmeal, and other foodstuffs to the sisters at the mission for the children in their care. In a similar act of hospitality grounded in social tradition, Moberly had, on three separate occasions, offered glasses of whiskey to the lay brothers and priests at the mission. On each occasion, the whiskey was accepted. Based on the mission's previous acceptance of both food and liquor, Moberly regarded Rapet's accusations of improper behaviour as hollow.

Father Rapet's most damning charge against Moberly, however, was that the post hosted a "wild dance" during the Christmas season in which the men of the district became drunk and rowdy. Although it was customary for the officer in charge to host the annual New Year's dance, the 1892 New Year's Eve Grand Ball was held at the house of a Mr. McDermott because Moberly's young son was ill. Moberly and his family neither hosted nor attended the dance. Nevertheless, Moberly argued that had all been well at his house, he would indeed have hosted the ball because of its importance to the community as a defining, annual cultural event and because it was the HBC's "custom to give a few dances to the people of and about the north."[4]

Moberly went on to detail a number of other cultural traditions that he promoted while in charge of the Île à la Crosse post, some that honoured his own cultural sensibilities, some that honoured Company traditions, and others that honoured and affirmed Metis values. Moberly's account of these events sheds further light on the various socio-cultural and religious expressions operating in the district. Moberly, for instance, kept what he referred to as the "Old English" custom of decorating a Christmas tree with ornaments for his children. Christmas trees were rather unusual in the English River District, and the tree generated a great deal of interest among people in the community. Moberly invited a dozen adults to visit his home to view the tree and share a bottle of port wine to toast the season. At nine o'clock on the evening of that visit, Moberly's wife requested that one of the visiting servants play his fiddle so that their two young daughters could dance. Moberly felt that when Rapet accused him of corrupting the populace, the priest had merged these two events – the New Year's dance at McDermott's house and the small social gathering at his own – into one extremely distorted description of the holiday season's events. Moberly further rejected the notion that he had encouraged debauchery among the Metis of the northwest, reiterating to Macdougal that neither he nor any of his employees had ever insulted the Church or interfered with its religious mission among the local Aboriginal communities. It was Moberly's opinion that any Company action hostile to the clergy or the Church in the district would be a serious misstep because all the servants were Catholic.

The dual activities of economy and religion – the Company and the Church – were powerful forces in the northwest throughout the nineteenth century. Local people engaged in all aspects of the trade, for it was the only commercial economy in which to pursue a living, and they were equally connected to the Roman Catholic Church. Both institutions were integral to the ways in which the Metis nurtured and cultivated a worldview predicated on familial relationships and grounded in reciprocal support. By the closing decades of the nineteenth century, however, there was an obvious and growing friction between the Roman Catholic mission and the HBC over issues of the other's alleged behaviour, particularly perceptions of immorality or hypocrisy. Church officials believed that the HBC was a corrupting influence on the local Metis and Indian populations, while the HBC felt that the Church was expecting communities to transform behaviours and values that had long been compatible with the trade environment. Both institutions believed the other was interfering with the local populace to the detriment of their own goals and attitudes.

It is unwise to underestimate the influence that these two institutions held in the northwest, for their agents and practitioners extracted material and cultural wealth and often demanded conformity to social and religious norms based on values practised thousands of miles away. Other scholars have chronicled the negative impact of the fur trade and Christianity on Aboriginal society, but what is often missing from discussions of colonialism and economic imperialism is the story of response, reaction, and assertion of autonomy via alternative forms of power, such as that which could be found in the strength of wahkootowin.[5] Without ignoring the importance of those European institutions in shaping the histories of Aboriginal societies, it is equally important to understand how Aboriginal people shaped their daily activities based on their own cultural norms and expectations.

By the 1820s, the region's families had coalesced into a pattern of intergenerational intermarriage that united families as they moved across the northwest. At the same time, the number of outsider males entering the district was significantly reduced in the wake of the Company's restructuring after it merged with the North West Company in 1821.[6] This ushered in a new economic era that contributed, however unintentionally, to the growth of an independent spirit among Metis families throughout western Canada. Marcel Giraud concludes that between 1820 and 1850 the Metis faced economic uncertainty because of global market forces that reduced the Company's profit margin and resulted in an organizational restructuring.[7] After conducting audits of English River District financial returns from the 1870s to the 1890s, ethnoarchaeologists Robert Jarvenpa and Hetty Jo Brumbach concur with Giraud's findings but further note that Metis self-sufficiency and economic independence increased in this later period because of renewed fur trade competition from American companies and new competition from the Church.[8] Within this newly competitive environment, the HBC still required a solid and dependable work force, so district officials like Moberly cultivated a relationship with the local Metis to gain their loyalty while also encouraging their self-sufficiency. Jarvenpa and Brumbach conclude that when the HBC at Île à la Crosse determined it could only afford to feed a small number of servants, it required some full-time employees to support themselves and their families so the Company could limit or even cease the issuing of rations. The Metis adapted by becoming more economically selective, with some families freighting, trapping, trading independently, or seeking employment at the mission.[9]

This chapter, then, is an exploration of how the Metis of the district used tensions between the HBC and the Church to promote their own socio-cultural interests. It was in this contested space of competing authorities that the Metis pursued a range of secularized social activities such as dancing, drinking, and feasting that may or may not have been preceded by a religious ritual, such as a wedding, feast day, or funeral, and asserted a right to refuse to work on religious days such as those associated with saints. Overall, however, Metis families were loyal to the local institutions and were headed by men and women who had mostly good relationships with the superiors operating those organizations. Still, the familial loyalty integral to the society's values could be at odds with the HBC and mission hierarchies, especially when large families asserted cultural solidarity in the work and religious spaces of their homeland. The Metis expressed their socio-cultural identity in a manner that reaffirmed their values and commitment to one another in this space, which was, by the end of the century, in flux. As the mission and Company bickered with each other and focused on their own needs, the Metis asserted themselves in ways that ran counter to the goals and aspirations of these institutions.

Just as Christian religious ceremonies such as Sabbath observances and baptisms were performed prior to the arrival of missionaries in 1846, the secular and religious traditions of the district were also well established by mid-century. Historian Eric Hobsbawm's distinction between custom and tradition, defining the former as what people do and the latter as the paraphernalia and rituals or behaviours that demonstrate the action, is useful here. The relevance of traditions, according to Hobsbawm, is that they unify people by fostering social cohesion through customs rooted in a common set of beliefs and conventions – the values of a society.[10] The power of Catholic rituals and secular activities that found an outlet in the post economy should be understood in such terms. Combined, all these celebrations appealed to Metis people because of their emphasis on family, whether living or spiritual, natural or fictive. It was within this context that dancing, music, food, and liquor served as important symbols that confirmed the familial relationship. While exercised at various times of year for all types of occasions, these secular customs were never more important than at Christmas and New Year's. As the 1892 exchange between Moberly and Rapet demonstrates, the holiday season was a catalyst for a great number of intra-institutional conflicts. While Christmas was perhaps the most important religious date on the district's Christian calendar because it celebrated the birth of Jesus, the central character in the Catholic Church's theological conceptualization of the Holy Family, it also marked the beginning of annual secular celebrations at New Year's, a series of feasts and dances that signified a reaffirmation of community togetherness. While the festivities held at this time of year offered some respite from the constant labour, the holidays also drew together families from across the district, and individual members travelled large distances to celebrate their shared values.

The Christmas season began as early as 22 December, when people from across the English River District arrived at Île à la Crosse, some staying several days into the new year to spend time with their extended families.[11] In addition to the arrival of Metis, it was not unusual to have Cree and Dene families visit for Christmas Mass and to conduct business at the post. Indians typically returned to their wintering grounds between Christmas and New Year's Day; Metis often remained behind to partake in annual New Year's celebrations.[12] Île à la Crosse post journals record that on 22 December 1889, the men and women of the district – including Mr. McAuley from Green Lake, Mrs. Sinclair and Pierriche Laliberte from Portage La Loche, Magloire Maurice from Souris River, Alexandre Laliberte from Canoe Lake, and Charles Lafleur from Buffalo Narrows – arrived for Christmas celebrations (presumably accompanied by their families). A year later, many of these same people arrived again, but by 29 December George Dreaver of Green Lake, Pierriche Laliberte, Raphaël Grandin, Baptiste Laliberte, Magloire Maurice, and Charles Lafleur had already returned to their own regions within the district.[13] HBC records make clear that while Metis servants were expected to work on Christmas Eve, they were annually afforded time off on Christmas Day.[14] In addition to time off from their work, the Company gave "the people of the Establishment" rations of dried meat and barley.[15] After 1846, one of the incentives for spending the holiday season at Île à la Crosse was the opportunity to hear and participate in the Church's Christmas Mass at midnight on 24 December. While encouraging attendance at Christmas Mass, Oblate priests like Rapet unsuccessfully attempted to ban secular celebrations, such as New Year's Eve dances, that involved alcohol and fiddle music, claiming that such activities led to immorality.

New Year's celebrations became important public displays of camaraderie between families and local HBC officials. As such, this holiday received a great deal of attention in the HBC records, particularly as it reflected the involvement of HBC personnel and goods. However, what is only alluded to in these records is the extent to which the families carried on their celebrations away from the post and in the family-defined communities across the district. These events began with invitations extended to relatives and HBC servants throughout the English River District to join New Year's Eve festivities at the Île à la Crosse post. New Year's was an important time for the HBC to affirm the connections between Île à la Crosse and its many outposts, and it afforded the families working at and between those posts an opportunity to travel and socialize.[16] In 1826, Chief Factor George Keith gave a detailed description of typical New Year's celebrations at Île à la Crosse, which began early on the morning of 1 January.

According to Keith's account of the day, the annual ritual began at dawn, when all the men from the post arrived outside the factor's home to salute him with two rounds from their "Indian guns." After the salute, the men were invited in. Keith fed them, and they all toasted the day and the New Year with liquor from the post's supply. The factor played his role as the most senior Company official in the region and provided the men and their sons with tobacco, rum, and other spirits, along with flour cakes and pemmican. As the men departed, Keith recorded that they discharged their weapons in a farewell salute, thanked him for his generosity, and then embarked on a day-long round of visiting with family and friends in the community. Following their male relatives, the ladies of the post, dressed in their best clothes, were greeted by Keith at his house with a kiss on each cheek before he formally introduced them to "their own sex of the Masters house," who visited with them and likewise served food and liquor to celebrate the day.[17] Like their male relatives, the ladies were served spirits (diluted with water for the more refined tastes of women), port wine, flour cakes, and pemmican. The women usually visited with the chief factor's wife for a couple of hours before, like their male relatives, they departed to visit relatives and friends. That evening, everyone reassembled at the post for the annual New Year's Grand Ball, hosted by the senior officer and his family. The day following the New Year's celebrations was often spent resting from the previous day's activities and preparing for another dance held on the evening of the 2nd, and sometimes another on the 3rd. It is not clear whether these other dances were, like the New Year's balls, held annually, although it appears that there was some tradition to the celebrations. They are mentioned in post journals in 1823, 1825, 1832, 1837, and 1865.[18]

While dances offended the clergy's sense of morality and proper behaviour, the Île à la Crosse post openly hosted and supported these events. Dances were held for a variety of occasions – from celebrating a job well done to providing a social diversion in the midst of a life of demanding physical labour and the more sedate religious rituals offered by the Church. In September 1892, James Nicol Sinclair of Green Lake, an accomplished fiddler, invited Moberly, his wife and son, and George Dreaver to "come and favour us with your company at 4 o'clock PM" for a feast and dance at the post. Sinclair added that if his guests were unable to arrive for the feast, he hoped that they would make it by six or seven o'clock that evening to join the dance.[19] The arrival of a visitor in the community was further cause for extending hospitality, no matter the length of the visit. One of the most important visitors to Île à la Crosse in the nineteenth century was Governor George Simpson, who stopped over while on an inspection tour of the Company's trade districts immediately after the 1821 merger. Simpson arrived at Île à la Crosse in the fall of 1822 and spent several weeks at the post before leaving for the Athabasca District. The occasion was marked by social activities such as pheasant hunting and several dances held in the governor's honour, to which the families were invited. On 16 November, Keith wrote that, prior to Simpson's departure, a ball was held "for the people in consideration of the Governor's departure."[20] Similarly, when the nuns first arrived at Île à la Crosse or when bishops visited the district (see Chapter 4), feasts were held in their honour.

While dancing and other secular social celebrations developed into Metis cultural tradition, these activities, lacking support from the Roman Catholic clergy, became a source of conflict between the Metis congregation, their spiritual guides, and oftentimes the HBC. Nothing, not even church services the next morning, could derail a much-anticipated dance. On Sunday 11 October 1890, the Île à la Crosse clerk noted that church services were not well attended that day because so many were resting after the previous night's dance.[21]

It is often difficult to separate religion from secular social events because the spiritual and social were so intertwined in the lives of Metis people in the northwest. Religious ceremonies such as weddings and funerals were often preceded or followed by social events such as dances and wakes that served as central markers in the life cycle of families. According to post records, on 15 January 1901 the people of Sakitawak had a feast at Nehiyo-wahkasi (Sandy Point) for Louison Roy and Couronne Maurice's daughter, Angèle, who had been married the day before. According to the mission records, on 14 January, Angèle Roy married Jean Baptiste Pietassiw (Durocher), the son of André dit Pietassiw (or Piyettasiw) Durocher and Pauline Natomagan (also known as Pauline Lariviere).[22] This branch of the Durocher family traced its lineage back to Assiniy or Old Amable Durocher and his wife, Augustine, one of the region's first-generation couples. While the actual wedding took place at the mission, the feast and dance celebrating the union occurred across the lake at Nehiyo-wahkasi (Sandy Point), where the Larivieres lived near Morins and Natomagans in the nineteenth century. Dances and feasts occurred after wedding ceremonies and away from the mission, within the social spaces of the families, and both events were central to the act of marriage because social occasions such as these were necessary to celebrate and maintain relatedness. Ritual and ceremony – whether secular or religious in nature – had important roles in the facilitation and creation of a Metis cultural identity in the region. A wedding dance and feast away from the mission and within the domestic sphere of local families reinforced the distinction between landscapes and social spheres in the district.

As a result, and despite the Church's protestations throughout the nineteenth century, the Metis continued to use social events such as dances and feasts, just as they used religious rites, to draw the community together in both celebration and commemoration of family. The people of the northwest accepted aspects of the Roman Catholic Church (as they had accepted aspects of the fur trade) that were compatible with the values of wahkootowin and fit within the framework of familial alliances and responsibility. Philip Spaulding notes that the Roman Catholic clergy were unsuccessful in their attempts to change the values, behaviours, and basic cultural attitudes of the Metis of Île à la Crosse, concluding that "their actual influence in changing ... ingrained cultural practices was limited."[23] Spaulding's findings are supported by the ethnographic writings of Father Marius Rossignol, who recorded his experience with the marital practices of his Metis congregants in the northwest.[24] Historically, parents arranged marriages in a manner that strategically connected families economically, politically, and socially, but they also ensured that husband and wife were a good match. Both sets of parents sought partners for their children who were good workers and providers, regardless of gender. However, the young did not always agree with their parents' selections. According to Rossignol, in such circumstances he was sometimes asked to intercede and speak with the young people. On one such occasion, Rossignol accepted the task of talking to a young woman about accepting the man selected for her, but he proved to be unaware of Metis cultural and moral sensibilities and was chastized for his insensitivity to their values. The father of the young man explained to Rossignol that he wanted his son to marry the daughter of his sister, but the young woman was resistant. Although Rossignol agreed to speak to her, he also put forward an alternative plan, suggesting that the young man instead marry the available daughter of his father's brother. Despite ministering to this community for decades and sharing with them the intimate aspects of his faith, Rossignol was unaware that his solution proposed a culturally incestuous marriage. The horrified father informed the priest that the suggested potential couple was actually brother and sister and that such a union would destroy the family. The young man's marriage to the daughter of his father's sister was not incestuous, however, because according to Metis and Cree concepts of family, which did not mimic a Western conception of biologically determined family relationships, these two people were not considered to be biological relatives.[25] Despite having a presence in the region since the mid-nineteenth century, the clergy had not altered the community's perception of who was and who was not a member of a natural family or how wahkootowin governed all relationships within the community. Furthermore, and just as important, in this customary system of arranged marriages, the clergy was not expected to participate except to reinforce the decisions already made by the parents of a potential couple.

Perhaps the reason the Church was unable to influence the ingrained Metis social or cultural values was because it was not strictly the guardian of the values of home and family. By the 1850s, the clergy began engaging in commercial economic enterprises and, as a result, the Metis may have regarded their messages about Homeness and moral behaviour as inconsistent or compromised. The subtext of Rapet and Moberly's argument in 1892 was the Church's increasing interference in the trade economy as a competitor. In Moberly's opinion, Rapet's accusations about immorality and interference with the missionization process were motivated by revenge because Moberly had opposed the priest's efforts to engage in trade among the Cree at Nehiyo-wapasi – a region under the care of Alexandre Laliberte, the husband of Chief Raphaël Iron's daughter, Mary Isabelle (Elizabeth) Iron. In other words, the HBC was blocking the Church's attempt to violate the Company's monopoly, not interfering with the Church's religious mission. Perhaps as a result of Moberly's letter, on 13 June 1892 he received a response from Rapet. Moberly recorded that there was now an end to "all the unpleasant feelings between them," and he planned to meet with the mission to make arrangements to settle the matter by purchasing all their accumulated furs. Furthermore, the missionaries were to withdraw from the fur trade and, when possible and without causing conflict with their Christian ideals, promise to use their influence to support rather than compete with the HBC.[26] Moberly closed the matter by stating that he hoped in the future he and Rapet would be able to solve their problems without involving either of their superiors.[27]

The mission, although primarily a place of religious instruction and spiritual support, needed to be financially self-sustaining because it supported a complement of priests, nuns, and brothers, along with the children in the orphanage and school and infirm patients at the hospital. As a matter of policy, the HBC ceased to provide transportation for the missionaries and their supplies in the mid-1850s, so the Saint-Jean-Baptiste mission at Île à la Crosse had to develop an alternative means of transporting its goods, personnel, and equipment in and out of the district.[28]

At the same time, the Anglican Church at Red River was pressuring the HBC to expel the Oblates from the North so that the Anglicans could control the religious instruction in all fur districts. The HBC decided not to expel the Roman Catholic Church from Rupert's Land, likely because so many of its servants, as well as the rest of the Aboriginal population, were Catholic. However, the Anglican Church did manage to convince the Company to refuse to shelter the Catholic clergy at its posts or transport them on HBC brigades. Bishop Taché eventually persuaded Simpson to reverse the orders against aiding his clergy, but by then the priests in the English River District felt an uneasiness, which grew to be general distrust, whenever they had to depend on the HBC for assistance.[29] Instead, the mission developed a fairly sophisticated array of transportation routes, gardens and grain fields, saw and gristmills, and cattle herds. By the 1860s, for instance, Father Vital Grandin had overseen construction of a trail – really, a two-hundred-mile road – between Île à la Crosse, Green Lake, and Fort Carlton so that the mission no longer had to rely on the canoes and brigades of the HBC to transport its goods and equipment.[30] Several decades later, lay brothers were operating a sawmill at Beauval on Lac La Plonge and Amisko-sipi.[31] More damaging to the HBC-mission relationship, however, was the Roman Catholic Church's move into the fur trade economy as an open competitor. According to Robert Jarvenpa's audit of the post's account books, this event is best understood as a new trade war in the English River District. The mission's involvement in fur trading in the English River District mimicked, in many ways, the old NWC/HBC, and later Revillon Frères/HBC, competition. In short, the mission overreached economically and began operating like any other fur company, which, as we have seen, compromised its ability to establish a moral tone for both the people and the Company.[32]

When it became an economic competitor of the HBC, the mission began hiring local people as extra labourers, taking employees away from the Company. This created a situation in which the Metis had some choice in terms of employment and were able to assert a certain manoeuvrability, exploiting the competition between the two institutions by offering their labour and trading their goods and services to whichever best served their interests at the moment. For instance, some families moved back and forth between the HBC and the mission, engaging and disengaging as labourers whenever it suited them, just as they had done decades earlier with the North West Company. In the 1890s, Sister Hearn wrote to inform Moberly that Father LeGoff had just employed Vincent Daigneault, John

Thomas Corrigal, and Robbie Gardiner at the mission. According to
Sister Hearn, these three men considered themselves to belong to the
mission, so much so that they had applied to the priest for provisions, just
as they would have expected from the Company.[33] (These three men,
significantly, were all related through marriage. Gardiner and Corrigal
were Vincent Daigneault's sons-in-law, having converted to Catholicism
in order to marry his daughters Eliza and Sophie, respectively – see Chapter 4 and Figure 6.1.) Men who chose to be employed by the mission also
had the option to leave the Church's employ and re-engage with the
Company when it suited them. On 10 May 1865, Samuel McKenzie, chief
trader at Île à la Crosse, recorded that François Roy had finally left the
mission, where he had been employed, to come over to the Company and
enter service as a steersman.[34]

The range of activities in which local men were employed included
provisioning, transportation, wood cutting, and trading. Men employed
by the mission also engaged in activities specific to the needs of the Church,
including constructing and installing stations of the cross at sites throughout the district and occasionally exhuming and reburying bodies in mission
cemeteries when churches were moved and rebuilt. In June 1890, the priest
at Île à la Crosse had the people of Nehiyo-wapasi exhume and transfer
the bodies of about thirty deceased Catholics from the Canoe Lake mission
to the new cemetery at the rebuilt mission station. The same thing was
done in May 1897 at Green Lake, where eight bodies were exhumed from
a burial place near the chapel and re-interred at the community's cemetery
on the edge of Lac Vert itself.[35]

Metis families' ability to engage with either the Company or the Church,
or pursue independent economic activities, was the result of the Company's
policies and actions in the latter half of the century. The Company
needed reliable labourers but nevertheless sought to reduce the numbers
of men employed. This meant that there was a fairly large group of men
in the English River District who, if not engaged with the mission, would
have been unemployed or underemployed. Faced with the prospect of this
significant group of men with large families to support, the HBC took
creative steps to harness the labour pool. By the latter half of the nineteenth
century, the new economic environment gave rise to a new or reconceived
group of labourers known as the freemen. Despite their name, freemen
were not independent operators trading for their own profit but rather a
component of the Company's commercial operations.[36]

The freemen, because of their association with Metis communities, and
as a particular class of labourers, have received a significant amount of

scholarly attention. Historian John Foster argues that the French Canadian freemen class developed in the late eighteenth and early nineteenth centuries as a consequence of their wintering activities, which fostered an ethos of independence and an attitude that permitted them to act as "masters" of their own affairs and circumstances to such an extent that they ended their formal association with trading companies and truly became free.[37] According to Foster, freemen, or *l'homme libre*, established homes for themselves and their families apart from both the trading post and Indian bands, creating for the first time independent Metis communities. Heather Devine's study of the Desjarlais family further establishes this connection between freemen and Metis origins, and she argues that a freeman was a former employee of a trading company who, upon establishing a relationship *à la façon du pays* with an Indian woman, left the employ of that firm to operate in a trader capacity between bands and trade companies in the *pays d'en haut*.[38] More recently, Carolyn Podruchny has used the term to refer to former voyageurs – engagés, servants, and/ or workers – who chose to remain in the pays d'en haut and rely on a variety of economic strategies to survive, including trading, trapping, hunting, fishing, or short labour contracts with trade companies.[39] In all these instances, going free occurred in the eighteenth-century trade era at the height of competition in Rupert's Land, when there were multiple fur companies that strove to control the residency options and economic lives of their employees.

Prior to 1821, fur companies preferred that their retired servants leave the fur districts, fearing new competition if these experienced men remained inland. Shortly after the HBC and NWC merger, the Company began extending debt to freemen in the English River District for their summer and winter operations farther inland, expecting that the collected furs would be sold to the post at a reasonable price. Keith recorded in September 1823 that Jean Baptiste le Mai, a freeman in debt to the Company, left Île à la Crosse for Indian Lake. Less than a year later, Keith expressed concern over a "parcel of renegade freemen" around Lac Vert who had obtained supplies at Île à la Crosse for their summer outfits (see Glossary) and then left.[40] It is difficult to discern what separated an ordinary freeman from a "renegade." Perhaps renegades asserted greater independence from the Company than other freemen, who purchased goods on credit and returned faithfully to the post to pay off those debts with the product of their labour. Perhaps renegade freemen had a more literal interpretation of "free" than the Company did, and in the era between 1821 and 1840 they may have been more in line with the classical

freeman that Foster and Devine examine. These early definitions of freemen rang true in the northwest, at least as Metis society was emerging.
The economic and social environments of this early fur trade era were
mostly gone after 1821, completely so by the 1840s, so the concept of freemen evolved in HBC usage.

By the mid- to late nineteenth century, the act of going free from a trade
company had became a labour practice that the HBC encouraged and
incorporated into its operational structure. In the latter half of the century,
freemen were often retired or casually employed servants who continued
to live inland in fur districts like the English River and belonged to well-
established families that required their support. The basic roles of freemen
remained the same as in the earlier fur era, when the original freemen lived
apart from the posts and Indian communities and served as middlemen
between the two. Although they had no permanent contracts, HBC freemen performed occasional labour for the Company while pursuing other
economic opportunities. In the English River District, they served the
HBC as hunters, fishermen, and trappers, procuring provisions and furs
for the posts; operated commercial enterprises, such as freighting, transporting, or trading establishments; and occasionally sold their physical
labour to the Company for the same price as contracted servants. Giraud
argues that the prefix "free" was illusory because the HBC asserted a right
to expel these uncontracted servants from the territories where they lived
if they were judged offensive to the officers in charge. Such offences included a lack of discipline, refusal to respond to Company directives, or
competing against Company interests.[41] By the 1840s, freemen were not
classical French Canadian voyageurs, but rather Metis patriarchs and
matriarchs of large extended families invested in the homelands of their
maternal relations. The relationship between the HBC and freemen in the
English River District became increasingly complex over time as the character and definition of this economic class evolved to reflect new economic and, more importantly, social realities.

Between 1865 and 1870, Île à la Crosse began keeping an extensive list
of freemen in the district. By this time, the term may have indicated an
earlier usage that equated freemen with Metis, but there is not enough
information to determine precisely how it was being used when those lists
were compiled. The list of freemen over those five years included "the
Widow Morin" and many men who had once been regularly contracted
as HBC servants, including Pierre Laliberte, François Roy, Alex Robillard,
Vincent Daigneault, George C. Sanderson, and Joseph Girard.[42] Over

those five years, there was an average of thirteen freemen per year in the district (see Table 6.1), and their surnames were common to the region: Cook, Lafleur, Lariviere, McCallum, Merasty, Rat, Sylvestre, Touslesjour, and Herman. Furthermore, most of the names were those of the forty-three core Metis families, who were also known to be HBC servants at various points in their lives. Perhaps more interesting, however, were designations of "Est." associated with particular men and women. For example, in 1867 the freeman's balances included "Est. of Baptiste Jourdain," "Est. of Antoine Morin," and "Est. of Robert McKinnon." "Est." was a reference to "establishments" of freemen, which may refer to the basic organization of a hunting band, led by the patriarch and surrounded by his family, all working together, rather than to a trading house per se.

Like employment with the Company or mission, being a freeman was not a permanent condition. Men and women could move in and out of the freeman category as easily as they could engage or disengage with employers. The existence of the newly conceived freeman class, in conjunction with concepts embedded within wahkootowin, fostered among the Metis a level of financial self-determination and permitted the evolution of both a socio-religious and economic environment that they defined for themselves. With their increasing economic freedom and a continued assertion of socio-cultural confidence within this landscape, coupled with a growing tension between the Company and the mission, Metis servants asserted a right to refuse to engage in labour when it violated their sense of tradition or obligation. In particular, Metis labourers refused to work on the Sabbath, annual feast days, or any other religious occasion. In the 1820s, the Metis of Île à la Crosse and the other outposts began commemorating All Saints Day on 1 November, a holy day for remembering martyrs of the faith.[43] While not a mandatory religious obligation, Metis people of the district faithfully observed it and would not engage in any Company labour on that day. The Company had little choice but to adapt to this scheduled work stoppage.

In 1888, a fairly serious conflict arose between Chief Factor Joseph Fortescue and Father Rapet regarding Catholic servants' participating in Company work on a holy day. According to Company records, on 9 May 1888 the Beaver River route to Green Lake had finally thawed and become open for travel, so Fortescue planned for the first boats to be sent out of the district the next morning. This first trip south from Île à la Crosse had been pre-arranged by Fortescue in a broad sense, although the precise date of departure depended on an unpredictable spring thaw. However, the

TABLE 6.1 Freemen in the English River District, 1857–1870

	1857	1858	1859	1860	1861	1862	1863	1864	1865	1866	1867	1868	1869	1870
Anderson, William								X	X					
Bell, Thomas								X	X					
Cook, George	X	X	X	X	X	X	X	X	X	X	X	X	X	X
Cook, William	X	X					X	X	X	X	X	X	X	X
Cook, William [a]	X	X			X	X								
Daigneault, Vincent										X				
Desjarlais, Joseph	X	X	X	X	X	X								
Frog, John Pibor			X	X										
Girard, Joseph														X
Jourdain, Baptiste							X	X	X	X				
Jourdain, Baptiste, or Est. of											X	X	X	X
Jourdain, Baptiste Daigneault												X	X	
Lachance, Charles	X	X	X	X	X					X	X	X	X	X
Lafleur, Charles										X	X	X	X	X
Lafleur, Pierre							X	X	X	X				
Laliberte, Pierre										X	X			
Lariviere, Abraham							X	X	X	X	X	X	X	X
Malboeuf, Pierre	X	X	X	X	X									
McCallum, James												X	X	
McCallum, John												X	X	
McKay, Thomas									X	X				
McKenzie, Thomas	X	X	X	X	X									
McKinnon, Robert, or Est. of										X	X			
Mirasty, David			X	X	X	X								

Mirasty, Magloire

Mirasty, Philip

Morin, Antoine, or Est. of

Morin, Baptiste

Morin, Raphaël

Morin, Widow

Morriseau, Michel

Nepetappeanaise

Rat, William

Ray, William

Robillard, Alex

Roy, François

Rupert, George

Sanderson, George C.

Sanderson, William

Sasty, Charles

Stevens, George

Sylvestre, Jean Baptiste

Tapecappo, Louison

Tawepissime, Michel

Testawich, Michel or Est. of

Touslesjour, André

SOURCE: Abstracts of Servants Accounts, Hudson's Bay Company Archives B.89/g/1, file 1.

boats were expected to depart in early to mid-May. While making these plans, Fortescue was unaware and, more importantly, uninformed until the early morning hours of 10 May, just as the boats were to depart, that an obligatory Catholic feast day fell in early May.[44]

The priests, Fortescue was told, regretted the situation and stated that although they understood the Company boats were to depart as soon as the waters were clear, plans for a 10 May departure were a complete surprise to them. Fortescue found this explanation most perplexing because he had offered Father Teston passage on those boats days earlier so that the priest could visit the Saint-Julien mission at Lac Vert. Teston had declined the offer, not because of a feast day but rather because he feared too many people were already travelling in the brigade and there would be insufficient room for him in either of the two boats. At no time between the 9th, when the boats were being loaded, and the 10th, just prior to departure, did anyone – servants or priests – inform Fortescue of a conflict between the Company's schedule and the Catholic religious calendar. So he was surprised, on the morning of the 10th, when some freemen contracted with the Company to man the boats told him that Father Rapet had warned everyone not to work because it was a holy day. Although the first boat departed prior to the unexpected announcement, the remainder of those gathered on the shore immediately quit and went to church for services, stranding the second boat.

HBC officer William Cornwallis King was present on that day and described the conflict as a problem of two stubborn personalities, Fortescue and Father Rapet, rather than an issue of institutional policy. According to King,

> The boatmen explained their position in regard to their command to go to church. Fortescue insisted that the trip must be made, and rightly. He spoke to Père Rapport [sic], accusing him of upsetting the business of the Company. Père Rapport declared he was not interfering with the men, saying he merely told them that this day was an important church holy day, though it was not compulsory for them to give up work. Fortescue insisted on the brigade leaving for Green Lake on scheduled time. The men refused to go until the next day.[45]

In King's account, he says he suggested to Fortescue that the trip be postponed, arguing that forcing the Metis to work on a holy day would only cause them to become "sulky and resentful," further hindering timely delivery of the cargo. King surmised that if they were permitted to attend church, the men would then do their best to make up the lost time because, he believed, "These men had pride in their skill as boatmen and in keeping their record."[46] Fortescue, however, refused to relent and demanded that the men depart that morning as planned. Predictably, not one man returned for duty. King stated that he then went to the Metis workers to tell them that at midnight, when the holy day ended, he expected them to report for service and depart immediately. This is precisely what happened. King was of the opinion that Fortescue, while a great officer, was a poor trader because he did not understand how his employees thought or felt about themselves, and he too often let such problems get the best of him.[47] Perhaps because he was Anglican, Fortescue was removed socially and spiritually from the population. However, Moberly was also Anglican and made great effort to accommodate the needs of the local populace. Fortescue was non-Aboriginal, had not been raised in a trade environment, and seemed to be detached from the lived experiences of the servant class. Born in Middlesex, England, he began his career with the HBC as an apprentice clerk at Moose Factory and spent most of his career at James Bay or Red River before being stationed as a chief factor at Île à la Crosse for four years in the late 1880s. Moberly, who was also non-Aboriginal, was raised in northern Ontario among Native communities, and this early experience influenced the manner in which he chose to live his later life in the West.

Justifying his actions to Joseph Wrigley, a Winnipeg-based HBC commissioner, Fortescue lamented that no one had had the courtesy to inform him sooner of the day's religious significance. Moreover, from Fortescue's point of view, Thomas Desjarlais, one of the Catholic servants employed that morning, had not stated any objection to travelling on 10 May until quite late the day before. Upon hearing of the problem, Fortescue claimed that he immediately wrote Father Teston to seek a resolution, but he said that he received no reply until six o'clock the next morning, when, for the first time, he was informed that the servants would not work.[48] From Fortescue's perspective, the priest's behaviour toward the HBC was intolerable. In his letter to Wrigley, Fortescue asked HBC officials in Winnipeg to request that the bishop of St. Boniface provide an outline of exactly how many days the Catholic servants were to be freed from their work for church festivals and services so that he could more effectively plan his year. Furthermore, Fortescue wrote (rather unconvincingly) that if the matter were not resolved, the Company should dismiss all Roman Catholic servants and employ only Protestants in the future because the Company would otherwise have no authority to command its own men.[49] This last statement was more a demonstration of frustration and false bravado than a sensible suggestion, given that the district's local labour pool was almost entirely Catholic and Metis and that even non-Catholic and non-Metis could and did convert and acculturate to community standards and expectations regarding familial obligations and responsibilities.[50]

Indeed, the very existence of the missions in the district was at least partially attributable to Metis people, who requested their presence, became congregants, and assisted in Church construction and support with labour and donations of physical space. In the early 1870s, after Cyprien Morin, the son of Antoine Morin and Pélagie Boucher, moved to the Lac Prairie region to become a rancher and farmer, he contributed his land, labour, and finances to the construction of the first Roman Catholic Church in the area. Adjacent to that mission was (and still is) St. Cyprien cemetery.[51] While the cemetery is seemingly named for Cyprien Morin, an act of naming that may be attributable to his contributions to the very establishment of the Church, it should be noted that Cyprien himself was likely named for St. Cyprien, the bishop of Carthage who contributed much of his personal fortune to the poor in the third century.[52] Like his namesake, Cyprien Morin came to be known among the Metis as a benefactor of the Roman Catholic Church in the northwest. The connection between the Metis of the region and the Church was doubtless too great for the HBC to break.

On 29 May 1888, Father Rapet wrote an official apology to Fortescue, expressing his hope that the mission and Company could remain on friendly terms despite the recent conflict. Rather ungraciously, Fortescue replied that relations had been friendly prior to the recent incident, implying that the Church alone was responsible by its recent behaviour. It took another month for goodwill to be restored between the institutions, when Father Rapet finally conceded that Fortescue had not been adequately informed of a potential problem regarding a May departure date and that something should have been done sooner to prevent the Company from inconvenience. Fortescue accepted this concession and regarded the matter resolved.[53]

The argument between Fortescue and Rapet, as presented in the HBC records, focuses on how each institution interpreted the incident. However, the key players in this drama – the Metis – were often ignored by both men, even though it was ultimately their decisions and actions that dictated whether the boats moved. The priests told the Metis boatmen that their presence was not required at church on 10 May, yet they refused to depart or work in any capacity that day, suggesting, perhaps, that the reason for their attendance was as much social as it was religious. Church activities afforded an opportunity for families to gather and, after services, to host a large communal feast. Interestingly, King reported that Rapet declared he had not "interfered" with the men – a phrase used four years later by Moberly to describe his dealings with Rapet. This shared belief that institutions were interfering with each other obscures what was happening within the Metis community. The Metis undoubtedly recognized that the Company and mission were focused on each other and worried about harm to their institutional interests, and this allowed the Metis to exploit tensions to suit their own interests.

When clergy demanded time off for religious observances, the request was normally granted by the HBC, but when conflicts arose, such as the incident in 1888, Metis servants asserted a right to do as they pleased in their homeland. Based on the records, it is often difficult to determine on whose initiative the men were released from service, but it is apparent that the Metis released themselves whenever it suited their collective interests to join together as a community instead of work. In response, the Company and Church negotiated an uneasy acceptance that there were specific times of the year when men would not work in order to participate in secular social activities centred on families.[54] From the emotional and intellectual distance of Winnipeg, HBC officials reminded their officer in charge at Île à la Crosse that he had a responsibility to maintain good relationships with the clergy for the sake of the trade, which meant, by extension, he had to maintain a good relationship with the overwhelmingly Catholic local populace, which was free by this time to seek alternative employment opportunities. For instance, in 1886, Wrigley wrote to Fortescue to remind him that it was his duty to facilitate the attendance of those in the Company's employ, as well as the Indians in the district, at church services. Apparently Fortescue had had a series of conflicts with Father Rapet prior to 1888, and Wrigley, while sympathetic, wanted his chief factor to establish a more harmonious relationship with the mission.[55] Within his directives, Wrigley specifically identified the Metis servants and Indians, populations that by this time were closely intertwined, as critical to the restoration and functioning of that relationship.

Similarly, it was in the mission's best interest that relations with the Company were cordial and professional, because although the Metis provided labour, financial support, and sometimes their spaces to the mission, the Church also depended on the HBC for some of its needs. For example, at the turn of the twentieth century, when the threat of flooding at Île à la Crosse was particularly strong, the priest turned to the

HBC to help the mission relocate. In December 1900, Thomas Anderson reported to Prince Albert that because the mission was located at the tip of the peninsula on Lac Île à la Crosse, where the land was lowest, it was at risk of being submerged by high waters when the lake thawed in the spring. Consequently, the priests were considering moving the mission five or six miles away to a more suitable location, but they needed to purchase some land from the HBC in order to do so.[56] The missionaries' fears were well founded. In 1901 the peninsula flooded between early June and the end of October, when the lake froze over again. On 13 July 1901, Mother Vicar Eugéne Letellier arrived to visit the sisters and assess the situation, although she had already requested permission from the superior general of the Order in Montreal to have the Grey Nuns removed from Île à la Crosse.[57] Permission was not obtained until December, by which time it was too late to move, so the request was withdrawn. The flood prevented the planting or harvesting of gardens, and the clergy and those they supported went hungry that winter. J. Chisholm, HBC inspector of agencies in Prince Albert, notified Île à la Crosse that in anticipation of the hardship and distress during the coming winter, the Indian Department had instructed the post to provide relief measures to the people of the region, the costs of which would be borne by the federal government. The Indian Department sent the mission and boarding school flour, tea, and bacon rations to distribute to employees and other charges. Metis and Indian populations not connected to the institutions were also to receive a gratuity of the same rations. Chisholm instructed the officials at Île à la Crosse not to encourage applications for relief and to use their discretion in determining the quantities of the rations.[58] In October 1901, thirteen of the mission's cows were butchered so that the missionaries, students, and others associated with the mission would not starve to death that winter. By April 1902, the remaining cows were so emaciated that they could not produce milk.[59] The Church's land request was forwarded to C.C. Chipman, the HBC commissioner in Winnipeg, who, in 1902, notified Île à la Crosse officials that the mission would be able to lease a reasonable amount of land indefinitely from the Company at a nominal rent, with the stipulation that these lands would only be used for Church – presumably meaning religious – purposes.[60]

Dealing with the mission and Company in a business context was a bit of a quandary for the Metis. On the one hand, the community people had the power to control their labour and social activities, deciding when and how to work as well as how to express themselves culturally. But they also relied on these two institutions to assist them with financial matters, specifically with transacting their wills and investing their savings and pensions to support their families. The death of Michel Bouvier Sr. and the subsequent dealings with his financial arrangements were an unpleasant reminder that the HBC and mission were not always to be trusted, whereas family and community could always be relied on. Surrendering financial autonomy – necessary because the Metis had no access to other financial institutions inside or outside the district – ensured that true autonomy remained elusive.

At five o'clock on the evening of 23 February 1890, Michel Bouvier Sr. died at eighty-two years of age. In preparation for the funeral rites, his sons-in-law, Vincent Daigneault and Thomy (Thomas) Lariviere, made his coffin, while HBC servant Joseph Roy dug the grave at the mission cemetery. People from throughout the district travelled to Saint-Jean-Baptiste in Île à la Crosse for the funeral, to be held at the mission on 25 February 1890. Wakes for the dead, which occurred before funerals at the mission, were equally important socio-cultural mechanisms to commemorate death and celebrate life. Although death signified the fracturing of a family, the initial commemoration, the wake, united the remaining family with the wider community in a social bond that celebrated the continuity of wahkootowin. So just as the Roy-Durocher wedding was commemorated by a dance and, as noted in Chapter 5, the family of Old Bruce hosted a wake during which the HBC men sat through the night with the body and toasted his life and their relationships as friends and colleagues, the people of the northwest came together to honour Michel Bouvier Sr. and his family.

Bouvier was born in the northwest sometime between 1801 and 1811 and worked as a steersman, guide, carpenter, interpreter, freeman, and general labourer over the course of sixty-six years in the HBC's employ at Île à la Crosse.[61] Michel Sr. may have been the son of Jean Baptiste Bouvier, who was listed as an employee at the Canadian establishment in the HBC's district census of 1821. Jean Baptiste Bouvier worked for the HBC as late as 1833, surviving the layoffs associated with the 1821 merger between the NWC and HBC. Two Jean Baptistes and a Michel Bouvier are listed in the 1833 English River Abstracts of Servants Accounts. The Jean Baptistes are Jr. and a Sr., presumably Michel Sr.'s father and brother. By the 1841 outfit, both Jean Baptistes disappear from the English River District account books, leaving only Michel.[62]

Michel Sr. and his wife, Julie Desjarlais, were one of Île à la Crosse's first-generation couples, having married and established their small family in the early 1830s. Julie Desjarlais had been previously married to Louison

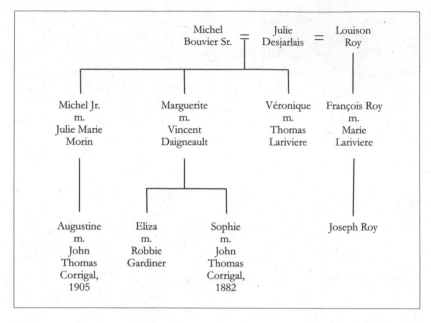

FIGURE 6.1　Bouvier genealogy

Roy, with whom she had one son, François Roy, who was a voyageur and fisherman married to Marie Lariviere. The Joseph Roy who dug Michel Sr.'s grave, then, was his grandson by his wife's first marriage.[63] The children and grandchildren of Michel Bouvier Sr. and Julie Desjarlais matured and married into other large HBC families with strong social ties to still more families – Indian and Metis – throughout the district and with a devotion to the Church. According to Company, Church, scrip, and census records, Michel and Julie Bouvier had three children together – Michel Jr. (b. 1838, Île à la Crosse), who married Julie Marie Morin; Marguerite (b. 1842, Île à la Crosse), who married Vincent Daigneault; and Véronique (b. 1857, Île à la Crosse), who married Thomas Lariviere (see Figure 6.1).[64]

The three Bouvier children and their spouses contributed to the establishment of second- and third-generation families by linking themselves and then their children to local families, such as the Morins and Larivieres, and by establishing alliances with incoming outsider males throughout the nineteenth century. By 1863, Michel Jr. was listed in the Abstracts of Servants Accounts as a Company employee, serving on HBC boats and as a general labourer. However, unlike his father, Michel Jr. was a temporary servant who rarely sold furs to the HBC, which suggests that he and his family likely lived close to the post and mission rather than in more remote parts of the district or even across the lake.[65] That he served as a fisherman and carpenter for those two institutions, jobs requiring a more consistent presence in the village, adds to the likelihood that he lived near the post. In 1868 at Île à la Crosse, Michel Jr. married Julie Marie Morin, the daughter of Raphaël Morin and Elizabeth (Betsy) Cook, and they had fourteen children.[66]

Around 1866, daughter Marguerite married Vincent Daigneault, an occasional HBC servant and freeman originally from Montreal, with whom she had ten children. Like his brother-in-law, Vincent was first listed in the Abstracts of Servants Accounts in the 1863 outfit for English River and worked as a midman and general labourer for two years before becoming a freeman. Remaining inland after his contract expired, Daigneault occasionally worked for the Company well into the 1880s as a cow herder and carpenter before contracting with the mission in the early 1890s, along with his two sons-in-law, John Corrigal and Robbie Gardiner.[67] Véronique, Michel Sr. and Julie's youngest child, married Thomas or Thomy Lariviere of Souris River, the adopted son of Abraham Lariviere and Mary Petawchamwistewin (also known as Ee-Ya-Nis), in 1875 at Île à la Crosse (see Photo 6.1). Thomy first appeared in the Abstracts of Servants Accounts in 1864 as a midman, rising to the rank of guide a decade later.[68] The Bouvier children each established families that connected them to the HBC and the mission through their labour and commitment to the ideals of the Church. Significantly, these three related men – Corrigal, Daigneault, and Gardiner – began working for the mission at about the time that the family patriarch died, an incident that underscores the manner in which families attempted to care for one another.

According to post records, in the days leading up to his death, Michel Sr. sent for Isaac Cowie, junior chief trader at Île à la Crosse, and a Mr. Archie to serve as witnesses to his last will and testament. As they assembled, Bouvier declared before his family and the two witnesses that each of his three children should receive $100, with the remainder of the estate going to his "old wife." Cowie wrote that Julie Desjarlais Bouvier would probably give a certain portion of the sum intended for her to the mission because of her piety and sense of responsibility to the Church.[69] Michel Sr.'s death, like John Harper's, encouraged his heirs to begin putting their own affairs in order so that the family would not be left destitute by the passing of their patriarch. Like Charlotte Harper (see Chapter 5), the Bouviers asked the HBC for assistance, but they also turned to the Church, and the story of their dealings with the central religious and

PHOTO 6.1   Born in 1831 in the vicinity of Île à la Crosse, Abraham Lariviere was perhaps the son of François Lariviere (b. 1797) of L'Assomption, Quebec, who became a servant of the trade in 1820 and retired at Red River. According to the *Liber Animarum* for Île à la Crosse, Abraham was an old Metis and a patriarch of the Lariviere family. He married a Cree woman, Mary Petawchamwistewin, also of Île à la Crosse, and adopted her son, Thomas (Thomy), in 1842. Lariviere's family shared ties with Larivieres from the Green Lake region. In addition to Thomas, Abraham also adopted Samuel Misponas (originally L'Esperance), and he and Mary had seven more children. In this photo, Lariviere is sitting in the priest's residence at Île à la Crosse in front of a picture that depicts Lacombe's or the Catholic ladder, a drawing that was used to teach Aboriginal converts in North America about the virtues of Roman Catholicism. In Lacombe's drawing, two paths represent the choices that face an individual. The path of evil is represented by idolatry, paganism, and the seven capital sins, while the path of righteousness is exemplified by the virtues and sacraments of the Roman Catholic Church. | *"Abraham Lariviere," Oblates of Mary Immaculate, Visite Pastorale, Île à la Crosse* | St. Boniface Historical Society, N3507

economic institutions in the English River District underscores the interaction between Western and Aboriginal cultural values in the nineteenth century. The Bouvier family and their extended families had a history of working for the HBC and also of supporting the Church with their piety and labour. The legacy of the Bouvier family's closeness to the Church is evident in the village's spatial configuration. Historically, the mission was located at the end of the peninsula on Lac Île à la Crosse's shoreline, in an area called Bouvierville because, by all accounts, the family had always lived near the mission, not out on the land or nearer the post.[70] Perhaps it was because they lived near the mission grounds that their engagement as Church labourers was an easy transition. They supplied the missionaries with fish, worked in their gardens, and supported the Church with their devotion and financial contributions.

After serving over six decades in the HBC's service, Michel Sr. retired from the fur trade in the late 1880s and began collecting a Company pension of £40 per year. The Company guaranteed his pension in a written agreement that specified the amount paid to him for the rest of his life as long as he lived in the district. This pension became the subject of a great deal of discussion after his death and framed an important narrative about the intersection of familial expectations and interests, the Roman Catholic mission, and the HBC. Bouvier's pension was a special case for the HBC because, unlike others, it was apparently an expense borne by the district, not the central administration in Winnipeg, and it specified that the retired servant remain in the district. In his will, Michel Sr. was apparently referring to his accumulated personal savings as the source for his survivors' future financial security, but it is unclear how he amassed that sum of money. Was he able to save some of his wages and invest wisely, or was it based on his pension?

In August 1890, six months after the senior Bouvier's death, George C. Sanderson, the Île à la Crosse carpenter, contacted W. Beacher, the Company's Winnipeg accountant, asking that the status of Bouvier's bequest to his family be reviewed. At this stage, some confusion arose over the issue of Bouvier's pension versus his accumulated savings. The family believed that the Company had managed their patriarch's savings, but the official response from Winnipeg did not address the savings, dealing instead with the pension. The Company was under the mistaken impression that the family wanted the pension to continue and be distributed to them in perpetuity. Beacher informed Sanderson that when Bouvier died, the pension was stopped because, without the commissioner's written approval, there was no authority to continue dispensing it to the Bouvier family. Furthermore, according to Beacher, if Sanderson sought additional information regarding any monies belonging to Bouvier, he needed to contact the commissioner directly.[71] With the exception of the pension, Beacher had no knowledge of any savings held by the Company to be distributed to Michel Bouvier Sr.'s heirs.

By November 1890, the estate was still not settled, and the Bouviers were still asserting their intentions to retrieve monies rightfully belonging to them. Julie Desjarlais Bouvier (who was now living with her daughter Marguerite and son-in-law Vincent Daigneault) and two of her children, Michel Jr. and Marguerite, were by this time borrowing from the Île à la Crosse mission as they awaited distribution of the estate. In a letter to Moberly in November 1890, the mission requested reimbursement for the Bouvier family's debts, stating that Julie Desjarlais owed $13.15, Michel Jr. $5.00, and Marguerite $4.00. There is nothing to indicate why the mission believed the Company was responsible for repayment except that the Bouviers had an outstanding claim with the Company. Nineteen months after the elder Bouvier's death, Moberly was still trying to arrange with Winnipeg the settlement of the estate for the benefit of the heirs, while the family continued to rely on the mission for financial support. In turn, local officers in charge paid the Church out of the district's accounts and then charged it against the Bouvier family's inheritance, which officials in Winnipeg still claimed to have no knowledge of.[72] Local HBC officials like Moberly and Sanderson did what they could to help the Bouviers. There was no reason for Moberly to pay debts owed to the mission except, perhaps, his sense of obligation to this family that had worked hard for the HBC for over six decades. Charging the repayment against their accounts would have been standard procedure and required of Moberly. His persistent letter writing to Winnipeg on behalf of the Bouviers is evidence of his effort to assist this family within the authority of his position.

Over two years after his death, Michel Bouvier's estate was still not settled, and now the Bouvier children formally wrote to Moberly on their mother's behalf, requesting information about the inheritance. They further asked that the Company take the necessary steps to check on their accounts, inform them what debts needed to be paid, and indicate how much money remained in the estate. On 12 November 1892 – two weeks after Julie Desjarlais Bouvier's death – Donald A. Smith in Winnipeg finally released the inheritance and credited it to that year's English River District outfit. The total balance in the Bouvier estate was £112.60 ($563.00).[73] Chief Factor Lawrence Clarke of Prince Albert notified

Moberly that the money was to be divided equally between the children, but only after all debts to the HBC were repaid. Clarke added that Moberly was not to pay the mission until given instructions to do so. By this time, according to the Company accounts, the Bouvier family owed the mission $506.95 (£101.39) and the HBC another $148.10 (£29.62), for a total owing of $655.05 (£131.01).[74] After the HBC was repaid, the Bouviers were left with $414.90, which was $92.05 less than their debt to the mission. It is unclear whether the HBC released the remaining funds to the mission, but the two-year delay before final dispersal of the estate was evidently extremely frustrating to the Bouviers. It is reasonable to assume that the family developed a significant degree of bitterness toward the local institutions that contributed to their growing indebtedness. It is also unclear whether the family actually owed those amounts. Presumably, the men – Vincent, Michel Jr., and Thomy – were all working for either the HBC or the mission during this time and were earning wages. But it is evident that the Winnipeg officials, unlike local officers, had no regard for the family's circumstances and had contributed to an increasing financial hardship when it had the ability to place in their hands a significant amount of money that would have established a more solid financial future for the Bouviers. The mission's dealings with the Company regarding the debt, furthermore, appear to have taken place without input from the Bouviers, surely leaving the family with some level of resentment toward the Church as well.

Yet within this uncertainty, the Metis had some overall measure of social, religious, and economic autonomy, which they asserted within their own sphere of influence in the English River District. The contested space between the Hudson's Bay Company and the Roman Catholic Church gave the local Metis an opportunity to assert an important form of political economy that supported their families and cultural expressions. Feasting, dancing, refusal to labour on religious days, arranged marriages, and other events and activities were all expressions of a cultural identity, but they were also important political assertions. The Metis community recognized and exploited the growing tensions between the HBC and mission, generating and tapping political and economic strength that would eventually threaten the Company's profitability and shake the mission's claim as arbitrator of morality. Traditions, secular or religious, were important outlets to communicate this self-determination to the priests and Company officials, who too often concentrated on the actions of the other institution while failing to realize how independent the Metis spirit had become by the end of the century. This contested space only widened throughout the century. As the following chapter demonstrates, the growth of a free-trading economy ensured that the HBC's dominance of the region's economy was never complete.

7

"I thought it advisable to furnish him"

Freemen to Free Traders in the
Northwest Fur Trade

In an 1892 post report submitted by Green Lake clerk George Dreaver to Chief Trader Henry J. Moberly at Île à la Crosse, Pierriche Laliberte and James Nicol Sinclair are described as retired and pensioned Company servants occasionally employed as freemen to deliver furs to local posts.[1] Dreaver advised, however, that the pensions be revoked and that Laliberte and Sinclair no longer be permitted to work for the Company as freemen because they were attempting to trade for their own gain in opposition to the Company's monopoly.[2] Moberly disagreed with the recommendation, asserting that revoking Laliberte's pension, and barring him from trading, would be a serious error. In a letter to Winnipeg, Moberly argued that Laliberte had "a huge part of his family married and settled in the vicinity of Green Lake, and by his keeping a small stock of goods, which are actually sold by some of his sons under his inspection, his sons are kept from taking Outfits to oppose the HBC from the Merchants at Prince Albert and as we gain by the Transaction in more ways than one, I thought it advisable to furnish him."[3] Moberly also suspected that Laliberte was trading against the HBC, but he nevertheless ensured that Pierriche obtained his trading outfit from Île à la Crosse that year (instead of getting it from Prince Albert, Lac La Biche, Fort McMurray, or Winnipeg) in an attempt to pre-empt any further action against the Company. In return for receiving his outfit from Île à la Crosse, Laliberte sold all the furs that he had collected at a reasonable price to the English

River District and, perhaps more importantly, employed some of his sons in his operations, keeping them from becoming free traders in opposition to the region's posts.[4]

The story of Pierriche Laliberte highlights how fluidly men moved across the HBC employment spectrum in the course of a lifetime. Two years prior to Dreaver and Moberly's exchange, Pierriche – the seventy-three-year-old husband of Sarazine Morin, patriarch of the Laliberte family, and postmaster of Portage La Loche – notified his superiors at Île à la Crosse that he wanted to retire from the service the following spring. Pierriche requested a Company pension and permission to retire near Lac Vert. To establish Laliberte's right to a pension, Moberly provided the administrative office in Winnipeg with information about Laliberte's age, length of service, and other particulars about his life and work for the Company. In turn, Moberly was informed that Laliberte owed $1,984 on his Company accounts, which would have to be paid in full when he retired.[5] After several further inquiries to Winnipeg, Laliberte was granted a pension in the fall of 1890, and he, Sarazine, and their granddaughter Adélaide moved to the Lac Vert region, where several sons and their families already resided. Although retired, Pierriche remained in the occasional employ of the Company as a freeman, collecting and delivering furs to the Lac Vert and Île à la Crosse posts until 1892, when it appeared that he began free trading.

As explained in the previous chapter, by mid-century there was an array of employment choices open to men and women in the English River District. At one end of the spectrum were the permanently contracted servants, such as chief factors, chief traders, clerks, postmasters, interpreters, boat builders, tripmen, and blacksmiths, who received annual wages, food rations, and/or housing in return for their services in these highly specialized positions. While a few local men or outsider males who had been incorporated into the local family system performed specialized jobs, none were chief factors, traders, or even clerks, with the exception of James Nicol Sinclair, who was chief trader at Lac Vert and stepfather-in-law to Pierriche Laliberte's son Louis (more commonly called Roy). Unlike Sinclair, chief factors and traders were usually Anglo-Protestants with little direct influence over wahkootowin in the northwest, although they certainly impacted the economic operations of families.

Local men with permanent contracts were normally assigned roles in the lower ranks of servants and officers as postmasters, interpreters, runners, and Indian traders in the district outposts. The position of postmaster was an especially popular assignment for the Aboriginal sons of former servants and was generally filled by family men like Pierriche Laliberte at Portage La Loche or his son Alexandre Laliberte at Canoe Lake. The position, a rank between interpreter and clerk, was created especially for men who had gained reputations of steadiness, honesty, and attention to duty. After 1832, postmasters were also "young Men the half breed sons or Relatives of Gentlemen in the Country who could not obtain admission to the Service as Apprentice Clerks."[6] Similarly, interpreters were often local men like Magloire Maurice who were proficient in several languages and well connected to local communities, while clerks required some basic literacy skills in order to maintain their post's records.

At the other end of the Company's employment spectrum were the hunters and fishermen, such as the Aubichon, Merasty, and Misponas men, who supplied the Company with its country produce. Often in these instances the oldest male ancestor in the family had been a Company man, but one who lived away from the posts, only occasionally coming in to a place like Île à la Crosse, yet still benefiting from having a working relationship with local officials.[7] In between these two extremes was the basic labouring class, men who were contracted to perform the manual labour necessary to operate the posts and, indeed, the districts.

Existing outside these official employment categories were the freemen and free traders. Freemen families were engaged in limited contracts with the HBC and were hired to guide, freight, interpret, trade, and transport – in short, they did much the same job as a contracted servant. Freemen, however, signed on only occasionally and/or seasonally rather than maintaining regular or permanent employment. Freemen were not free traders, who were independent operators trading solely for personal profit. While there is an obvious distinction between freemen and free traders, the boundary between the two sometimes became blurred in the late nineteenth century. The terms were sometimes used interchangeably, perhaps because the men themselves moved freely between the range of employment options available to them, and it was difficult for the Company to keep track of everyone's activities. Freemen could become free traders when it benefited the economic needs of their families and the socio-cultural notions embedded in the reciprocal family model. When freemen moved beyond a role defined, supported, or encouraged by the Company, they were quickly labelled free traders – a descriptor infused with negative connotations by the HBC. Additionally, because free traders had no regular salary or contract with the Company, they had no regular access to Company produce, rations, housing, or other amenities.[8] Men and women in the northwest often participated in an array of employment niches, following a strategy of economic choices that maximized the well-being of their families.

Familial relationships, such as those established by the Laliberte family, created a social framework and reflected the evolution of a Metis cultural identity that affected economic operations at Île à la Crosse and other posts throughout the district. The social behaviour and cultural values of Metis families expressed by wahkootowin influenced economic decisions such as those that inspired men like Pierriche to become first freemen and, later, free traders. By the end of the nineteenth century, Metis cultural identity had a role to play in determining the nature of trade relations within the home territories. Rather than being wholly shaped by the necessities of trade, the Metis worldview (which differed from that of the HBC's European and Canadian managers) centred on relatedness, emphasizing the potential for creating relationships that both augmented and challenged the HBC's authority over the fur trade. Furthermore, the HBC as an institution was incorporated, however unwillingly, into the Metis familial structure because of the holistic nature of this worldview. When they were in service and had a good economic relationship with the Company, the Metis strove to keep the HBC within their socio-cultural framework by treating it as a member of the family. They came to rely on it for a variety of needs, including investing savings, dispensing rations, and providing housing. However, when the HBC failed to act as a good relative – putting profits ahead of the interests of the people or dismissing servants because of economic downsizing – heads of families such as Pierriche had to locate alternative means to support their immediate and extended families. In either situation, regardless of whether they were servants of the Company or acting as freemen or free traders, the Metis sought to pursue their interests and those of their relatives, which may or may not have included the HBC, depending on the Company's own behaviour.

This chapter is an analysis of how families in the English River District asserted their greatest form of economic self-determination by becoming free traders in the latter half of the nineteenth century, overtly challenging the Company's authority in the trade economy. The Company's belief in the existence of free trading and the power of families to direct trade is evident in post journals and general correspondence – and in the minds of local officials, it was a very real threat to the HBC. Dreaver and Moberly both noted in 1892 that the threat of free trading did not rest with just one man but potentially involved his entire family and close colleagues. By the time Pierriche retired in 1890, many of his sons, a son-in-law,

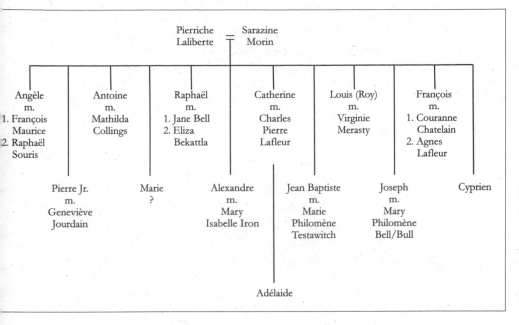

FIGURE 7.1   Laliberte genealogy

brothers-in-law, and other members of his extended family were employed by the Company in various capacities, several of them in the district's key trade and transport regions at Portage La Loche and Green Lake and as runners throughout the district, as noted on King's map (see Chapter 3). At least seven of Pierriche's nine sons worked closely with him in the English River District, assisting him with district trade operations until they were old enough to become servants with their own contracts and career paths (see Figure 7.1, as well as Chapter 3).

Pierriche Laliberte and his family may have been somewhat atypical. Few others in the district received such intense scrutiny by Company officials within the English River District's records. But the possibility that any Metis family wielded enough socio-economic power to threaten the Company's sense of economic security warrants a re-evaluation of the HBC's authority to direct the behaviour or choices of Metis families within this district.[9] I will explore more fully the influence of Metis family life on the fur trade, examining the experiences of several families, including the Lablibertes, Lafleurs, Janviers, and Delarondes, as they worked for and against the Company's interests in the region as servants, freemen, and free traders.

Pierriche Laliberte was one of the most discussed men in the English River District's records. He was first hired on with the Company in 1838 at twenty-one years of age, and he worked on and off for the Company in the district for almost his entire adult life. Although he retired periodically during his fifty-two years of labour, Pierriche regularly re-engaged with the Company in various capacities, including steersman, general labourer, trader, interpreter, and finally postmaster before becoming a freeman. As an HBC servant, Pierriche worked throughout the district at the larger posts of Île à la Crosse, Green Lake, and Portage La Loche. After his 1842 or 1843 marriage to Sarazine Morin, he became the head of an increasingly large family and was able to send at least two of his sons to St. Boniface College in Red River, an expensive venture for a servant whose highest rank was postmaster of a northern district's outpost. While his sons were in school in Manitoba, Laliberte paid the Company to have them return yearly on the spring brigades travelling to English River so that the family could maintain its closeness despite the separation.[10]

Attesting to the power of the Laliberte connections in the trade and Pierriche's particular effectiveness as a Company servant, French-speaking Pierriche was postmaster in a region critical to the transportation system of the district, and by extension the entire northern trade, despite being completely unable to read, write, or speak English to communicate with his largely English-speaking superiors. While Pierriche was working as an interpreter for Chief Trader Samuel McKenzie in 1857, Île à la Crosse chief factor George Deschambeault suggested that he be promoted to postmaster of Portage La Loche because he was "industrious, careful and interested."[11] Furthermore, "he can make wheels and carts, and I do not see a better hand in the country than this Pierre La Liberte. He is at the same time a first rate trader and all the Indians like and respect him."[12] Deschambeault's request was granted, and Pierriche was promoted that year. At Portage La Loche, he was responsible for overseeing the Portage La Loche brigade, maintaining Methy Portage, hiring men to support tasks associated with the portage, engaging in general trade duties, and travelling to Carlton when necessary to obtain dry goods for the post.[13]

It was not until he achieved the rank of postmaster in 1857 that Pierriche's potential to disrupt Company trade became a real possibility. HBC officers were faced with the prospect of an extremely skilled trader and manager, living inland, who had forged for himself a marital alliance with another large and well-connected family, the Morins, and who now had adult children beginning to forge their own alliances and further expand the family's connections to other HBC families and Indian communities. At the same time, the Company faced a growing threat to its monopoly in the form of free traders entering the English River District from Manitoba and northern Alberta. For example, Pierriche's son Alexandre dealt with William Venne, a free trader at Canoe Lake, who had gained the trade of several of that region's Indian families.[14] During the 1870s, François Maurice dealt with free traders in his territory at Portage La Loche. In a December 1873 letter, Île à la Crosse chief factor William McMurray notified Maurice that his (Maurice's) wife's uncle, Raphaël Morin, had returned to Île à la Crosse in the fall with an "astonishing ten cart loads" of goods from Manitoba, and it was believed that he would be travelling north in the spring to trade with the Dene.[15] McMurray further informed Maurice that two men, one named Primeau and the other Louis Mariou, had established themselves at Cold Lake and Goose Lake with a large supply of goods. McMurray was concerned that Primeau, who knew the Indians of the area quite well, would be particularly successful in his trading goals, and he wanted Maurice to send two of his most trustworthy men into those regions to collect the furs from a man named Delttaize and some other Dene men.[16]

In his 1874 retirement plan, Pierriche Laliberte expressed a desire to become a freeman, purchase his outfit from Manitoba, and operate on the Green Lake Road, which connected the English River District to Carlton. He asked McMurray to help him reach an agreement with the Company to obtain twenty draught oxen, harnesses and carts, and goods from Fort Garry at Red River. McMurray endorsed and forwarded the proposal to Winnipeg, adding his belief that Pierriche was "honest & reliable" and would make an excellent freighter. Furthermore, McMurray did not "think that Mr. Laliberte has any intentions of setting up as a 'free trader' if he can do otherwise."[17] Perhaps more importantly, according to McMurray, Laliberte "is besides connected with the Morins and others in this district – If he were to get a contract for Freight, his relatives would receive employment from him, and would thus be prevented from entering the service of our opponents."[18] In other words, by giving Laliberte a legitimate freeman's business to operate, the Company believed it would avoid facing opposition from his sons or extended relatives, who would be more inclined to support their relative than oppose the Company.

A year after retiring, Pierriche changed his mind and decided to re-engage for at least one more contract. In the spring of 1875, he also decided to have his two sons return from St. Boniface College to work with him in the district. McMurray directed officials in Winnipeg to make arrangements for the boys' travel to Lac Vert, with the understanding that Laliberte would repay all expenses.[19] The decision to bring his two sons home meant that Pierriche was not only able to employ his sons at Green Lake but also, and more importantly, could fortify the presence of his family network in the area through their social and economic efforts. This was surely a tactical manoeuvre intended to send a message to the Company not to trifle with the Laliberte family, as well as to strengthen the family by bringing all members together. This took on greater importance the next year when Pierriche began discussing his retirement yet again. By this time, Pierriche felt that, given the demands of his trading operation, his position as postmaster at Green Lake was requiring too much of him.[20]

The comments written about Laliberte's character in 1876-77 were much less flattering than those written two years earlier. Indeed, the Company no longer described him as "honest and reliable." Although still regarded as an excellent postmaster, his inability to read or write was now an "embarrassment" and a hindrance to the Company's reputation, one that made Green Lake a less reputable post.[21] The Company sought to relocate Pierriche to a smaller outpost, but he refused reassignment, indicating that he wanted Green Lake to be his retirement home.[22] Despite the Company's obvious lack of respect for Laliberte, McMurray must have believed that it was still beyond his capacity to force him out of the area, for Pierriche remained at Green Lake. Ideally, from a Company perspective, when Pierriche retired he should have left the English River District and gone to Manitoba or elsewhere, as he had done in 1849 (when he left the service and moved to Red River before re-engaging in 1851 as a steersman, which allowed him to return to the northwest).[23] This, perhaps, more than anything else, spoke to Laliberte's influence – he was able to prevent the Company from either relocating him from his adopted homeland or demoting him to a lower position. However, he was subsequently denied an opportunity to retire until his current contract ended, and so he remained managing the Green Lake post.

Despite friction with the Company over his retirement plans, in 1876 Laliberte continued to hope that he would be permitted to establish a freighting business as a freeman when his contract expired. However, he knew that he would need Company assistance to obtain contracts and procure goods to haul. Negative comments about Pierriche's literacy notwithstanding, McMurray supported Laliberte's post-retirement plans, and although he understood that the Company did not like to extend credit to individuals who were establishing their own business ventures, he wrote that in this case the HBC should make an exception. McMurray stated that as long as Laliberte received aid, he would not contribute to the betterment of actual free-trading opponents, and he cited Paul Delaronde Sr. as an example of that disreputable type of competitor. Delaronde, a known "Indian trader," was associated with Sarazine (Morin) Laliberte's sister Sophie and had just recently moved into the Lac Vert area. McMurray felt that Delaronde wanted Laliberte's assistance in his free-trading efforts. As part of his final plea, McMurray asked the Company to remember that Laliberte and his sons could not afford to lead an idle life at Lac Vert. They required something to occupy their time; otherwise they would surely begin their own free-trading operations.[24] Laliberte retired in the spring of 1876 and immediately went to Winnipeg to negotiate a freighting agreement with the Company for an operation in the English River District. He was obviously successful, because the next time he is mentioned in the Île à la Crosse records is in June 1877, when his men arrive at the post to begin freighting.

It is unclear what exactly occurred next, but by 1879 Laliberte was back in service at Green Lake, although no longer in charge of the post. According to Ewan McDonald, chief trader for Île à la Crosse from 1876 to 1883, Laliberte still desired to be a freighter and remain at Green Lake, but he took a contract as an assistant postmaster. McDonald further stated that he knew Laliberte had been "removed" from service by Company officials because his illiteracy and inability to speak or understand English made him incapable of managing the Green Lake post. Still, McDonald felt that Pierriche's ability to work effectively with the Indians and speak their language(s) made him a good employee and effective assistant to the new postmaster. Despite this ambivalence about his abilities, Laliberte remained in the Company's employ at Green Lake until June 1882. In that year, according to McDonald, Laliberte was still refusing to move away from Green Lake, even after his official retirement. With no other options, McDonald arranged for Laliberte to live in his own house, apart from the post, but on the understanding that he would have to look after his own living. The Company was clearly not committing itself to help Laliberte establish his own business or pay a pension that would support him and his large family.[25]

By the late 1880s, Pierriche Laliberte once again had a Company contract, this time as the postmaster at Portage La Loche. The 1889 Portage La Loche post report recorded that one of the HBC's houses was occupied by Pierriche, Sarazine, and an unnamed daughter, likely their granddaughter, Adélaide Lafleur, whom they raised after their daughter Catherine died in 1873.[26] Despite his often combative relationship with the Company, Pierriche was still regarded as a good and honest trader, although it was felt that, at seventy-two years of age, he was becoming too old for active service. Pierriche was not alone at the Portage La Loche post. Just as at Green Lake, his children continued to play a pivotal role in their father's career. His sons Baptiste and Antoine were at Portage La Loche with their families, as was his daughter Angèle and her family.[27]

In 1868, when their father was in charge of the Green Lake post, Pierre Jr. and Antoine were trading and transporting goods from Carlton to Green Lake and travelling to Île à la Crosse to obtain the year's outfit for their father's post.[28] Antoine eventually tended the Company's cattle at Methy Portage and hauled wood for the HBC in the winter, agreeing to be paid half the going rate for his work in the winter of 1890 on the condition that he be given any calves born under his care.[29] This arrangement reflected the significance of the Methy Portage transportation network and the importance of those servants who worked in that aspect of the business. By the time of the 1821 merger, one of the English River District's key operations was the trade and transport activity at Methy Portage. In 1823, the York boats, notable for their size and capacity, were in regular use on that portage, adding to the sheer physical labour required to transport furs, goods, and boats along it. The introduction of York boats necessitated the use of horses and oxen to transport goods and furs as well as to haul the boats across the portage. This, in turn, meant that entire communities like Portage La Loche and Bull's House, the feeding place for Methy Portage livestock, were devoted to the care and upkeep of animals and boats.[30] As a result, Company cattlekeepers like Antoine Laliberte, Robbie Gardiner, and Vincent Daigneault held critical positions in the late-nineteenth-century English River District trade. Unlike his brothers, Pierre Jr. was an occasional labourer and fisherman – perhaps a freeman – for the Company.[31] François, a man not discussed in much detail in Company records, was also a hunter, fisherman, and labourer in the Lac Vert area.[32]

All the Libertes listed on the sketch map had long and varied careers with the Company that were, because of their father's operations, troublesome for the HBC. Baptiste Laliberte was his father's successor as postmaster at Portage La Loche in 1890, after Pierriche's retirement, and was his brother Louis' (Roy) superior. The Company had apprenticed Baptiste with his father at Portage La Loche, and after a total of eight years in the service he was deemed reliable enough to be made a clerk in 1892. That was the same year his father was accused of free trading, and Moberly was concerned that Pierriche's sons might also become free traders if their father were not placated. It is unclear whether the promotion occurred because Baptiste threatened to leave the service entirely if he were not made a clerk and given a wage increase, but the timing of this threat is certainly significant.[33] In light of this, it is not surprising that Baptiste was re-engaged as postmaster on another three-year contract and at a higher rate of pay.[34] Like his father, Baptiste had an uneven relationship with the HBC, and the Company's assessment of him was that while he was a fairly good man, he was undoubtedly "under priestly influence and very likely assisting the Traders."[35]

Baptiste was not the only Laliberte son suspected of, or indeed engaged in, free trading. Alexandre served as Green Lake postmaster in 1892, an appointment that came after he had operated the outpost at Canoe Lake from 1888 to 1890. In the spring of 1899, Alexandre retired from the Company and took a position with a Prince Albert trader who, Company officials were convinced, had unduly encouraged Alexandre to retire. At some point, Alexandre was rehired by the Company, but he retired again in 1902 and began working for Revillon Frères. This was much to the Company's regret, for he, like his father, was an excellent trader.[36]

The sentiment expressed by Dreaver and Company officials in Winnipeg in 1892 – that Pierriche's pension be revoked and he no longer be permitted to work as a freeman because he was attempting to free trade – was at odds with the reality of life in the northwest. By this time, family loyalty often superseded loyalty to the Company because the power of those families was rooted in four generations of custom and tradition. Moberly understood this and knew it would be a mistake to withdraw Pierriche's pension because of the possibility that the Laliberte family might interpret the move as a call to economic arms, which might convince Pierriche to begin trading against the Company. The influence of Pierriche, the patriarch of the Laliberte extended family network, reached beyond his own children and potentially included his wife's relatives, the Morins, and other relatives created through the marriages of his sons and daughters.

In their homeland, servants' families forged large and powerful cultural, social, and spiritual alliances through the intrafamilial, intergenerational connections that impacted their economic decisions and, to no small degree, directed the Company's trade. As a result, because wahkootowin, as a system of values that influenced behaviours, was so pervasive throughout the region, Moberly had clear cause to warn the Company against revoking the elder Laliberte's pension. Moberly cautioned that not only would Pierriche engage in free trading if his pension were cancelled, but his sons would also begin trading against the Company in support of their father. The extent of the Laliberte employment with the Company gains significance when juxtaposed against the backdrop of family life. These men collectively derived their economic power by keeping their familial alliances solid and well connected. Through marriage, the Lalibertes were directly related to the Maurice, Souris, Lafleur, Jourdain, Collings, Bekattla, Iron, Testawitch, Merasty, Bell/Bull, and Chatelain families (see Figure 7.1). By the late 1870s, the Laliberte and Morin families were deeply entwined because of the marriage of Sarazine and Pierriche. Furthermore, five of Sarazine's younger brothers held contracts with the Company and lived throughout the district with equally large families, while two of her sisters were married to HBC servants.

From this first critical family alliance, the breadth of the Laliberte and Morin connections to other HBC families grew with each generation. Two of Pierriche and Sarazine's daughters were married to HBC servants, François Maurice and Charles Pierre Lafleur. The Laliberte sons were likewise connected to HBC or Indian families of the region. Pierre Jr. married Géneviève Jourdain, the daughter of Jean Baptiste Jourdain, another HBC servant from Montreal, and Margaret Bear (L'Ours), a Cree woman from the northwest. Antoine was first married to a woman who, although unnamed in the records, was the daughter of HBC servant George C. Sanderson. By the 1870s, Antoine may have married Mathilda Collings (also known by the surnames Fraser and/or Clement), about whom no other information was recorded. Raphaël was first married to Jane Bell or Bull of the northwest before marrying Eliza (or Aloïsa) Bekattla, daughter of hunter, trapper, and occasional HBC labourer George Bekattla and Nancy Kippling. Jean Baptiste was married to Marie Philomène Testawitch of Lac Vert. Louis (or Roy) Laliberte married Virginie Merasty, daughter of Bazile Merasty and Josephte Durocher, also of Lac Vert. In the Green Lake records, Roy was listed as the stepson-in-law of James Nicol Sinclair, the former HBC employee who was now married to Josephte Durocher and was also accused by the Company of free trading in 1892.[37] Joseph married Mary Philomène Bell or Bull, while François married first Couranne Chatelain of the northwest and later Agnes Lafleur of Sakitawak, the daughter of Baptiste Charlot Lafleur and Angélique Jourdain (see Figure 7.2).

Finally, at the district's southern end, Alexandre Laliberte was married to Mary Isabelle (or Elizabeth) Iron, daughter of Chief Raphaël Iron of Nehiyo-wapasi. Mary Isabelle's family connections made Alexandre of particular value to the Company.[38]

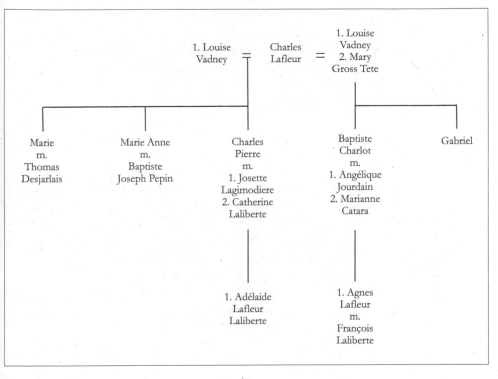

FIGURE 7.2   Lafleur genealogy

As these families spread out across the district, becoming associated with particular communities, their living arrangements reflected the early Cree and Dene heritages and distinct territorial boundaries within the region. Apart from the Lalibertes, the Morins were the only other family in the English River District to live at all three main posts – Île à la Crosse, Green Lake, and Portage La Loche – as well as smaller communities such as Devil's Lake, Lac la Caribou (Reindeer Lake) on the Shell River, and Lac Prairie. The Lafleur and Merasty families, for instance, were based at Sakitawak, Nehiyo-wapasi, and Lac Vert, while the Bekattla family was known to be from Portage La Loche, Bull's House, and Sakitawak. Although a relatively small family, the Bekattlas were well respected by other Metis families and the HBC throughout region. Many of these families, like the Irons, have been known historically as both Metis and Cree (or Dene). The Iron family were signatories to Treaty No. 10 in 1906 and became members of the Nehiyo-wapasi Cree Indian band, while James Nicol Sinclair's wife, Josephte Durocher, was a Treaty No. 6

signatory. The Sinclairs, Jourdains, and Girards were all well-established HBC families working in the Île à la Crosse and Green Lake areas. Based on these direct extended family connections to Indian and Metis communities throughout the northwest, the Company had every reason to be wary of the power that Pierriche and, by extension, the entire Laliberte family might exert in redirecting the trade and opposing the Company if they so chose.

Clearly, one of the HBC's greatest concerns was that experienced servants with equally experienced sons would disengage and become free traders and assist other trading firms. It was unlikely, in the latter half of the century, that retired servants, especially those born and raised inland, who were married and had families, would willingly or quietly retire to Europe, eastern Canada, or even Red River. Rather, they were more likely to engage in alternative economies in their own homelands and among their relatives. Throughout the nineteenth century, men and women engaged in a variety of economic activities to support themselves and fulfill roles important to the HBC, but it was not necessarily cost effective for the Company to assign these tasks to contracted servants. The economic niche of freemen, therefore, expanded in relevance and became a payment-for-service position, eventually contributing to the establishment of the free-trader class by the late 1850s. It was in this era that the term "freeman" officially indicated men retired from the service, however temporary that retirement might be, who lived inland and occasionally contracted with the Company as labourers and freighters or purchased trade outfits and then sold the furs they obtained back to the Company. Free traders, however, were involved with commercial trading outfits that infringed on the Company's monopoly, taking profits away from the post of origin while often supported and supplied by competing HBC trade districts, if not actual independent fur companies.

Certainly by the 1850s, American and small independent fur companies were openly operating throughout western and northern Canada. It appears that after 1870, free traders at Île à la Crosse purchased trade outfits from Lac La Biche, Fort McMurray, Prince Albert, and Winnipeg and then sold their furs to those locations, diverting fur returns and profits from the English River District. For instance, a July 1892 entry in the Île à la Crosse post journal notes that Michel Bouvier Sr. went to meet with American traders.[39] Several years later, the post report for the 1896-97 season noted that the post was experiencing competition from Lac La Biche, especially from Louis'on (or Louison) Janvier.[40] Similarly, a 1900 Portage La Loche letter from clerk John Bell titled a "Report of Fur Trade

Outfit, 1900" noted that two men, Marcelain and Lalonde, along with Elliam Gordon, had their traders in that region all winter, well stocked with provisions and dry goods. No details about Marcelain and Lalonde were given, but Gordon was described as being from Fort McMurray and, unlike the others, personally supervising his own business at Portage La Loche.[41] At roughly the same time, Revillon Frères, the Paris-based furrier, diversified its operations and began opening up fur posts in the Canadian subarctic to compete with the HBC.[42]

Issuing pensions to men such as Pierriche Laliberte was an effective investment to prevent having well-placed family men engage in free trading. The Company loathed doing it but believed that men who had drawn on their family connections to ensure steady and profitable trade for the HBC could easily use those same connections to support individual commercial endeavours. In a 1 June 1891 letter to the department office, Moberly made the following assessment of an unidentified pensioner:

> In consideration of the services rendered to the HBCo during a long life time and his honesty and good character as well as the fact that all his sons [as] long as they lived here always worked faithfully for the HBCo I have granted him a Pension of 50MB a year from this date as long as I remain in charge of Isle a la Crosse District and hope that my successor will continue the same as long as the old man lives. Now that his last son has died in our employment and he has no one to assist him in His Old Age.[43]

It is hard to know how many retired servants became freemen or engaged in free trading because analysis of this issue relies on comments made by HBC officers only when they felt that local operations were threatened, rather than on statistical data gleaned from English River District fur returns.

There was an undertone of insecurity in many of the Company's journal entries and letters concerning men retiring from service – how would these men generate a living? Who would ensure that they were cared for? Where would they live? Were retired servants on pensions unacknowledged freemen, and did they have greater potential to become free traders? In a January 1844 letter to George Simpson, Chief Factor Roderick McKenzie of Île à la Crosse noted that as of 1 June of that year, the contracts of ten men would expire, and he did not know how many would decide to renew, although he was told that many were determined to leave the service. McKenzie noted that "the greatest number of them are Natives of this District, and from Red River, and are very good men."[44] Although retired, former servants would need to continue working to support themselves and their families. At places like Île à la Crosse, Portage La Loche, or Green Lake, with few other economic options and possessing few other skills, they were likely to continue in the fur trade, thereby diverting trade from the Company as long as they were able to obtain outfits from the District's competitors. It was up to the HBC to determine how best to harness those energies and engender greater loyalty to the Company than to particular families.

Beginning in the 1840s, when free trade was first mentioned in the district, the Company determined that free traders were causing problems with the trade. There were limited options for non-Company employment in Sakitawak, and any former fur trade employees with relatives in English River who were laid off because of the merger had to locate alternative economic opportunities. Outside of gardening and limited grain crops, agriculture was not possible in this climate. Perhaps it was the lack of agricultural or non-fur trade employment opportunities that prompted some of the Morin family to move south to Lac Prairie, Sipisihk, and the Big River areas in the late nineteenth century, or perhaps being farther south gave them better access to transportation routes and alternative trade markets. It was certainly possible to hunt and fish in the English River District, and some people procured foods to trade to the Company and the mission. However, it was not feasible for many to engage in such a specific and limited pursuit. For men who had spent all their adult lives engaged in commercially driven occupations, who were used to purchasing luxury goods as well as necessities, and who had large numbers of dependants, free trading was surely an attractive alternative commercial economic pursuit. Free trading in the district also gave the men and their families an opportunity to remain in their homeland. Furthermore, as was the case with the free traders in the Red River region during the 1840s and 1850s, it is clear that the Metis of the English River District did not recognize the HBC's authority to control their personal economic endeavours – particularly when it was attempting to eliminate as many contracted positions as possible to improve its profit margin. This perceived betrayal surely promoted the increased attempts of families to engage in free-trading operations. From the perspective of the Metis community, the Company had benefited from the personal familial alliances that were the backbone of many of its operations. It was, after all, the alliances and connections forged by their relatives, not the HBC's monopoly, that had made trade profitable for the HBC.

While the numbers, or actual financial influence, of these men is not well articulated in the types of qualitative records used in this study, the increasing number of post report references to their activities and movements reveals the Company's concern over their influence in the region. By the mid-nineteenth century, free traders were described as "bands," with one man typically identified as being in charge. Presumably, these were extended family groups led by senior adult males, typically Metis families with intimate connections to Dene or Cree communities, most likely through extended family relationships across the district. An example of such an arrangement is provided by the Janviers of the Portage La Loche region, a family that was closely intermarried with the Dene of that territory and northern Alberta.

The Janvier family first appears in HBC records in the spring of 1845. While servants packed for the annual journey to York Factory with the winter's returns, the Île à la Crosse officer in charge was waiting for Baptiste Janvier and "Little Ice's Chipewyan" bands to arrive with their winter furs. The officers did not want to embark for York Factory until the furs from these two bands were part of Île à la Crosse's inventory. It is unclear whether Baptiste Janvier was working as a hunter, servant, or freeman, but "Janvier's band" made regular visits to Île à la Crosse throughout the 1840s and appeared to be operating in the capacity of freemen, with a fairly good relationship with the Company.[45] Some fifty years later, in February 1893, Moberly at Portage La Loche notified Île à la Crosse that a man in Louison (sometimes spelled Louis'on) Janvier's band – possibly a relative of Baptiste Janvier, but certainly the same Louis'on who free traded with support from Lac La Biche in the late 1890s – was trading contrary to the agreement that the Company had made with Baptiste. Moberly confiscated the man's goods and prepared an inventory to be sent to Île à la Crosse. So Louison Janvier was categorized as free trader rather than freeman, yet the Company continued to expect that his band would trade at Île à la Crosse, not Lac La Biche, Cold Lake, or Fort McMurray.[46]

While there were a number of Janvier families, at this time they are not adequately linked genealogically, so it is difficult to ascertain who belonged to what branch of the family. However, there was a Louis'on (born in 1807) who was the son of Old Janvier, a Canadian who married a Dene woman, Marguerite Pierriche or Piche.[47] According to the Oblates, the Janviers were a Metis family at Portage La Loche with strong connections to the region around Cold Lake (see Figure 7.3).[48] Louison was the brother of Pascal, Louise, Suzanne, and Marie Anne Janvier. According to records,

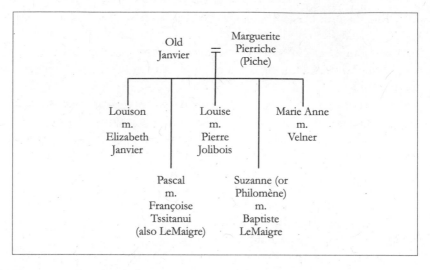

FIGURE 7.3   Janvier genealogy

he married Elizabeth Janvier (unfortunately, her parentage is unrecorded). Pascal married Françoise Tssitanui, reportedly the daughter of a Dene man and a Metis woman; Louise was married to Pierre Jolibois, whose father was, according to the Oblates, "a pure Dene" from the other side of Lake Athabasca; Suzanne married Baptiste LeMaigre from Portage La Loche, who was, according to the Oblates, Metis; and Marie Anne was married to a man known only as Velner and about whom nothing is known except that the Oblates described him as Metis of Cree ancestry.[49]

These family connections contributed to the Janvier family's reputation as a formidable force within the district. Decades later, Louison was supplied with trade goods by the HBC post at Lac La Biche, and since 1890 he had traded a great deal with Indians at Fort McMurray and Portage La Loche. According to Company representatives, his free-trading operation was successful because he belonged "to Portage La Loche ... related to many of the Indians there" and "[made] that an excuse for going among them."[50] Louison Janvier was therefore in regular competition with the HBC posts at Portage La Loche and Fort McMurray in the early 1890s, receiving his supplies from the HBC post at Lac La Biche and using his family connections to further his own economic agenda.[51] Janvier's enterprise in the region was so extensive that in the winter of 1892 he established independent winter posts at Portage La Loche, Jackfish Lake (twenty-three miles from Portage La Loche), Whitefish Lake (twenty miles from Portage

La Loche), and Swan Lake (on the headwaters of Clearwater River). According to Company officials in Winnipeg, when Janvier made his annual visits to Portage La Loche, he was actually paying higher prices for
furs than the HBC post there, which was why he was able to compete so
effectively against them. Yet much to the annoyance of Company representatives in the English River District, the HBC depot at Lac La Biche
continued to supply Janvier with goods throughout the 1890s. Not surprisingly, English River District officials demanded that this practice cease.
They felt that Winnipeg had a responsibility to stop Lac La Biche from
helping Janvier from infringing on Portage La Loche's trade and compel
him to trade at Île à la Crosse.[52]

The ability of free-trader bands to interfere with the Company's monopoly became significant enough in the second half of the century that Île
à la Crosse officials spent a great deal of time ruminating on how to neu-
tralize their effects. Beginning in the late 1840s, an apparent increase in
the amount of free trading taking place in the English River District was
reflected in a growing number of journal entries, letters, and district reports
on the topic. In the summer of 1847, Mr. McPherson at the Portage La
Loche post reported that a man named L'Esperance was starting his own
traffic in leather, although the man denied any such efforts. More troublesome, according to McPherson, was the fact that the Halfbreeds on the
Mackenzie River were obtaining skins from the Dene of Fort Chipewyan
and delivering them to their "countrymen" at the Portage. At best, Mc-
Pherson's crews claimed to have stopped about half this traffic in leather.[53]

To prevent free traders' movement into the district from other trade
territories or even Red River, the HBC's northern department began
policing travel routes and attempted to stop all men not contracted to
particular districts. Indeed, a notation at the top of the sketch map provides
important information about the operation of the trails: "12 Main Trails
run from Ile a la Crosse [sic] post which are guarded by 4 men with dog
teams always in readiness to follow up all opponents."[54] This description
suggests that the HBC was concerned that free traders were entering the
district and that the region needed to be on guard against their incursions.
In January 1854, George Deschambeault of Île à la Crosse notified Governor George Simpson that no free traders travelling by boat had been
able to enter the district the previous fall. There had been reports that at
least two boats were destined for Île à la Crosse, but Deschambeault heard
that Simpson's crews at Green Lake persuaded them to go in another
direction. Grateful for the assistance, Deschambeault further impressed
upon Simpson that if a large party of free traders from outside the district

chose to descend on Île à la Crosse, the post would have little defence because there were not enough contracted servants to prevent them from trading as they pleased nor enough goods to entice trade away from them.[55]

Despite all efforts to prevent their entrance into the English River District, free traders appeared at Deer's Lake and Lac La Ronge in 1856.[56] Pierre Bruce, for example, a man who had served the Company as an interpreter for at least sixteen years, had travelled to La Ronge and was seeking out furs from the Cree there.[57] According to Deschambeault,

> This man is a native of English River and will give us some trouble. I was told that he appears to be much interested for the welfare and prosperity of 'Mr. Samuel Indians' and is well known to be real adept at deception. I am informed that he brought an outfit of eight or nine pieces of Trade and has changed Entirely the Tariff of that Place. It is said that on his way up he collected a large pack of furs which he traded with Cumberland Indians a privilege which we have not even ourselves to trade with Indians of another District, but his ambition which has no bounds did more and I am sorry to say on account of the respect and regard we have for the Church Mission that this wanderer found a passage both for himself and Baggage into one of their Boats from Cumberland to Mr. Samuel's place.[58]

According to Deschambeault, Reverend Tate of the Church Missionary Society (CMS) attempted to prevent Bruce from taking passage in one of their boats, but the Indians manning the boat rejected Tate's authority and "actually threatened to leave Mr. Tate and his Boat if he objected to Embark Bruce and his property."[59] Deschambeault did not want Simpson to blame either the minister or the CMS for Bruce's actions because Tate had no power to prevent what had transpired.[60]

As a direct consequence of the incident with Bruce in La Ronge, Deschambeault immediately stocked both Green Lake and La Ronge with every conceivable trade good to compete more effectively against the free traders. Furthermore, the Company men in the district remained vigilant. Even as Deschambeault was writing to Simpson, he received word that Samuel McKenzie had sent two of his best men after some free traders. It was Deschambeault's opinion that the number of free traders was increasing and that their operations in the English River District were becoming so extensive that they would soon "overrun the whole country even to the Frozen Ocean with American goods."[61] Perhaps more damaging, the free traders supposedly did everything they could to corrupt the Indians of the district by telling them lies about the Company, although Deschambeault felt that most Indians would remain loyal to the Company and refuse to trade with the interlopers.[62]

According to Company officials, the free traders were causing great "acts of destruction" among Indians throughout the district by introducing alcohol to the trade. The worst offenders, according to Deschambeault, were "The Desjarlais."[63] It is unclear which Desjarlais was/were being referred to because there were several large families of Desjarlais spread throughout the northwest and into northern Alberta. Nevertheless, Deschambeault clearly felt that "The Desjarlais," more than any other free trader, had tainted the act of trading with his wickedness. In 1858, according to Deschambeault,

> The Desjarlais and the two Murderers of poor old Naulet [Paulet] Paul and of that poor little Englishman Houston at [T]he Pas are making themselves conspicuous among those who are working against the Company. Those scamps have so far escaped retribution for their crimes but leaving their wickedness and follies aside, It is nevertheless vexing and I should say almost beyond the limits of human endurance to see with our own eyes those Miscreants walking freely abroad with their hands in their pockets and a feather upon their caps much as to say they did not care a button either for law, justice or in fact any thing else.[64]

In the fall of 1862, Île à la Crosse was told to expect its first free trader that winter, a Charles McDermott of Red River.[65] Men at the post were also cautioned that others – how many was unknown – were on their way from Red River, and they needed to prepare for this incursion.[66] The free traders were possibly relocating because of the growing influx of eastern Canadian immigrants to the territory and the changes in the Red River area as Rupert's Land prepared to enter into Canadian Confederation, or perhaps the growing Metis free-trading class from Red River was simply trying to expand its operations.

The situation with free traders only worsened in the English River District throughout the 1880s. Île à la Crosse district reports for those years lament that so many free traders throughout the region were the cause of a greater evil: the free traders inspired Indians to all kinds of bad behaviour, including trading at night so that they could slip past the post unnoticed.[67] Baptiste Laliberte at Portage La Loche was facing opposition from two free traders, Peeche Pruden of Fort McMurray and another man from Lac La Biche. Furthermore, free trader William Venne was active in the Lac Vert region. In 1888, Venne was one of the Company's main opponents,

organizing a large business with three traders at Nehiyo-wapasi in opposition to Alexandre Laliberte, three more down the English River, and two
at Buffalo Lake. An Île à la Crosse post report from the late 1880s notes
that Venne had "gotten a hold of the Irons and Coulleneurs," despite
Alexandre Laliberte's marriage to the chief's daughter. This appears to have
been a bit of an exaggeration, as the report goes on to say that Alexandre,
because of his position, had indeed obtained a large number of furs from
his wife's family, but in return was distributing too much debt to them, a
practice that had to stop, regardless of Venne's presence.[68] It seems apparent that Alexandre was using the Company's resources to placate his relations. Venne also had a northern operation in the Moostoos-sipi region.
Baptiste Charlot Lafleur, a "headman," and two Indians from that region
were trading the produce from their hunts exclusively to Venne. To oppose
free traders, Île à la Crosse had to post both an interpreter and an additional man at Nehiyo-wapasi, an officer and fisherman at the Moostoos-sipi
winter post under Charles Pierre Lafleur, and additional men at the Souris
River post, as well as assigning men to visit the Indian communities
weekly or bi-weekly to obtain provisions and furs. As a result of these
measures, district expenses rose steadily.[69] The Company attempted to use
the power of the northwest's family structure to stop Venne's activities at
Nehiyo-wapasi and Baptiste Charlot Lafleur's at Moostoos-sipi. Venne's
operation called upon the Irons and Couillonneurs to trade with him
instead of the Green Lake post, so the Company placed Alexandre Laliberte at Canoe Lake in order to benefit from the familial loyalty he had
cultivated.

Ironically, Charles Pierre Lafleur, the man sent to Buffalo Narrows to
protect the region against free traders, was the brother of Baptiste Charlot
Lafleur – and he eventually became a free trader himself. Both Baptiste
Charlot and Charles Pierre Lafleur were the sons of HBC servant Charles
Lafleur and either Mary Grosse Tete or Louise Vadney, and their family
was known to have been from the Sakitawak region.[70] Charles Pierre
Lafleur was engaged as a Dene language interpreter after first signing on
with the Company in 1861. He served as postmaster at the Buffalo Narrows
outpost from 1888 to 1890, where he was charged with protecting the post
from free traders like his brother. While employed by the Company, Charles
Pierre became one of its highest-paid employees and was regarded as an
honest and trustworthy servant. After he was injured in the early 1890s,
he wanted to retire and requested a pension. In a letter to Henry Moberly at Île à la Crosse, C.C. Chipman of Winnipeg wrote that although
Lafleur was not old enough to receive a pension, he would be granted one

on account of his injury. The pension allotted to Lafleur was only £8 per year and was paid at the pleasure of the English River District accounts, not as an entitlement for his years of work or loyalty as a servant. Perhaps because he was still relatively young and the pension not especially generous, Charles Pierre was, by the late 1890s, a free trader, working in Prince Albert with Baker and Company. When Winnipeg officials learned of Lafleur's change in status, they alerted Île à la Crosse that the pension was to be cancelled immediately if proof was obtained that Lafleur was trading against the Company.[71] As already mentioned, pensions were Winnipeg's means of controlling former servants and preventing them from trading against Company interests. Yet in Lafleur's case, the Company's paltry recognition of his service had the opposite effect.

When Chief Commissioner Wrigley, in Manitoba, asked him to take charge of Île à la Crosse in the early 1890s, Henry John Moberly was advised that the region was in dire straits because it was overrun with free traders and plagued with unreliable servants. According to Wrigley, Île à la Crosse had "gone to the devil."[72] By 1891, Moberly was considering leaving the service himself but decided to remain for another three-year contract in order to be properly promoted and increase his pension, and so he agreed to take the job at Île à la Crosse. Upon his arrival, Moberly claimed to have dismissed "the ringleaders among the refactory servants, letting the rest understand I would tolerate no insubordination."[73] He then visited the district outposts to reorganize and return them to profitability before turning his attention back to the free traders. By the end of 1891, Moberly declared that Île à la Crosse was rid of free traders and the Company's predominance in trade was restored.[74] Interestingly, this was the same chief trader who had advised the Company not to cancel Pierriche Laliberte's pension and bar him from trading, actions that certainly would have alienated him and his large family from the Company. Moberly was the most sympathetic officer in the district and demonstrated his willingness to accommodate the Metis community's socio-cultural values on many occasions, as shown by his distribution of food to the mission, his hosting of dances, and his open participation in and defence of local traditions. Arguably, to restore the power of the English River District, Moberly needed to harness the more powerful families, like the Labertes, and convince them to remain loyal to the Company – a task that could only be accomplished if the Company itself acknowledged the cultural values embedded within Metis wahkootowin.

Moberly's optimism was short-lived, for free traders were still operating in the district two years later. In 1893, Moberly suggested to his superiors at Winnipeg that Magloire Maurice of Portage La Loche and another temporary labourer be sent to establish an outpost at Cree Lake (Sandy Lake) the following winter. According to Moberly, there were good furs in the Cree Lake area, and establishing an outpost there under a loyal servant would prevent the Indians from trading with free traders. Magloire Maurice, son of François Maurice and Angèle Laliberte, had been in charge at Pine River, but in the winter of 1892-93, Moberly put him in charge of Portage La Loche's newest winter outpost, Cree Lake, servicing a largely Dene population. Magloire, with over a decade of service, was deemed to be a good servant, so much so that he and his wife, Philomène Lariviere, lived in housing supplied by the Company.[75]

One of the most persistent and frequently discussed free traders of the period was Paul Delaronde Sr. Delaronde had children with his first wife, Marguerite Sinclair, in Manitoba.[76] However, he arrived in the Devil's Lake area in 1874 with Sophie Morin and lived with her, her family, and several of his adult children. (He later had a daughter with Sophie.) He is first noted in the post records when he was attempting to establish various commercial enterprises throughout the district. In September 1874, Chief Factor William McMurray of Île à la Crosse noticed the free-trading Delaronde, who had arrived at Green Lake well stocked with goods and provisions and had established himself near the post. McMurray estimated that the amount of supplies in Delaronde's possession would cause considerable trouble for the Company. After a year in the district, Delaronde had apparently managed to procure furs from the Cree around Lac Vert despite the HBC's best efforts to stop him. However, the Company felt that Delaronde would make little profit because he had extended too much credit to the Cree to entice them to his business. Delaronde did not spend the winter at Lac Vert that year, but the Company was sure that he would return and other free traders would follow. Indeed, Delaronde did return and challenged the Company in the northwest throughout the remainder of the decade.[77]

Company officials felt that at least part of the reason for Delaronde's success as a free trader was the behaviour of Ewan McDonald, chief trader at Île à la Crosse in the early 1880s, who was the target of a number of complaints levelled against him by local Indians. In one recorded incident, Chief Factor Lawrence Clarke was returning to Prince Albert from Edmonton in 1880 when he found three chiefs and their headmen from Île à la Crosse awaiting him. According to Clarke, he and the chiefs spoke for over twelve hours about McDonald's treatment of the Indians in his district. The chiefs said that they were so poorly treated, they were now refusing to trade with the Company as long as McDonald occupied his present position in their territory. Clarke then indicated in his report of the incident that Delaronde was trading for a company known as Ashdown and Agnew of Winnipeg and for an individual named Baptiste Stobart (a man also known in the Duck Lake region) in opposition to the Company, thereby giving Cree and Dene trappers of the northwest other opportunities to dispose of their furs. To calm the men in the short term, and as a show of good faith, Clarke gave each chief a $50 credit and the young men who accompanied them $25 to $35 of credit each, which was then taken out of Île à la Crosse's accounts. Clarke wrote to McDonald, relating the complaints about his conduct and notifying him that the commissioners in Winnipeg had also been informed of the trouble. Perhaps, Clarke suggested, McDonald should consider leaving the region voluntarily before the trade relationships were irrevocably destroyed.[78]

While his first year may not have been profitable, Delaronde's activities made enough of an impact on the Company that the HBC attempted to engage him as a servant in 1880. According to McDonald, Delaronde refused the offer because he said he would not take orders from any man. McDonald felt that the real reason was that he had already obtained a trading outfit for that year.[79] This theory has some merit, for in 1881 McDonald successfully signed Delaronde on as a freeman with his own outfit. However, Chief Moshonas of Pelican Lake told McDonald that the Indians of that region did not like Delaronde and preferred not to deal with him, so Delaronde operated to the south, at Green Lake.[80] Considering the seriousness of the complaints lodged against McDonald less than a year earlier, it is possible that he was attempting to salvage his own reputation by painting Delaronde as mistrusted by local Indians.

Delaronde's treatment of the Cree and Dene of the district could not have been too egregious because the Company was still outfitting him four years later. For the 1884 trading season, Delaronde and the Company continued their work arrangement, but beginning in 1885 he was regularly engaged as a clerk at £100 per annum. More importantly, from the Company's perspective, by supplying his yearly outfits, the HBC ensured Delaronde became indebted to it. Roderick Ross at Île à la Crosse was notified that if Delaronde was unable to pay off his debts by the end of the 1884 trading season, he would be obliged to hand over his cattle to the Company at market rates as repayment.[81] Slowly, the Company gained control of Delaronde's behaviour and economic choices. In May 1888, Joseph Fortescue at Île à la Crosse wrote to Clarke and said that Delaronde, once a thorn in Ewan McDonald's side, was now beaten and broken.[82]

The uneasy relationship between Delaronde and the Company continued throughout the late 1880s until 1893, when Delaronde was ready to relocate away from Lac Vert after almost twenty years. In March 1893, Henry Moberly informed Winnipeg that Delaronde had sought permission to establish a store at Muskeg Lake, southwest of Prince Albert and near Carlton, having already built himself a house there on an acre of land. Supporting Delaronde's request, Moberly laid out a justification for permitting the new arrangement. He wrote that Muskeg Lake was a community of thirteen Indian families and a Roman Catholic mission that employed eleven to twelve men on a farm, so a local customer base existed. Prior to the establishment of a post at Lac Prairie, all supplies for Muskeg Lake had to be transported a considerable distance from Prince Albert or Carlton, so the opening of an outpost was not only feasible, but desirable. Furthermore, according to the mission priests, "settlers" were expected to arrive shortly, and a store was required to support the growing population. Finally, Moberly felt that granting Delaronde permission would add to the Shell River outpost's profits without too much additional expense for the Company. The store was built on Delaronde's land and open for business once a week. When Delaronde was not there, the local priest opened the store without expecting to be compensated. According to Moberly, the only thing required of the Company was to supply an outfit of groceries.[83] By the time they wrote to Winnipeg, Moberly and Delaronde had already established a solid plan that would benefit both Delaronde and the Company, and as he prepared for the transition to running a store, he was supplied with another three-year contract as HBC clerk. Muskeg Lake was near the Shell River/Devil's Lake region, where Delaronde's brother-in-law, Raphaël Morin, had established himself in the 1880s, and near Lac Vert, where many more relatives such as the Lalibertes now lived.[84]

Paul Delaronde disappears from available records until the 1900-01 season, when, to the Company's surprise, he resumed his earlier career as their opponent, having received his last outfit on credit from Winnipeg.[85] The 1900-01 district report for Green Lake reported that Paul Delaronde was the Company's "most persistent opponent [and] with his sons and relatives reaches almost every camp tributary to Lac Vert. His experience must be out of proportion to his trade and he cannot, I think, be making headway. He gives more trouble than all of the other petty traders in this section."[86] Delaronde had three sons – Alexandre, Paul Jr., and William – all of whom later married Morin women (see Chapter 3). The interconnections between the Laliberte, Morin, and Delaronde families were complicated and grew in size over successive generations, a reality that was clear to local Company officials by the late nineteenth century. These three families had equally complicated relationships with the HBC; the men moved from being loyal servants to realizing that their interests were better served in the capacity of either freemen or free traders. Just as important, the Company recognized their value, as demonstrated by comments about the power of Pierriche Laliberte to influence his extended relatives in the district and by attempts to hire men like Paul Delaronde Sr.

The English River District's men and their families moved fluidly through the employment spectrum during their lifetime, serving the Company in ways that suited their own circumstances. During the latter half of the nineteenth century, Pierriche Laliberte went from being a postmaster at Portage La Loche, with over five decades of service to the Company, to a freeman freighting in the Green Lake region of the district. He was then rehired as postmaster of Lac Vert prior to his final retirement in the 1890s. Conversely, Laliberte's brother-in-law Paul Delaronde Sr. went from being a free trader to a Company servant and then an HBC-contracted freeman in the Lac Vert area during the same time period before opening a trading establishment under the Company's supervision near Muskeg Lake. It is clear that, from the beginning, certain men – whether servants, freemen, or free traders – in the English River District and its subsidiary posts enjoyed an influence that both furthered and frustrated Company ambitions. As trying as the families could be, the HBC attempted to appeal to their sensibilities, as expressed through wahkootowin, when it suited Company interests. The HBC was a powerful economic force and, therefore, is often described as having irrevocably altered the economies of Aboriginal societies and imposed dependency. Yet evidence suggests that families in the northwest exerted a certain level of self-determination, at least until the early 1900s. A cultural worldview that emphasized familial loyalty ensured that the HBC was never fully secure in the region, and local families played no small part in influencing the nature of trade relations for much of the nineteenth century.

Conclusion

"Hope for the future that a way of being would not be lost"

Nimoshom is standing
cap in hand
waving good-bye
a yellow bus
with me in it
leaving Sakitawak
lake on Missinipi
the big water
Kistapinanik
My destination

reassurance
is a story
he was there
a long time ago
working for Revillon Frére [sic]
after the family broke ties
with the Hudson's Bay Company

and then he expressed
hope for the future
that a way of being would not be lost

that place
would not be forgotten
that a language
would not be lost
Nitanis, ahpotikwimina
kamistahitimisoyon

such sadness
in his voice
I never forgot

Rita Bouvier, "Leaving Home"[1]

This poem by Rita Bouvier, a descendant of the nineteenth-century Bouvier family, is about leaving home, but it nevertheless reflects a hopeful outlook for the future because it is an invocation to home, to family, to language, to place – to all those things that comprise wahkootowin. Nimoshom, Bouvier's grandfather, expresses his desire that, although people will leave home, their way of life – the place, the language, and the sense of belonging to this homeland – will not be lost. The act of writing gives life to memories and serves as a reminder of the richness of the cultural identity bequeathed to the contemporary Metis community by its ancestors. Nimoshom ("my grandfather"), nitanis ("my girl"), Sakitawak (Île à la Crosse), and Missinipi are particular references to home and identity grounded in family and are used to transport readers to a time and place not their own, just as mention of the Hudson's Bay Company and Revillon Frères links them to the region's economic history.

Understanding this Metis society requires an appreciation for place and for the way families organized themselves in relation to their homeland. Aboriginal cultural identity is enshrined, in the words of Raymond Fogelson, in "narratives of ethnogenesis," in which territories become "a home area where life was lived, and as the final resting place of mortal remains."[2] Contemporary Aboriginal writers like Bouvier often privilege stories of historical, even mystical, landscapes when they reference family and community because of the land's historical importance to a people's sense of self, their sense of belonging. Perhaps most significantly, such a tool establishes connections to the histories of their ancestors.[3] In a manner similar to Bouvier, when Lawrence Ahenakew described a family reunion at Nehiyo-wahkasi (Sandy Point), he also referenced family and homeland as being integral to his personal identity and, just as importantly, the cornerstone of how he would teach his own children and grandchildren about a place and people that they will never know as intimately. The use of family stories located in a particular place is an important means of imprinting in others a memory of family and of passing community histories on to future generations. In the world of Metis in the northwest, family histories rooted in a specific place is at the core of the community's sense of self as well as its economic and religious history. It grounds all relationships. Sakitawak was the centre of this historic community socially and economically because of its location on Missinipi, transforming it in the late eighteenth century into a gateway to both southerly and northerly transportation corridors.

The historical reality of the region's trade economy was that it involved entire families; men, women, and children all worked in the HBC's sphere of influence in a variety of capacities: as servants, unpaid casual labourers, freemen, and, eventually, in open opposition as free traders. Specifically, Bouvier invokes her family's socio-economic history: "he was there a long time ago working for Revillon Frére [sic] after the *family* broke ties with the Hudson's Bay Company" [emphasis added]. The Bouvier family understood, and passed on this knowledge to their descendants, that the relationship with the Company was not solely that of employee-employer, but rather involved the entire family. In the first half of the twentieth century, Marcel Giraud concludes, "between the members of these [Metis] clans, for such in effect they were, deeply attached to the country of the West where they had always lived, a kind of esprit de corps could develop, similar to that animating the groups of families into which the native tribes were divided; relatives and followers would develop a solidarity between them and would side with anyone among them who thought himself wronged by the head of the post."[4] Giraud regards the Metis as clannish, a trait he considers to be a cultural weakness that resulted in their political and economic decline and eventual social marginalization by the midtwentieth century. Nevertheless, despite his negative assessment, Giraud reveals an enduring Metis cultural attitude, one that promoted fierce loyalty to one another, to their families, and to their land. This idea of Metis cultural and economic solidarity, values embedded in wahkootowin, itself a worldview linking land, family, and identity in one interconnected web of being, appears to have been ubiquitous in Metis communities across Canada, and it continues to be a theme commonly pursued in studies of Metis society. Diane Payment, for instance, observes in her study of the Batoche Metis along the South Saskatchewan River that "the network of 'la parenté' (kinship) promoted solidarity, social stability, and continuity."[5] In the case of the northwest, although the families were spread out across the region, each was connected to the other through generations of intermarriage; each was a part of the region's economic and religious histories; and each was in some manner tied to the early trade relationship, first with the pedlars from Montreal and then with the HBC. This early trade was, of course, centred at Lac Île à la Crosse, the heart of this subarctic homeland, to which all the families can trace their ancestry.

The cultural identity of Aboriginal peoples hinged on their ability to connect the present and future to the past, and their relationship to place served as the common thread integral to all stories. Just as the families of the northwest were traceable intergenerationally, they were also traceable to Île à la Crosse. However, throughout the nineteenth century, as their families grew in size and as the Company required their labour, they radiated outward from this central depot and moved throughout the region, trading, transporting, and procuring food stuff and furs for the post, rooting their communities in the homeland of their Cree and Dene mothers and grandmothers. The notion of relatedness integral to Metis communities was, of course, a principle passed to them by these mothers and grandmothers. As Cree, Dene, and eventually Metis women married outsider adult male fur traders, they brought to their marriages attitudes and beliefs – a worldview – about family and social life that influenced the creation and shape of this particular Metis socio-cultural identity. French, Scottish, and English traders certainly contributed attitudes, ideas, and behaviours from their homelands that influenced their family life in the district, but it was an indigenous worldview that shaped the cultural expression of Metis wahkootowin.[6] Metis families lived in the lands of their maternal relatives and, as was the case in the northwest, spoke the languages of those maternal cultures. Land and language were the cornerstones on which their worldview or philosophy of life developed. As the northwest's proto-generation took shape in the late eighteenth and early nineteenth centuries, those early couples raised their children according to the socio-cultural values of wahkootowin. Four subsequent generations of Metis from this region lived, laboured, and established for themselves a society that privileged familial relationships, in turn using them as the basis for determining appropriate behaviour and interaction with all outsiders, whether male fur traders, fur trade companies, or the Roman Catholic Church. Historian Nicole St-Onge explores many of the same ideas about Metis identity, but from a different starting point. In her work on both Saint-Laurent and St-Paul des Saulteaux, she argues that there were greater similarities between those two Metis parishes and their Saulteaux relatives than with other French- or English-speaking Metis parishes in Red River.[7] What the present study has attempted to do is explore the Aboriginality of the Metis of the northwest as rooted in a maternal ancestry indigenous to the region and subsequently expressed through the values and behaviours integral to wahkootowin.

Beginning in the late eighteenth century, several patterns emerged that defined living arrangements, familial identification, religiosity, and economic expectations. Wahkootowin is the interpretive lens best suited to evaluate these patterns because it is culturally grounded in Cree philosophy or *nehiyaw tahp sinowin* (the Cree way of seeing the world), which itself encompasses the dual, although not mutually exclusive, aspects of behaviour and worldview. While the proto-generation quite literally gave birth to the Metis people, it was the four subsequent generations who remained in the lands of their mothers and grandmothers and truly created a new society. An intergenerational evaluation of Metis genealogies from the district exposes regional matrilocal residency patterns and patronymic connections at the community level. A construction of the genealogical history of this region revealed forty-three core families. They are regarded as core because they were traceable intergenerationally; they were linked to each other through marriage, adoption, and other socially constructed relationships; they remained closely linked to Cree and Dene populations in the region; they operated in a variety of economic niches central to the operation of the fur trade; and they were Roman Catholic. Furthermore, each generation incorporated outsider male fur traders who sought to marry women born to the region and remain in the region as fathers, husbands, and sons-in-law. While we cannot know exactly how these men felt or why they joined this new society, we do know that they married, lived, and died in their adopted communities and homeland. In short, they acculturated. Within each generation, alliances with First Nations communities were reaffirmed as Cree and Dene women and men married Metis people. Throughout the nineteenth century, the ties between these Aboriginal communities were regularly strengthened through marriage patterns, religious conversions, family work groups, and other socio-cultural events that reaffirmed familial and community unity.

While wahkootowin was the dominant cultural system of the region, it was neither hegemonic nor coercive. Rather, its power lay in its appeal to human sociability, to be a part of family, to be connected to something greater than oneself. Because wahkootowin was a cultural system that not only permitted but also encouraged the incorporation of new peoples and compatible ideas, it was necessarily adaptable and transformative. This is not, however, to argue that the Metis always welcomed, embraced, or controlled adaptation, but that wahkootowin afforded a means for families and individuals to respond to new possibilities, be they positive or negative. As a result, in order to become part of the family structure in the northwest that largely defined itself as Catholic, for example, outsider males (and in at least one instance a woman) took the necessary step to join the institution that marked the community's religious identity. Acceptance of Catholicism, in turn, put one on a path of acceptance. Catholicism as a religion that also privileged family – natural and spiritual – and Homeness was wholly compatible with the worldview of the Metis, and, as such, was easily incorporated into the region's prevailing socioreligious structures. The acculturation of individuals, institutions, and ideas via wahkootowin connected people through intermarriage, religious conversion, acceptance of a godparent's role, and engagement in the sociocultural life of the community, which, in turn, framed relationships with outsiders.

The idea of acculturation should not, as often happens, be confused with assimilation. Acculturation processes do not overwhelm and consume other peoples or cultures, but rather permit the possibility of cultural fusion and sharing. There were, of course, degrees of acculturation and acceptance of wahkootowin by outsiders, and indeed there were instances when the collision of wahkootowin with outside elements, both secular and sectarian, resulted in outright conflict. However, there were also instances when outside influences and/or individuals were easily incorporated, and significant shifts from one world to another occurred.

By evaluating the history of the region within a generational framework of families, we can see how those families grew in size, radiated outward from Sakitawak into other parts of the territory, and organized themselves in a regionally defined matrilocal system according to local patronymic connections. In this study of family life and structure in the northwest, the term "matrilocal" was necessarily expanded to reflect a regional reality in which women remained in the district, anchoring their families to the land and socializing children in the worldview that they and their mothers had inherited. While women served as the regional social anchor, evaluation of particular communities within the region highlighted the patronymic connections used to distinguish branches of families identifiable with specific locations within the territory. Between 1800 and 1912 (or thereabouts), there were five generational cohorts in the northwest. Members of the proto-generation, although important because of their contribution to the birth of a first generation, were not themselves Metis, and so this study focuses more on the four subsequent generations. The first generation, born between 1810 and 1830, established a way of life different from that of their parents. They were born inland, in a space that they transformed into their homeland by intermarrying with one another and beginning those trends common to the forty-three core families. By the time the first generation reached adulthood, members were raising their own children in the social and economic atmosphere of the fur trade – the economic activity that had brought their own fathers into the region – and had incorporated the basic elements of Roman Catholicism into their lives. The second and third generations, born in the 1830s-1850s and 1860s-1880s, respectively, were, like their parents and grandparents, committed to the social life, spiritual heritage, and economic patterns that supported and defined their homeland.

The birth and maturation of the fourth generation marked a new era in the history of Metis in the northwest, occurring at a time when the paths and interests of the people and the institutions associated with religion and economy began to diverge and old patterns were increasingly found wanting by all parties in the region. Born between the 1890s and the 1920s, the fourth generation, like the proto-generation, is difficult to fully assess because it, too, is only partially documented. During the scrip era, members of the fourth generation were the children of established families, so only some appear in baptismal records, and fewer still are in the marriage records of the early 1900s. The record of the fourth generation is incomplete, but it nevertheless reveals new avenues for exploring Metis history through the interpretive lens of wahkootowin. In the fourth generation, many of the older patterns reappeared, such as the acculturation of outsider males into the regional family structure defined by women and the persistence of the socio-economic relationships developed and maintained by trading families. However, significant events introduced new challenges for families living according to this worldview and, therefore, for the ability of families to respond. Such events included the extension of Treaty No. 6 into the northwest, when Green Lake became a part of the 1889 adhesion; the issuance of scrip in that part of the territory; the subsequent negotiation of Treaty No. 10; and another round of scrip distribution in the remainder of the district in 1906 and 1907.

The issuance of scrip and the signing of treaties, first at Green Lake and later at Île à la Crosse and Portage La Loche, drew a line across the northwest for the first time and divided treaty and non-treaty people geopolitically and legally. While the English River District continued to exist as an administrative region for the HBC, the treaty boundaries segmented people into new zones of differing responsibilities and rights. Where culture had once bound communities and family as a social unifier, Canadian law now had the potential to disrupt old alliances, alter expectations, and create categories of haves and have-nots. Historically, there had certainly been differences between being Cree, Dene, or Metis, yet well into the twentieth century those divisions were often muted because of a shared language, lineage, and, in some instances, economic mode of life. Raphael Marceland, a Dene elder from Birch Narrows First Nation, provided some insight into how wahkootowin operated in practical terms in northwestern Saskatchewan during the course of his lifetime:

> I speak Cree too, that's where I learned it, in Clear Lake. I'm a Dene but we live all together. Nowadays they say Half-breed, Treaty and non-Treaties. In Clear Lake we live all together and there was no such thing. We were like one family. If they shot a moose, everybody got a piece of meat, they don't take it to their homes and put it away like we do now and dump it in the deep-freeze. And they don't feed nobody. In those days everybody shared, everybody had a piece of meat out of that moose. There was no such thing as Treaty or non-Treaty them days.[8]

Marceland made note of several important socio-cultural unifiers within the region at a time when one would expect to find division. He noted that Cree was spoken throughout the region regardless of cultural background; he emphasized the ethic of sharing with everyone; and he lamented the problems that arose when people forgot their obligations to one another and paid greater attention to the divisions created by Canadian legal definitions. And most importantly, Marceland framed his sense of responsibility and obligation as a cultural value that was shared by others throughout the region, regardless of legal status, ancestry, religion, or race. What remains evident is that the sense of connectedness to the region, to place, to family has not been truly lost, even if the actual connections themselves have been transformed by contemporary influences and mores.

Wahkootowin made the northwest a Metis community through the development and maintenance of relationships forged by mixed-ancestry people within the territories of their Cree and Dene grandmothers. Without the establishment of those familial ties and alliances, Metis people would not have been able to create for themselves a homeland in what were Cree and then Dene traditional territories. The Metis of the northwest were able to create a space for themselves within the region, in part, because of the religious and economic lifestyles of their paternal and maternal ancestors. More importantly, they were able to carve out a territorial niche because of the principles embodied in their socio-cultural expression of family. Wahkootowin was their means of evaluating and negotiating the economic, political, and spiritual demands of two external and competing institutions. At the intersection of these indigenous community values and institutional expectations in economic, political, or cultural spheres, the Metis expressed their self-determination and forged a society different from, but compatible with, that of their ancestors.

Appendix

Godparents, 1867–1912

Godfather	Godmother	Date of baptism	Baptized	Father of baptized	Mother of baptized
Vincent Daigneault	Marguerite Bouvier	16 May 1867	Joseph Miameskosinaguseshyini	Joseph Miameska	Elise Assenis
Vincent Daigneault	Marguerite Bouvier	25 May 1867	Joseph Natomagan	Baptiste Natomagan	Elise
Antoine [illegible]	Marguerite Bouvier	30 May 1867	Louis Carlekis	Louis Carlekis	Magdeleine
Baptiste Morin	Marianne Angelique Lafleur	30 Aug 1867	Flora Hope	John Hope	Emilie
Raphaël Morin		10 Oct 1867	Sophie Lariviere	Abraham Lariviere	Marie Patasseta (?)
Raphaël Morin and François Roy		illegible	Jean [illegible]	Louis	Magdeleine
Raphaël Morin	Marie Lafleur	2 Apr 1868	Pierre Baptistcho	Baptistcho	Marie Elsishayase (?)
Baptiste [illegible]	Julie Morin	19 May 1868	Joseph Morin	Cyprien Morin	Marie Cook
Thomas Lariviere	Marguerite Morin	16 May 1869	Narcisse LaFleur	Baptiste Lafleur	Angélique Jourdain
Baptiste Morin	Esther Gerard	25 May 1868	D'Edouard	Major D'Edouard	Marguerite Crise
Pierre Morin	Géneviève Louison	6 July 1868	Philomène McAllen	James McAllen	Marie Abraham
Raphaël Morin	Marguerite Assinaboine	5 Sept 1868	Marie Joseph Aubichon	Baptiste Aubichon	Philomène Gerard
Louis Morin	Betse Ekinsootshineoisfwew	15 Nov 1868	Philomène Linklater	Peter Linklater	Marie Morin
Michel Bouvier Sr.	Julie Bouvier	24 Dec 1868	James Nipteponayu		
Louis Morin	Madam Deschambeault	6 Jan 1869	George Alexandre Laliberte	Antoine Laliberte	Marie Aubichon
Michel Bouvier Sr.	Julie Bouvier	7 Feb 1869	John Catfish	Ahouis	[illegible]
Michel Bouvier Sr.	Julie Bouvier	9 Feb 1869	Marie Desjarlais	Thomas Desjarlais	Marie Lafleur
Cyprien Morin	Marie Cook	19 May 1869	Cyprien Laliberte	Pierriche Laliberte	Sarazine Morin
Louis Morin	Marguerite Jourdain	21 May 1869	Cyprien Laliberte	Joseph Laliberte	Marie Lafleur
Vincent Danis [?]	Julie Bouvier	9 June 1869	Manuel Mallet	Antoine Mallet	Magdeleine

Godfather	Godmother	Date of baptism	Baptized	Father of baptized	Mother of baptized
Raphaël Morin	Julie Bouvier	19 June 1869	Julie Bouvier	Michel Bouvier Jr.	Julie Bouvier
Baptiste Morin	Bessie Morin	12 Oct 1869	Marie Josephine Casdeze	Alexis Montagnais	Angélique Casdeze
Pierre Malboeuf	Marie Morin	24 Mar 1870	Marie Philomène Morin	Raphaël Morin	Betsy Cook
Vincent [illegible]	Betse Morin	15 June 1870	[illegible] Robillard	[illegible] Robillard	illegible
Baptiste Morin	Angélique Jourdain	18 June 1870	Louis Jourdain	Louis Jourdain	Marguerite McKay
Pierre Marie Morin	Marie Lariviere	10 July 1870	Sophie Miamiskusinakwsi	Baptiste Miamiskusinakwsi	Elise Assenis
Pierriche Laliberte	Sarazine Morin	13 Aug 1870	Alexis Laliberte	Joseph Laliberte	Marie Lafluer
Raphaël Morin	Marie Roy	29 Aug 1870	William Hope	John Hope	Emilie
Raphaël Morin	Madam Deschambeault	7 Sept 1870	Marie Elizabeth Sara Spencer	William Spencer	Caroline Small
Pierre Morin	Elise	16 Sept 1870	Marie	Pierre	[illegible]
Cyprien Morin	Julie Bouvier	20 Sept 1870	Louis Zéphrin	Louis Morin	Marguerite Jourdain
Frederic Durocher	Julie Bouvier	22 Sept 1870	Maria Malboeuf	Louis Malboeuf	Marguerite Passain
Pierre Morin	Sophie Welle	25 Dec 1870	Joseph Montagnais	Grand Bapt. Montagnais	Marian Csemmaredda (?)
Pierre Morin	Sophie Welle	28 May 1871	Joseph Billette	Paul Billette	Justine Montagnais
	Caroline Morin	1 June 1871	Michel Ya'ias	Louison Ya'ias	Elise
Pierre Marie Morin	Rosalie Walle	1 June 1871	Alexandre Marcel	Marcel	Adelaide
Pierre Morin	Véronique Bouvier	1 June 1871	Abraham Tchyalgere	Louis Tchyalgere	Madeleine Thagultsell
	Véronique Bouvier	5 June 1871	Joseph Daotsare	Baptiste Daotsare	Marie Tsekwitsi
Pierre Marie Morin	Sophie Welle	6 June 1871	Marie Philomène Deneyou	Michel Deneyou	Catherine Edekusi
Pierre Marie Morin	Sophie	12 June 1871	Samuel	Thomas	Marguerite
Michel Bouvier Sr.	Julie Bouvier	4 Aug 1871	Maria Christine Mallette	Arene Mallette	Madeleine
Pierre Morin	Marie Cook	4 Sept 1871	Pierre Marie Roy	François Roy	Marie
Pierriche Malboeuf	Julie Bouvier	10 Sept 1871	Marie Catfish	John Catfish	Marie Lapatte
Louis Roy	Marguerite Bouvier	23 Sept 1871	Jean Baptiste [blank]	Michel [blank]	Catherine Roy

Father	Mother	Date	Child	Godfather	Godmother
Cyprien Morin	Marie Cook	28 Nov 1871	Marie Jourdain	Louis Jourdain	Marguerite McKay
Pierriche Laliberte	Sarazine Morin	6 June 1872	Joseph Lafleur	Baptiste Lafleur	Angélique Jourdain
Pierriche Laliberte	Sarazine Morin	6 June 1872	Rosalie	Jami Petit Ours	Cawiskuttew
Louis Morin	Angélique Morin	6 June 1872	Sophie	Jami Petit Ours	Cawiskuttew
Louis Morin	Marguerite Jourdain	6 June 1872	Louis	Jami Petit Ours	Cawiskuttew
	Véronique Bouvier	17 June 1872	Marie Louise Egou	Samuel Egou	Marguerite Klasta (?)
	Véronique Bouvier	24 June 1872	Marie Flora E'talshemez	E'talshemez	Tsekowi yuzi
Baptiste Morin	Caroline Morin	24 June 1872	Jean Baptiste Billette	Paul Billette	Marie
Pierre Morin	Sarazine Morin	16 Sept 1872	Sarazine Morin	Louison Morin	[blank] Jourdain
Jean Bapt. Payette	Caroline Morin	22 Oct 1872	Marie Agnês Morin	Raphaël Morin	Betsy Cook
Pierre Gerard	Véronique Bouvier	8 Jan 1873	Jean Marie Martial Desjarlais	Chamas Desjarlais	Marie Lafleur
	Marie Morin	24 Feb 1873	Angêle Catfish	John Catfish	Marie Lapatte
	Véronique Bouvier	7 May 1873	Josephine Kapikhawakiswin	François Kapikhawakiswin	Françoise Makégou
Pierre Morin	Véronique Bouvier	24 May 1873	Elizabeth Jourdain	Jean Baptiste Jourdain	Ann Bekattla
		11 June 1873	Adam Tchyanlgwa	Louis Tchyanlgwa	Madeleine
	Caroline Morin	19 June 1873	Joseph Oliver Montagnais		Chakeltess (?)
	Véronique Bouvier	24 June 1873	Marie Josephine Tsinae'iaze	Tsinae'iaze	Sara Nenn'iaze
Pierriche Laliberte	Caroline Morin	24 June 1873	Louis Lisa Echiléairi iaze	Echiléairi iaze	Dzenn Eézé
Baptiste Morin	Sarazine Morin	12 Aug 1873	Cyrille Laliberte	Pierre Laliberte	Deneyuille
	Marguerite Roy	1 Oct 1873	Joseph Jourdain	Joseph Jourdain	Géneviève Jourdain
	Sarazine Morin	14 Oct 1873	Géneviève Petit Ours	François Petit Ours	Aloisa Bruce
Louis Morin	Pélagie Morin	30 Nov 1873	Joseph Misponas	Samuel Misponas	Sizakkapess
Alexandre Morin	Marguerite Jourdain	15 Dec 1873	Jerome Manilokaiwasis	Manilokaiwasis	Véronique Attahew
	Marguerite	18 Feb 1874	François Bouvier	Michel Bouvier Jr.	Marguerite Petit Ours
Alexandre Morin	Caroline Morin	29 May 1874	Charles Joseph Lariviere	David Lariviere	Julie Morin
		12 June 1874	Wiliam Egou	Samuel Egou	Marie Durocher
Alexandre Morin	[illegible] Morin	7 June 1874	Pierre Morin	Zéphrin Morin	Marguerite Kkasba
		17 June 1874	Alexandre Nartheniaze	Joseph Nattheniaze	Madeleine Girard / Agathe Dapazéla

▼ Godparents, 1867–1912

Godfather	Godmother	Date of baptism	Baptized	Father of baptized	Mother of baptized
Alexandre Morin	Sarazine Morin	19 June 1874	Julien Montagnais	Thomas Montagnais	Mary Montagnais
P. Laliberte	Sarazine Morin	2 Oct 1874	Marie Delaronde	Paul Delaronde	Sophie Morin
Pierre Aubichon	Caroline Morin	6 Oct 1874	François Kiweyakomew	Kiweyakomew	
Baptiste Morin	Caroline Morin	2 Mar 1875	Jean Bapt. Durocher dit Assion	d'Assion Durocher	Pauline
Pierre Morin	Anne Sassthe	16 Mar 1875	Patrice Dassalabe	Dassalabe	Susan Yaze
Michel Bouvier Sr.	Julie Bouvier	11 Aug 1875	Louis Michel Jourdain	Louis Jourdain	Marguerite McKay
[illegible]	Julie Bouvier	2 Apr 1876	Elie Augustine Roy	François Roy	Marie Lariviere
	Marguerite Morin and Sister Marguerite Marie	7 Apr 1876	Marguerite Marie McKay	.	
Zéphrin Morin	Madeleine Girard	9 May 1875	Jean Baptiste Morin	Raphaël Morin	Betsy Cook
Louis Morin	Marguerite Jourdain	9 May 1875	Marie Louise Merasty	George Merasty	Cecile Durocher
	Sophie Morin	13 May 1876	Sophie Petit Ours	François Petit Ours	blank
Zéphrin Morin	Madeleine Girard	13 May 1876	Eliza Merasty	Alfred Merasty	Kanikamowitomi
Paul Grégeau	Pélagie Morin	3 June 1877	Rose Dapazale	Joseph Dapazale	Philomene Thu'tennuei
Paul Grezaud	Julie Morin	15 June 1877	Paul Echindke yua	Echindke yua	Tsandess
Joseph Jourdain	Marguerite Morin	22 Jan 1878	Suzanne Opikokew	Joseph Opikokew	Isabelle Wiyabaskusk
	Pélagie Morin	5 Apr 1878	Marie Billette	Paul Billette	Justine
	Pélagie Morin	14 Apr 1878	Marguerite Estalthennen	Jacob Estalthennen	Rose Echilekwiez
Vincent Daigneault	Julie Bouvier	17 May 1878	Johny Thomas Kyplain	Thomas Kyplain	Sophie
Pierre Malboeuf	Julie Morin	26 July 1878	Norbert Maurice	François Maurice	Angele Laliberte
Joseph Morin	Virginie Merasty	2 Aug 1878	Alphonse Mangeur du lard	Michel Mangeur du lard	Paulette Billette
Henry McKay	Pélagie Morin	12 Oct 1878	Sara Estalthennen	Amiphelon Estalthennen	Malanie Essethyuw
Vincent Daigneault	Pélagie Morin	5 May 1880	Antoine Bebbaedipinan	Nodente Bebbaedipinan	Sara Nakkize

Father	Mother	Date	Child	Godfather	Godmother
Wulle Morin	Philomène Lariviere	30 May 1880	Marie Angèle Durocher	Pierre Durocher	Caroline Lariviere
Wulle Morin	Marie Lucia	2 June 1880	Vital Piwicha	Piwicha	Catherine Thacheza (?)
Wulle Morin	Josephine Lafleur	9 June 1880	Jean Baptiste Tadelthiye	Peter Tadelthiye	Marie Dzemnape
Joseph Morin	Philomène Malboeuf	11 June 1880	Jean Baptiste Tssinaiaze	Jean Tssinaiaze	Marie Edthenpòn nundsòn
Pierriche Laliberte	Sarazine Morin	1 Sept 1880	Johny Sinclair	James Nicol Sinclair	Josephte Durocher
Thomas Desjarlais	Julie Bouvier	21 Feb 1881	Elie Roy	François Roy	Marie Lariviere
Vincent Daigneault		9 June 1881	Willibrov Faraud	Samuel Faraud	Henriette Eketcho
	Julie Bouvier	22 Jan 1882	Joseph Couyounner	François Couyounner	Françoise Maskedom Iskwew
Brother Marcilly	Julie Bouvier	20 May 1882	John MacLeod	Donald MacLeod	Mary MacLeod
	Julie Bouvier	18 July 1885	Athanase Roy	François Roy	Marie Lariviere
J.B. Rapet	Julie Bouvier	13 Nov 1885	Jean Baptiste [not listed]	Peter Moise	Angélique
	Julie Bouvier	25 May 1886	Philippe Jacob	François Jacob	Julia Ikkeilzik
	Julie Bouvier	22 Nov 1886	Etienne Clement	Laurent Deneyou	Elise
	Véronique Morin	8 June 1887	Véronique Saltaye	Peter Saltaye	Marie
François Daigneault	Véronique	14 Jan 1888	Ambroise Jacobson	François Jacobson	Julie Ikkeilzik
	Julie Bouvier	20 Feb 1888	Louise Caisse	Louis Caisse	Sophie Lariviere
Charles Maurice	Julie Bouvier	18 May 1888	Charles Bouvier	Michel Bouvier Jr.	Julie Morin
Pierre Marie Isla	Véronique Morin	18 May 1888	Pierre Marie Bouvier	Michel Bouvier Jr.	Julie Morin
François Daigneault	Véronique Morin	29 May 1889	Aloysia Corrigal	James Daigneault	Sophie Daigneault
Archibald Linklater	Julie Bouvier	21 July 1889	Mary Anna Bella McDermet	Andrew Miles McDermet	Ellen Flett
Baptiste Lafleur	Véronique Morin	27 Sept 1889	Marie Octavie Aubichon	Modeste Aubichon	Marie Anne Desjarlais
François Daigneault	Véronique Morin	22 Dec 1889	Thomas Daigneault	Vincent Daigneault	Marguerite Bouvier
	Augustine Bouvier	17 Mar 1891	Beatrice Maurice	Magloire Maurice	Philomène Lariviere
François Daigneault	Sister Lajoie	19 Sept 1892	Marie Marguerite Roy	Louison Roy	Courrone Maurice
Brother Marcilly	Julie Bouvier dite Can.	4 Oct 1892	Felix François Caisse	Charles dit Ladébcauch Caisse	Augustine Bouvier

▲ Godparents, 1867–1912

Godfather	Godmother	Date of baptism	Baptized	Father of baptized	Mother of baptized
François Daigneault	Véronique	24 Mar 1893	Ambroise Gardiner	Robert Gardiner	Eliza/Lucia Daigneault
	Julie Bouvier	12 June 1893	Joseph Mangeur du lard	Charlie Mangeur du lard	Sara Nakkiye
Charles dit Ladébeauch Caisse	Augustine Bouvier	1 July 1893	Jules Bouvier	Joseph Bouvier	Caroline Lafleur
Vincent Daigneault	Véronique Morin	18 Feb 1894	Alexis Durocher	Prosper Desjarlais	Pauline Durocher
Martial Desjarlais	Eliza/Lucia Daigneault	30 Oct 1894	William Alfred Maurice	Charles Maurice	Julie Bouvier dite Can.
Martial Desjarlais	Octavie Bouvier	15 Dec 1894	Marie Sarazine Bouvier	François Bouvier	Marie Rose Laliberte
Brother Lacroix	Octavie Bouvier	10 June 1895	Robert Corrigal	Thomas Corrigal	Lucia Vincena
Vincent Daigneault	Julie Bouvier	8 Oct 1895	Joseph Desjarlais	Martial Desjarlais	Octavie Bouvier
Vincent Daigneault	Véronique Morin	1 Oct 1896	Ambroise Roy	Prosper Roy	Catherine Lafleur
Vincent Daigneault	Augustine Bouvier	19 Jan 1897	Hélène Bouvier	François Bouvier	Marie Rose Laliberte
Vincent Daigneault	Marguerite Bouvier	10 Feb 1897	Marguerite Malboeuf	Pierriche Malboeuf	Pélagie Morin
	Julie Bouvier	4 June 1897	Joseph Charles McCallum	Charles McCallum	Agnès Lafleur
Pierre Maurice	Julie Bouvier	12 June 1897	Alfred Aubichon	Julien Aubichon	Rosalie Maurice
Vincent Daigneault	Marguerite Bouvier	13 Aug 1897	Hermaline Daigneault	Vincent Daigneault Jr.	Eliza Merasty
William Daigneault	Véronique	14 Aug 1897	Marius Robert Gardiner	Robert Gardiner	Eliza/Lucia Daigneault
Joseph Mitchan	Augustine Bouvier	24 Aug 1897	Felix Caisse	Louis Caisse	Sophie
Vincent Daigneault Jr.	Eliza Merasty	13 Dec 1897	Anna Piwabiskus	Jean Piwabiskus	Marguerite Marie Daigneault
Pierre Daigneault	Julie Bouvier	18 Dec 1897	Oliver Bouvier	Joseph Bouvier	[blank] Lafleur
Prosper Roy	Augustine Bouvier	27 Mar 1898	Pierre Marie Bouvier	Michelis Bouvier	Julie Morin
	Octavie Bouvier	28 May 1898	Emilie Marie Opikokew	Jean Baptiste Opikokew	Eliza Desjarlais
François Daigneault	Courrone Maurice	15 Aug 1898	Edouard Marie Lariviere	Louis Lariviere	Marguerite Marie Roy
Joseph Lariviere	Agnès Morin	10 Dec 1898	Aldina Marie Lariviere	Thomy Lariviere	Véronique Bouvier

François Roy	Caroline Morin	24 Apr 1899	Clementine Bedshhidelkkezhi	Raphaël Bedshhidelkkezhi	Hélène Roy
J.W. Harris	Octavie Bouvier	24 Apr 1899	Marguerite Marie Malboeuf	Pierre Malboeuf	Pélagie Morin
Vincent Daigneault	Marguerite Bouvier	31 May 1899	Marie Madeleine Corrigal	John Thomas Corrigal	Sophie Daigneault
[illegible]	Octavie Bouvier	8 June 1899	Emile Opikokew	Jean Baptiste Opikokew	Eliza Desjarlais
François Daigneault	Véronique Morin	7 Nov 1899	Marie Agnès Desjarlais	Martial Desjarlais	Octavie Bouvier
[illegible]	Augustine Bouvier	5 Apr 1900	Patrice Opikokew	Jonas Opikokew	Marie
Zéphrin Joannisis	Marie Elizabeth Bouvier	13 Aug 1900	Christine Droutzana	Baptiste Droutzana	Marie Fisher
François Maurice	Pélagie Morin	22 Nov 1900	Ernest Maurice	François Maurice	Josephine Couillonneur
Jérémie Caisse	Véronique Morin	8 Jan 1901	Ermeline Bouvier	Joseph Bouvier	Caroline Lafleur
Prosper Daigneault	Marie Elizabeth Bouvier	19 Mar 1901	Jérémie Maurice	Charles Maurice	Marie Julie Bouvier
Philippe You	Marie Rose Laliberte	23 Mar 1901	Alexandre Daigneault	Vincent Daigneault Jr.	Eliza Merasty
Joseph Daigneault	Octavie Bouvier	28 June 1901	Rosa Roy	Prosper Roy	Marie Catherine Lafleur
	Marie Elizabeth Bouvier	30 June 1901	Joseph Lafleur	Charles McCallum	Agnès Lafleur
Prosper Daigneault	Julie Bouvier	16 Aug 1901	Emile Corrigal	John Thomas Corrigal	Sophie Daigneault
Prosper Daigneault	Hélène Campbell	27 Aug 1901	Alex. Thomas Raoul Roy	Elie Roy	Marguerite Marie McCallum
Prosper Daigneault	Eliza Merasty	6 Nov 1901	Rosa Bouvier	François Bouvier	Marie Rose Laliberte
Joseph Daigneault	Véronique Caisse	7 Nov 1901	Willie Gardiner[George]	Robbie Gardiner	Eliza Merasty
Baptiste Mitchon	Augustine Bouvier	18 Nov 1901	Anastasie Ikkeilzik	Martial Ikkeilzik	Charlotte Harper
Joseph Daigneault	Lucia Aubichon	28 June 1902	Leon Malboeuf	Cyprien Malboeuf	Liza Janvier
Pierriche Malboeuf	Pélagie Morin	22 Apr 1903	Clementine Desjarlais	Prosper Desjarlais	Valerie Malboeuf
	Octavie Bouvier	8 Jan 1903	Joseph Bouvier	François Bouvier	Marie Rose Laliberte
Louis Lariviere	Julie Morin	18 July 1903	Jean Marie Laliberte	Jean Baptiste Laliberte	Marie Testawitch
François Daigneault	Josephine Maurice	2 Feb 1904	Joseph August Durocher	Jean Baptiste Durocher	Angèle Roy
François Daigneault	Véronique Morin	24 Apr 1904	Henri Maurice	Celestin Maurice	Catherine Lariviere
Alex Laliberte	Pélagie Morin	4 May 1904	Gregoire Malboeuf	Cyprien Malboeuf	Aloisa Janvier
Pierre Daigneault	Aloisa Daigneault	6 May 1904	Ambroise Morin	Paul Morin	Catherine Daigneault
William Gardiner	Octavie Bouvier	25 May 1904	Jules Caisse	Charles Caisse	Marie Rose Maurice

▶ Godparents, 1867–1912

Godfather	Godmother	Date of baptism	Baptized	Father of baptized	Mother of baptized
Martial Desjarlais	Octavie Bouvier	10 July 1904	Emilie Daigneault	Pierre Daigneault	Clementine Malboeuf
Felix Morin	Catherine Marguerite Daigneault	27 Oct 1904	Ambroise Corrigal	John Thomas Corrigal	Sophie Daigneault
François Daigneault	Marguerite Daigneault	15 Mar 1905	Cyprien [Bouvier]		Augustine Bouvier
George Bekattla	Caroline Morin	31 Mar 1905	Joseph Alex Lafleur	Baptiste Lafleur	Marianne
Pierre Malboeuf	Caroline Morin	3 Apr 1905	Marguerite Marie Kerbriand	Auguste Kerbriand	Yvonne
Felix Morin	Octavie Aubichon	12 Apr 1905	Clementine Desjarlais	Prosper Desjarlais	Valerie Malboeuf
Thomas Daigneault	Aloisa Janvier	14 June 1905	Fredrick Alcrow	Joe Alcrow	Josephine Lafleur
Joseph Daigneault	Sophie Daigneault	1 Jan 1906	Ambroise Morin	Felix Morin	Catherine Daigneault
Oscar Roy	Caroline Morin	7 Feb 1906	Gilbert Didzepe	Pierre Didzepe	Lizette Shayhoene (?)
Pierre Daigneault	Christine Malboeuf	12 May 1906	John James Desjarlais	Louis Desjarlais	Marie Aubichon
François Laliberte	Octavie Bouvier	24 May 1906	Philomène Bouvier	Joseph Bouvier	Caroline Lafleur
François Daigneault	Catherine McCallum	13 June 1906	Gaspard Joseph Bouvier	Prosper Bouvier	Sarazine McCallum
Jules Morin	Catherine Daigneault	28 June 1906	Alfred Gardiner	Robert Gardiner	Eliza Daigneault
Joseph Lariviere	Agnès Morin	30 June 1906	Agnès Lariviere	Louis Lariviere	Marguerite Marie Roy
Thomas Daigneault	Eliza Merasty	7 Sep 1906	Louis Opikokew	Jean Baptiste Opikokew	Eliza Desjarlais
Narcisse Lafleur	Véronique Morin	16 Sep 1906	Jules [Maurice]		Euphemie Maurice
Narcisse Lafleur	Véronique Morin	16 Sep 1906	Olivier Opikokew		Valerie Opikokew Natowew
Joseph Lafleur	Marianne Bouvier	11 Dec 1906	Pélagie Gardiner	William Gardiner	Elmire Malboeuf
William Daigneault	Marguerite Marie Laliberte	3 Mar 1907	Marie Clara Daigneault	Vincent Daigneault Jr.	Eliza Merasty
William Gardiner	Véronique Morin	17 Apr 1907	Magdeleine Morin	Jules Morin	Jeanne Gardiner
Jules Morin	Flora Caisse	27 July 1907	Hélène Jonas Thapalgwe	Jonas Thapalgwe	Marie Louise
Thomas Daigneault	Madam Pierre Daigneault	4 Aug 1907	Jean Marie Malboeuf	Cyprien Malboeuf	Liza Janvier
Joseph Daigneault	Jeanne Gardiner	12 Aug 1907	Ambroise Lafleur	Joseph Lafleur	Elmire Corrigal

Date	Child	Father	Mother	Godfather	Godmother
27 Aug 1907	Hermeline Desjarlais	Prosper Desjarlais	Valerie Malboeuf	Joseph Daigneault	Catherine Daigneault
20 Sep 1907	Cecile Piwabiskus	Basile Piwabiskus	Marie Bouvier	François Daigneault	Julie Morin
22 Sep 1907	François Desjarlais	Martial Desjarlais	Octavie Bouvier	Prosper Daigneault	Josephine Maurice
23 Jan 1908	Jules Desjarlais	Louis Desjarlais	Marie Aubichon	Pierre Daigneault	Clementine Malboeuf
15 Mar 1908	Jean Marie Malboeuf	Daniel Malboeuf	Marie Jourdain	Felix Morin	Clementine Malboeuf
16 Apr 1908	Emilien Guinay	Joseph Guinay	Isobelle Youville	[blank] Bouvier	Marianne Bouvier
6 June 1908	Marie Rose Marguerite Morin	Felix Morin	Marguerite Daigneault	Vincent Daigneault Jr.	Eliza Merasty
11 June 1908	Marie Agnès Aubichon	Jonas Aubichon	Corrine Lariviere	Thomas Lariviere	Véronique Bouvier
20 June 1908	Hermeline Caisse	Jérémie Caisse	Anna Ross	Pierre Gerard	Véronique Morin
11 July 1908	Marguerite Marie Boyd	Andrew Boyd	Celeste Lariviere	William Daigneault	Marie Testawitch
20 July 1908	Adélaide Caisse	Charles Caisse	Marie Rose Maurice		Marianne Bouvier
1 Oct 1908	Anne Gardiner	Robert Gardiner	Eliza/Lucia Daigneault	William Gardiner	Marie Rose Bouvier
31 Oct 1908	Vitaline Roy	Elie Roy	Eliza Corrigal	François Roy	Véronique Bouvier
26 Dec 1908	Adélaide Maurice	Charles Maurice	Julie Bouvier	Charles Caisse	Augustine Bouvier
14 Jan 1909	François Xavier Daigneault	Vincent Daigneault Jr.	Eliza Merasty	Jules Morin	[blank] McCallum
24 Jan 1909	William Melchoir Malboeuf	Cyprien Malboeuf	Eliza Janvier	William Daigneault	Sarazine McCallum
6 Mar 1909	Albert Lariviere	François Lariviere	Sophie Charlebois Natomagan	Thomas Daigneault	Marie
6 June 1909	Augustin Joseph Philippe Malboeuf	Daniel Malboeuf	Marie Jourdain	Joseph Daigneault	Flora Caisse
4 Sep 1909	Flora Desjarlais	Louis Desjarlais	Marie Aubichon	Philippe Halcrow	Octavie Bouvier
5 Sep 1909	Joseph Henri Bekartla	Thomas Bekartla	Marie Anne	François Roy	Caroline Morin
9 Nov 1909	François Gardiner	Robert Gardiner	Eliza/Lucia Daigneault	Alexis Durocher	Marianne Bouvier
11 Dec 1909	Leon Desjarlais	Prosper Desjarlais	Valerie Malboeuf	Prosper Roy	Julie Bouvier
17 Dec 1909	Pierre Joachim Morin	Jules Morin	Jane Gardiner	Ambroise Morin	Marguerite Marie Laliberte
17 Jan 1910	Philippe Antoine Lafleur	Joseph Lafleur	Elmire Corrigal	William Daigneault	Marguerite McCallum
4 Feb 1910	Agathe Celina Laliberte	Norbert Laliberte	Josephine Gerard	William Daigneault	Véronique Morin
14 Feb 1911	Marie Melanie Victorie Roy	Philippe Roy	Flora Caisse	Joseph Daigneault	Marguerite Marie Laliberte
6 Apr 1910	Marguerite Marie Billette	Jean Baptiste Billette	Nancy Sillne	Louis Morin	Elizabeth Jourdain
29 July 1910	Jean Marie Lamp Desjarlais	Martial Desjarlais	Octavie Bouvier	Monian Morin	Angèle Roy

▼ Godparents, 1867–1912

Date of baptism	Baptized	Father of baptized	Mother of baptized	Godfather	Godmother
14 Oct 1910	Zéphrin Morin	Felix Morin	Catherine Daigneault	Jules Morin	Véronique Morin
14 Oct 1910	Adeline Halcrow	Samuel Halcrow	Hélène Laliberte	Charlot Maurice	Julie Morin
1 Dec 1910	Magloire Gazaire François Morin	Louis Morin	Hélène Maurice	Zéphrin Morin	Madeleine Girard
26 Dec 1910	Zéphrin Bouvier	Prosper Bouvier	Sarazine McCallum	Louis Morin	Véronique Morin
4 Mar 1911	Ernest Daigneault	Joseph Daigneault	Maria Louisa		Catherine Marguerite Daigneault
26 Apr 1911	Jean Marie Didzepe	Simon Didzepe	Catherine 'iaze	Pierriche Malboeuf	Pélagie Morin
21 July 1911	Alexandre Maurice	François Maurice	Marie Adele Laliberte	Pierriche Malboeuf	Pélagie Morin
12 Dec 1911	Albert Daigneault	Prosper Daigneault	Josephine Maurice	Thomas Daigneault	Clementine Malboeuf
14 Dec 1911	Marie Philomene Desjarlais	Louis Desjarlais	Marie Aubichon	Pierre Daigneault	Octavie Daigneault
24 Dec 1911	Marie Vitaline You	Philippe You	Madeleine Piwabiskus	Joseph Daigneault	Marguerite Marie
23 Mar 1912	Marie Alphonsine Couillonneur	François Couillonneur	Rosalie Piwabiskus	Felix Morin	Marguerite Marie Morin
9 Apr 1912	Anastasie Ross	Joseph Ross	Marie Philomène Iron	[illegible] Morin	M. Elizabeth You
14 Aug 1912	Melanie Maskinut	Benjamin Maskinut	Josephte Kret	Joseph Desjarlais	Hélène Bouvier
23 Sep 1912	Gilbert Caisse	Jérémie Caisse	Annie Ross	William Daigneault	Marie Catherine Roy
19 Dec 1912	Ambroise Guinay	Joseph Guinay	Isobelle Youville	Ambroise Gardiner	Hélène Bouvier

Glossary

Canadian | A term that is used rather broadly within fur trade records to refer to traders from the St. Lawrence region. It refers to those men born in and based out of Canada who engaged in the trade – as opposed to those men who worked for the HBC, a London-based company that imported many of its servants from Great Britain and other European countries before 1821.

The term "Canadian" therefore applies to French, Scottish, and Aboriginal people who were part of the St. Lawrence trade network.

chief factor | The term "factor" is from the Latin, "he who does," and was a person who professionally acted as the representative of another individual or other legal entity. Within the HBC, a chief factor was the highest rank in the officer class. Chief factors were responsible for the management of several outposts and of other ranking officers. Only chief traders could be promoted to the position of chief factor.

chief trader | The HBC officer responsible for actual fur bartering. Chief traders were generally promoted to their position after they had honed their skills as a clerk in the service of the Company for at least fifteen to twenty years. Chief trader was the second-highest position in the trade districts.

clerk | The lowest rank of officer of the HBC. After a five-year apprenticeship, most clerks were placed in charge of smaller fur-trading outposts to administer the day-to-day tasks of trading and outpost maintenance. Clerks provided the work-force from which future chief traders and factors were recruited.

district | The HBC divided the administrative stucture of its trade into districts. Each district had an inland headquarters under the command of a district master or chief factor. The names, boundaries, and even headquarters of districts changed over time.

free trader | When freemen moved beyond a role defined and supported by the HBC, they became free traders. Free traders were involved with commercial trading outfits that infringed on the Company's monopoly, taking profits away from the post of origin. Free traders were often supported and supplied by competing HBC trade districts, if not actual independent fur companies. The free traders' ability to work independently from the HBC and outside its jurisdictional control at Red River resulted in the trial of Pierre Guillaume Sayer in 1849. The HBC convicted Sayer of trafficking in furs and opposing the Company's monopoly. Although convicted, Sayer was released when an armed body of Metis surrounded the courthouse. The Metis concluded that the monopoly had been broken, and they declared that the trade was now free.

freemen | In the latter half of the nineteenth century, freemen were often retired or casually employed servants who continued to live inland in fur districts like the English River and belonged to well-established families that required their support. Although they had no permanent contracts, HBC freemen performed occasional labour for the Company while pursuing other economic opportunities, such as subsistence hunting and fishing. Among the roles fulfilled in the HBC's commercial enterprise in the English River District, they served as hunters and trappers, procuring provisions and furs for the posts; they operated commercial enterprises, such as freighting, transporting, or trading establishments; and occasionally they sold their physical labour to the Company for the same price as contracted servants. Freemen were not independent operators trading for their own profit but, rather, were a component of the Company's commercial operations. However, freemen only signed on occasionally and/or seasonally rather than maintaining regular or permanent employment.

Indian trader | An HBC trader who dealt directly with Indian traders and communites to pursue and maintain the trade relationship.

Metis | Note that in this work "Metis" is written without an acute accent over the "e." The reason for this choice is that "Métis" typically implies a specific historical circumstance, associated with both French and Catholic influences, that originated with the eastern trade routes prior to the fall of New France and the Scottish takeover of the St. Lawrence trade. The term "Halfbreed," also known as "country born," has historically referred to English and Scottish mixed-bloods who came out of the Hudson's Bay Company trade.

Use of an unaccented "Metis" signifies that the term is being used to encompass all mixed-descent people in the English River District. The use of the unaccented word is meant to denote mixed-descent people who created communities for themselves that were separate and distinct from both their Indian and European ancestors, regardless of their association with fur companies or European/Euro-Canadian paternity. The Metis of the English River District are predominantly, although not exclusively, from French and Cree forebears, but there are also those with Dene, Scottish, English, Blackfoot, and Iroquois heritages. Furthermore, using "Métis," I believe, privileges their Frenchness over their Aboriginal heritages or alternative European lineages. Regardless of either maternity or paternity, the Metis of the English River District were all members of the family and lived according to the values articulated by wahkootowin.

There is a rich historiography dealing with the use of the term "Metis." See in particular John Foster, "The Métis: The People and the Term," *Prairie Forum* 3, 1 (1978): 79-90; Jennifer S.H. Brown, "Fur Traders, Racial Categories and Kinship Networks," in *Papers of the 6th Algonquian Conference, 1974,* ed. William Cowan (Ottawa: National Museums of Canada, 1975), 209-22; Gerhard Ens, *Homeland to Hinterland: The Changing Worlds of the Red River Metis in the Nineteenth Century* (Toronto: University of Toronto Press, 1996); and Nicole St-Onge, *Saint-Laurent, Manitoba: Evolving Metis Identities, 1870-1914* (Regina: Canadian Plains Research Center, 2004), and "Uncertain Margins: Métis and Saulteaux Identities in St-Paul des Saulteaux, Red River, 1821-1870," *Manitoba History* (October 2006): 1-8.

Michif | Classically, Michif is described as a blended language of Cree (and/or Saulteaux) and French and is an area of study that has received a great deal of scholarly attention in recent years. There has been some debate as to whether the language spoken in Île à la Crosse was actually Michif. The leading scholar in the field, Peter Bakker, has argued that the people of Île à la Crosse did not speak Michif. Instead, he concluded that their language "must be considered Cree, with some borrowings from French." However, at the National Michif Conference held in Saskatoon, Saskatchewan, in March 2008, organizers acknowledged the existence of a distinct Michif dialect that was far more influenced by the Cree language than others. This new dialect is being referred to as "Île à la Crosse Michif." Michif speakers within the Metis community are currently exploring the notion that, as a language family, Michif has regional and/or local dialect variations. To a lesser degree, scholars have also examined Bungi, a blend of Cree and Gaelic spoken by British Metis in the Red River area in the nineteenth century.

outfit | A fur trade outfit is both the annual goods a post or individual trader was given to trade and the annual cycle around which the HBC trade was structured. An outfit ran from 1 June of one year to 31 May of the next year.

postmaster | The position of postmaster was an especially popular assignment after 1832 for the Aboriginal sons of former servants. Postmaster, a rank between interpreter and clerk, was created especially for men who had gained reputations of steadiness, honesty, and attention to duty.

runner | A type of labourer most often used during competitive periods, when a lot of trading was conducted in Indian encampments rather than at the posts. These labourers ensured the smooth movement of goods and furs between outposts and the main depots.

servant | An HBC employee obligated to give service to the Company under the terms of a contract.

tripmen/trippers | The terms "tripmen" and "trippers" are interchangeable and were a part of the HBC's lexicon. The terms refer to those men who were hired specifically to work in the transport system. Therefore, they served a similar function to that of the voyageurs of the St. Lawrence trade network. Tripmen or trippers manned the York boat and Red River cart brigades.

wahkootowin | Relative, relationship, kinsmanship, or simply relation. There are various derivatives of wahkootowin, including wakotuhisoo (he forms a relationship), wakottuwok (they are related), or wakomakun (close relation), that have similar but more precise meanings, depending on required usage. There is considerable variation in spelling, including wahkootowin, wakottuwin, and wahko'towin, reflecting the newness of Roman orthography's application of the Cree language and the lack of standardization.

In 2003-04, wahkootowin was used as the framework for Saskatchewan's First Nations and Metis Justice Commission during an inquiry into the relationship between Saskatchewan Aboriginal peoples and the provincial justice system. The Commission took as its motto "meyo wahkotowin," or "one community," indicating that in order for meaningful change to occur, the people of the province must regard themselves as members of a shared community, not two solitudes.

York boat | Modelled after fishing boats from the Orkney Islands, Scotland, this style of boat was designed and used by the HBC to transport furs and goods throughout Rupert's Land. Because York boats were larger and heavier than the NWC's trade canoes, which were manned by voyageurs, they could carry greater quantities of furs and goods. Approximately forty-six feet long and capable of carrying six tons of cargo, the York boat was too large to carry across a portage. It was dragged across land and water by trippers. In the case of the Methy Portage, the tripmen emptied the York boats, carried the cargo across a path cut through the brush, and then, using oxen kept especially for that purpose, dragged the empty canoe across that same path.

Notes

1 Lawrence Ahenakew, interview, Sandy Point, Lake Île à la Crosse, August 1999, The Virtual Museum of Metis History and Culture, http://www.metismuseum.ca (emphasis added). The interview text has been altered slightly from the interview transcript as it appears at the Virtual Museum of Metis History and Culture in order to make it more concise and readable. Ahenakew's sentiment and tone, however, have not been changed.

2 The Michif/Cree place names used by the people of the region to name and describe their homeland, their space, their history will be privileged over French and English place names as much as possible.

3 Sakitawak is both the village and lake known since 1776 as Île à la Crosse to both English and French speakers.

4 Ahenakew, interview (emphasis added).

5 While indigenous names survive for the specific places in this study, no known name in Cree, Michif, or any other Aboriginal language exists for the region as a whole. I use the term "the northwest" to refer to the larger place or space occupied and used by the Metis – their homeland – and use the phrase "the English River District" for those spaces utilized by trade companies and the Catholic Church. There is obviously some geographic overlap between the two, but the intent is to emphasize that different people conceptualized the space in distinct intellectual and spiritual ways based on notions of either belonging or being an outsider.

6 J.R. Miller, "From Riel to the Métis," *Canadian Historical Review* 69, 1 (1988): 14. See also Trudy Nicks and Kenneth Morgan, "Grand Cache: The Historic Development of an Indigenous Aboriginal Métis Population," in *The New Peoples: Being and Becoming Metis in North America,* ed. Jacqueline Peterson and Jennifer S.H. Brown (Winnipeg: University of Manitoba Press, 1985), 163-81.

7 Carolyn Podruchny, "Baptizing Novices: Ritual Moments among French Canadian Voyageurs in the Montreal Fur Trade, 1780-1821," *Canadian Historical Review* 83, 2 (2002): 173-74.

8 The term "style of life" was coined in 1953 by anthropologist Robert R. Redfield and has maintained some resonance since. Historian Lawrence W. Levine, for example, drew inspiration from Redfield in his study of the cultural traditions of African Americans derived from their West African ancestors. Levine criticized others for ignoring the songs, sermons, and storytelling traditions of African slaves, thereby rendering inarticulate in the historical record an articulate people. See Robert R. Redfield, *The Primitive World and Its Transformations* (Ithaca, NY: Cornell University Press, 1953), 51-53; and Lawrence W. Levine, *The Unpredictable Past: Explorations in American Cultural History* (New York: Oxford University Press, 1993), 36.

9 Redfield, *The Primitive World*, 51-53.

10 Clifford Geertz, *The Interpretation of Cultures* (New York: Basic Books, 1973), 50-51.

11 See Peter Bakker, *A Language of Our Own: The Genesis of Michif, the Mixed Cree-French Language of the Canadian Métis* (New York: Oxford University Press, 1997); John C. Crawford, "What Is Michif? Language in the Metis Tradition," in *The New Peoples: Being and Becoming Metis in North America,* ed. Jacqueline Peterson and Jennifer S.H. Brown (Winnipeg: University of Manitoba Press, 1981), 231-42; Patrick C. Douaud, *Ethnolinguistic Profile of the Canadian Métis,* Mercury Series – Canadian Ethnology Service, Paper 99 (Ottawa: National Museum of Man, 1985); Margaret R. Stobie, "Background of the Dialect Called Bungi," *Historical and Scientific Society of Manitoba* 3, 24 (1967-68): 65-75; and Stobie, "The Dialect Called Bungi," *Canadian Antiques Collector* 6, 8 (1971): 20.

12 David Thompson, *David Thompson's Narrative, 1784-1812,* ed. Richard Glover (Toronto: Champlain Society, 1962), 73.

13 See R. Faries, ed., *A Dictionary of the Cree Language, as Spoken by the Indians in the Provinces of Quebec, Ontario, Manitoba, Saskatchewan and Alberta. Based upon the Foundation Laid by E.A. Watkins, 1865,* rev. ed. (Toronto: General Synod of the Church of England in Canada, 1938); Gérard Beaudet, *Cree-English English-Cree Dictionary = Nehiyawe mina Akayasimo, Akayasimo mina Nehiyawe ayamiwini-masinahigan* (Winnipeg: Wuerz Publishing, 1995); H.C. Wolfart and Freda Ahenakew, *The Student's Dictionary of Literary Plains Cree: Based on Contemporary Texts* (Winnipeg: Algonquian and Iroquoian Linguistics, 1998); and Anne Anderson, ed., *Plains Cree Dictionary in the "Y" Dialect* (s.i.: s.n., 1975). Elders such as Maria Campbell carry and share the teachings specific to wahkootowin today as part of their responsibilities as teachers within the Metis community. Specifically, Campbell, in her role as an instructor at various universities across Canada, has brought the teachings about wahkootowin into the classroom to further understandings of indigenous literature, knowledge and methods, and history. Some of these teachings have been published and are available in texts designed to promote cultural teachings, such as Grace McKay Jolly, Alice Aby, and Stan Cuthand, *Kisewatotatowin: Loving, Caring, Sharing, Respect,* 2nd ed. (Saskatoon: Aboriginal Parent Program, 1998), a parenting handbook published to assist in strengthening young families. Campbell has further written about wahkootowin in her bi-monthly newspaper column for *Eagle Feather News.* See, for instance, Campbell, "We Need to Return to the Principles of Wahkotowin," *Eagle Feather News,* November 2007, p. 5.

14 Ella Cara Deloria, *Speaking of Indians* (1944; repr., Lincoln: University of Nebraska Press, 1998), 24.

15 Ibid., 24-25.
16 Morgan, the father of kinship studies, established the method and practice of evaluating Aboriginal family, and therefore social life, in his *Systems of Consanguinity and Affinity of the Human Family*, vol. 17 (Washington: Smithsonian Contributions to Knowledge, 1871). A proliferation of Aboriginal kinship studies followed Morgan's model. See also Morgan's *Ancient Society* (New York: Holt, 1877); Henry S. Sharp, "The Kinship System of the Black Lake Chipewyan" (PhD diss., Duke University, 1973); Scott Rushforth, *Bear Lake Athabascan Kinship and Task Group Formation*, Canadian Ethnology Service, Paper 96 (Ottawa: National Museum of Canada, 1984); David M. Schneider, *A Critique of the Study of Kinship* (Ann Arbor: University of Michigan Press, 1984); Linda Stone, *Kinship and Gender: An Introduction* (Boulder, CO: Westview Press, 1997); and Thomas R. Trautmann, *Lewis Henry Morgan and the Invention of Kinship* (Berkeley: University of California Press, 1987).
17 Raymond J. DeMallie, "Kinship: The Foundation for Native American Society," in *Studying Native America: Problems and Prospects*, ed. Russell Thornton (Madison: University of Wisconsin Press, 1998), 306.
18 Sharp, "The Kinship System of the Black Lake Chipewyan," 58; Sharp, *Chipewyan Marriage*, Canadian Ethnology Service, Paper 58 (Ottawa: National Museum of Canada, 1979), 3-5; Emile Petitot, *The Amerindians of the Canadian Northwest in the Nineteenth Century*, ed. Donat Savoie (Ottawa: Northern Science Research Group, Dept. of Indian Affairs and Northern Development, 1970), 69-70. The manner in which these ideas of relatedness were best applied to non-Indians was explored in Richard White's *The Middle Ground: Indians, Empires, and Republics in the Great Lakes Region, 1650-1815* (Cambridge: Cambridge University Press, 1991).
19 Mark Nuttall, "Choosing Kin: Sharing Subsistence in a Greenlandic Hunting Community," in *Dividends of Kinship: Meanings and Uses of Social Relatedness*, ed. Peter Schweitzer (London: Routledge, 2000), 46; and Gary Clayton Anderson, *Kinsmen of Another Kind: Dakota-White Relations in the Upper Mississippi Valley, 1650-1862* (Lincoln: University of Nebraska Press, 1984), xi.
20 Reminiscences about Aboriginal, specifically Native American, family life from the nineteenth century can be found in Arlene Hirschfelder, ed., *Native Heritage: Personal Accounts by American Indians, 1790 to Present* (New York: Macmillan, 1995).
21 These ideas were explored in Winona Stevenson, "'Ethnic' Assimilates 'Indigenous': A Study in Intellectual Colonialism," *Wicazo Sa Review* (1998): 33-51, and applied to a contemporary circumstance.
22 See, for instance, Sonia Blouin, "Entre frères et cousins: l'expérience familiale des voyageurs de la seigneurie de Rivière-du-Loup dans le commerce des fourrures, 1788-1821" (master's thesis, University of Ottawa, 2003); Françoise Noël, *Family Life and Sociability in Upper and Lower Canada, 1780-1870: A View from Diaries and Family Correspondence* (Montreal/Kingston: McGill-Queen's University Press, 2003); and Nancy Christie, ed., *Households of Faith: Family, Gender, and Community in Canada, 1760-1969* (Montreal/Kingston: McGill-Queen's University Press, 2002).
23 The missions in the region maintained community genealogies separate from the registries. These books identified the community's families and gave, in most instances, a brief description of each family's origins in the region and a generational genealogy that was useful as a means to cross-reference the data contained within the registries.
24 Gerhard J. Ens, *Homeland to Hinterland: The Changing Worlds of the Red River Metis in the Nineteenth Century* (Toronto: University of Toronto Press, 1996).

25   Natalie Zemon Davis, *The Return of Martin Guerre* (Cambridge, MA: Harvard University Press, 1983), 1.

26   Ibid., 5.

27   Carlo Ginzburg, *The Cheese and the Worms: The Cosmos of a Sixteenth-Century Miller,* trans. John and Anne C. Tedeschi (Baltimore: Johns Hopkins University Press, 1980); and Ginzburg, *Clues, Myths, and the Historical Method,* trans. John and Anne C. Tedeschi (Baltimore: Johns Hopkins University Press, 1986).

28   Ginzburg, *Clues, Myths,* 98, 103.

29   Marcel Giraud, *The Metis in the Canadian West,* trans. George Woodcock (Edmonton: University of Alberta Press, 1986); 2:329.

30   Ibid.

31   Sylvia Van Kirk, *Many Tender Ties: Women in Fur Trade Society in Western Canada, 1670-1870* (Winnipeg: Watson and Dwyer, 1980); and Jennifer S.H. Brown, *Strangers in Blood: Fur Trade Company Families in Indian Country* (Vancouver: UBC Press, 1980).

32   Diane Payment, *"The Free People – Otipemisiwak": Batoche, Saskatchewan, 1870-1930* (Ottawa: Canadian Parks Service, 1990).

33   Martha Harroun Foster, *We Know Who We Are: Métis Identity in a Montana Community* (Norman: University of Oklahoma Press, 2006); Susan Sleeper-Smith, *Indian Women and French Men: Rethinking Cultural Encounter in the Western Great Lakes* (Amherst: University of Massachusetts Press, 2001); Tanis C. Thorne, *The Many Hands of My Relations: French and Indian on the Lower Missouri* (Columbia: University of Missouri Press, 1996); and Lucy Eldersveld Murphy, *A Gathering of Rivers: Indians, Métis, and Mining in the Western Great Lakes, 1737-1832* (Lincoln: University of Nebraska Press, 2000).

34   Frits Pannekoek, *A Snug Little Flock: The Social Origins of the Riel Resistance, 1869-1870* (Winnipeg: Watson and Dwyer, 1991).

35   Irene M. Spry, "The Métis and Mixed-Bloods of Rupert's Land before 1870," in *The New Peoples: Being and Becoming Metis in North America,* ed. Jacqueline Peterson and Jennifer S.H. Brown (Winnipeg: University of Manitoba Press, 1981), 97.

36   Heather Devine, *The People Who Own Themselves: Aboriginal Ethnogenesis in a Canadian Family, 1660-1900* (Calgary: University of Calgary Press, 2004), 14.

37   John Foster, "Wintering, the Outsider Adult Male and the Ethnogenesis of the Western Plains Métis," *Prairie Forum* 19, 1 (1994): 1-14, reprinted in Theodore Binnema, Gerhard J. Ens, and R.C. MacLeod, eds., *From Rupert's Land to Canada* (Edmonton: University of Alberta Press, 2001), 179-92.

38   Arthur J. Ray's *Indians in the Fur Trade: Their Role as Trappers, Hunters, and Middlemen in the Lands Southwest of Hudson Bay, 1660-1870* (Toronto: University of Toronto Press, 1974) examined the role of Indian peoples in the fur trade, but his work did not focus the same attention on the Metis. Frank Tough's *"As Their Natural Resources Fail": Native Peoples and the Economic History of Northern Manitoba, 1870-1930* (Vancouver: UBC Press, 1996) placed greater emphasis on the role of the Metis, focusing on the northern Manitoba trade experience. Jennifer S.H. Brown's *Strangers in Blood* furthered Ray's "fur trade as social history" by examining how Hudson's Bay Company and North West Company structures influenced social development at the posts. In terms of mission histories, there are numerous biographies of priests and other missionaries that credit the clergy with saving the Metis from themselves. See, for example, Brian Owens and Claude M. Roberto, eds., *The Diaries of Bishop Vital Grandin, 1875-77,* trans. Alan D. Ridge, 2 vols. (Edmonton: Historical Society of Alberta, 1989); and Thérèse Castonguay, s.g.m., *A Leap in Faith: The Grey Nuns*

Ministries in Western and Northern Canada, 2 vols. (Edmonton: Grey Nuns of Alberta, 1999). There are also studies of missions and their role in the colonization and settlement of western Canada that regard the Church's role and significance in influencing social behaviour. See Raymond J. Huel, *Proclaiming the Gospel to the Indians and the Métis* (Edmonton: University of Alberta Press, 1996).

39 Conversely, non-core families cannot be traced intergenerationally nor linked to other families in the region, which reduces the chances of fitting them into any of the other categories that fit the core families. Non-core families, in short, lack the necessary records to link them to larger patterns, either because they were not members of the regional family structure or because of weaknesses in the record that prevent demonstration of any connections. It is, therefore, possible that some core families were missed because at this time meaningful connections cannot be made.

40 Nicole St-Onge, "Uncertain Margins: Métis and Saulteaux Identities in St-Paul des Saulteaux, Red River, 1821-1870," *Manitoba History* (October 2006): 1-8. St-Onge challenges the generally held belief that Metis society is endogamous, with men occasionally marrying Indian women and Metis women doing the same with European traders. St-Onge's examination of some of the Red River census records reveals the possibility that Metis women also married Indian men.

41 Robert Jarvenpa, "The Hudson's Bay Company, the Roman Catholic Church, and the Chipewyan in the Late Fur Trade Period," in *Le Castor Fait Tout: Selected Papers of the 5th American Fur Trade Conference, 1985,* ed. Bruce Trigger, Toby Morantz, and Louise Dechêne (Montreal: Lake St. Louis Historical Society, 1987), 485-517; and Arthur J. Ray, *The Canadian Fur Trade in the Industrial Age* (Toronto: University of Toronto Press, 1990). Jarvenpa indicates that fur returns for the English River District had indeed diminished by the late nineteenth century. This conclusion, as Ray notes, corresponds to general Canadian fur trade trends in the same period.

CHAPTER 1: THE SOCIAL LANDSCAPES OF THE NORTHWEST

1 Robert Longpré, *Ile-a-la-Crosse, 1776-1976* (Île à la Crosse, SK: Ile-a-la-Crosse Bi-Centennial Committee, Ile-a-la-Crosse Local Community Authority, 1976), 1.

2 Hood's description was published in Alexander Henry, *Alexander Henry's Travels and Adventures in Canada and the Indian Territories between the Years 1760 and 1776,* ed. James Bain (Edmonton: Hurtig Publishers, 1969), 328. The Franklin expedition, 1819-22, located the exact position of the mouth of the Coppermine River and mapped the shoreline of the Polar Sea.

3 The work of Sylvia Van Kirk, *Many Tender Ties: Women in Fur Trade Society in Western Canada, 1670-1870* (Winnipeg: Watson and Dwyer, 1980), and Jennifer S.H. Brown, *Strangers in Blood: Fur Trade Company Families in Indian Country* (Vancouver: UBC Press, 1980), has most succinctly and extensively established this reality in the North American fur trade. Also see Arthur J. Ray, "Reflections of Fur Trade Social History and Metis History in Canada," *American Indian Culture and Research Journal* 6, 2 (1982): 91-107; Susan Sleeper-Smith, *Indian Women and French Men: Rethinking Cultural Encounter in the Western Great Lakes* (Amherst: University of Massachusetts Press, 2001); and Heather Rollason Driscoll, "'A Most Important Chain of Connection': Marriage in the Hudson's Bay Company," in *From Rupert's Land to Canada,* ed. Theodore Binnema, Gerhard Ens, and R.C. Macleod (Edmonton: University of Alberta Press, 2001), 81-107.

4 Richard White, *The Middle Ground: Indians, Empires, and Republics in the Great Lakes Region, 1650-1815* (Cambridge: Cambridge University Press, 1991).

5 David Thompson, *David Thompson's Narrative, 1784-1812,* ed. Richard Glover (Toronto: Champlain Society, 1962), 104.

6 Frank J.P. Crean, *New Northwest Exploration: Report of Exploration, Seasons of 1908 and 1909* (Ottawa: Department of the Interior, 1910), 31.

7 The Frobishers and Henry the Elder first established their partnership in 1774. Harry W. Duckworth, ed., *The English River Book: A North West Company Journal and Account Book, 1796,* Rupert's Land Record Society Series (Montreal/Kingston: McGill-Queen's University Press, 1990), xi; Gordon Charles Davidson, *The North West Company* (Berkeley: University of California Press, 1918), 239; and W. Kaye Lamb, ed., *Sixteen Years in the Indian Country: The Journal of Daniel Williams Harmon, 1800-1816* (Toronto: Macmillan, 1957), 114.

8 See Hetty Jo Brumbach and Robert Jarvenpa, *Ethnoarchaeological and Cultural Frontiers: Athapascan, Algonquian, and European Adaptations in the Central Subarctic* (New York: Peter Lang, 1989), 32.

9 David W. Friesen, *The Cree Indians of Northern Saskatchewan: An Overview of the Past and Present* (Saskatoon, 1973), 7; and Greg Marchildon and Sid Robinson, *Canoeing the Churchill: A Practical Guide to the Historic Voyageur Highway* (Regina: Canadian Plains Research Center, 2002), 26.

10 Thompson, *Narrative,* 58. Thompson was at Cumberland House in 1787, and he began mapping the area in 1789. From 1793 to 1796, Thompson surveyed other regions of northern Saskatchewan. At the end of this period, he was expected to spend more time procuring furs rather than engaging in cartography. In 1797, Thompson joined the NWC and left the North. He returned in 1799, at which time he married Charlotte Small. Thompson's presence in the Île à la Crosse area ended in 1799, when he was sent west as a surveyor. It is likely that Thompson's observations for the region were made between 1793 and 1796.

11 Ibid., 107. Thompson's description of the Dene migration is rather sanitized; these types of territorial shifts were anything but peaceful. The Cree and the Dene had a history of violent confrontation, at Île à la Crosse and across the region. The story of Thanadelthur, the "Dene Slave woman," is a good representation of the level of violence and conflict. See Sylvia Van Kirk, *Many Tender Ties,* for a discussion of the friction between these two indigenous groups and the role that Thanadelthur played in the HBC expansion of trade. See also Patricia A. McCormack's, "The Many Faces of Thanadelthur: Documents, Stories, and Images," in *Reading beyond Words: Contexts for Native History,* ed. Jennifer S.H. Brown and Elizabeth Vibert (Peterborough, ON: Broadview Press, 2003), 329-64.

12 Friesen, *Cree Indians,* 7. Arthur S. Morton likewise noted that smallpox had been present in northern Saskatchewan between 1782 and 1783. See Morton, *A History of the Canadian West to 1870-71,* 2nd ed. (Toronto: University of Toronto Press, 1973), 335. For a more detailed examination of the social, political, economic, and cultural effects of epidemics on Aboriginal people, see Jody Decker, "'We Shall Never Be Again the Same People': The Diffusion and Cumulative Impact of Acute Infectious Diseases Affecting the Natives on the Northern Plains of the Western Interior of Canada, 1774-1839" (PhD diss., York University, 1989); Maureen Lux, *Medicine That Walks: Disease, Medicine, and Canadian Plains Native People, 1880-1940* (Toronto: University of Toronto Press, 2001); and Paul Hackett, *A Very Remarkable Sickness: Epidemics in the Petit Nord to 1846* (Winnipeg: University of Manitoba Press, 2002).

13 Friesen, *Cree Indians,* 7.

14 See Brumbach and Jarvenpa, *Ethnoarchaeological and Cultural Frontiers;* Robert Jarvenpa, "The People of Patuanak: The Ecology and Spatial Organization of a Southern Chipewyan Band" (PhD diss., University of Minnesota, 1974); Jarvenpa, *The Trappers of Patuanak: Toward a Spatial Ecology of Modern Hunters* (Ottawa: National Museum of Canada, 1980); Richard Wuorinen, *A History of Buffalo Narrows* (Buffalo Narrows: Buffalo Narrows Celebrate Saskatchewan Committee, 1981); Davidson, *North West Company;* and D.N. Sprague and R.P. Frye, *The Genealogy of the First Metis Nation: The Development and Dispersal of the Red River Settlement, 1820-1900* (Winnipeg: Pemmican Publications, 1983), 79.

15 Thompson, *Narrative,* 101.

16 Ibid., 106.

17 Jarvenpa, *Trappers of Patuanak,* 35-41.

18 The recording of this Dene oral narrative took place at Cold Lake, Alberta, in the late nineteenth century. The story of the Arctic Giant was told to other missionaries, including Bishop Alexandre-Antoine Taché, who heard the story at Île à la Crosse in 1851. It was told to others again in 1879 by Chief Uldayé at Cold Lake. See Émile Petitot, *The Amerindians of the Canadian Northwest in the Nineteenth Century,* ed. Donat Savoie (Ottawa: Northern Science Research Group, Dept. of Indian Affairs and Northern Development, 1970), 35; Petitot, *Les Litteratures Populaires de Toutes les Nations,* vol. 23 (Paris: Maisonneuve Frères et Ch. Leclerc, 1894), 423-24; and James G.E. Smith, "Historical Changes in the Chipewyan Kinship System," in *North American Indian Anthropology,* ed. Raymond J. DeMallie and Alfonso Ortiz (Norman: University of Oklahoma Press, 1994), 49-81.

19 Lawrence J. Burpee, *The Search for the Western Sea: The Story of the Exploration of North Western America,* rev. ed. (Toronto: Macmillan, 1935), 1:317-19; Davidson, *North West Company,* 39; Stewart W. Wallace, *The Pedlars from Quebec and Other Papers on the Nor'Westers* (Toronto: Ryerson Press, 1954), 13; Marcel Giraud, *The Metis in the Canadian West,* trans. George Woodcock (Edmonton: University of Alberta Press, 1986), 1:188; and James K. Smith, *David Thompson: Fur Trader, Explorer, Geographer* (Toronto: Oxford University Press, 1971), 37.

20 Longpré, *Ile-a-la-Crosse,* 1; and Davidson, *North West Company,* 230.

21 Burpee, *Western Sea,* 1:vii; and Lloyd Keith, ed., *North of Athabasca: Slave Lake and Mackenzie River Documents of the North West Company, 1800-1821* (Montreal/Kingston: McGill-Queen's University Press, 2001), 76.

22 Keith, *North of Athabasca,* 76.

23 Ibid.

24 Davidson, *North West Company,* 11.

25 See Wallace, *Pedlars from Quebec,* 13; Lamb, *Sixteen Years,* 113; Giraud, *Metis,* 1:178-79; Smith, *David Thompson,* 37; and Burpee, *Western Sea,* 1:xxviii.

26 Pond was born in Milford, Connecticut, around 1739 or 1740 and had a varied career, including serving as a soldier with a Connecticut regiment, before becoming a fur trader, explorer, and cartographer. He began his trade career with his father at Detroit, Michigan, and worked throughout Minnesota and Wisconsin. Through his business, he became acquainted with Alexander Henry, Simon McTavish, and the brothers Thomas, Benjamin, and Joseph Frobisher. Despite his accomplishments, he died in relative obscurity and poverty in his birthplace. Barry M. Gough, "Peter Pond," *Dictionary of Canadian Biography Online,* http://www.biographi.ca.

27 Arthur S. Morton, *Under Western Skies: A Series of Pen-Pictures of the Canadian West in Early Fur Trade Times* (Toronto: T. Nelson, 1937); Edith I. Burley, *Servants of the Honourable Company: Work, Discipline, and Conflict in the Hudson's Bay Company, 1770-1879* (Toronto: Oxford University Press, 1997); Marchildon and Robinson, *Canoeing the Churchill,* 85-87.

28 For detailed descriptions of the ebb and flow of posts of the major companies in northwestern Saskatchewan, see Ernest Voorhis, *Historic Forts and Trading Posts of the French Regime and of the English Fur Trading Companies* (Ottawa: Department of the Interior, 1930); Duckworth, *The English River Book,* xv; Burpee, *Western Sea,* 1:322-23, 330; Smith, *David Thompson,* 37; Florida A. Town, *The North West Company: Frontier Merchants* (Toronto: Umbrella Press, 1999), 23; Giraud, *Metis,* 1:189; Wallace, *Pedlars from Quebec,* 15-16; and Davidson, *North West Company,* 238.

29 Giraud, *Metis,* 1:180, 197.

30 Morton, *Canadian West,* 337; Edward J. McCullough and Michael Maccagno, *Lac La Biche and the Early Fur Traders* (Edmonton: Canadian Circumpolar Institute, 1991), 54; and W. Kaye Lamb, "Sir Alexander MacKenzie," *Dictionary of Canadian Biography Online,* http://www.biographi.ca.

31 Longpré, *Ile-a-la-Crosse,* 1-5; McCullough and Maccagno, *Lac La Biche,* 17; and Giraud, *Metis,* 1:197.

32 Burpee, *Western Sea,* 1:499.

33 James G. McGregor, *Peter Fidler: Canada's Forgotten Explorer, 1769-1822* (Calgary: Fifth House, 1998), 28, 174-75.

34 Peter Fidler, Journal of Exploration and Survey, 1789-1806, Hudson's Bay Company Archives (hereafter HBCA) E.3/1.

35 Burpee, *Western Sea,* 1:178-79.

36 In 1808, the NWC seized and burned the HBC's Île à la Crosse post. The Company was unable to rebuild until the following year. Entries for 9 and 21 June 1810, Île à la Crosse Post Journal, 1810-11, HBCA B.89/a/2.

37 Entries for 14 August 1805 and 18-21 August 1805, Île à la Crosse Post Journal, 1805-06, HBCA B.89/a/1. It is not clear precisely what Linklater meant when he said the fortunes of the HBC had improved since Churchill Factory had been destroyed. Perhaps he was simply attempting to reassure his clients that the Company had not been destroyed and was still prepared to trade.

38 Entry for 22 September 1805, ibid.

39 McGregor, *Peter Fidler,* 28, 174-75. See also Morton, *Under Western Skies,* 196-97; and Morton, *Canadian West,* 520. Unfortunately, the given names for these men are not provided. Mr. Black was likely Samuel Black, a NWC employee who was assigned to northern territories such as the English River and Athabasca districts in the early nineteenth century.

40 Morton attributed the HBC's difficulties to an uneven competition between cultural groups. He surmised that Peter Fidler could never have successfully competed against the NWC's Highland Scots culture led by McTavishs, McDermotts, McGillivrays, Mackenzies, and Campbells. Morton, *Under Western Skies,* 196.

41 Correspondence between Mr. Fidler and Canadians, 23 January-23 July 1811, Île à la Crosse Correspondence Inward, 1810-11, HBCA B.89/c/1.

42 Letter from W. Henry to P. Fidler, 11 July 1810, ibid.

43 See also the letters of 9-10 October 1820, Île à la Crosse Correspondence Book, 1820, HBCA B.89/b/1. This series of letters details one of the final incidents between the HBC and NWC, wherein John Clarke, chief factor of the HBC, and John Thompson of the NWC disputed the events involving a Cree man at Nehiyo-wapasi. At issue was which company the man should trade with. Clarke felt the HBC had negotiated an arrangement, while Thompson stated that the man was in debt to the NWC and that it was to be paid off first before any new deal could be struck. The HBC men involved accused the NWC of threatening violence against the Cree man if he did not go back with them to his father's hunting territory. The traders eventually decided they would have to seek out the man for his version of events. There is no indication of the final resolution of this event.

44 Longpré, *Ile-a-la-Crosse*, 6-12.

45 Brumbach and Jarvenpa, *Ethnoarchaeological and Cultural Frontiers*, 39, 41. Bull's House was located on the Dillon River/White Fish River.

46 Eric W. Morse, *Fur Trade Canoe Routes of Canada: Then and Now* (Toronto: University of Toronto Press, 1984), 93-94; Burpee, *Western Sea*, 1:xxvii-xxix, 317-26; and McCullough and Maccagno, *Lac La Biche*, 23.

47 Carolyn Podruchny has detailed the eighteenth-century voyageur routes between Montreal and Athabasca and the early manifestations of the Athabasca Brigade, which was modelled on the earlier Grand Portage system. See Podruchny, *Making the Voyageur World: Travelers and Traders in the North American Fur Trade* (Toronto: University of Toronto Press, 2006). See also Burley, *Servants*, 8, 218-19; Morse, *Fur Trade Canoe Routes*, 93; and Sprague and Frye, *Genealogy*, 19.

48 William Cornwallis King, *Trader King as Told to Mary Weekes* (1949; repr., Regina: Fifth House, 2007), 41.

49 Ibid.

50 Morton, *Under Western Skies*, 127-30; Burley, *Servants*, 218-19; and Marchildon and Robinson, *Canoeing the Churchill*, 85-87.

51 Ibid.; and J.P. Turner, "The La Loche Brigade," *The Beaver* 274 (December 1943): 32-36.

52 King, *Trader King*, 23-28. Emphasis in original.

53 Ibid., 26.

54 Town, *Northwest Company*, 23; Wallace, *Pedlars*, 15-16; and Burpee, *Western Sea*, 1:326.

55 Morton, *Canadian West*, 451.

56 Ibid., 347, 704.

57 Carol M. Judd, "Alexis Bonami (Bonamis), *dit* Lespérance (L'Espérance)," *Dictionary of Canadian Biography Online*, http://www.biographi.ca; scrip application of Abraham Lariviere, 25 September 1906, Île à la Crosse, Library and Archives Canada (hereafter LAC), RG 15, vol. 1354; scrip application of Samuel Le Esperance, 16 June 1907, Île à la Crosse, LAC, RG 15, vol. 1010, file 1495306; and Turner, "La Loche Brigade," 33.

58 Records for these men exist in a variety of archives located in such places as Quebec and the United Kingdom.

59 Thompson, *Narrative*, 73, 107.

60 Ibid., 75.

61 Ibid., 74.

62 Ibid., 128.

63 Ibid., 194.

64 Ibid., 103.

65 Ibid.
66 Ibid., 103-4.
67 Ibid., 104.
68 Entry for 6 July 1810, Île à la Crosse Post Journal, 1810-11, HBCA B.89/a/2.
69 Entries for 7 July-8 July 1810, ibid.; and correspondence between Mr. Fidler and Canadians, 24 May 1811, Île à la Crosse Correspondence Inward, 1810-11, HBCA B.89/c/1.
70 Correspondence between Mr. Fidler and Canadians, 24 May 1811, ibid.
71 Ibid.
72 Entries from 6 July to 6 August 1811, Île à la Crosse Post Journal, 1810-11, HBCA B.89/a/2.
73 Peter Fidler, Journal of Exploration and Survey, 1789-1806, HBCA E.3/1.
74 Letter from W. Henry to P. Fidler, 11 July 1810, Île à la Crosse Correspondence Inward, 1810-11, HBCA B.89/c/1.

CHAPTER 2: SOCIAL CONSTRUCTION OF THE METIS FAMILY

1 A more in-depth treatment of women as an unpaid but necessary source of labour for the HBC can be found in Brenda Macdougall, "'The Comforts of Married Life': Metis Family Life, Labour, and the Hudson's Bay Company," *Labour/Le Travail* 61 (Spring 2008): 9-40. ·
2 "Belanger, Charles Eugêne (b. 1881) (fl. 1902-1936)," Hudson's Bay Company Archives (hereafter HBCA) Search File.
3 Charles Eugêne's father, Horace Belanger Sr., began his career with the Company in 1853 as an apprentice clerk and served as chief factor at Norway House in the 1880s and 1890s. Belanger Sr. drowned at Sea River Falls, Nelson River, on 1 October 1892. "Belanger, Horace (1836-1892) (fl. 1853-1892)," HBCA Search File; letter to Angus McKay from R.H. Hall, 26 January 1907, Île à la Crosse Correspondence Inward, 1903-10, HBCA B.89/c/8. See also Frank Tough, *"As Their Natural Resources Fail": Native Peoples and the Economic History of Northern Manitoba, 1870-1930* (Vancouver: UBC Press, 1996), 273.
4 Letter to McKay from Hall, 26 January 1907, ibid.
5 Ibid.
6 Letter to C.E. Belanger from Hall, 26 January 1907, ibid.
7 Ibid.
8 For a history of Revillon Frères, see Marcel Sexé, *Two Centuries of Fur Trading, 1723-1923: Romance of the Revillon Family* (Paris: Draeger Frères, 1923).
9 Letter to McKay from Hall, 26 September 1907, Île à la Crosse Correspondence Inward, 1903-10, HBCA B.89/c/8. Interestingly, Belanger's history of resigning and re-engaging several times mimicked the career of his grandfather-in-law, Pierriche Laliberte, who followed the same pattern in the late nineteenth century.
10 Ibid.
11 Herbert G. Gutman, *The Black Family in Slavery and Freedom, 1750-1925* (New York: Vintage Books, 1976), 31.
12 Grace McKay Jolly, Alice Aby, and Stan Cuthand, *Kisewatotatowin: Loving, Caring, Sharing, Respect,* 2nd ed. (Saskatoon: Aboriginal Parent Program, 1998), 63.
13 Richard Slobodin, *Metis of the Mackenzie District* (Ottawa: Canadian Research Centre for Anthropology, 1966), 70-71, 163-64.
14 This comment about the birth of the Metis was most typically made by early Metis activists and scholars such as Duke Redbird, *We Are Métis: A Metis View of the Development of a Native Canadian People* (Willowdale, ON: Ontario Metis and Non-Status Indian

Association, 1980); and D. Bruce Sealey and A.S. Lussier, *The Metis: Canada's Forgotten People* (Winnipeg: Manitoba Métis Federation Press, 1975), when the idea of Metis was transformed from that of an ethnicity into a nation. See, for instance, Jacqueline Peterson, "Many Roads to Red River: Metis Genesis in the Great Lakes Region, 1680-1815," in *The New Peoples: Being and Becoming Metis in North America,* ed. Jacqueline Peterson and Jennifer S.H. Brown (Winnipeg: University of Manitoba Press, 1985), 37-71.

15 Entry for 1 November 1822, Île à la Crosse Post Journal, 1822-23, HBCA B.89/a/5.

16 Report by George Keith for the English River District, 1824-25, Île à la Crosse Post Journal, 1824-25, HBCA B.89/a/8.

17 Ibid.

18 Entry for 1 November 1822, Île à la Crosse Post Journal, 1822-23, HBCA B.89/a/5; entry for 25 October 1824 and an undated entry, Île à la Crosse Post Journal, 1824-25, HBCA B.89/a/8.

19 Entry for 13 January 1825, Île à la Crosse Post Journal, 1825-26, HBCA B.89/a/9.

20 Letter to John Spencer from George Keith, 6 April 1826, Île à la Crosse Correspondence Book, 1825-26, HBCA B.89/b/3.

21 Entry for 31 May 1844, Île à la Crosse Post Journal, 1843-45, HBCA B.89/a/23.

22 Philip T. Spaulding, "The Metis of Ile-a-la-Crosse" (PhD diss., University of Washington, 1970).

23 Ibid., 85; and Philip T. Spaulding, "The Social Integration of a Northern Community: White Mythology and Metis Reality," in *A Northern Dilemma: Reference Papers,* ed. Arthur K. Davis (Bellingham: Western Washington State College, 1967), 101-2.

24 There were Belangers in the English River District in the late 1700s, and at least one child from that family continued to live in the region. A Belanger woman born in the northwest was cited as the wife of Antoine Laliberte, one of the early Canadian fur traders from Quebec.

25 See Irene M. Spry, "The Métis and Mixed-Bloods of Rupert's Land before 1870," in *The New Peoples: Being and Becoming Metis in North America,* ed. Jacqueline Peterson and Jennifer S.H. Brown (Winnipeg: University of Manitoba Press, 1981), 95-118.

26 *Liber Animarum,* Mission N.D. de la Visitation vicarait de Keewatin La Loche, Saskatchewan, St. Boniface Historical Society. This book was reconstituted in June 1927 because the mission de la Visitation burned down.

27 Ibid., translation provided by Gilles Lesage, executive director of the Société historique de Saint-Boniface.

28 The information we have on Old Montgrand is derived from the scrip records of his children. See the scrip application of Louison Montgrand, 10 September 1906, Library and Archives Canada (hereafter LAC), RG 15, vol. 1360; and Canadian census return, 1901, for Portage La Loche, LAC.

29 While a close examination of Cree and Dene kinship is not within the scope of this study, for more detailed information on the subject, see James G.E. Smith, "Historical Changes in the Chipewyan Kinship System," in *North American Indian Anthropology,* ed. Raymond J. DeMallie and Alfonso Ortiz (Norman: University of Oklahoma Press, 1994), 49-81; Henry S. Sharp, "The Kinship System of the Black Lake Chipewyan" (PhD diss., Duke University, 1973); Regina Flannery, "Cross-Cousin Marriage among the Cree and Montagnais of James Bay," *Primitive Man* 2 (1938): 29-33; A. Irving Hallowell, "Kinship Terms and Cross-Cousin Marriage of the Montagnais-Naskapi and the Cree," *American Anthropologist* 34, 2 (1932): 171-99; Alfred Louis Kroeber, "Athabascan Kin Term Systems,"

American Anthropologist 39 (1937): 602-8; Elaine Hay, *Dene Hélot'ine Kinship* (Saskatoon: Saskatchewan Indian Cultural Centre, 1998); David Meyer, *The Red Earth Crees, 1860-1960,* Canadian Ethnology Service, Paper 100 (Ottawa: National Museum of Canada, 1985); David G. Mandelbaum, *The Plains Cree: An Ethnographic, Historical, and Comparative Study* (1940; repr., Regina: Canadian Plains Research Center, 1979); and Scott Rushforth, *Bear Lake Athabascan Kinship and Task Group Formation,* Canadian Ethnology Service, Paper 96 (Ottawa: National Museum of Canada, 1984).

30 Regina Flannery, "The Position of Women among the Eastern Cree," *Primitive Man* 8 (1934): 86.
31 Sharp, "Kinship System," 2-3.
32 Spaulding, "Social Integration," 101-2.
33 Mandelbaum, *Plains Cree;* Meyer, *Red Earth Crees,* 82-85, 106; and Robert A. Brightman, *A Grateful Prey: Rock Cree Human-Animal Relationships* (Berkeley: University of California Press, 1993), 11.
34 See M. Rossignol, OMI, "Cross-Cousin Marriage among the Saskatchewan Cree," *Primitive Man* 2 (1938): 26-28; and Richard J. Preston, "Eastern Cree Notions of Social Grouping," in *Papers of the 11th Algonquian Conference,* ed. William Cowan (Ottawa: Carleton University Press, 1980), 40-48.
35 See Smith, "Historical Changes," 53-58; Hetty Jo Brumbach and Robert Jarvenpa, *Ethnoarchaeological and Cultural Frontiers: Athapascan, Algonquian, and European Adaptations in the Central Subarctic* (New York: Peter Lang, 1989), 258-59, 300; and Jennifer S.H. Brown and Laura Peers, "'There Is No End to Relationships among the Indians': Ojibwa Families and Kinship in Historical Perspective," *History of the Family* 4, 4 (2000): 532. Loretta Fowler examined how the Gros Ventre of Fort Belknap Reservation regarded their cultural identity, symbolized it internally, and, more importantly, created it through interactions with the Assiniboine with whom they shared the reservation. Historically, Gros Ventre and Assiniboine people of northern Montana shared the same territory (and, later, reservation), intermarried extensively, and borrowed from each other's cultural ceremonies and customs. Because they shared a land base and were both Plains peoples, Fowler concluded, the Gros Ventre and Assiniboine shared some general conceptualizations, values, and broad understandings about social relations, the supernatural, and the overall reservation experience. Yet, despite all this, these two peoples remained culturally distinct because they had different interpretations of past events and circumstance. See Loretta Fowler, *Shared Symbols, Contested Meanings: Gros Ventre Culture and History, 1778-1984* (Ithaca, NY: Cornell University Press, 1987), 197, 224.
36 Gutman, *Black Family,* xxi.
37 Scrip applications of Raphaël Laliberte and Eliza Percatler (spelled Percateler), 12 September 1906, LAC, RG 15, vol. 1353; parish registers from Mission de Saint-Jean-Baptiste (1867-1912), Ile à la Crosse, Saskatchewan; and Canadian census return, 1901, for Île à la Crosse, LAC.
38 Canadian census return, 1901, for Île à la Crosse, LAC; and scrip application of Raphaël Laliberte, 12 September 1906, LAC, RG 15, vol. 1353.
39 Scrip application of Raphaël Laliberte, ibid.
40 Scrip applications of Augustine Montgrand Laliberte, Joseph Montgrand, and Boniface Montgrand, 10 September 1906, LAC, RG 15, vol. 1360.
41 Harry W. Duckworth, ed., *The English River Book: A North West Company Journal and Account Book, 1796,* Rupert's Land Record Society Series (Montreal/Kingston: McGill-

Queen's University Press, 1990), 156; and parish registers, Mission de Saint-Jean-Baptiste (1867-1912).

42 Scrip application of Louis Caisse, 20 September 1906, LAC, RG 15, vol. 1339; parish registers, Mission de Saint-Jean-Baptiste (1867-1912).

43 The historical spelling for "Natomagan" was "Nanatomagan." Furthermore, "Ikkeilzik" appears to have become "Kenzie."

44 David Thompson makes reference to the Cree conquering "martial" tribes of the Great Plains and taking possession of the entire region stretching from the subarctic to the Plains. Glover, the editor of Thompson's narrative, felt that the martial tribes he referred to were the Blackfoot, Blood, and Piegan, who Thompson indicated lived in the north. David Thompson, *David Thompson's Narrative, 1784-1812*, ed. Richard Glover (Toronto: Champlain Society, 1962), 107.

45 Nicole St-Onge, "Uncertain Margins: Métis and Saulteaux Identities in St-Paul des Saulteaux, Red River 1821-1870," *Manitoba History* (October 2006): 1-8.

46 *Liber Animarum*, Mission de Saint-Jean-Baptiste, Île á la Crosse, vicarait de Keewatin La Loche, Saskatchewan, St. Boniface Historical Society.

47 Scrip application of François Herman, 10 September 1906, LAC, RG 15, vol. 1351; scrip application of Elizabeth Touslesjour (spelled "Toutlejour"), 13 July 1907, LAC, RG 15, vol. 1012, file 1521716; and Canadian census returns, 1891 for Île à la Crosse, Portage La Loche, LAC.

48 *Liber Animarum*, Mission de Saint-Jean-Baptiste, Île á la Crosse, vicarait de Keewatin La Loche, Saskatchewan, St. Boniface Historical Society.

49 Parish registers, Mission de Saint-Jean-Baptiste (1867-1912).

50 Ibid.; and scrip application of Marie Isabelle Iron Laliberte, 22 September 1906, LAC, RG 15, vol. 1023, file 1598555.

51 Heather Devine, *The People Who Own Themselves: Aboriginal Ethnogenesis in a Canadian Family, 1660-1900* (Calgary: University of Calgary Press, 2004), 224-30.

52 Gutman, *Black Family,* 95.

53 Parish registers, Mission de Saint-Jean-Baptiste (1867-1912); parish registers, Saint-Julien (1875-1912), Green Lake, Saskatchewan; parish registers, Mission de la Visitation (1890-1912), Portage La Loche, Saskatchewan; Canadian census returns, 1881, 1891, 1901 for Île à la Crosse, Green Lake, and Portage La Loche, LAC.

54 Scrip applications for different Joseph Larivieres on 28 June 1907 (LAC, RG 15, vol. 994, file 1313219), 21 September 1906 (LAC, RG 15, vol. 1354), 26 September 1906 (LAC, RG 15, vol. 1354), 14 July 1900 (LAC, RG 15, vol. 1354), 2 July 1907 (LAC, RG 15); scrip application of Thomas Lariviere, n.d. (LAC, RG 15); Canadian census return, 1891, for Green Lake, LAC; and parish registers, Mission de Saint-Jean-Baptiste (1867-1912).

55 Parish registers, Mission de Saint-Jean-Baptiste (1867-1912).

56 Devine notes that the use of "dit" or "dite" was an old French, and later French Canadian, practice required to differentiate between branches of a family because of the other common francophone Catholic practice of naming children for male or female saints. Devine, *People Who Own Themselves,* 224-25.

57 *Liber Animarum*, Mission N.D. de la Visitation vicarait de Keewatin La Loche, Saskatchewan, St. Boniface Historical Society.

58 Scrip application of William Archie, 25 September 1906, LAC, RG 15, vol. 1005, file 1430910; and parish registers, Mission de Saint-Jean-Baptiste (1867-1912).

59 Scrip application of Véronique Morin, 22 October 1877, LAC, RG 15, vol. 558, file 167788.

60 Charles Mair, *Through the Mackenzie Basin: An Account of the Signing of Treaty No. 8 and the Scrip Commission, 1899* (Edmonton: University of Alberta Press, 1999), 70-71.

61 Furthermore, the raising of children by grandparents was (and is) a common cultural practice in Metis and Cree communities throughout western Canada, regardless of whether their parents are dead.

62 Scrip applications of Catherine Jolibois Montgrand, 10 September 1906, LAC RG 15, vol. 1360; scrip applications of Alexandre Herman and Julien Herman, 11 September 1906, LAC RG 15, vol. 1351; and parish registers, Mission de Saint-Jean-Baptiste (1867-1912).

63 Barthélémy's mother, Jeanne, was associated with five men – John Cummings, Paul Ket, Napoléon Girard, Joseph Billette or Diaze, and Harry/Henry LeMaigre. Jeanne married LeMaigre in 1910 at Portage La Loche, but it is unclear if the other relationships were common-law unions, were entered into according to the custom of the country, or took place at the same time or over discrete periods of time. Nor is it known how long each relationship lasted. The only thing clear is that none of the possible marriages, expect that to LeMaigre, was sanctioned by the Church. We also know that Napoléon was alive, but no longer with Jeanne, at the time their son Barthelémy was married in 1911. Parish registers, Mission de Saint-Jean-Baptiste (1867-1912); scrip application of Bartholomy Cummings, 24 September 1906, LAC, RG 15, vol. 1342; and Meadow Lake Diamond Jubilee Heritage Group, *Heritage Memories: A History of Meadow Lake and Surrounding Districts* (North Battleford, SK: Turner-Warwick Printers, 1981).

64 Parish registers, Mission de Saint-Jean-Baptiste (1867-1912); scrip application of Bartholomy Cummings, 24 September 1906, LAC, RG 15, vol. 1342; scrip application of Adélaide Lafleur Le Jarre, 15 June 1900, LAC, RG 15; and scrip application of Clara McKay McCallum, 21 September 1906, LAC, RG 15, vol. 1358.

65 Similar conclusions about Metis self-identification have been observed in other study areas. See D.V. Burley, G.A. Horsfal, and J.D. Brandon, *Structural Considerations of Metis Ethnicity: An Archeological, Architectural and Historical Study* (Vermillion: University of South Dakota Press, 1992), 15, 34-35.

66 Ritualized ways of establishing family reinforced a social value that asserted that family members could exist with or without biological relationships. Without social value, cultural concepts like adoption have no meaning. According to Patricia C. Albers, Sioux genealogical connections offered the possibility of collaboration and support for all daily activities, particularly working relationships. These genealogical connections themselves became working relationships that inspired social interaction. That is, genealogy became the primary idiom through which Aboriginal peoples ordered their social relations of production, trade, war, ceremony, and recreation. Family systems themselves were a form of language with meanings that both shaped and responded to social values and established cultural identity. David M. Schneider, *A Critique of the Study of Kinship* (Ann Arbor: University of Michigan Press, 1984), 54-55, 60; and Patricia Albers, "Sioux Kinship in a Colonial Setting," *Dialectical Anthropology* 6 (1982): 253-69.

CHAPTER 3: RESIDENCY AND PATRONYMIC CONNECTIONS ACROSS THE NORTHWEST

1 Scrip application of Raphaël Morin, 1 March 1887/17 October 1887, Library and Archives Canada (hereafter LAC), RG 15, vol. 557, file 167727.

2 Scrip application of Marie Morin, 8 March 1889, LAC, RG 15, vol. 682, file 320835.

3 Scrip application of Sophie Morin Linklater, 8 March 1899, LAC, RG 15, vol. 1360.

4 Canadian census returns, 1881, 1901 for Lac Vert (Green Lake), LAC; and scrip application of Pélagie (spelled "Pilagie") Morin, 22 October 1887, LAC, RG 15, vol. 558, file 167786.

5 Scrip application of Pélagie Morin, ibid.; and Canadian census returns, 1881, 1901 for Green Lake, LAC.

6 Greg Marchildon and Sid Robinson, *Canoeing the Churchill: A Practical Guide to the Historic Voyageur Highway* (Regina: Canadian Plains Research Center, 2002), 140-42.

7 This information is derived from Michael J. Durocher, who maintains a website about himself, his family, and where he came from. See http://metis.tripod.com.

8 There were Belangers in the English River District in the late 1700s, and at least one child from that family continued to live in the region. A Belanger woman born in the northwest was cited as the wife of Antoine Laliberte, one of the early Canadian fur traders from Quebec.

9 Île à la Crosse District Report, 1889, Hudson's Bay Company Archives (hereafter HBCA), B.89/e/8.

10 Carolyn Podruchny's recent work on the French Canadian voyageur class recounts many of the stereotypes that are at the base of popular depictions of the Metis. Indeed, it is often difficult to separate the images of the French Canadian voyageurs from their Metis descendants. Podruchny, *Making the Voyageur World: Travelers and Traders in the North American Fur Trade* (Toronto: University of Toronto Press, 2006), 1-3.

11 W. Kaye Lamb, ed., *Sixteen Years in the Indian Country: The Journal of Daniel Williams Harmon, 1800-1816* (Toronto: Macmillan, 1957), 197-98.

12 Alexander Ross, *The Fur Hunters of the Far West*, ed. Kenneth A. Spaulding (1855; repr., Norman: University of Oklahoma Press, 2001), 196.

13 Alexander Ross, *The Red River Settlement: Its Rise, Progress, and Present State* (1856; repr., Minneapolis: Ross and Haines, 1957), 191.

14 J.G. Kohl, *Kitch-Gami: Life among the Lake Superior Ojibwa* (1860; repr., St. Paul: Minnesota Historical Society, 1985), 260. In the original French: "Où je reste? Je ne peux pas te le dire. Je suis Voyageur – je suis Chicot, monsieur. Je reste partout. Mon grand-père était Voyageur: il est mort en voyage. Mon père était Voyageur: il est mort en voyage. Je mourrai aussi en voyage, et un autre Chicot prendra ma place. Such is our course of life." According to Kohl, "chicot," the name given by French Canadians to half-burnt stumps, became a nickname for the Metis because of their complexion. The chicot with whom Kohl was speaking was himself Metis or of mixed-ancestry and was using the term to refer not only to himself but to others like him as well. Thanks to Dr. Nicole St-Onge at the University of Ottawa for the English translation from the original French.

15 See Jennifer S.H. Brown, *Strangers in Blood: Fur Trade Company Families in Indian Country* (Vancouver: UBC Press, 1980); Jacqueline Peterson, "Prelude to Red River: A Social Portrait of the Great Lakes Metis," *Ethnohistory* 25, 1 (1978): 41-67; John Foster, "The Origins of the Mixed Bloods in the Canadian West," in *The Prairie West: Historical Readings*, ed. R. Douglas Francis and Howard Palmer (Edmonton: Pica Pica Press, 1985), 86-99; and Foster, "The Plains Metis," in *The Canadian Experience*, ed. R. Bruce Morrison and C. Roderick Wilson (Toronto: McClelland and Stewart, 1986), 315-403.

16 Scrip application of Pélagie Morin, 22 October 1887, LAC, RG 15, vol. 558, file 167786. "Montagnais" was a term used by French speakers to indicate the Dene, also known as Chipewyan, people.

17 At least two women carrying the Boucher surname remained in the English River District well after Louis' retirement. In addition to Pélagie, there was a Marguerite Boucher,

likely Pélagie's sister, who subsequently married Jean Baptiste Riel at Île à la Crosse. Marguerite and Jean Baptiste were the parents of Jean Louis Riel, father of the nineteenth-century Metis political leader Louis Riel. However, Marguerite's life at Île à la Crosse ended early – by 1821 she was dead. After Jean Louis' birth at Île à la Crosse in 1817, the family lived in English River for another five years and then left for Quebec after the HBC and NWC merged. Jean Louis married Julie Lagimodière in 1844 at Red River, and their son Louis was born that same year. The couple's next child to live past infancy was Sara Riel, who became a Grey Nun and served at the mission at Île à la Crosse from 1872 until her death in 1883. Harry W. Duckworth, ed., *The English River Book: A North West Company Journal and Account Book, 1796,* Rupert's Land Record Society Series (Montreal/Kingston: McGill-Queen's University Press, 1990); and A.G. Morice, OMI, *Dictionnaire historique des Canadiens et des Métis français de L'Ouest* (Montreal: Chez Granger Freres, 1908).

18 Scrip application of Raphaël Morin, 1 March 1887/17 October 1887, LAC, RG 15, vol. 557, file 167727; and Canadian census returns, 1881, 1891 for Green Lake, LAC.

19 Scrip application of Raphaël Morin, ibid.

20 Île à la Crosse District Report, 1862, HBCA B.89/e/4. The entry states that only thirty-six men worked in the district; however, the numbers provided add up to forty.

21 Île à la Crosse District Report, 1889, HBCA B.89/e/8.

22 "Report to the Chief Commissioner at Fort Garry" from Samuel McKenzie, 1 June 1872, Île à la Crosse Correspondence Book, 1872-75, HBCA B.89/b/4.

23 "Remarks Regarding the HB Posts in Upper English River District," by William McMurray, 10 January 1873, Île à la Crosse Correspondence Book, 1872-75, HBCA B.89/b/4.

24 Ibid. Bull's House (present-day Dillon) was at some point moved to the south shore of Little Buffalo Lake.

25 Ibid.

26 "Sketch Map of the English River District," 1895, HBCA B.89/e/17. William Cornwallis King, *Trader King as Told to Mary Weekes* (1949; repr., Regina: Fifth House, 2007), xiii-xiv. King was first stationed at Île à la Crosse in 1885-86.

27 Canadian census returns, 1881 for Green Lake and 1901 for Île à la Crosse, town, LAC.

28 Île à la Crosse Post Report, 1890, HBCA B.167/e/2.

29 Letter to Pierriche Laliberte from Walter West [Best], Île à la Crosse, 1 June 1877, Île à la Crosse Correspondence Book, 1877-81, HBCA B.89/b/4-9 [6].

30 Entry for 10 August 1888, Île à la Crosse Post Journals, 1888, HBCA B.89/e/6.

31 Île à la Crosse Post Reports, 1888-90, HBCA B.89/e/10a.

32 Canadian census return, 1891, for Green Lake, LAC.

33 Scrip application of Eliza Percatler (spelled Percateler), 12 September 1906, LAC, RG 15, vol. 1353; and parish registers, Mission de Saint-Jean-Baptiste (1867-1912), Île à la Crosse, Saskatchewan.

34 Canadian census return, 1901, for Île à la Crosse, town, LAC.

35 Scrip application of Louis Caisse, 20 September 1906, LAC, RG 15, vol. 1339; and parish registers, Mission de Saint-Jean-Baptiste (1867-1912).

36 Canadian census returns, 1901 for Île à la Crosse, town, and 1891 for Green Lake, LAC; and scrip application of Pierre Girard, 2 July 1907, LAC, RG 15, vol. 1023, file 1598983.

37 Scrip application of Madeleine Girard-Morin, 21 October 1887, LAC, RG 15, vol. 556, file 167701.

38 Scrip application of Pierre Girard, 2 July 1907, LAC, RG 15, vol. 1023, file 1598983; and parish registers, Saint-Julien (1875-1912), Green Lake, Saskatchewan.

39 Scrip application of Louis Laliberte, 22 October 1887, LAC, RG 15, vol. 557, file 167742.

40 Île à la Crosse Post Report, 1900-01, HBCA B.89/e/20; letter to Bell, Prince Albert, from Thomas Anderson, Île à la Crosse, 5 February 1902, Île à la Crosse Correspondence Book, 1899-1902, HBCA B.89/b/21; and Île à la Crosse Post Reports, 1888-90, HBCA B.89/e/10a.

41 Paul Hurly, "Beauval, Saskatchewan: An Historical Sketch," *Saskatchewan History* 33 (1980): 103-5.

42 Nothing is known about Marguerite Sinclair except for an alternative spelling of her last name – Quinclair. Sophie Morin, as noted in the previous chapter, was the daughter of Antoine Morin and Pélagie Boucher, and therefore was the sister of Sarazine Morin Laliberte and sister-in-law of Pierriche Laliberte.

43 Scrip application of Pierre Laliberte Sr., 22 October 1887, LAC, RG 15, vol. 556, file 167712. Antoine did not file a scrip application and was listed in his son's application, as was the surname of his wife. In the absence of a church record of the event, and unless otherwise stated in another source, I will still use the terms "married" or "marriage" for couples with long-term associations with each other in order to reflect the existence of enduring relationships, as demonstrated by births of children. Although the Belanger woman is not given a first name or identified in any other way, her husband and children identified her as a Halfbreed from the northwest. Scrip applications of Pierre Laliberte Sr., ibid., and Serazine Laliberte Morin, 22 October 1887, LAC, RG 15, vol. 557, file 167746.

44 Îsle à la Crosse Post Journals, 1865-1904, HBCA B.89/a/36-38.

45 Scrip application of Serazine Laliberte Morin, 22 October 1887, LAC, RG 15, vol. 557, file 167746.

46 Scrip application of Pierre Laliberte Sr., 22 October 1887, LAC, RG 15, vol. 556, file 167712; and Canadian census returns, 1881, 1891, 1901 for Lac Vert (Green Lake), LAC.

47 Scrip applications of Pierre Laliberte Sr., ibid., and Serazine Laliberte Morin, 22 October 1887, LAC, RG 15, vol. 557, file 167746.

48 Scrip applications of Josephine Maurice Natomagan, 26 June 1907, LAC, RG 15, vol. 1023, file 1599001; Marie Angèle Maurice Archie, 25 September 1906, LAC, RG 15, vol. N/A; Rosalie Maurice Aubichon, 21 September 1906, LAC, RG 15, vol. 1334; Célestine Maurice, 19 September 1906, LAC, RG 15, vol. 1357; Charles Maurice, ibid.; François Maurice, 19 September 1906, LAC, RG 15, vol. N/A; Magloire Maurice, 20 September 1906, ibid.; Norbert Maurice, 20 September 1906, LAC, RG 15, vol. 1357; Pierre Maurice, 19 September 1906, LAC, RG 15, vol. N/A; Lucia Maurice Meraste, 12 July 1900, ibid.; Carmine (spelled also as Courrone) Maurice, 21 September 1906, LAC, RG 15, vol. 1365. Also parish registers, Mission de Saint-Jean-Baptiste (1867-1912), and Mission de la Visitation (1890-1912), Portage La Loche, Saskatchewan.

49 Scrip applications of Angèle Laliberte Souris, LAC, RG 15, vol. 1367, N/A; Angèle Souris, 27 June 1907, LAC, RG 15, vol. 991, file 1247280; and Raphaël Souris, 21 September 1906, LAC, RG 15, vol. 1367.

50 Canadian census return, 1901, for Île à la Crosse, town, LAC; and letter to John McTavish, Fort Garry, from William McMurray, Île à la Crosse, 14 March 1874, Île à la Crosse Correspondence Book, 1872-91, HBCA B.89/b/4.

51 Scrip applications for Marie Morin, 8 March 1889, LAC, RG 15, vol. 682, file 320835; Sophie Morin Linklater, 8 March 1899, LAC, RG 15, vol. 1360; and Pélagie (spelled Pilagie) Morin, 22 October 1887, LAC, RG 15, vol. 558, file 167786.

52　Scrip application of Pélagie Morin, 22 October 1887, LAC, RG 15, vol. 558, file 167786. The surname Lanonde given on the application is likely Laronde or Delaronde, and it is possible that Sophie and Jadule (spelled Judule) both married Delarondes from Red River.

53　Scrip application of Raphaël Morin, 1 March 1887-17 October 1887, LAC, RG 15, vol. 557, file 167727. Raphaël and Betsy were married at Île à la Crosse at around 1850.

54　Ibid., and Canadian census returns, 1881, 1891 for Lac Vert (Green Lake), LAC.

55　Meadow Lake Diamond Jubilee Heritage Group, *Heritage Memories: A History of Meadow Lake and Surrounding Districts* (North Battleford, SK: Turner-Warwick Printers, 1981), 179.

56　Parish registers, Saint-Julien (1875-1912) and Mission de Saint-Jean-Baptiste (1867-1912); and scrip applications of Zéphrin (spelled Zephirin) Morin dit Catholique, 12 July 1900, LAC, RG 15, vol. 1360, and Madeleine Girard Morin, 21 October 1887, LAC, RG 15, vol. 556, file 167701.

57　Parish registers, Saint-Julien (1875-1912) and Mission de Saint-Jean-Baptiste (1867-1912); scrip applications of Marguerite Jourdain Morin, 22 October 1887, LAC, RG 15, vol. 558, file 167774; and Canadian census returns, 1891 for Green Lake and 1901 for Île à la Crosse, LAC.

58　A William Linklater built one of the first HBC posts at Sandy Point on Lac Île à la Crosse in the late eighteenth/early nineteenth century. It is unlikely that Sophie married this particular William Linklater, but she may well have married his son.

59　Scrip application of Sophie Morin Linklater, 8 March 1899, LAC, RG 15, vol. 1360; Canadian census returns, 1891 for Green Lake, LAC; and parish registers, Saint-Julien (1875-1912).

60　Scrip application of Sophie Morin Linklater, ibid.

61　Nicole St-Onge, *Saint-Laurent, Manitoba: Evolving Metis Identities, 1870-1914* (Regina: Canadian Plains Research Center, 2004), 38.

62　Ibid., 38, 66. Paul Delaronde's first wife, according to St-Onge's research, was listed in the 1891 census at Saint-Laurent as the forty-eight-year-old widow of Paul Delaronde. She headed a household that included her son William, who was then working as a salaried farmhand.

63　Beginning with the pioneering work of Lewis Henry Morgan, kinship studies have long been about the degrees of relatedness rather than the social and cultural meaning behind the relationships. Lewis Henry Morgan, *Systems of Consanguinity and Affinity of the Human Family*, vol. 17 (Washington: Smithsonian Contributions to Knowledge, 1871); Lewis Henry Morgan, *Ancient Society* (New York: Holt, 1877); Michael Asch, *Kinship and the Drum Dance in a Northern Dene Community* (Edmonton: Boreal Institute for Northern Studies, 1989); Scott Rushforth, *Bear Lake Athabascan Kinship and Task Group Formation*, Canadian Ethnology Service, Paper 96 (Ottawa: National Museum of Canada, 1984); Henry S. Sharp, *Chipewyan Marriage*, Canadian Ethnology Service, Paper 58 (Ottawa: National Museum of Canada, 1979); and Henry S. Sharp, "The Kinship System of the Black Lake Chipewyan" (PhD diss., Duke University, 1973).

64　Richard Slobodin, *Metis of the Mackenzie District* (Ottawa: Canadian Research Centre for Anthropology, 1966), 57.

65　Diane Payment, *"The Free People – Otipemisiwak": Batoche, Saskatchewan, 1870-1930* (Ottawa: Canadian Parks Service, 1990), 38.

66　Ibid., 43.

CHAPTER 4: FAMILY, ACCULTURATION, AND ROMAN CATHOLICISM

1 Letter to Henry J. Moberly, Île à la Crosse, from George Dreaver, Green Lake, 21 October 1893, Île à la Crosse Correspondence Inward, 1893-1902, Hudson's Bay Company Archives (hereafter HBCA) B.89/c/7.

2 Letter from Dreaver to Moberly, 15 February 1893, ibid.

3 Canadian census returns, 1881, 1891, 1901, for Green Lake, Library and Archives Canada (hereafter LAC).

4 See Raymond J. Huel, *Proclaiming the Gospel to the Indians and the Métis* (Edmonton: University of Alberta Press, 1996). There are, of course, non-Catholic Metis communities on the Red River, such as St. Andrews. See Frits Pannekoek, *A Snug Little Flock: The Social Origins of the Riel Resistance, 1869-1870* (Winnipeg: Watson and Dwyer, 1991); Kenneth S. Coates and William R. Morrison, "'More than a Matter of Blood': The Federal Government, the Churches and the Mixed Blood Populations of the Yukon and Mackenzie River Valley, 1890-1950," in *1885 and After: Native Society in Transition,* ed. F. Laurie Barron and James B. Waldram (Regina: Canadian Plains Research Center, 1986), 253-77; Keith Widder, *Battle for the Soul: Métis Children Encounter Evangelical Protestants at Mackinaw Mission, 1823-1837* (East Lansing: Michigan State University Press, 1999); Sylvia Van Kirk, "'What If Mama Is an Indian?' The Cultural Ambivalence of the Alexander Ross Family," in *The New Peoples: Being and Becoming Metis in North America,* ed. Jacqueline Peterson and Jennifer S.H. Brown (Winnipeg: University of Manitoba Press, 1985), 207-17; and James B. Waldram, "'The Other Side': Ethnostatus Distinction in Western Subarctic Native Communities," in *1885 and After,* ed. Barron and Waldram, 279-95.

5 Mary Jordan, *To Louis from Your Sister Who Loves You, Sara Riel* (Toronto: Griffin House, 1974), 58. The four priests were Alexandre Taché, Henri Faraud, Louis-François Laflèche, and Vital Grandin.

6 Rufus Redmond Earle, "A Trip to Île-à-la-Crosse in 1915," *Saskatchewan History* 39, 1 (1986): 31.

7 M. Rossignol, OMI, "The Religion of the Saskatchewan and Western Manitoba Cree," *Primitive Man* 11 (1939): 68-69.

8 See, for instance, Martha McCarthy, *From the Great River to the Ends of the Earth: Oblate Missions to the Dene, 1847-1921* (Edmonton: University of Alberta Press, 1995), xviii.

9 Robert Jarvenpa, "The Development of Pilgrimage in an Inter-Cultural Frontier," in *Culture and Anthropologic Tradition: Essays in Honour of Robert F. Spencer,* ed. Robert H. Winthrop (London: University of America Press, 1990), 177-203.

10 Widder, *Battle,* 65; John Foster, "Wintering, the Outsider Adult Male and the Ethnogenesis of the Western Plains Metis," *Prairie Forum* 19, 1 (1994): 1-14, reprinted in Theodore Binnema, Gerhard J. Ens, and R.C. Macleod, ed., *From Rupert's Land to Canada* (Edmonton: University of Alberta Press, 2001), 186.

11 McCarthy, *Great River,* 32-33; Gaston Carriére, OMI, "The Oblates and the Northwest, 1845-1861," *Canadian Catholic Historical Association Study Sessions* (1970): 45-46; A.G. Morice, OMI, *History of the Catholic Church in Western Canada: From Lake Superior to the Pacific,* 2 vols. (Toronto: Masson, 1910); Carolyn Podruchny, *Making the Voyageur World: Travelers and Traders in the North American Fur Trade* (Toronto: University of Toronto Press, 2006); Podruchny, "'Dieu, Diable, and the Trickster': Voyageur Religious Syncretism in the pays d'en haut, 1770-1821," *Etude Oblates de l'Ouest* 5 (2000): 75-92; Podruchny,

"Baptizing Novices: Ritual Moments among French Canadian Voyageurs in the Montreal Fur Trade, 1780-1821," *Canadian Historical Review* 83, 2 (2002): 165-95.

12 Podruchny, "'Dieu, Diable,'" and "Baptizing Novices." On 24 March 1909, an infant from the Lariviere family was buried at Île à la Crosse. The baby was born at Souris River and was reportedly privately baptized by Thomy Lariviere. There was a similar incident with a child, Turommé Durocher, who was buried on 24 December 1909. The child, whose parents were Jean Baptiste Durocher and Angèle Roy, was baptized and buried on the same day, although the baptism was done privately. Finally, on 24 August 1912, Jean Baptiste Maurice, son of Celestin Maurice and Catherine Lariviere, was buried while the priests were absent from the mission. Parish registers, Mission de Saint-Jean-Baptiste (1867-1912), Île à la Crosse, Saskatchewan.

13 David Thompson, *David Thompson's Narrative, 1784-1812*, ed. Richard Glover (Toronto: Champlain Society, 1962), 74-75.

14 Ibid., 75-76.

15 Ibid., 107.

16 Ibid., 75.

17 Allan Greer, *Mohawk Saint: Catherine Tekakwitha and the Jesuits* (New York: Oxford University Press, 2005).

18 Ibid., 99.

19 Terrance L. Craig, *The Missionary Lives: A Study in Canadian Missionary Biography* (New York: Brill, 1997), 28.

20 See Widder, *Battle*, xiii.

21 "Brother" is a generic name that originally referred to all members of a religious community but is now generally used to identify those religious men who do not, or will not, receive holy orders. Both brothers and lay brothers (those with no plan to take holy orders) served in Île à la Crosse. For a more complete discussion of this aspect of missionary behaviour, see Craig, *Missionary Lives*.

22 Although the actual personification of Wisakejak varies between Aboriginal cultural traditions, many other Aboriginal societies have a generalized description of a trickster figure (e.g., Wolverine, Raven, Glooscap, Coyote) whose actions are used to teach the values, laws, and accepted behaviours/practices of the people. Saskatchewan Cree elder Stan Cuthand, in a short piece entitled "On Nelson's Text" in Jennifer S.H. Brown and Robert Brightman's *"The Orders of the Dreamed": George Nelson on Cree and Northern Ojibwa Religion and Myth, 1823* (Winnipeg: University of Manitoba Press, 1988), notes that, "In the period when the world was being peopled by mortals, the stories of the trickster grew up. There are many names for this same kind of character in Cree and other languages. Wisahkecahk, Cahkapes, and Ayas in Cree, Nannabush of the Ojibway, Napi of the Blackfeet, and Iktomi of the Assiniboine, are all personages to which the trickster stories are attributed" (190-91). See also Basil Johnston, *Ojibway Heritage* (Toronto: McClelland and Stewart, 1981) and Edward Ahenakew, "Cree Trickster Tales," *Journal of American Folk-Lore* 42, 166 (1929): 309-13.

23 Note that there is a distinction being drawn here between the "mother earth" of New Age thought and "mother for the earth" as a way of expressing a family relationship with the land/earth. In Cree spiritual traditions, the notion that the world (as opposed to the earth) is a mother (and not a father) is not contentious – life springs from women, not men, and as the world gives life to all bio-systems, it too is female and not male. See Michael Asch, *Kinship and the Drum Dance in a Northern Dene Community* (Edmonton: Boreal Institute

for Northern Studies, 1989); Robert A. Brightman, *Grateful Prey: Rock Cree Human-Animal Relationships* (Berkeley: University of California Press, 1993); Huel, *Proclaiming;* and David G. Mandelbaum, *The Plains Cree: An Ethnographic, Historical, and Comparative Study* (1940; repr., Regina: Canadian Plains Research Center, 1979).

24 Raymond J. DeMallie, "Kinship and Biology in Sioux Culture," in *North American Indian Anthropology,* ed. Raymond J. DeMallie and Alfonso Ortiz (Norman: University of Oklahoma Press, 1994), 125-46.

25 Rossignol, "Religion," 70.

26 Ibid., 67-71.

27 *Treaty No. 10 and Reports of Commissioners* (Ottawa: Queen's Printer, 1966).

28 McCarthy, *Great River,* 32-33; letters from R. McKenzie, Île à la Crosse, 2 March 1844 and 10 January 1845, Governor George Simpson's Correspondence Inward, HBCA D.5/10.

29 McCarthy, *Great River,* 33.

30 Robert Choquette, *The Oblate Assault on Canada's Northwest* (Ottawa: University of Ottawa Press, 1995), 41, 55; McCarthy, *Great River,* 32.

31 Carriére, "The Oblates," 46; Jarvenpa, "Development of Pilgrimage," 181; Morice, *History,* 1:205; Choquette, *Oblate Assault,* 41.

32 Kay Cronin, *Cross in the Wilderness* (Vancouver: Mitchell Press, 1960), 2; Christopher Vecsey, *The Paths of Kateri's Kin* (Notre Dame, IN: University of Notre Dame Press, 1997), 296.

33 In 1848, Taché and Laflèche were joined at Île à la Crosse by Father Henri Faraud. McCarthy, *Great River,* 32-33; Carriére, "The Oblates," 45-46, 49; Morice, *History,* 2:205; Arthur S. Morton, *Under Western Skies: A Series of Pen-Pictures of the Canadian West in Early Fur Trade Times* (Toronto: T. Nelson, 1937), 132; and Choquette, *Oblate Assault,* 41.

34 Morice, *History,* 1:249.

35 Choquette, *Oblate Assault,* 42, 92.

36 McCarthy, *Great River,* 108-9.

37 Letter from George Deschambeault, Île à la Crosse, 20 February 1853, Governor George Simpson's Correspondence Inward, HBCA D.5/36.

38 John Webster Grant, *Moon of Wintertime: Missionaries and the Indians of Canada in Encounter since 1534* (Toronto: University of Toronto Press, 1984).

39 Thérèse Castonguay, s.g.m., *A Leap in Faith: The Grey Nuns Ministries in Western and Northern Canada* (Edmonton: Grey Nuns of Alberta, 1999), 2:17.

40 Castonguay, *Leap in Faith,* 2:22-24.

41 Ibid.

42 Ibid., 2:24; and letter from Hospice St. Joseph, n.d., Thursday afternoon, Correspondence Inward, Île à la Crosse, 1871-85, HBCA B.89/c/2.

43 Castonguay, *Leap in Faith,* 2:25; and letter from Hospice St. Joseph, n.d., Thursday afternoon, ibid.

44 Castonguay, *Leap in Faith,* 2:25.

45 Ibid.

46 Frank J.P. Crean, *New Northwest Exploration: Report of Exploration, Seasons of 1908 and 1909* (Ottawa: Department of the Interior, 1910), 31, 33, 35; Frank J. Dolphin, *Indian Bishop of the West: The Story of Vital Justin Grandin, 1829-1902* (Ottawa: Novalis, 1986), 108; McCarthy, *Great River,* xix.

47 A Sister of Charity of Montreal, *Notes and Sketches Collected from a Voyage in the North West for the Furtherance of a Charitable Object* (Montreal: F. Callahan, Book and Job Printer, 1875), 23.

48 Crean, *New Northwest Exploration,* 33, 35.

49 These figures came from letters shared between Sara and her brother, Louis Riel, and while the numbers are not mathematically accurate, they indicate that fish remained a staple despite the vegetable gardens. Jordan, *To Louis,* 95.

50 Letter to Father Rapet from Joseph Fortescue, 30 May 1888, Île à la Crosse Correspondence Outward, 1888-91, HBCA B.89/b/15; William Cornwallis King, *Trader King as Told to Mary Weekes* (1949; repr. Regina: Fifth House, 2007), 170.

51 The other three sacraments are Holy Eucharist, penance, and holy orders.

52 While the first permanent mission was founded at Île à la Crosse in 1846, no records survive for the English River District prior to 1865 because of a number of fires at the mission site. Furthermore, the missions for Green Lake and Portage La Loche were founded after the one in Île à la Crosse. Île à la Crosse's and Portage La Loche's records end in 1912, and Green Lake's are unavailable after 1911 because of an error in photographing the records for microfilm.

53 It should be noted that the Roman Catholic registries for the parishes of Île à la Crosse, Green Lake, and Portage La Loche were accessed through the Mormon church's Family History Centre. At the time I was doing my research, I could not access the registries through either the local churches or the Oblate archives but was fortunate to locate them through the Mormon collection and access the microfilm at the Saskatoon Mormon Temple's reading room. The original records are now housed at St. Boniface Historical Society in Winnipeg, MB.

54 In Red River, the Catholic Church competed for congregants with other Christian denominations, such as Anglicanism, and later Methodism and Presbyterianism, and so its ability to control the marital patterns and faiths of a couple marrying was less successful than in a community such as Île à la Crosse, where the Church was the dominant religion.

55 It is difficult to determine how many non-Catholic servants entered the district during this period, which would provide a better sense of the total possible number of conversions.

56 Entry for 21 November 1824, Île à la Crosse Post Journal, 1824-25, HBCA B.89/a/8.

57 Entry for 31 October 1824, ibid.

58 Ibid. Nineteen-year-old James Douglas from Lanark had been listed as a clerk at the Canadian (NWC) establishment in the 1821-22 HBC census.

59 Entry for 10 June 1849, Île à la Crosse Post Journal, 1849-52, HBCA B.89/a/27; entry for 29 May 1855, Île à la Crosse Post Journal, 1855-56, HBCA B.89/a/29; entry for 5 August 1861, Île à la Crosse Post Journal, 1861, HBCA B.89/a/31; entry for 3 April 1863, Île à la Crosse Post Journal, HBCA B.89/a/33; entry for 4 December 1864, Île à la Crosse Post Journals, 1864-65, HBCA B.89/a/35; and entries for 29 December 1889 and 13 September 1890, Île à la Crosse Post Journal, 1889-96, HBCA B.89/a/36 and 37.

60 Entry for 29 May 1855, Île à la Crosse Post Journal, 1855-56, HBCA B.89/a/29.

61 Raymond J. Huel, "The Oblates of Mary Immaculate in the Canadian North West: Reflections on 150 Years of Service, 1845-1995," in *Proceedings of the Fourth Symposium on the History of the Oblates in Western and Northern Canada* (Edmonton: Western Canadian Publishers, 1996), 19.

62 Entry for 17 September 1865, Île à la Crosse Post Journal, 1864-65, HBCA B.89/a/35.

63 Ibid.

64 24 September 1865, ibid.

65 At the end of May, Grandin visited Green Lake, Cree Lake, Canoe Lake, and Waterhen Lake, and by the beginning of June he was at Île à la Crosse, where he spent the remainder

of the month. Brian Owens and Claude M. Roberto, eds., *The Diaries of Bishop Vital Grandin, 1875-77*, vol. 1, trans. Alan D. Ridge (Edmonton: Historical Society of Alberta, 1989).

66 Ibid.

67 Baptismal registry, parish registers, Mission de Saint-Jean-Baptiste (1867-1912).

68 Sara Riel's mother was Julie Lagimodière. Sara's time in Île à la Crosse was not long, but there is a sense that she had a meaningful impact. Of the sisters sent to Île à la Crosse, Sara was one of only two or three who may have been Metis and from the Manitoba region. The great majority of Grey Nuns were sent to the English River District from Quebec. By the time of Sara's death of tuberculosis in December 1883, she had changed her name to Sister Marguerite Marie, believing that the Blessed Marguerite Marie, the apostle of the Sacred Heart, had saved her from a fatal case of pneumonia. This was the second believed intervention of the Blessed Marguerite Marie in Île à la Crosse, as she was said to have cured Father Prosper Legeard of an illness in 1871. Castonguay, *Leap in Faith*, 2:28.

69 Rossignol, "Religion," 67-71.

70 Ibid. See also Robert A. Brightman, *Acoohkiwina and Acimowina: Traditional Narratives of the Rock Cree Indians* (Regina: Canadian Plains Research Center, 2007). Brightman explores the different genres of Rock Cree oral tradition and details the protocols for providing offerings to various spirit beings as an example of the reciprocal responsibility within all relationships.

71 Parish registers, Mission de Saint-Jean-Baptiste (1867-1912).

72 Ibid.

73 Green Lake (English River District) Post Report, 1897, HBCA B.84/e/6. Because of Dreaver's abilities, Beeston recommended that he be transferred to Fort Chipewyan, a more important post in another district.

74 Canadian census returns, 1891, for Green Lake, LAC.

75 Ibid.

76 Letter to Henry J. Moberly from George Dreaver, 6 June 1892, Île à la Crosse Correspondence Inward, 1890-92, HBCA B.89/c/4. Emphasis in original.

77 Letter to Moberly from Dreaver, 22 March 1893, Île à la Crosse Correspondence Inward, 1892-1901, HBCA B.89/c/6.

78 Letter from Eden Colvile, Île à la Crosse, 29 July 1849, Governor George Simpson Correspondence Inward, HBCA D.5/25.

79 Entries for 13 November 1864, 27 November 1864, and 5 February 1865, Île à la Crosse Post Journals, 1864-65, HBCA B.89/a/35; entry for 26 October 1862, Île à la Crosse Post Journal, 1862, HBCA B.89/a/32; and entry for 18 October 1865, Île à la Crosse Post Journal, 1864-65, HBCA B.89/a/35.

80 Canadian census returns, 1881, 1891, 1901, for Île à la Crosse, Green Lake, and Portage La Loche, LAC.

81 Robert Jarvenpa provides an excellent study based on this interpretation in "The Hudson's Bay Company, the Roman Catholic Church, and the Chipewyan in the Late Fur Trade Period," in *Le Castor Fait Tout: Selected Papers of the 5th American Fur Trade Conference, 1985*, ed. Bruce Trigger, Toby Morantz, and Louise Dechêne (Montreal: Lake St. Louis Historical Society, 1987), 485-517.

82 Sylvia Van Kirk explores ideas of class and race in her most recent article, "Colonized Lives: The Native Wives and Daughters of Five Founding Families of Victoria," in *In the Days of Our Grandmothers: A Reader in Aboriginal Women's History in Canada*, ed. Mary-Ellen

Kelm and Lorna Townsend (Toronto: University of Toronto Press, 2006), 170-99. See also Van Kirk, "'What If Mama,'" 207-17.

83   Entry for 8 July 1855, Île à la Crosse Post Journal, 1855-56, HBCA B.89/a/29. There were three priests in Île à la Crosse at that time, so the priest in question was either Prosper Legeard, Julien Moulin, or Valentin Vegreville.

84   Entry for 1 November 1903, Île à la Crosse Post Journal, 1896-1904, HBCA B.89/a/38.

CHAPTER 5: FAMILY, LABOUR, AND THE HBC

1   In 1862 alone, over the course of one and a half weeks, the women and young people harvested 990 kegs of potatoes to feed a substantial residential population at Île à la Crosse. Entries for 22 September-1 October 1862, Île à la Crosse Post Journal, 1862, Hudson's Bay Company Archives (hereafter HBCA) B.89/a/32.

2   Entry for 22 September 1862, ibid.; entry for 29 June 1831, Île à la Crosse Post Journal, 1831-32, HBCA B.89/a/14; and entry for 9 May 1890, Île à la Crosse Post Report, HBCA B.89/e/10b.

3   Entry for 28 November 1824, Île à la Crosse Post Journal, 1824-25, HBCA B.89/a/8; entry for 10 October 1843, Île à la Crosse Post Journal, 1842-43, HBCA B.89/a/22; entries for 13 December 1844 and 18 June 1845, Île à la Crosse Post Journal, 1843-45, HBCA B.89/a/23; and entries for 5, 6, and 9 July 1861 and 4-6 August 1861, Île à la Crosse Post Journal, 1861, HBCA B.89/a/31.

4   Entry for 29 June 1831, Île à la Crosse Post Journal, 1831-32, HBCA B.89/a/14; entry for 9 October 1843, Île à la Crosse Post Journal, 1842-43, HBCA B.89/a/22; and entry for 22 July 1844, Île à la Crosse Post Journal, 1843-45, HBCA B.89/a/23.

5   Entry for 5 February 1834, Île à la Crosse Post Journal 1834-35, HBCA B.89/a/16; and entries for 3 and 6 February 1823, Île à la Crosse Post Journal, 1822-23, HBCA B.89/a/5.

6   There is no record of Augustine having a daughter (or of Julie Marie having a grand-daughter) named Eliza. It is unclear if Eliza is Augustine's daughter or if she is just Julie Marie's granddaughter. Given the nature of the mission records and lack of detail in the post journal entries, it is not possible to gain information about Eliza. Additionally, Augustine had a relationship with a Baptiste Quatremoulin before her association with either Charles dit Ladébeauch Caisse or John Thomas Corrigal. Scrip applications of J.T. Corrigal, 22 September 1906, and Augustine Bouvier Corrigal, 24 September 1906, Library and Archives Canada (hereafter LAC), RG 15, vol. 1342; and parish registers, Mission de Saint-Jean-Baptiste (1867-1912), Île à la Crosse, Saskatchewan.

7   Parish registers, Mission de Saint-Jean-Baptiste (1867-1912); scrip applications of Caroline Lafleur, 24 September 1906, and Marguerite Lafleur-Boyer, 18 June 1900, LAC, RG 15, vol. 1337.

8   Jean Baptiste Bouvier was likely the father of Michel Bouvier Sr. Jean Baptiste was listed as being forty-one years old, nineteen years a Canadian employee, from L'Ours or Maska, and employed as a middleman in the 1821-22 Company census at the Canadian Establishment. In 1826, Jean Baptiste was a fisherman at the HBC post. Michel Bouvier Sr. was identified as having been born in 1811 or 1812 in the North-West Territory, so, conceivably, Jean Baptiste was his father. Abstracts of Servant's Accounts, 1833-64, HBCA B.89/g/1, file 1; scrip applications of Michel Bouvier and Julie Bouvier-Morin, 22 September 1906, LAC, RG 15, vol. 1337; and parish registers, Mission de Saint-Jean-Baptiste (1867-1912).

9   Parish registers, Mission de Saint-Jean-Baptiste (1867-1912).

10 Scrip applications of William Gardiner, 24 September 1906, and Lucia Gardiner, 21 September 1906, LAC, RG 15, vol. 1348; and parish registers, Mission de Saint-Jean-Baptiste (1867-1912).

11 The name Misponas is a phonetic variation of L'Esperance. At some point the French surname L'Esperance, which translates as "the hope" or "the promise," became the surname Misponas in the English River District, for which there appears to be no translation.

12 Scrip application of Louis Caisse, 20 September 1906, LAC, RG 15, vol. 1339; and parish registers, Mission de Saint-Jean-Baptiste (1867-1912).

13 Beatrice Medicine, "American Indian Family," *Journal of Ethnic Studies* 18, 4 (1981): 17-19.

14 M. Rossignol, OMI, "Property Concepts among the Cree of the Rocks," *Primitive Man* 12 (1939): 69.

15 Robert A. Brightman, *A Grateful Prey: Rock Cree Human-Animal Relationships* (Berkeley: University of California Press, 1993), 12.

16 Richard J. Preston, "Eastern Cree Notions of Social Grouping," in *Papers of the 11th Algonquian Conference*, ed. William Cowan (Ottawa: Carleton University Press, 1980), 43; and Bernard Bernier, *The Social Organization of the Waswanipi Cree Indians* (Montreal/Kingston: McGill-Queen's University Press, 1968), 9.

17 Robert Jarvenpa, *The Trappers of Patuanak: Toward a Spatial Ecology of Modern Hunters* (Ottawa: National Museum of Canada, 1980), 3, 41; James G.E. Smith, "Historical Changes in the Chipewyan Kinship System," in *North American Indian Anthropology*, ed. Raymond J. DeMallie and Alfonso Ortiz (Norman: University of Oklahoma Press, 1994), 58.

18 Philip T. Spaulding, "The Metis of Ile-a-la-Crosse" (PhD diss., University of Washington, 1970), 96-98.

19 Île à la Crosse Post Report, 1888, HBCA B.89/e/6.

20 The two studies that stand as seminal works regarding fur trade companies and families are, of course, Jennifer S.H. Brown's *Strangers in Blood: Fur Trade Company Families in Indian Country* (Vancouver: UBC Press, 1980), and Sylvia Van Kirk's *Many Tender Ties: Women in Fur Trade Society in Western Canada, 1670-1870* (Winnipeg: Watson and Dwyer, 1980).

21 See Van Kirk, *Many Tender Ties*, in particular for a discussion of the role of white women in Rupert's Land.

22 For biographical information on Simpson and his marriage, see James Raffin, *Emperor of the North: Sir George Simpson and the Remarkable Story of the Hudson's Bay Company* (Toronto: HarperCollins, 2007).

23 Entry for 25 December 1824, Île à la Crosse Post Journal, 1824-25, HBCA B.89/a/8.

24 Letter to Henry J. Moberly from Sisters of St. Joseph Hospice, 31 December 1892, Île à la Crosse Correspondence Inward, HBCA B.89/c/4.

25 Letter to Moberly from Sister Agnès, n.d., Île à la Crosse Correspondence Inward, 1893-1902, HBCA B.89/c/7.

26 For more about the First Nations kin-based task economy in the subarctic, see Bernier, *Social Organization*, and Scott Rushforth, *Bear Lake Athabascan Kinship and Task Group Formation*, Canadian Ethnology Service, Paper 96 (Ottawa: National Museum of Canada, 1984).

27 Entries for 3 and 6 February 1823, Île à la Crosse Post Journal, 1822-23, HBCA B.89/a/5; and for 2 October 1824, Île à la Crosse Post Journal, 1824-25, HBCA B.89/a/8.

28 On 18 September 1865, the women of the fort were recorded as being busy knitting nets for the fisheries. Île à la Crosse Post Journal, 1864-65, HBCA B.89/a/35.

29 Entries for 6 July-6 August 1810, Île à la Crosse Post Journal, 1810-11, HBCA B.89/a/2; and correspondence between Mr. Fidler and Canadians, 24 May 1811, Île à la Crosse Correspondence Inward, 1810-11, HBCA B.89/c/1.

30 Entry for 11-15 April 1890, Île à la Crosse Post Journal, 1889-96, HBCA B.89/a/36 and 37. The contemporary spelling for the surname Case is Caisse, while Malbeuaf is Malboeuf.

31 Scrip applications of Carmine Maurice, 21 September 1906, LAC, RG 15, vol. 1365; Raphaël Souris, 21 September 1906, LAC, RG 15, vol. 1367; Angèle Souris, 27 June 1907, LAC, RG 15, vol. 991, file 1247280; Ambroise McKay, 24 September 1906, LAC, RG 15, vol. 1358; Anna Jourdain, 24 September 1906, LAC, RG 15, vol. 1352; and parish registers, Mission de Saint-Jean-Baptiste (1867-1912).

32 In her scrip application, Mary identified her father as John Sinclair, a halfbreed. However, in church records she is often identified as Pilon or Pilow. Scrip application of Mary Caisse, 24 September 1906, LAC, RG 15, vol. 1339; and parish registers, Mission de Saint-Jean-Baptiste (1867-1912).

33 Entry for 10 February 1892, Île à la Crosse Post Journal, 1889-96, HBCA B.89/a/36 and 37.

34 Entry for 15 February 1892, Île à la Crosse Post Journal, 1889-96, ibid. The given name Marcial is more typically spelled Martial.

35 Scrip applications of François Xavier Daigneault, 20 September 1906, LAC, RG 15, vol. 1343; Charles Maurice, 19 September 1906, LAC, RG 15, vol. 1357; Raphaël Souris, 21 September 1906, LAC, RG 15, vol. 1367; and parish registers, Mission de Saint-Jean-Baptiste (1867-1912), and parish registers, Mission de la Visitation (1890-1912), Portage La Loche, Saskatchewan.

36 Arthur J. Ray has presented the most in-depth research dealing with the relationship between the HBC and its Native, primarily Indian, personnel. See his *Indians in the Fur Trade: Their Role as Trappers, Hunters, and Middlemen in the Lands Southwest of Hudson Bay, 1660-1870* (Toronto: University of Toronto Press, 1974). Furthermore, Brown's *Strangers in Blood* provides a succinct examination of the Company's stratification, which was based largely on the model of the English household with a patriarch, his wife and children, and a number of unmarried young female servants and male apprentices.

37 Frank Tough, *"As Their Natural Resources Fail": Native Peoples and the Economic History of Northern Manitoba, 1870-1930* (Vancouver: UBC Press, 1996), 7.

38 Ibid., 269.

39 Abstracts of Servants Accounts, 1833-64, HBCA B.89/g/1, file 1.

40 Tough, *Natural Resources*, 58.

41 Letter from Mr. Laliberte, n.d., Île à la Crosse Correspondence Inward, 1886-89, HBCA B.89/c/3.

42 Entries for 19-20 April 1823, Île à la Crosse Post Journal, 1822-23, HBCA B.89/a/5.

43 Abstracts of Servants Accounts, 1833-64, HBCA B.89/g/1, file 1. This census may not have been an actual accounting of the men at the establishments on the day the census was taken but rather a reflection of the places where each man was employed. Some switched employers regularly. As of the 1821 merger, it was plausible that an individual had, in fact, worked for both companies in that calendar year. It is difficult to regard the duplication of the name Patrick Cunningham as an error because there were a number of other names also duplicated in the Abstracts of Servants Accounts for 1821.

44 Entries for 19-20 April 1823, Île à la Crosse Post Journal, 1822-23, HBCA B.89/a/5.

45 Letter from Roderick Mackenzie, Île à la Crosse, 8 January 1850, Governor George Simpson's Correspondence Inward, HBCA D.5/27.

46 Parish registers, Mission de Saint-Jean-Baptiste (1867-1912).

47 Ibid.

48 The name Tastawitch was likely Testawitch. There was a Michel Testawitch in the English River District who was married to Sophie Lachance. This couple had a daughter, Marie Philomène Testawitch, who married Jean Baptiste Laliberte. It is probable that Margaret Testawitch was the sister of Marie Philomène. Additionally, the surname may in fact be Iroquois, not Dene, according to descendants of that family. The actual etymology of the name is unknown. Letter to R. Pamlet, Assistant Commissioner, from Henry J. Moberly, 25 November 1893, Île à la Crosse Correspondence Book, 1892-94, HBCA B.89/b/19.

49 In the Île à la Crosse mission records, there is a record of Hélène Harper giving birth to a daughter, Celina-Marie, whose father was a Willie Biggs to whom Hélène was not married. Parish registers, Mission de Saint-Jean-Baptiste (1867-1912).

50 Letter to Pamlet from Moberly, 25 November 1893, Île à la Crosse Correspondence Book, 1892-94, HBCA B.89/b/19.

51 Alternate spellings for Ikkeilzik are Elkeze, Elkelzek, and Elkezi.

52 Handwritten scrip application for Pierre Malboeuf, 12 July 1900, LAC, RG 15, vol. 1357; and parish registers, Mission de Saint-Jean-Baptiste (1867-1912).

53 Ray detailed this economic model based on semi-social assumption of responsibility, first in *Indians in the Fur Trade,* and then in *The Canadian Fur Trade in the Industrial Age* (Toronto: University of Toronto Press, 1990), 67-68, 137-39. The HBC offered economic assistance, particularly to Indian traders, in traditional or ceremonial forms, such as proffering debts, "gifting," and issuing relief to the sick and destitute.

54 Memo from Christie, Inspecting Chief Factor, to Wm. McMurray, n/d 1872, Île à la Crosse Correspondence Inward, 1871-85, HBCA B.89/c/2.

55 Ibid.

56 Ibid.

57 Letter to Joseph Fortescue from James Nicol Sinclair, 25 September 1885, Île à la Crosse Correspondence Inward, 1871-85, HBCA B.89/c/2.

58 Letter to Charles Lafleur from Moberly, 2 April 1892, Île à la Crosse Correspondence Book, 1891-93, HBCA B.89/b/18.

59 Letter from William McMurray to François Maurice, 12 December 1873, Île à la Crosse Correspondence Book, 1872-91, HBCA B.89/b/4. Joseph Vadnoit had thirty-eight years in the service and was employed at Portage La Loche.

60 The type of food to be obtained from Prince Albert was not specifically identified.

61 Île à la Crosse Post Report, 1888, HBCA B.89/e/6.

62 Ibid.

63 Ray, *Canadian Fur Trade,* 210-11.

64 Letter from R. Mackenzie, Île à la Crosse, 4 January 1844, Governor George Simpson's Correspondence Inward, HBCA D.5/10; letters from Mackenzie, 2 March 1841 and 22 February 1843, Governor George Simpson's Correspondence Inward, HBCA D.5/6. Glyndwr Williams, ed., *Hudson's Bay Miscellany, 1670-1870,* vol. 30 (Winnipeg: Hudson's Bay Record Society, 1975); HBCA Search File, Roderick Mackenzie (senior C.F.), #2.

65 Williams, *Hudson's Bay Miscellany,* 186.

66 Ibid.

67 Letter from R. Mackenzie, Île à la Crosse, 8 January 1850, Governor George Simpson's Correspondence Inward, HBCA D.5/27; letter from Samuel McKenzie, Île à la Crosse, 15 January 1853, Governor George Simpson's Correspondence Inward, HBCA D.5/36. By

1873, Samuel, who had served as a chief trader at Île à la Crosse from 1864 to 1871, was retired from the service and living with his four children at Prince Albert. Samuel's wife, Anne, had died by the early 1870s.

68 Letter from Thomas Hodgson, Île à la Crosse, 31 May 1848, Governor George Simpson's Correspondence Inward, HBCA D.5/22.

69 Letter from R. Mackenzie, Île à la Crosse, 14 June 1848, Governor George Simpson's Correspondence Inward, ibid.

70 W.L. Morton, "The Proceedings in the Convention, 3-5 February 1870," in *Manitoba: The Birth of a Province,* ed. W.L. Morton (Winnipeg: Manitoba Historical Records Society, 1984), 20.

71 Ibid., 22-24.

Chapter 6: Competition, Freemen, and Contested Spaces

1 Letter to J. Macdougal from Henry J. Moberly, 2 ? 1892, Île à la Crosse Correspondence Book, 1891-93, Hudson's Bay Company Archives (hereafter HBCA) B.89/b/18.

2 Ibid.

3 Ibid.

4 Ibid. Mr. McDermott was likely Andrew Miles McDermott, an accountant stationed in the English River District in the 1880s and 1890s.

5 Arthur S. Morton, *A History of the Canadian West to 1870-71,* 2nd ed. (Toronto: University of Toronto Press, 1973); Gordon Charles Davidson, *The North West Company* (Berkeley: University of California Press, 1918); Richard Slobodin, *Metis of the Mackenzie District* (Ottawa: Canadian Research Centre for Anthropology, 1966); Ron Bourgeault, "The Indian, the Metis and the Fur Trade: Class, Sexism and Racism in the Transition from 'Communism' to Capitalism," *Studies in Political Economy* 12 (1983): 45-80; Arthur J. Ray, "Reflections of Fur Trade Social History and Metis History in Canada," *American Indian Culture and Research Journal* 6, 2 (1982): 91-107; Gaston Carriére, OMI, "The Oblates and the Northwest, 1845-1861," *Canadian Catholic Historical Association Study Sessions* (1970): 35-66; M. Rossignal, OMI, "The Religion of the Saskatchewan and Western Manitoba Cree," *Primitive Man* 11 (1939): 67-71; and Christopher Vecsey, *The Paths of Kateri's Kin* (Notre Dame, IN: University of Notre Dame Press, 1997).

6 For studies addressing the structure of the pre- and post-merger HBC, see Frank Tough, *"As Their Natural Resources Fail": Native Peoples and the Economic History of Northern Manitoba, 1870-1930* (Vancouver: UBC Press, 1996); Arthur J. Ray, *The Canadian Fur Trade in the Industrial Age* (Toronto: University of Toronto Press, 1990); and Edith I. Burley, *Servants of the Honourable Company: Work, Discipline, and Conflict in the Hudson's Bay Company, 1770-1879* (Toronto: Oxford University Press, 1997).

7 Marcel Giraud, *The Metis in the Canadian West,* trans. George Woodcock (Edmonton: University of Alberta Press, 1986), 2:330.

8 Robert Jarvenpa and Hetty Jo Brumbach, "Occupational Status, Ethnicity and Ecology: Metis Adaptations in a Canadian Trading Frontier," *Human Ecology* 13, 3 (1985): 325.

9 Ibid.

10 Eric Hobsbawm, "Inventing Tradition," in *The Invention of Tradition,* ed. Eric Hobsbawm and Terrence Ranger (Cambridge: Cambridge University Press, 1983), 1-14.

11 Entry for 23 December 1889, Île à la Crosse Post Journal, 1889-96, HBCA B.89/a/36 and 37; and entry for 23 December 1903, Île à la Crosse Post Journal, 1896-1904, HBCA B.89/a/38.

12 Entry for 25 December 1824, Île à la Crosse Post Journal, 1824-25, HBCA B.89/a/8; entry for 24 December 1831, Île à la Crosse Post Journal, 1831-32, HBCA B.89/a/13; entry for 25 December 1864, Île à la Crosse Post Journal, 1864-65, HBCA B.89/a/35; and entry for 22-23 December 1889, Île à la Crosse Post Journal, 1889-96, HBCA B.89/a/36 and 37.

13 Entries for 22 December 1889 and 22 and 29 December 1890, Île à la Crosse Post Journal, 1889-96, HBCA B.89/a/36 and 37.

14 Entry for 25 December 1824, Île à la Crosse Post Journal, 1824-25, HBCA B.89/a/8; entry for 24 December 1831, Île à la Crosse Post Journal, 1831-32, HBCA B.89/a/13; entry for 25 December 1864, Île à la Crosse Post Journal, 1864-65, HBCA B.89/a/35; and entry for 22-23 December 1889, Île à la Crosse Post Journal, 1889-96, HBCA B.89/a/36 and 37.

15 Entry for 25 December 1824, Île à la Crosse Post Journal, 1824-25, HBCA B.89/a/8.

16 New Year's celebrations in other fur districts have been recounted by others, including Barbara Benoit, "Mission at Ile-a-la-Crosse," *The Beaver* (Winter 1990): 40-50; and Diane Payment, *"The Free People – Otipemisiwak": Batoche, Saskatchewan, 1870-1930* (Ottawa: Canadian Parks Service, 1990).

17 Entry for 1 January 1826, Île à la Crosse Post Journal, 1825-26, HBCA B.89/a/9. See also entries for 1 January 1825 (Post Journal, 1824-25, HBCA B.89/a/8), 1 January 1826 (Post Journal, 1825-26, HBCA B.89/a/9), 1 January 1832 (Post Journal, 1831-32, HBCA B.89/a/13), 1 January 1840 (Post Journal, 1839-40, HBCA B.89/a/19), 1 January 1843 (Post Journal, 1842-43, HBCA B.89/a/22); 1 January 1890 (Post Journal, 1889-96, HBCA B.89/a/36 and 37), and 1 January 1904 (Post Journal, 1896-1904, HBCA B.89/a/38).

18 Entries for 3 January 1823 (Île à la Crosse Post Journal, 1822-23, HBCA B.89/a/5), 2 January 1825 (Post Journal, 1825-26, HBCA B.89/a/9), 2 January 1832 (Post Journal, 1831-32, HBCA B.89/a/13), 2 and 3 January 1865 (Post Journal, 1864-65, HBCA B.89/a/35), and 13 January 1837 (Post Journal, 1836-38, HBCA B.89/a/17b).

19 Letter from James Nicol Sinclair to Moberly, 13 September 1892, Île à la Crosse, Correspondence Inward, 1890-92, HBCA B.89/c/4.

20 Entry for 16 November 1822, Île à la Crosse Post Journal, 1822-23, HBCA B.89/a/5.

21 Entry for 11 October 1890, Île à la Crosse Post Journal, 1889-96, HBCA B.89/a/36 and 37.

22 *Liber Animarum*, Mission de Saint-Jean-Baptiste, Île á la Crosse, vicarait de Keewatin La Loche, Saskatchewan, St. Boniface Historical Society. At some stage in Pauline's father's life, he went from being known as Charles Lariviere to Charles Natomagan.

23 Philip T. Spaulding, "The Metis of Ile-a-la-Crosse" (PhD diss., University of Washington, 1970), 56.

24 M. Rossignol, OMI, "Cross-Cousin Marriage among the Saskatchewan Cree," *Primitive Man* 2 (1938): 26-28; Rossignol, "Property Concepts among the Cree of the Rocks," *Primitive Man* 12 (1939): 61-70; and Rossignol, "The Religion of the Saskatchewan and Western Manitoba Cree," *Primitive Man* 11 (1939): 67-71.

25 Rossignol's article "Cross-Cousin Marriage" offers an anthropological assessment of marriage patterns among the Cree and Metis Cree of Île à la Crosse. The marriage options presented in this example are known, in academic terminology, as "cross-cousin" versus "parallel cousin" marriages. The terms refer to the relationships of the parents of individuals deemed eligible to marry. In the instance of cross-cousins, the parents are of different genders – brothers and sisters. Conversely, parallel cousins are sons and daughters of parents of the same gender, either two brothers or two sisters. In the case of the people of the English River District, in anthropological terms, cross-cousin marriages were acceptable while parallel cousin marriages were deemed incestuous. Rossignol, "Cross-Cousin Marriage," 26-28.

26 Letter to C.C. Chipman from Moberly, n.d., ca. 1892, Île à la Crosse Correspondence Book, 1891-93, HBCA B.89/b/18.

27 Letter to C.C. Chipman from Moberly, n.d., 1892, ibid.; letter to Macdougal from Moberly, 2 ? 1892, ibid.; letter to Rev. Pere Rapet from Moberly, 13 June 1892, ibid.; and letter to Chipman from Moberly, 18 June 1892, ibid.

28 Robert Choquette, *The Oblate Assault on Canada's Northwest* (Ottawa: University of Ottawa Press, 1995), 55.

29 Frank J. Dolphin, *Indian Bishop of the West: The Story of Vital Justin Grandin, 1829-1902* (Ottawa: Novalis, 1986), 86.

30 Ibid., 108.

31 Frank J.P. Crean, *New Northwest Exploration: Report of Exploration, Seasons of 1908 and 1909* (Ottawa: Department of the Interior, 1910), 33, 35.

32 See Robert Jarvenpa, "The Hudson's Bay Company, the Roman Catholic Church, and the Chipewyan in the Late Fur Trade Period," in *Le Castor Fait Tout: Selected Papers of the 54th American Fur Trade Conference, 1985,* ed. Bruce Trigger, Toby Morantz, and Louise Dechêne (Montreal: Lake St. Louis Historical Society, 1987), 485-517.

33 Letter to Moberly from Sister Hearn, n.d., Île à la Crosse Correspondence Inward, 1893-1902, HBCA B.89/c/7.

34 Entry for 10 May 1865, Île à la Crosse Post Journal, 1864-65, HBCA B.89/a/35.

35 In this final instance, there was a record of the bodies being transferred: the deceased woman of Bazil Durocher and his son; an infant of Louis Morin; an infant of Paul Grezaud; an infant of François Lariviere; an infant of James McCallum; an infant of Petit Roy Laliberte; and an infant of Pierre Durocher. According to the parish register, two years earlier the bodies of Jean Baptiste Aubichon and Pierriche Laliberte were likewise moved under the guidance of Jean Baptiste Payette and Pierre Laliberte Jr. Parish registers, Saint-Julien (1875-1912), Green Lake, Saskatchewan; and parish registers, Mission de Saint-Jean-Baptiste (1867-1912), Île à la Crosse, Saskatchewan.

36 Perhaps the most comprehensive description of the freemen is found in Giraud's *Metis in the Canadian West.* The best-known incident of a freeman becoming a free trader was the famous trial of Pierre Guillame Sayer at Red River in 1849. The buffalo hunters of the Plains also worked for no one but themselves and commonly challenged the Company's monopoly. For more on freemen, see Heather Devine, "Les Desjarlais: Aboriginal Ethnogenesis and Diaspora in a Canadien Family" (PhD diss., University of Alberta, 2001), 129-32.

37 John Foster, "Wintering, the Outsider Adult Male and the Ethnogenesis of the Western Plains Métis," *Prairie Forum* 19, 1 (1994): 1-14, reprinted in Theodore Binnema, Gerhard J. Ens, and R.C. MacLeod ed., *From Rupert's Land to Canada* (Edmonton: University of Alberta Press, 2001), 179-92.

38 Heather Devine, *The People Who Own Themselves: Aboriginal Ethnogenesis in a Canadian Family, 1660-1900* (Calgary: University of Calgary Press, 2004), 4.

39 Carolyn Podruchny, *Making the Voyageur World: Travelers and Traders in the North American Fur Trade* (Toronto: University of Toronto Press, 2006), xi.

40 Entry for 25 September 1822, Île à la Crosse Post Journal, 1822-23, HBCA B.89/a/5; entry for 28 May 1825, Île à la Crosse Post Journal, 1824-25, HBCA B.89/a/8; and letter from Roderick Mackenzie, Île à la Crosse, 2 March 1844, Governor George Simpson's Correspondence Inward, HBCA D.5/10, fos. 331-33.

41 Giraud, *Metis,* 2:322-23.

42 Freeman's Balances, English River District, 1857-70, HBCA B.89/z/1, fos. 27-42.

43 Entry for 1 November 1820, Île à la Crosse Post Journals, 1819-20, HBCA B.89/a/4; Greg
Dues, *Catholic Customs and Traditions: A Popular Guide* (Mystic, CT: Bayard, 2003), 17-18.

44 Letter to Joseph Wrigley, HBC Commissioner, 10 May 1888, Île à la Crosse Correspondence
Inward, 1888-91, HBCA B.89/b/15.

45 William Cornwallis King, *Trader King as Told to Mary Weekes* (1949; repr., Regina: Fifth
House, 2007), 170.

46 Ibid.

47 Ibid.

48 Letter to Father Rapet from Joseph Fortescue, 30 May 1888, Île à la Crosse Correspondence
Outward, 1888-91, HBCA B.89/b/15.

49 Letter to Wrigley, 10 May 1888, ibid. Thomas Desjarlais was an HBC labourer and bows-
man married to Marie Lafleur, daughter of Charles Lafleur and Louise Vadney. Her
brother, Charles Pierre, was the postmaster for Moostoos-sipi.

50 Letters to Rapet from Fortescue, 30 May 1888, and to Wrigley, 10 May 1888, ibid.

51 Meadow Lake Diamond Jubilee Heritage Group, *Heritage Memories: A History of Meadow
Lake and Surrounding Districts* (North Battleford, SK: Turner-Warwick Printers, 1981),
179.

52 St. Cyprien (or Thascius Caecilius Cyprianus) was born in the third century to a wealthy
North African family, converted to Catholicism, and was eventually made bishop of the
early Catholic Church prior to his eventual martyrdom as a result of his faith.

53 Letter to Wrigley from Fortescue, 18 June 1888, Île à la Crosse Correspondence Outward,
1888-91, HBCA B.89/b/15.

54 Entry for 31 October 1819, Île à la Crosse Post Journal, 1819-20, HBCA B.89/a/4; entry for
1 November 1822, Île à la Crosse Post Journal, 1822-23, HBCA B.89/a/5; and entry for 7
June 1855, Île à la Crosse Post Journal, 1855-56, HBCA B.89/a/29.

55 Letters to Fortescue from Wrigley, 2 August 1886 and 13 November 1886, Île à la Crosse
Correspondence Inward, 1871-85, HBCA B.89/c/3.

56 Letter to Bell, Prince Albert, from Thomas Anderson, Île à la Crosse, 1 December 1900,
Île à la Crosse Correspondence Outward, 1899-1902, HBCA B.89/b/21.

57 Initially, the nuns were to leave the district entirely. The mother house in Montreal felt
that the environmental conditions at Île à la Crosse had become too dangerous for the
sisters and were interfering with their ability to minister to the people of the region. The
sisters, however, did not actually abandon the Île à la Crosse mission until 3 September
1905, when they were replaced by the Sisters of St. Joseph of Lyons – the Black Nuns – who
stayed only a year before relocating to Beauval, where a new school was built. The Black
Nuns remained at Beauval until they were replaced by the Grey Nuns in 1909. There were
no Grey Nuns in Île à la Crosse again until 21 September 1917, when a new boarding school
was built there. Paul Hurly, "Beauval, Saskatchewan: An Historical Sketch," *Saskatchewan
History* 33 (1980): 103; Rose Arsenault, RSR, *A Religious History of St. John the Baptist Parish Ile a la Crosse 150 Years,* http://www.jkcc.com/rcnuns.html.

58 Letter to Anderson, Île à la Crosse, from J. Chisholm, Prince Albert, 4 October 1901, Île
à la Crosse Correspondence Inward, 1893-1902, HBCA B.89/c/7.

59 Thérèse Castonguay, s.g.m., *A Leap in Faith: The Grey Nuns Ministries in Western and
Northern Canada* (Edmonton: Grey Nuns of Alberta, 1999), 2:31.

60 Letter from Chipman, Winnipeg, to the Officer in Charge, Île à la Crosse, 2 January 1902, Île à la Crosse Correspondence Inward, HBCA B.89/c/7.

61 Abstracts of Servants Accounts, 1833-64, HBCA B.89/g/1, file 1; and entries for 23 and 24 February 1890, Île à la Crosse Post Journal, 1889-96, HBCA B.89/a/36 and 37.

62 Abstracts of Servants Accounts, ibid.

63 *Liber Animarum,* Mission Saint-Jean-Baptiste, Île á la Crosse, vicarait de Keewatin La Loche, Saskatchewan, St. Boniface Historical Society.

64 Canadian census returns, 1881, 1891, 1901, for Île a la Crosse, Library and Archives Canada (hereafter LAC); Parish registers, Mission de Saint-Jean-Baptiste (1867-1912); scrip applications of Michel Bouvier, 22 September 1906, LAC, RG 15, vol. 1337; Marguerite Bouvier Daigneault, 20 September 1906, LAC, RG 15, vol.1343; Véronique Bouvier Lariviere, 28 June 1907, LAC, RG 15, vol. 1026, file 1599097; and Jarvenpa and Brumbach, "Occupational Status."

65 Abstracts of Servant's Accounts, 1833-64, HBCA B.89/g/1, file 1; scrip application of Michel Bouvier, 22 September 1906, LAC, RG 15, vol. 1337; and Canadian census returns, 1881, 1891, 1901, for Île à la Crosse, LAC. Michel Bouvier Jr. was also one of four men whose lives and histories were thoroughly researched by Robert Jarvenpa and Hetty Jo Brumbach. See Jarvenpa and Brumbach, "Occupational Status."

66 Scrip application of Michel Bouvier, 22 September 1906, LAC, RG 15, vol. 1337.

67 Abstracts of Servant's Accounts, 1833-64, HBCA B.89/g/1, file 1; scrip application of Vincent Daigneault Jr., 20 September 1906, LAC, RG 15, vol. 1343; and Canadian census returns, 1881, 1891, 1901, for Île à la Crosse, LAC.

68 Abstracts of Servant's Accounts, 1833-64, ibid.; scrip application of Thomas Lariviere, 28 June 1907, LAC, RG 15, vol. 1023, file 1598985; and Canadian census returns, 1881, 1891, 1901, for Portage La Loche, LAC.

69 Entry for 22 February 1890, Île à la Crosse Post Journal, 1889-96, HBCA B.89/a/36 and 37. Although there is no clear indication who Mr. Archie was, he may have been either William Archie, who, although not an employee of the Company, was a man who knew quite a bit about medicinal plants, or, more likely, Archibald Linklater, the Company accountant, who went to live in the Prince Albert settlement between the 1880s and 1891.

70 The Bouvier living arrangement is part of the contemporary community's collective memory. As far back as current residents can remember, Bouviers have lived near the mission.

71 Entries for 23 and 24 February 1890, Île à la Crosse Post Journal, 1889-96, HBCA B.89/a/36 and 37; and letter from George C. Sanderson, Île à la Crosse, to W. Beacher, Winnipeg, 7 August 1890, Île à la Crosse Correspondence Inward, 1890-92, HBCA B.89/c/4.

72 Letter to Moberly from Rapet, 4 November 1890, ibid.

73 The Company records refer to money inconsistently in either dollars or pounds sterling, making it difficult to determine actual amounts. The conversion of pounds sterling to Canadian dollars is based on an approximation of £1 equaling $5.

74 Letters to Lawrence Clarke, Prince Albert, from Moberly, 5 September 1891 and 28 December 1892, and to Beecher from Moberly, 29 December 1892, Île à la Crosse Correspondence Book, 1891-93, HBCA B.89/b/185; letters to Moberly from Rapet, 2 November 1892, and to Moberly from HBC accountant, Winnipeg, 12 November 1892, Île à la Crosse Correspondence Inward, 1890-92, HBCA B.89/c/4; and entry for 30 October 1892, parish registers, Mission de Saint-Jean-Baptiste (1867-1912).

CHAPTER 7: FREEMEN TO FREE TRADERS IN THE NORTHWEST FUR TRADE

1 Letters to H.J. Moberly from George Dreaver, Green Lake, 6 September 1890 and 16 October 1890, Île à la Crosse Correspondence Inward, 1890-92, Hudson's Bay Company Archives (hereafter HBCA) B.89/c/4; and Green Lake (Lac Vert) Post Report, 1892, HBCA B.84/e/3.
2 Green Lake Post Report, 1892, ibid.
3 Letter to C.C. Chipman, HBC Chief Commissioner, from Moberly, 8 December 1892, Île à la Crosse Correspondence Book, 1891-93, HBCA B.89/b/18.
4 Ibid.
5 Letter to Moberly from J. Wrigley, Winnipeg, 22 August 1890, Île à la Crosse Correspondence Inward, 1890-92, HBCA B.89/c/4.
6 Glyndwr Williams ed., *Hudson's Bay Miscellany, 1670-1870,* vol. 30 (Winnipeg: Hudson's Bay Record Society, 1975), 232.
7 Hetty Jo Brumbach and Robert Jarvenpa, *Ethnoarchaeological and Cultural Frontiers: Athapascan, Algonquian, and European Adaptations in the Central Subarctic* (New York: Peter Lang, 1989), 227-29.
8 Ibid.
9 In his study of the Sioux during the colonial fur trade, Gary Clayton Anderson reached much the same conclusion. See the introduction of *Kinsmen of Another Kind: Dakota-White Relations in the Upper Mississippi Valley, 1650-1862* (Lincoln: University of Nebraska Press, 1984), ix-xxiv. This is not, however, to argue that the economic mechanisms were either developed or controlled by the Metis. There was, of course, as Frank Tough pointed out, a world market that determined the overall scope of trade by setting prices, determining values of furs, and marketing them to consumers worldwide, and the Metis of the English River District likely had little knowledge of or interest in this world market. See *"As Their Natural Resources Fail": Native Peoples and the Economic History of Northern Manitoba, 1870-1930* (Vancouver: UBC Press, 1996).
10 Letter to John McTavish, Fort Garry, from William McMurray, 14 March 1874, Île à la Crosse Correspondence Book, 1872-91.
11 Letter from George Deschambeault, 26 April 1857, Governor George Simpson's Correspondence Inward, HBCA D.5/43.
12 Ibid.
13 Letter from Deschambeault, 21 January 1859, Governor George Simpson's Correspondence Inward, HBCA D.5/48, fos. 97-98; entries for 25 November 1864, Île à la Crosse Post Journal, 1864-65, HBCA B.89/a/35.
14 Letters to Chipman from Moberly, 2 April 1892 and 30 June 1892, Île à la Crosse Correspondence Book, 1891-93, HBCA B.89/b/18; Green Lake Post Reports, 1892, HBCA B.84/e/3; and letter to Baptiste Laliberte from Moberly, 17 June 1893, Île à la Crosse Correspondence Book, 1892-94, HBCA B.89/b/19.
15 Letter to F. Maurice from McMurray, 12 December 1873, Île à la Crosse Correspondence Book, 1872-91, HBCA B.89/b/4-9[4].
16 Ibid.
17 Letter to James A. Grahame, HBC Chief Commissioner, from McMurray, 5 December 1874, Île à la Crosse Correspondence Book, 1872-91, HBCA B.89/b/4.
18 Ibid.

19 Letter to John McTavish from McMurray, 10 July 1875, Île à la Crosse Correspondence Book, 1872-91, HBCA B.89/b/4.

20 Letters to McTavish from McMurray and to Grahame from McMurray, both dated 10 March 1876, Île à la Crosse Correspondence Book, 1875-77, HBCA B.89/b/5.

21 Letter to McTavish from McMurray, 10 March 1876, ibid.

22 Letter to Ewan McDonald from Grahame, 15 September 1879, Île à la Crosse Correspondence Book, 1877-81, HBCA B.89/b/4-9[6].

23 By now the Red River settlement was a thriving community shaped by retired HBC servants and their Aboriginal families. Servants like Pierriche Laliberte and his family were encouraged by Company officials to retire to Red River as a means of removing these potential competitors from their trade districts.

24 Letters to McTavish and Grahame from McMurray, both dated 10 March 1876, Île à la Crosse Correspondence Book, 1875-77, HBCA B.89/b/5.

25 Letter to McTavish from McMurray, 20 May 1876, ibid.; letter to Pierre Laliberte from Walter West, Île à la Crosse, 1 June 1877, Île à la Crosse Correspondence Book 1877-81, HBCA B.89/b/6; letter to Grahame from McDonald, 15 September 1879, ibid.; and letter to Grahame from McDonald, 6 October 1881, Île à la Crosse Correspondence Book, 1881-85, HBCA B.89/b/7.

26 Portage La Loche Post Report, 1889, HBCA B.167/e/1.

27 Entries for 4-5 June 1889, Île à la Crosse Post Journal, 1889-96, HBCA B.89/a/36 and 37; and Green Lake Post Report, 1889, HBCA B.89/e/1.

28 Letters to Pierre Laliberte, Green Lake, from McMurray, 10 December 1872 and 24 February no year, Île à la Crosse Correspondence Book, 1872-75, HBCA B.89/b/4.

29 Letter to Moberly from Dreaver, 16 October 1890, Île à la Crosse Correspondence Inward, 1890-92, HBCA B.89/c/4.

30 See Edith I. Burley, *Servants of the Honourable Company: Work, Discipline, and Conflict in the Hudson's Bay Company, 1770-1879* (Toronto: Oxford University Press, 1997), 7-8; and Greg Marchildon and Sid Robinson, *Canoeing the Churchill: A Practical Guide to the Historic Voyageur Highway* (Regina: Canadian Plains Research Center, 2002), 93-96.

31 Canadian census returns, 1881 and 1891, for Lac Vert (Green Lake), Library and Archives Canada (hereafter LAC).

32 Canadian census returns, 1891, for Lac Vert, LAC.

33 Île à la Crosse Post Report, 1890, HBCA B.167/e/2.

34 Île à la Crosse Post Reports, 1888-90, HBCA B.89/e/10a.

35 Île à la Crosse Post Report, 1897, HBCA B.89/e/19.

36 Île à la Crosse Post Report, 1900-01, HBCA B.89/e/20; letter to Bell, Prince Albert, from Thomas Anderson, Île à la Crosse, 5 February 1902, Île à la Crosse Correspondence Book, 1899-1902, HBCA B.89/b/21; and Île à la Crosse Post Reports, 1888-90, HBCA B.89/e/10a.

37 Letters to Moberly from Dreaver, 6 September 1890 and 16 October 1890, Île à la Crosse Correspondence Inward, 1890-92, HBCA B.89/c/4; and Green Lake Post Report, 1892, HBCA B.84/e/3.

38 Île à la Crosse Post Report, 1900-01, HBCA B.89/e/20; letter to Bell from Anderson, 5 February 1902, Île à la Crosse Correspondence Book, 1899-1902, HBCA B.89/b/21; and Île à la Crosse Post Reports, 1888-90, HBCA B.89/e/10a.

39 Île à la Crosse Post Journals, 1889-96, HBCA B.89/a/36 and 37.

40 Portage La Loche Post Report, 1896, HBCA B.167/e/3.

41 Letter from John Bell to the officer in charge of Cumberland House, n.d., 1900. Portage La Loche Correspondence Book, 1895-1901, HBCA B.167/b/1.

42 The history of Revillon Frères is interesting because, unlike other small trading firms, it launched the most comprehensive assault on the HBC monopoly in the subarctic since the era of the NWC (although the competition was decidedly less violent in nature). For a full survey of that company's history, see Marcel Sexé, *Two Centuries of Fur Trading, 1723-1923: Romance of the Revillon Family* (Paris: Draeger Frères, 1923).

43 Circulars from Department Office, 1 June 1891, from Moberly, Île à la Crosse Correspondence Inward, 1893-1902, HBCA B.89/c/7.

44 Letter from Roderick McKenzie, Île à la Crosse, 2 January 1844, Governor George Simpson's Correspondence Inward, HBCA D.5/10, fos. 20-21.

45 Entry for 22 May 1845, Île à la Crosse Post Journal, 1843-45, HBCA B.89/a/23; and entries for 15 September 1849 and 11 October 1849, Île à la Crosse Post Journal, 1849-52, HBCA B.89/a/27.

46 Île à la Crosse Post Report, 1892, HBCA B.89/e/15.

47 If this is the same Louis'on who was free trading in the 1890s, he would have been in his late eighties or early nineties. There are a few possible explanations. There may have been two men named Louis'on Janvier born in different generations, or the date given for Louis'on's birth could have been off significantly, for birth dates were often estimates based on how old an individual appeared to be to the recorder.

48 *Liber Animarum,* Mission N.D. de la Visitation vicarait de Keewatin La Loche, Saskatchewan, St. Boniface Historical Society.

49 Ibid.; and scrip application of Pascal Janvier, 6 September 1906, LAC, RG 15, vol. 1352.

50 Île à la Crosse Post Report, 1892, HBCA B.89/e/15; Canadian census returns, 1891, for Portage La Loche, LAC. In the 1891 census returns, there was a Louison who was listed as being eighty-five years of age and married to Elizabeth. In the 1901 census for the Chipewyan section of the Île à la Crosse census, the Janviers are all listed as "Chipeweyan Breeds," but in the 1881 Portage La Loche census they are listed as "French Breeds."

51 Île à la Crosse Post Report, 1892, HBCA B.89/e/15.

52 Letter from Moberly to William Gardiner, 27 February 1893, Île à la Crosse Correspondence Inward, 1893-1902, HBCA B.89/c/7; letter to Officer in Charge, Île à la Crosse, English River District, from Wrigley, 13 May 1890, Île à la Crosse Correspondence Inward, 1890-92, HBCA B.89/c/4; Île à la Crosse Post Report, 1892, HBCA B.89/e/15.

53 Letter from M. McPherson, Portage La Loche, 25 July 1847, Governor George Simpson's Correspondence Inward, HBCA D.5/20. In this era, the L'Esperance in question was either Alexis, the leader of the famed La Loche brigade, or his son Samuel, a hunter in the Lac au Serpent region of English River. The name L'Esperance was at some point transformed into the Cree name Misponas, which continues to appear today in Île à la Crosse. There are no families in northwestern Saskatchewan with the name L'Esperance.

54 "Sketch Map of the English River District," 1895, HBCA B.89/e/18.

55 Letter from Deschambeault, 24 January 1854, Governor George Simpson's Correspondence Inward, HBCA D.5/43.

56 Ibid.

57 For a number of years, the Lac La Ronge post was part of the English River District and therefore administered by Île à la Crosse. Letter from Deschambeault, 10 January 1856, Governor George Simpson's Correspondence Inward, HBCA D.5/41, fos. 14-17.

58 Ibid.

59 Ibid.

60 Ibid.

61 Deschambeault's fears were greater than the reality of the free traders' ability or influence over market forces or transport routes. Realistically, until market forces dictated increased fur prices or transportation networks were improved, free traders could not have had a great deal of influence. However, even when there are significant changes and improvements in these two forces, as there were in the post-1870 era, the HBC was still able to dominate the trade economy. Letter from Deschambeault, 10 January 1856, Governor George Simpson's Correspondence Inward, HBCA D.5/41, fos. 14-17.

62 Letter from Deschambeault, 10 January 1856, Governor George Simpson's Correspondence Inward, HBCA D.5/41, fos. 14-17.

63 There are too many Desjarlais in the English River District for a positive identification, but the one being referred to here may actually have been a member of the "Le Desjarlais" from Heather Devine's *The People Who Own Themselves: Aboriginal Ethnogenesis in a Canadian Family, 1660-1900* (Calgary: University of Calgary Press, 2004).

64 Letter from Deschambeault, 16 January 1858, Governor George Simpson's Correspondence Inward, HBCA D.5/46.

65 Charles may have been the father of Andrew Miles McDermott, an HBC employee in English River in the 1880s and 1890s.

66 Entry for 15 September 1862, Île à la Crosse Post Journal, 1862, HBCA B.89/a/32.

67 Île à la Crosse Post Report, 1888-90, HBCA B.89/e/10a.

68 Ibid.

69 10 August 1888 to Wrigley, Île à la Crosse Post Reports, 1888, HBCA B.89/e/6.

70 *Liber Animarum*, Mission Saint-Jean-Baptiste, Île á la Crosse, vicarait de Keewatin La Loche, Saskatchewan, St. Boniface Historical Society. Charles Lafleur apparently had two wives, Louise Vadney and Mary Grosse Tete. It is difficult to determine which woman was the mother of which child.

71 Île à la Crosse Post Report, 1892, HBCA B.89/e/15; letter from Chipman to N.C. King, Île à la Crosse, 25 March 1896, Île à la Crosse Correspondence Inward, 1892-1901, HBCA B.89/c/6; and letter from Chipman to Moberly, 8 February no year, Île à la Crosse Correspondence Inward, 1893-1902, HBCA B.89/c/7.

72 Henry John Moberly, *When Fur Was King* (London: J.M. Dent and Sons, 1929), 175.

73 Ibid., 176.

74 Ibid.

75 Letter to Chipman from Moberly, 17 June 1893, Île à la Crosse Correspondence Book, 1892-94, HBCA B.89/B/19.

76 Nothing is known about Marguerite Sinclair except that an alternative spelling for her last name was Quinclair. Sophie Morin was the daughter of Antoine Morin and Pélagie Boucher and therefore the sister of Sarazine Morin Laliberte and sister-in-law of Pierriche Laliberte. Scrip application of William Delaronde, 11 July 1900, LAC, RG 15, vol. 1343.

77 Letters to Roderick McFarlane, Fort Chipewyan, from McMurray, 2 December 1874, and to Grahame from McMurray, 30 June 1875, Île à la Crosse Correspondence Book, 1872-91, HBCA B.89/b/4.

78 Letter to McDonald from Lawrence Clarke, 10 October 1880, Île à la Crosse Correspondence Inward, 1871-85, HBCA B.89/c/2; and letter to Clarke from McDonald, 1 November 1880, Île à la Crosse Correspondence Book, 1877-81, HBCA B.89/b/6.

79 Letter to Grahame from McDonald, 1 October 1880, Île à la Crosse Correspondence Book, 1877-81, HBCA B.89/b/6.

80 Letter to Clarke from McDonald, 22 July 1881, Île à la Crosse Correspondence Book, 1881-85, HBCA B.89/b/7.

81 Letter to Roderick Ross from Clarke, 16 October 1884, Île à la Crosse Correspondence Inward, 1871-85, HBCA B.89/c/2.

82 Letter to Clarke from Joseph Fortescue, 10 May 1888, Commissioner's Office, Inward Correspondence, HBCA D.20/59/20.

83 Letter to Chipman from Moberly, 31 March 1893, Île à la Crosse Correspondence Book, 1892-94, HBCA B.89/b/19.

84 Scrip application of Raphaël Morin, 1 March 1887/17 October 1887, LAC, RG 15, vol. 557, file 167727; scrip application of Sophie Morin Linklater, 8 March 1899, LAC, RG 15, vol. 1360; parish registers, Mission de Saint-Jean-Baptiste (1867-1912), Île à la Crosse, Saskatchewan; and scrip application of Marie Agnis deLaronde, 5 July 1900, LAC, RG 15, vol. 1360.

85 Letter to Chipman from Moberly, 31 March 1893, Île à la Crosse Correspondence Book, 1892-94, HBCA B.89/b/19; and letters to Moberly from Clarke, 4 October 1893, and from Clarke to Anderson, 24 December 1901, Île à la Crosse Correspondence Inward, 1893-1902, HBCA B.89/c/7.

86 Green Lake Post Report (English River District), 1900-01, HBCA B.84/e/7.

CONCLUSION

1 Rita Bouvier, *Blueberry Clouds* (Saskatoon: Thistledown Press, 1999), 11. Rita Bouvier is the granddaughter of Joseph Bouvier and Flora Gardiner, a marriage that established another link between the Bouvier, Gardiner, and Daigneault families. Joseph Bouvier was the son of Joseph Alexandre Michel (Michelis) Bouvier and Caroline Lafleur. Michelis was the son of Michel Bouvier Jr., and Julie Marie Morin. Flora Gardiner was the daughter of Robert (also spelled Roby or Robbie) Gardiner and Eliza Daigneault, who was the daughter of Vincent Daigneault and Marguerite Bouvier. Michel Jr. and Marguerite were brother and sister.

2 Raymond D. Fogelson, "Perspectives on Native American Identity," in *Studying Native America: Problems and Prospects,* ed. Russell Thornton (Madison: University of Wisconsin Press, 1998), 48.

3 See, for instance, Janet Campbell Hale, *Bloodlines: Odyssey of a Native Daughter* (New York: HarperCollins, 1994); Leslie Marmon Silko, *Yellow Woman and the Beauty of the Spirit: Essays on Native American Life Today* (New York: Simon and Schuster, 1996); Gerald Vizenor, *Manifest Manners: Postindian Warriors of Survivance* (Hanover, CT: Wesleyan University Press, 1994); Thomson Highway, *Kiss of the Fur Queen* (Toronto: Doubleday Canada, 1998); Craig S. Womack, *Red on Red: Native American Literary Separatism* (Minneapolis: University of Minnesota Press, 1999); and Louis Owens, *Mixedblood Messages: Literature, Film, Family, Place* (Norman: University of Oklahoma Press, 1998).

4 Marcel Giraud, *The Métis in the Canadian West,* trans. George Woodcock (Edmonton: University of Alberta Press, 1986), 2:330.

5 Diane Payment, *"The Free People – Otipemisiwak": Batoche, Saskatchewan, 1870-1930* (Ottawa: Canadian Parks Service, 1990), 311.

6 Jennifer S.H. Brown's *Strangers in Blood: Fur Trade Company Families in Indian Country* (Vancouver: UBC Press, 1980) provides an excellent, comprehensive description of how

the North West Company and Hudson's Bay Company structures were shaped by French, English, and Scottish ideals of family life that, in turn, influenced types of Metis communities.

7 Nicole St-Onge, *Saint-Laurent, Manitoba: Evolving Metis Identities, 1870-1914* (Regina: Canadian Plains Research Center, 2004), and "Uncertain Margins: Métis and Saulteaux Identities in St-Paul des Saulteaux, Red River, 1821-1870," *Manitoba History* (October 2006): 1-8.

8 Marlene Miller, ed., *Voices of the Elders* (Meadow Lake: Meadow Lake Tribal Council, 2006), 11.

Bibliography

PRIMARY SOURCES

Manuscripts

Church of Jesus Christ of Latter Day Saints Family History Search Centre
—. Parish registers, Saint-Julien (1875-1912), Lac Vert (Green Lake), Saskatchewan.
—. Parish registers, Mission de Saint-Jean-Baptiste (1867-1912), Île à la Crosse, Saskatchewan.
—. Parish registers, Mission de la Visitation (1890-1912), Portage La Loche, Saskatchewan.
Hudson's Bay Company Archives (HBCA)
—. B.39/a/5a, Nottingham House Athepesecoue Lake Journal also Astronomical and Meteorological Observations made at the same place by Peter Fidler.
—. B.84/a/1-7, Green Lake (English River), Post Journals, 1799-1930.
—. B.84/c/1-2, Green Lake (English River), Correspondence Inward, 1879-85.
—. B.84/e/1-7, Green Lake (English River), District Reports, 1889-1901.
—. B.84/z/1-2, Green Lake (English River), Miscellaneous, 1883-1900.
—. B.89/a/1-38, Île à la Crosse, Post Journals, 1805-1904.
—. B.89/b/1-23, Île à la Crosse, Correspondence, 1820-75.
—. B.89/c/1-8, Île à la Crosse, Correspondence Inward, 1810-62.
—. B.89/e/1-21, Île à la Crosse, District Reports, 1822-64.
—. B.89/f/1, Île à la Crosse, Lists of Servants, 1865-82.
—. B.89/z/1-6, Île à la Crosse, Miscellaneous, 1814-1903.
—. RG 3/4A/7, Île à la Crosse Fort Superior, 18 March 1929.
—. B.167/a/1-7, Portage La Loche, Post Journals, 1872-93.
—. B.167/b/1, Portage La Loche, Correspondence, 1895-1901.
—. B.167/c/1, Portage La Loche, Correspondence Inward, 1879-1911.
—. B.167/e/1-5, Portage La Loche, District Reports, 1889-1901.
—. B.167/z/1, Portage La Loche, Miscellaneous, 1834-70.
—. B.239/k/1, Minutes of Council Meetings, 1821-31.

–. D.5/1-48, Governor George Simpson's Correspondence Inward.

–. D.20/59, Commissioner's Office, Correspondence Inward, 1890.

–. E.3/1-2, Peter Fidler, Journal of Exploration and Survey, 1789-1806.

Library and Archives Canada (LAC)

–. RG15, Series DII 8c, Scrip Applications, 1886-1906, volumes 1333-71.

–. RG15, Series DII 8m, North-West Half-Breeds and Original White Settlers, Registers and Indexes, 1877-1927, volumes 1425-1555.

–. Canadian census returns, 1881, 1891, 1901, Île à la Crosse.

–. Canadian census returns, 1881, 1891, 1901, Green Lake.

–. Canadian census returns, 1881, 1891, 1901, Portage La Loche.

Société historique de Saint-Boniface (SHSB)

–. *Liber Animarums*. Mission Notre Dame de la Visitation vicarait de Keewatin La Loche, Saskatchewan.

–. *Liber Animarums*. Mission de Saint-Jean-Baptiste, Île à la Crosse, vicarait de Keewatin La Loche.

Published Primary Records

Burpee, Lawrence J. *The Search for the Western Sea*. London: Alston Rivers, 1908.

–. *The Search for the Western Sea: The Story of the Exploration of North Western America*. Rev. ed. 2 vols. Toronto: Macmillan, 1935.

Crean, Frank J.P. *New Northwest Exploration: Report of Exploration, Seasons of 1908 and 1909*. Ottawa: Department of Interior, 1910.

Duckworth, Harry W., ed. *The English River Book: A North West Company Journal and Account Book, 1796*. Rupert's Land Record Society Series. Montreal/Kingston: McGill-Queen's University Press, 1990.

Earle, Rufus Redmond. "A Trip to Île-à-la-Crosse in 1915." *Saskatchewan History* 39, 1 (1986): 31.

Henry, Alexander. *Alexander Henry's Travels and Adventures in Canada and the Indian Territories between the Years 1760 and 1776*. Edited by James Bain. Edmonton: Hurtig, 1969.

Hirschfelder, Arlene, ed. *Native Heritage: Personal Accounts by American Indians, 1790 to Present*. New York: Macmillan, 1995.

Keith, Lloyd, ed. *North of Athabasca: Slave Lake and Mackenzie River Documents of the North West Company, 1800-1821*. Montreal/Kingston: McGill-Queen's University Press, 2001.

King, William Cornwallis. *Trader King as Told to Mary Weekes*. 1949. Reprint, Regina: Fifth House, 2007.

Kohl, J.G. *Kitch-Gami: Life among the Lake Superior Ojibwa*. 1860. Reprint, St. Paul: Minnesota Historical Society, 1985.

Lamb, W. Kaye, ed. *Sixteen Years in the Indian Country: The Journal of Daniel Williams Harmon, 1800-1816*. Toronto: Macmillan, 1957.

Mair, Charles. *Through the Mackenzie Basin: An Account of the Signing of Treaty No. 8 and the Scrip Commission, 1899*. Edmonton: University of Alberta Press, 1999.

Moberly, Henry John. *When Fur Was King*. London: J.M. Dent and Sons, 1929.

Morice, A.G., OMI. *Dictionnaire historique des Canadiens et des Métis français de L'Ouest*. Montreal: Chez Granger Freres, 1908.

–. *History of the Catholic Church in Western Canada: From Lake Superior to the Pacific*. 2 vols. Toronto: Masson, 1910.

Owens, Brian, and Claude M. Roberto, eds. *The Diaries of Bishop Vital Grandin, 1875-77.* Translated by Alan D. Ridge. Vol. 1. Edmonton: Historical Society of Alberta, 1989.

Petitot, Émile. *The Amerindians of the Canadian Northwest in the Nineteenth Century.* Edited by Donat Savoie. Ottawa: Northern Science Research Group, Dept. of Indian Affairs and Northern Development, 1970.

–. *Les littératures populaires de toutes les nations.* Vol. 23. Paris: Maisonneuve Frères et Ch. Leclerc, 1894.

Ross, Alexander. *The Fur Hunters of the Far West.* Edited by Kenneth A. Spaulding. 1855. Reprint, Norman: University of Oklahoma Press, 2001.

–. *The Red River Settlement: Its Rise, Progress, and Present State.* 1856. Reprint, Minneapolis: Ross and Haines, 1957.

Sister of Charity of Montreal. *Notes and Sketches Collected from a Voyage in the North West for the Furtherance of a Charitable Object.* Montreal: F. Callahan, Book and Job Printer, 1875.

Thompson, David. *David Thompson's Narrative, 1784-1812.* Edited by Richard Glover. Toronto: Champlain Society, 1962.

Williams, Glyndwr, ed. *Hudson's Bay Miscellany 1670-1870.* Vol. 30. Winnipeg: Hudson's Bay Record Society, 1975.

Secondary Sources

Ahenakew, Edward. "Cree Trickster Tales." *Journal of American Folk-Lore* 42, 166 (1929): 309-13.

Albers, Patricia. "Sioux Kinship in a Colonial Setting." *Dialectical Anthropology* 6 (1982): 253-69.

Anderson, Anne, ed. *Plains Cree Dictionary in the "Y" Dialect.* S.I.: s.n., 1975.

Anderson, Gary Clayton. *Kinsmen of Another Kind: Dakota-White Relations in the Upper Mississippi Valley, 1650-1862.* Lincoln: University of Nebraska Press, 1984.

Arsenault, Rose, RSR. *A Religious History of St. John the Baptist Parish Ile a la Crosse 150 Years.* http://www.jkcc.com/rcnuns.html.

Arthur, Elizabeth. "Angelique and Her Children: Papers and Records." *Thunder Bay Historical Society* 6 (1978): 30-34.

Asch, Michael. *Kinship and the Drum Dance in a Northern Dene Community.* Edmonton: Boreal Institute for Northern Studies, 1989.

Bakker, Peter. *A Language of Our Own: The Genesis of Michif, the Mixed Cree-French Language of the Canadian Métis.* New York: Oxford University Press, 1997.

Beaudet, Gérard. *Cree-English English-Cree Dictionary = Nehiyawe mina Akayasimo, Akayasimo mina Nehiyawe ayamiwini-masinahigan.* Winnipeg: Wuerz Publishing, 1995.

Benoit, Barbara. "Mission at Ile-a-la-Crosse." *The Beaver* (Winter 1990): 40-50.

Bernier, Bernard. *The Social Organization of the Waswanipi Cree Indians.* Montreal/ Kingston: McGill-Queen's University Press, 1968.

Bhabha, Homi K. *The Location of Culture.* London: Routledge, 1994.

Blouin, Sonia. "Entre frères et cousins: L'expérience familiale des voyageurs de la seigneurie de Rivière-du-Loup dans le commerce des fourrures, 1788-1821." Master's thesis, University of Ottawa, 2003.

Bourgeault, Ron. "The Indian, the Metis and the Fur Trade: Class, Sexism and Racism in the Transition from 'Communism' to Capitalism." *Studies in Political Economy* 12 (1983): 45-80.

Bouvier, Rita, "Leaving Home." *Blueberry Clouds.* Saskatoon: Thistledown Press, 1999.

Brightman, Robert A. *Acoohkiwina and Acimowina: Traditional Narratives of the Rock Cree Indians.* Regina: Canadian Plains Research Center, 2007.

—. *Grateful Prey: Rock Cree Human-Animal Relationships.* Berkeley: University of California Press, 1993.

Brown, Jennifer S.H. *Strangers in Blood: Fur Trade Company Families in Indian Country.* Vancouver: UBC Press, 1980.

Brumbach, Hetty Jo, and Robert Jarvenpa. *Ethnoarchaeological and Cultural Frontiers: Athapascan, Algonquian, and European Adaptations in the Central Subarctic.* New York: Peter Lang, 1989.

Burley, D.V., G.A. Horsfal, and J.D. Brandon. *Structural Considerations of Metis Ethnicity: An Archeological, Architectural and Historical Study.* Vermillion: University of South Dakota Press, 1992.

Burley, Edith I. *Servants of the Honourable Company: Work, Discipline, and Conflict in the Hudson's Bay Company, 1770-1879.* Toronto: Oxford University Press, 1997.

Campbell, Maria. "We Need to Return to the Principles of Wahkootowin." *Eagle Feather News,* November 2007.

Carrière, Gaston, OMI. "The Oblates and the Northwest, 1845-1861." *Canadian Catholic Historical Association Study Sessions* (1970): 35-66.

Castonguay, Thérèse, s.g.m. *A Leap in Faith: The Grey Nuns Ministries in Western and Northern Canada.* Vol. 2. Edmonton: Grey Nuns of Alberta, 1999.

Choquette, Robert. *The Oblate Assault on Canada's Northwest.* Ottawa: University of Ottawa Press, 1995.

Christie, Nancy, ed. *Households of Faith: Family, Gender, and Community in Canada, 1760-1969.* Montreal/Kingston: McGill-Queen's University Press, 2002.

Coates, Kenneth S., and William R. Morrison. "'More than a Matter of Blood': The Federal Government, the Churches and the Mixed Blood Populations of the Yukon and Mackenzie River Valley, 1890-1950." In *1885 and After: Native Society in Transition,* edited by F. Laurie Barron and James B. Waldram, 253-77. Regina: Canadian Plains Research Center, 1986.

Craig, Terrence L. *The Missionary Lives: A Study in Canadian Missionary Biography.* New York: Brill, 1997.

Crawford, John C. "What Is Michif? Language in the Metis Tradition." In *The New Peoples: Being and Becoming Metis in North America,* edited by Jacqueline Peterson and Jennifer S.H. Brown, 231-42. Winnipeg: University of Manitoba Press, 1981.

Cronin, Kay. *Cross in the Wilderness.* Vancouver: Mitchell Press, 1960.

Cuthand, Stan. "On Nelson's Text." In *"The Orders of the Dreamed": George Nelson on Cree and Northern Ojibwa Religion and Myth, 1823,* edited by Jennifer S.H. Brown and Robert A. Brightman, 189-98. Winnipeg: University of Manitoba Press, 1988.

Davidson, Gordon Charles. *The North West Company.* Berkeley: University of California Press, 1918.

Davis, Natalie Zemon. *The Return of Martin Guerre.* Cambridge, MA: Harvard University Press, 1983.

Decker, Jody. "'We Shall Never Be Again the Same People': The Diffusion and Cumulative Impact of Acute Infectious Diseases Affecting the Natives on the Northern Plains of the Western Interior of Canada, 1774-1839." PhD diss., York University, 1989.

Deloria, Ella Cara. *Speaking of Indians.* 1948. Reprint, Lincoln: University of Nebraska Press, 1998.

DeMallie, Raymond J. "Kinship and Biology in Sioux Culture." In *North American Indian Anthropology*, edited by Raymond J. DeMallie and Alfonso Ortiz, 125-46. Norman: University of Oklahoma Press, 1994.

–. "Kinship: The Foundation for Native American Society." In *Studying Native America: Problems and Prospects*, ed. Russell Thornton, 306-56. Madison: University of Wisconsin Press, 1998.

Devine, Heather. "Les Desjarlais: Aboriginal Ethnogenesis and Diaspora in a Canadien Family." PhD diss., University of Alberta, 2001.

–. *The People Who Own Themselves: Aboriginal Ethnogenesis in a Canadian Family, 1660-1900*. Calgary: University of Calgary Press, 2004.

Dolphin, Frank J. *Indian Bishop of the West: The Story of Vital Justin Grandin, 1829-1902*. Ottawa: Novalis, 1986.

Douaud, Patrick C. *Ethnolinguistic Profile of the Canadian Métis*. Mercury Series – Canadian Ethnology Service, Paper 99. Ottawa: National Museum of Man, 1985.

Dues, Greg. *Catholic Customs and Traditions: A Popular Guide*. Mystic, CT: Bayard, 2003.

Ens, Gerhard J. *Homeland to Hinterland: The Changing Worlds of the Red River Metis in the Nineteenth Century*. Toronto: University of Toronto Press, 1996.

Faries, R., ed. *A Dictionary of the Cree Language, as Spoken by the Indians in the Provinces of Quebec, Ontario, Manitoba, Saskatchewan and Alberta. Based upon the Foundation Laid by E.A. Watkins, 1865*. Rev. ed. Toronto: General Synod of the Church of England in Canada, 1938.

Flannery, Regina. "Cross-Cousin Marriage among the Cree and Montagnais of James Bay." *Primitive Man* 2 (1938): 29-33.

–. "The Position of Women among the Eastern Cree." *Primitive Man* 8 (1934): 81-86.

Fogelson, Raymond D. "Perspectives on Native American Identity." In *Studying Native America: Problems and Prospects*, edited by Russell Thornton, 40-59. Madison: University of Wisconsin Press, 1998.

Foster, John. "The Metis: The People and the Term." *Prairie Forum* 3, 1 (1978): 79-90.

–. "The Origins of the Mixed Bloods in the Canadian West." In *The Prairie West: Historical Readings*, edited by R. Douglas Francis and Howard Palmer, 86-99. Edmonton: Pica Pica Press, 1985.

–. "The Plains Metis." In *The Canadian Experience*, edited by R. Bruce Morrison and C. Roderick Wilson, 315-403. Toronto: McClelland and Stewart, 1986.

–. "Wintering, the Outsider Adult Male and the Ethnogenesis of the Western Plains Metis." *Prairie Forum* 19, 1 (1994): 1-14. Reprinted in Theodore Binnema, Gerhard J. Ens, and R.C. Macleod, eds., *From Rupert's Land to Canada*, 179-92. Edmonton: University of Alberta Press, 2001.

Foster, Martha Harroun. *We Know Who We Are: Métis Identity in a Montana Community*. Norman: University of Oklahoma Press, 2006.

Fowler, Loretta. *Shared Symbols, Contested Meanings: Gros Ventre Culture and History 1778-1984*. Ithaca, NY: Cornell University Press, 1987.

Friesen, David W. *The Cree Indians of Northern Saskatchewan: An Overview of the Past and Present*. Saskatoon, 1973.

Geertz, Clifford. *The Interpretation of Cultures*. New York: Basic Books, 1973.

Ginzburg, Carlo. *The Cheese and the Worms: The Cosmos of a Sixteenth-Century Miller*. Translated by John and Anne C. Tedeschi. Baltimore: Johns Hopkins University Press, 1980.

—. *Clues, Myths, and the Historical Method*. Translated by John and Anne C. Tedeschi. Baltimore: Johns Hopkins University Press, 1986.

Giraud, Marcel. *The Metis in the Canadian West*. Translated by George Woodcock. 2 vols. Edmonton: University of Alberta Press, 1986.

Gough, Barry M. "Peter Pond." *Dictionary of Canadian Biography Online*. http://www.biographi.ca.

Grant, John Webster. *Moon of Wintertime: Missionaries and the Indians of Canada in Encounter since 1534*. Toronto: University of Toronto Press, 1984.

Greer, Allan. *Mohawk Saint: Catherine Tekakwitha and the Jesuits*. New York: Oxford University Press, 2005.

Gutman, Herbert G. *The Black Family in Slavery and Freedom, 1750-1925*. New York: Vintage Books, 1976.

Hackett, Paul. *A Very Remarkable Sickness: Epidemics in the Petit Nord to 1846*. Winnipeg: University of Manitoba Press, 2002.

Hale, Janet Campbell. *Bloodlines: Odyssey of a Native Daughter*. New York: HarperCollins, 1994.

Hallowell, A. Irving. "Kinship Terms and Cross-Cousin Marriage of the Montagnais-Naskapi and the Cree." *American Anthropologist* 34, 2 (1932): 171-99.

Hay, Elaine. *Dene Hélot'ine Kinship*. Saskatoon: Saskatchewan Indian Cultural Centre, 1998.

Highway, Thomson. *Kiss of the Fur Queen*. Toronto: Doubleday Canada, 1998.

Hobsbawm, Eric. "Inventing Tradition." In *The Invention of Tradition*, edited by Eric Hobsbawm and Terrence Ranger, 1-14. Cambridge: Cambridge University Press, 1983.

Holland, Lynda. *The Dene Elders Project: Stories and History from the Westside*. La Ronge, SK: Holland-Dalby Educational Consulting, 2002.

Holland, Lynda, and Mary Ann Kkailther. *They Will Have Our Words: The Dene Elders Project*. Vol. 2. La Ronge, SK: Holland-Dalby Educational Consulting, 2003.

Huel, Raymond J. "The Oblates of Mary Immaculate in the Canadian North West: Reflections on 150 Years of Service, 1845-1995." In *Proceedings of the Fourth Symposium on the History of the Oblates in Western and Northern Canada*. Edmonton: Western Canadian Publishers, 1996.

—. *Proclaiming the Gospel to the Indians and the Métis*. Edmonton: University of Alberta Press, 1996.

Hurly, Paul. "Beauval, Saskatchewan: An Historical Sketch." *Saskatchewan History* 33 (1980): 102-10.

Jarvenpa, Robert. "The Development of Pilgrimage in an Inter-Cultural Frontier." In *Culture and Anthropologic Tradition: Essays in Honour of Robert F. Spencer*, edited by Robert H. Winthrop, 177-203. London: University of America Press, 1990.

—. "The Hudson's Bay Company, the Roman Catholic Church, and the Chipewyan in the Late Fur Trade Period." In *Le Castor Fait Tout: Selected Papers of the 5th American Fur Trade Conference, 1985*, edited by Bruce Trigger, Toby Morantz, and Louise Dechêne, 485-517. Montreal: Lake St. Louis Historical Society, 1987.

—. "The People of Patuanak: The Ecology and Spatial Organization of a Southern Chipewyan Band." PhD diss., University of Minnesota, 1974.

—. *The Trappers of Patuanak: Toward a Spatial Ecology of Modern Hunters*. Ottawa: National Museum of Canada, 1980.

Jarvenpa, Robert, and Hetty Jo Brumbach. "Occupational Status, Ethnicity and Ecology: Metis Adaptations in a Canadian Trading Frontier." *Human Ecology* 13, 3 (1985): 309-29.

Johnston, Basil. *Ojibway Heritage*. Toronto: McClelland and Stewart, 1981.

Jordan, Mary. *To Louis from Your Sister Who Loves You, Sara Riel*. Toronto: Griffin House, 1974.

Judd, Carol M. "Alexis Bonami (Bonamis), *dit* Lespérance (L'Espérance)." *Dictionary of Canadian Biography Online*. http://www.biographi.ca.

Kroeber, Alfred Louis. "Athabascan Kin Term Systems." *American Anthropologist* 39 (1937): 602-8.

Lamb, W. Kaye. "Sir Alexander MacKenzie." *Dictionary of Canadian Biography Online*. http://www.biographi.ca.

Levine, Lawrence W. *The Unpredictable Past: Explorations in American Cultural History*. Oxford: Oxford University Press, 1993.

Longpré, Robert. *Ile-a-la-Crosse, 1776-1976*. Île à la Crosse, SK: Ile-a-la-Crosse Bi-Centennial Committee, Ile-a-la-Crosse Local Community Authority, 1976.

Lux, Maureen. *Medicine That Walks: Disease, Medicine, and Canadian Plains Native People, 1880-1940*. Toronto: University of Toronto Press, 2001.

Macdougall, Brenda. "'The Comforts of Married Life': Metis Family Life, Labour, and the Hudson's Bay Company." *Labour/Le Travail* 61 (Spring 2008): 9-40.

MacLeod, Margaret Arnett. "Red River New Year." *The Beaver* (December 1953): 43-47.

Mandelbaum, David G. *The Plains Cree: An Ethnographic, Historical, and Comparative Study*. 1940. Reprint, Regina: Canadian Plains Research Center, 1996.

Maranda, Pierre. *French Kinship: Structure and History*. Paris: Mouton, 1974.

Marchildon, Greg, and Sid Robinson. *Canoeing the Churchill: A Practical Guide to the Historic Voyageur Highway*. Regina: Canadian Plains Research Center, 2002.

McCarthy, Martha. *From the Great River to the Ends of the Earth: Oblate Missions to the Dene, 1847-1921*. Edmonton: University of Alberta Press, 1995.

McCormack, Patricia A. "The Many Faces of Thanadelthur: Documents, Stories, and Images." In *Reading beyond Words: Contexts for Native History*, edited by Jennifer S.H. Brown and Elizabeth Vibert, 329-64. Peterborough, ON: Broadview Press, 2003.

McCullough, Edward J., and Michael Maccagno. *Lac La Biche and the Early Fur Traders*. Edmonton: Canadian Circumpolar Institute, 1991.

McGregor, James G. *Peter Fidler: Canada's Forgotten Explorer, 1769-1822*. Calgary: Fifth House, 1998.

McKay Jolly, Grace, Alice Aby, and Stan Cuthand. *Kisewatotatowin: Loving, Caring, Sharing, Respect*. 2nd ed. Saskatoon: Aboriginal Parent Program, 1998.

Meadow Lake Diamond Jubilee Heritage Group. *Heritage Memories: A History of Meadow Lake and Surrounding Districts*. North Battleford, SK: Turner-Warwick Printers, 1981.

Medicine, Beatrice. "American Indian Family." *Journal of Ethnic Studies* 18, 4 (1981): 13-23.

Meyer, David. *The Red Earth Crees, 1860-1960*. Canadian Ethnology Service, Paper 100. Ottawa: National Museum of Canada, 1985.

Miller, J.R. "From Riel to the Métis." *Canadian Historical Review* 69, 1 (1988): 1-20.

Miller, Marlene, ed. *Voices of the Elders*. Meadow Lake: Meadow Lake Tribal Council, 2006.

Morgan, Lewis Henry. *Ancient Society*. New York: Holt, 1877.

–. *Systems of Consanguinity and Affinity of the Human Family*. Vol. 17. Washington: Smithsonian Contributions to Knowledge, 1871.

Morin, Gail. *Métis Families: A Genealogical Compendium.* Pawtucket, RI: Quintin Publications, 1996.

Morse, Eric W. *Fur Trade Canoe Routes of Canada: Then and Now.* Toronto: University of Toronto Press, 1984.

Morton, Arthur S. *A History of the Canadian West to 1870-71.* 2nd ed. Toronto: University of Toronto Press, 1973.

–. *Under Western Skies: A Series of Pen-Pictures of the Canadian West in Early Fur Trade Times.* Toronto: T. Nelson, 1937.

Morton, W.L., ed. *Manitoba: The Birth of a Province.* Winnipeg: Manitoba Historical Records Society, 1984.

Murphy, Lucy Eldersveld. *A Gathering of Rivers: Indians, Métis, and Mining in the Western Great Lakes, 1737-1832.* Lincoln: University of Nebraska Press, 2000.

Nicks, Trudy, and Kenneth Morgan. "Grand Cache: The Historic Development of an Indigenous Aboriginal Métis Population." In *The New Peoples: Being and Becoming Metis in North America,* edited by Jacqueline Peterson and Jennifer S.H. Brown, 163-81. Winnipeg: University of Manitoba Press, 1985.

Noël, Françoise. *Family Life and Sociability in Upper and Lower Canada, 1780-1870: A View from Diaries and Family Correspondence.* Montreal/Kingston: McGill-Queen's University Press, 2003.

Nuttall, Mark. "Choosing Kin: Sharing Subsistence in a Greenlandic Hunting Community." In *Dividends of Kinship: Meanings and Uses of Social Relatedness,* edited by Peter Schweitzer, 33-60. London: Routledge, 2000.

Owens, Louis. *Mixedblood Messages: Literature, Film, Family, Place.* Norman: University of Oklahoma Press, 1998.

Pannekoek, Frits. *A Snug Little Flock: The Social Origins of the Riel Resistance, 1869-1870.* Winnipeg: Watson and Dwyer, 1991.

Payment, Diane. *"The Free People – Otipemisiwak": Batoche, Saskatchewan, 1870-1930.* Ottawa: Canadian Parks Service, 1990.

Peterson, Jacqueline. "Many Roads to Red River: Metis Genesis in the Great Lakes Region, 1680-1815." In *The New Peoples: Being and Becoming Metis in North America,* edited by Jacqueline Peterson and Jennifer S.H. Brown, 37-71. Winnipeg: University of Manitoba Press, 1985.

–. "Prelude to Red River: A Social Portrait of the Great Lakes Metis." *Ethnohistory* 25, 1 (1978): 41-67.

Podruchny, Carolyn. "Baptizing Novices: Ritual Moments among French Canadian Voyageurs in the Montreal Fur Trade, 1780-1821." *Canadian Historical Review* 83, 2 (2002): 165-95.

–. "'Dieu, Diable, and the Trickster': Voyageur Religious Syncretism in the pays d'en haut, 1770-1821." *Etude Oblates de l'Ouest* 5 (2000): 75-92.

–. *Making the Voyageur World: Travelers and Traders in the North American Fur Trade.* Toronto: University of Toronto Press, 2006.

Preston, Richard J. "Eastern Cree Notions of Social Grouping." In *Papers of the 11th Algonquian Conference,* edited by William Cowan, 40-48. Ottawa: Carleton University Press, 1980.

Raffin, James. *Emperor of the North: Sir George Simpson and the Remarkable Story of the Hudson's Bay Company.* Toronto: HarperCollins, 2007.

Ray, Arthur J. *The Canadian Fur Trade in the Industrial Age*. Toronto: University of Toronto Press, 1990.

–. *Indians in the Fur Trade: Their Role as Trappers, Hunters, and Middlemen in the Lands Southwest of Hudson Bay, 1660-1870*. Toronto: University of Toronto Press, 1974.

–. "Reflections of Fur Trade Social History and Metis History in Canada." *American Indian Culture and Research Journal* 6, 2 (1982): 91-107.

Redbird, Duke. *We Are Métis: A Metis View of the Development of a Native Canadian People*. Willowdale, ON: Ontario Metis and Non-Status Indian Association, 1980.

Redfield, Robert R. *The Primitive World and Its Transformations*. Ithaca, NY: Cornell University Press, 1953.

Rollason Driscoll, Heather. "'A Most Important Chain of Connection': Marriage in the Hudson's Bay Company. In *From Rupert's Land to Canada*, edited by Theodore Binnema, Gerhard J. Ens, and R.C. Macleod, 81-107. Edmonton: University of Alberta Press, 2001.

Rossignol, M., OMI. "Cross-Cousin Marriage among the Saskatchewan Cree." *Primitive Man* 2 (1938): 26-28.

–. "Property Concepts among the Cree of the Rocks." *Primitive Man* 12 (1939): 61-70.

–. "The Religion of the Saskatchewan and Western Manitoba Cree." *Primitive Man* 11 (1939): 67-71.

Rushforth, Scott. *Bear Lake Athabascan Kinship and Task Group Formation*. Canadian Ethnology Service, Paper 96. Ottawa: National Museum of Canada, 1984.

Schama, Simon. *Dead Certainties: Unwarranted Speculations*. Toronto: Vintage Press, 1992.

Schneider, David M. *A Critique of the Study of Kinship*. Ann Arbor: University of Michigan Press, 1984.

Sealey, D. Bruce, and A.S. Lussier. *The Métis: Canada's Forgotten People*. Winnipeg: Manitoba Métis Federation Press, 1975.

Sexé, Marcel. *Two Centuries of Fur Trading, 1723-1923: Romance of the Revillon Family*. Paris: Draeger Frères, 1923.

Sharp, Henry S. *Chipewyan Marriage*. Canadian Ethnology Service, Paper 58. Ottawa: National Museum of Canada, 1979.

–. "The Kinship System of the Black Lake Chipewyan." PhD diss., Duke University, 1973.

Shoumatoff, Alex. *The Mountain of Names: A History of the Human Family*. New York: Simon and Schuster, 1985.

Silko, Leslie Marmon. *Yellow Woman and the Beauty of the Spirit: Essays on Native American Life Today*. New York: Simon and Schuster, 1996.

Sleeper-Smith, Susan. *Indian Women and French Men: Rethinking Cultural Encounter in the Western Great Lakes*. Amherst: University of Massachusetts Press, 2001.

Slobodin, Richard. *Metis of the Mackenzie District*. Ottawa: Canadian Research Centre for Anthropology, 1966.

Smith, James G.E. "Historical Changes in the Chipewyan Kinship System." In *North American Indian Anthropology*, edited by Raymond J. DeMallie and Alfonso Ortiz, 49-81. Norman: University of Oklahoma Press, 1994.

Smith, James K. *David Thompson: Fur Trader, Explorer, Geographer*. Toronto: Oxford University Press, 1971.

Spaulding, Philip T. "The Metis of Ile-a-la-Crosse." PhD diss., University of Washington, 1970.

—. "The Social Integration of a Northern Community: White Mythology and Metis Reality." In *A Northern Dilemma: Reference Papers,* edited by Arthur K. Davis, 91-111. Bellingham: Western Washington State College, 1967.

Sprague, D.N., and R.P. Frye. *The Genealogy of the First Metis Nation: The Development and Dispersal of the Red River Settlement, 1820-1900.* Winnipeg: Pemmican Publications, 1983.

Spry, Irene M. "The Métis and Mixed-Bloods of Rupert's Land before 1870." In *The New Peoples: Being and Becoming Metis in North America,* edited by Jacqueline Peterson and Jennifer S.H. Brown, 95-118. Winnipeg: University of Manitoba Press, 1981.

Stanley, George F.G. *The Birth of Western Canada: A History of the Riel Rebellions.* 1936. Reprint, Toronto: University of Toronto Press, 1992.

Stevenson, Winona. "'Ethnic' Assimilates 'Indigenous': A Study in Intellectual Colonialism." *Wicazo Sa Review* (1998): 33-51.

Stobie, Margaret R. "Background of the Dialect Called Bungi." *Historical and Scientific Society of Manitoba* 3, 24 (1967-68): 65-75.

—. "The Dialect Called Bungi." *Canadian Antiques Collector* 6, 8 (1971): 20.

Stone, Linda. *Kinship and Gender: An Introduction.* Boulder, CO: Westview Press, 1997.

St-Onge, Nicole. *Saint-Laurent, Manitoba: Evolving Metis Identities, 1870-1914.* Regina: Canadian Plains Research Center, 2004.

—. "Uncertain Margins: Métis and Saulteaux Identities in St-Paul des Saulteaux, Red River, 1821-1870." *Manitoba History* (October 2006): 1-8.

Thorne, Tanis C. *The Many Hands of My Relations: French and Indian on the Lower Missouri.* Columbia: University of Missouri Press, 1996.

Tough, Frank. *"As Their Natural Resources Fail": Native Peoples and the Economic History of Northern Manitoba, 1870-1930.* Vancouver: UBC Press, 1996.

Town, Florida A. *The North West Company: Frontier Merchants.* Toronto: Umbrella Press, 1999.

Trautmann, Thomas R. *Lewis Henry Morgan and the Invention of Kinship.* Berkeley: University of California Press, 1987.

Treaty No. 10 and Reports of Commissioners. Ottawa: Queen's Printer, 1966.

Turner, J.P. "The La Loche Brigade." *The Beaver* 274 (December 1943): 32-36.

Van Kirk, Sylvia. "Colonized Lives: The Native Wives and Daughters of Five Founding Families of Victoria." In *In the Days of Our Grandmothers: A Reader in Aboriginal Women's History in Canada,* edited by Mary-Ellen Kelm and Lorna Townsend, 170-99. Toronto: University of Toronto Press, 2006.

—. *Many Tender Ties: Women in Fur Trade Society in Western Canada, 1670-1870.* Winnipeg: Watson and Dwyer, 1980.

—. "'What If Mama Is an Indian?' The Cultural Ambivalence of the Alexander Ross Family." In *The New Peoples: Being and Becoming Metis in North America,* edited by Jacqueline Peterson and Jennifer S.H. Brown, 207-17. Winnipeg: University of Manitoba Press, 1985.

Vecsey, Christopher. *The Paths of Kateri's Kin.* Notre Dame, IN: University of Notre Dame Press, 1997.

Vizenor, Gerald. *Manifest Manners: Postindian Warriors of Survivance.* Hanover, CT: Wesleyan University Press, 1994.

Voorhis, Ernest. *Historic Forts and Trading Posts of the French Regime and of the English Fur Trading Companies.* Ottawa: Department of the Interior, 1930.

Waldram, James B. "'The Other Side': Ethnostatus Distinction in Western Subarctic Native Communities." In *1885 and After: Native Society in Transition,* edited by F. Laurie Barron and James B. Waldram, 279-95. Regina: Canadian Plains Research Center, 1986.

Wallace, Stewart W. *The Pedlars from Quebec and Other Papers on the Nor'Westers.* Toronto: Ryerson Press, 1954.

White, Richard. *The Middle Ground: Indians, Empires, and Republics in the Great Lakes Region, 1650-1815.* Cambridge: Cambridge University Press, 1991.

Widder, Keith R. *Battle for the Soul: Métis Children Encounter Evangelical Protestants at Mackinaw Mission, 1823-1837.* East Lansing: Michigan State University Press, 1999.

Womack, Craig S. *Red on Red: Native American Literary Separatism.* Minneapolis: University of Minnesota Press, 1999.

Wuorinen, Richard. *A History of Buffalo Narrows.* Buffalo Narrows: Buffalo Narrows Celebrate Saskatchewan Committee, 1981.

Index of Names

See also the subject index on p. 321.

Note: "(f)" indicates a figure; "HBC" refers to Hudson's Bay Company; "(p)" indicates a photograph; "(t)" indicates a table

Index of Subjects

Printed and bound in Canada by Friesens

Set in Garamond by Artegraphica Design Co. Ltd.

Copy editor: Audrey McClellan

Proofreader: Lesley Erickson

Cartographer: Andrew Dunlop

Genealogical charts: Neil Soiseth

Indexer: Perry Millar

ENVIRONMENTAL BENEFITS STATEMENT

UBC Press saved the following resources by printing the pages of this book on chlorine free paper made with 100% post-consumer waste.

TREES	WATER	SOLID WASTE	GREENHOUSE GASES
9	4,004	243	831
FULLY GROWN	GALLONS	POUNDS	POUNDS

Calculations based on research by Environmental Defense and the Paper Task Force.
Manufactured at Friesens Corporation